D0344270

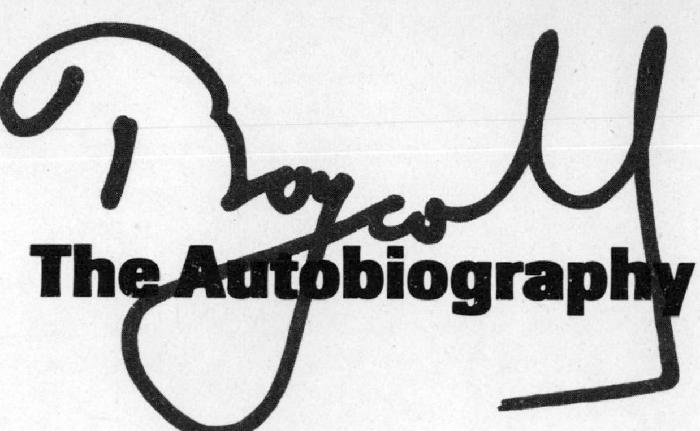

The Autobiography

Boycott

The Autobiography

Best Wishes

M
MACMILLAN
LONDON

My thanks and appreciation to Terry Brindle for his help and contribution in the writing of my book.

Copyright © Geoffrey Boycott 1987

All rights reserved. No reproduction, copy or transmission of this publication may be made without written permission. No paragraph of this publication may be reproduced, copied or transmitted save with written permission or in accordance with the provisions of the Copyright Act 1956 (as amended). Any person who does any unauthorised act in relation to this publication may be liable to criminal prosecution and civil claims for damages.

First published 1987 by
MACMILLAN LONDON LIMITED
4 Little Essex Street London WC2R 3LF
and Basingstoke

Associated companies in Auckland, Delhi, Dublin, Gaborone, Hamburg, Harare, Hong Kong, Johannesburg, Kuala Lumpur, Lagos, Manzini, Melbourne, Mexico City, Nairobi, New York, Singapore and Tokyo

British Library Cataloguing in Publication Data

Boycott, Geoffrey
Boycott : the autobiography.
1. Boycott, Geoffrey 2. Cricket players—
Great Britain—Biography
I. Title
796.35′8′0924 GV915.B6/

ISBN 0–333–44899–5

Typeset by Wyvern Typesetting Limited, Bristol

Printed by Butler and Tanner Limited, Frome, Somerset

Contents

‘If a man does not keep pace with his companions,
perhaps it is because he hears a different drummer.
Let him step to the music which he hears,
however measured or far away.’

Henry Thoreau, *Walden*

1

Early Days

Jane Boycott, née Speight, produced her first delivery – appropriately enough – at precisely 11 a.m. on 21 October 1940. By all accounts it was an easy birth, expertly conducted by the local midwife Nurse Day in the front room of No. 8 Earl Street, Fitzwilliam, the home of my maternal grandmother. The result was a boy weighing in at eight pounds, who already had a shock of hair and who would be called Geoffrey because Mum liked the name.

Dad was a miner's son born at Dawley near Telford in Shropshire, the third of eight children. His father moved to the Yorkshire coalfield in search of work when Dad was just a boy. We lived in Ackworth for a few years, then moved to No. 45 Milton Terrace, Fitzwilliam, a stone's throw from where I was born and the house in which I would spend the next forty years. Apart from the number on the door it was indistinguishable from any other red-brick, terraced house in the neighbourhood: a Coal Board house with two small rooms downstairs and three smaller ones above. As houses go, it wasn't much to write to the National Trust about. But it was home, which was infinitely more important. A place of warmth and movement and caring, a little part of a true community, which seems hopelessly outmoded and old-fashioned now but which was in many ways better than the society which is overtaking and replacing it.

I went back to Milton Terrace a little while ago, driving through the South Yorkshire lanes in a car which is probably worth more than the house where I grew up. I may have moved away from Fitzwilliam but I have never grown apart from its people or the memories. I couldn't even if I wanted to.

The house is boarded up now, the small back garden is overgrown with weeds and littered with rubbish, the upstairs windows have been smashed and plaster is peeling off the bedroom walls. Most of the houses in the terrace and many in the neighbourhood are in the same state; the local pit has closed and because the area has lost its main source of employment, a lot of people have moved away.

Dad was a simple, easygoing man who spent most of his energies just earning a decent living. My impression of him as I grew up was that he seemed to spend most of his time working and seemed almost permanently tired. Mum was the driving force in bringing us up, and by the time I was old enough to appreciate Dad's company fully his health was failing. He was a big man with big, powerful miner's hands and he only once hit me, which was probably just as well. It was a cuff, nothing more, but I felt as though my head was coming off. Mum told him off; it was all right for her to hit us but that wasn't his job. They rarely saw me play in top cricket, though both went to my first Test at Headingley. I would have liked to take them to Lord's, to show them round, take them into the tavern and the Long Room. Dad would have loved that, but I never got the chance. I wish I had.

I do remember that Dad bought me a rabbit, a great big blue-grey thing it was, and as a kid I made a big fuss of feeding and watering it or guarding it when it was allowed to roam free in the garden. Funny how you remember things like that. I was only two months old when Mum bought an artificial Christmas tree for my first Christmas – five foot tall with a fairy on top and candles on every branch. I still have that.

I was the last son at home, and after my father died I felt a strong sense of responsibility. In most respects I had probably grown closer to Mum than I was to Dad as the years went by. She didn't like it too much when we were besieged by the press, but the constant stream of messages and telephone calls also helped her to keep in touch with the outside world, which I think she quite enjoyed. She was also a marvellous cook, especially of fruit pies. Her mince pies at Christmas were a work of art and I developed a sweet tooth which I still have today. Not that anybody makes sweets the way mother used to make 'em . . .

I suppose that, as kids in the post-war depression and in a community which could never have been described as prosperous, we were poor and underprivileged. Disadvantaged would probably be the modern word, though of course nobody had heard of it then. All we knew was that we had clothes on our backs, enough food to eat and a rugged affection from our parents which was no less warm – and probably more lasting – for being laced with discipline. We led a knockabout, simple existence bordered by breakfast at one end of the day and an unwilling bedtime at the other.

As a baby and a toddler I had, unlikely as it may sound, a head of beautiful long curls, carefully combed and much admired until somebody mistook me for a little girl in boots and Mum decided the curls would have to go. I also had a distinctive turn of the bottom lip which would much later in life be described, accurately I think, as a wonky grin. The lip is still with me; had Mum had just a little more foresight she might have saved some of the hair . . .

My younger brother Tony had a head of pure white hair as a kid which gave him an angelic look – so it had its uses. He used to go round to the local shop cadging the odd orange, apple or bag of broken biscuits – 'and one for our kid, please' – and succeeded more often than not. He was also a game little devil who took an early fancy to a drop of the hard stuff, in his case the beer that my grandad used to get in refillable bottles from the local off-licence. Since Tony kept me in oranges, apples and broken biscuits, the least I could do was help him out when we visited Grandad. The beer bottle sat enticingly on the sideboard – my job was to keep Grandad occupied in conversation while Tony skilfully uncorked the bottle and had a swig. He became quite adept at it and Grandad wasn't mobile enough to pose a threat.

Grandad's garden, I recall, possessed an air raid shelter. At least that's what we called it, an above-ground structure that became our hideout when we wanted to drink lemonade, eat sweets and smoke gut-wrenching cigarettes by candlelight. There were never enough sweets and treats in life because food was rationed for many years after the war, so a couple of hedonistic hours in Grandad's shelter was a big event.

My other pleasures, not necessarily in order of priority, were the cinema, train-spotting and games, chiefly football and cricket. A radio was a rarity and nobody had a television: I must have been nine or ten before I actually saw a set and then it became the focus of a big night out – a bus trip to my Aunty Annie in Brierley, where we enjoyed a special tea watching the children's programmes. Afterwards we would stroll to the bus stop with Tony on Uncle Jack's shoulders. Jack made sure we caught the bus safely and Mum or Dad would be waiting when we got to the other end. The whole thing was quite an adventure.

Annie's and Jack's TV set was enormous, at least the cabinet was. It looked like a wardrobe and the valves were probably the size of jam jars – but the screen was tiny by modern standards. It couldn't have been bigger than ten inches but it was 3D and cinemascope rolled into one as far as we were concerned. The screen superstars of the day were Muffin the Mule and the Bumblies, a double-jointed string puppet and a collection of balloon-shaped oddities that lived, as I recall, in the ceiling. We never saw a string, never questioned the unlikely creation of a delightfully potty Michael Bentine. It was real while it lasted, and wonderful.

So was the cinema, a source as far as we were concerned of pure, unadulterated enjoyment. Pictures then were all about glamour and dazzle. The fashion for deeply 'significant' films had not yet developed and would undoubtedly have sailed over our heads if it had. We went to see Ethel Merman in *Call Me Madam*, John Wayne in just about everything, Victor Mature – stars of the sort of pictures that modern-day intellectuals would probably dismiss as superficial. True enough, the good guys always won, the cavalry always arrived in the nick of time and nobody who died actually looked hurt. But that was what we wanted. I cannot remember ever going to the cinema then and coming away disappointed. I was an absolute sucker for it all, unashamedly and without reservation. The streets outside might be cold and badly lit, the realities of the world might be harsh but cinema was an escape into a more glamorous world.

The Plaza – Fitzwilliam was not overburdened with imagination – has predictably disappeared, its site now occupied by a betting shop and a unisex hair salon. But I'll never forget how we dashed for the first three rows of seats, anxious that grown-ups shouldn't beat us to it and blissfully unaware that they had reasons of their own for wanting to be as far from the front as possible. Space was at a premium and the cinema was usually full at weekends, so the first three rows were practically within touching distance of the screen. We sat wide-eyed and with heads thrown back like so many patients in a dentist's chair, gorging ourselves on sweets – Grandma and Grandad used to pool their coupons until we felt quite spoiled – and relishing the make-believe world in front of us.

It may not be entirely coincidental that Mike Parkinson, an old friend of mine and a Barnsley boy, established an affection for the cinema very similar to my own. There may have been something in the lifestyle of communities like ours which made people of our generation seek escapism – the contrast between pithead villages and Hollywood is stark and obvious enough. But I doubt that any of us was aware of it at the time. We were too young to intellectualise it and too busy living our lives to give much thought to what we might be missing.

A little later, in my teens, I used to regret not going to university. I had a sense of missing out on some of the advantages which it then appeared others had. But as I've got older I've realised that growing up in a community like Fitzwilliam did me a lot of good. In many ways I was lucky to experience a sense of belonging and togetherness which seems to have been lost in so much of life nowadays. We had never heard of community spirit – that's the sort of catch-phrase which seems most used when genuine community spirit is missing. Our sense of community was spontaneous. It was simply a way of life.

There may have been murders and muggings, rapes and assaults, but in our young lives we never heard of them. The thought that we might be in danger if we ventured far from home or if we went out after dark never occurred to us. As a youngster smitten by train-spotting, I used to run over to Fitzwilliam station to watch the 9.30 p.m. from London whistle through. It was a streak – a specially streamlined class of locomotive much prized by spotters – and it dashed through the station in a thunderous second while I stood on the steps and tried to read the name and number by the light of a gas lamp. All I remember was the din and the smoke and the glow of the firebox in the dark. Then I would run home, without a care in the world.

I cannot remember going home and finding the door locked. Doors were locked in our neighbourhood only when the last person went to bed. There was simply no need to lock up at any other time and the rent collector or the familiar man from the Prudential could be sure of finding his money on the kitchen table if people weren't at home.

Families helped each other out, not showily but because that was the right and accepted thing to do. Everybody knew everybody, the streets were always full of kids and happenings. The houses might be primitive by modern standards but they were homes – and always warm. That was partly the nature of the neighbourhood and partly because, as a mining community, we received free coal. An active miner would receive a ton a month. That sounds a lot but we had to have an open fire every day of the year, winter and summer, to feed the back-boiler and produce hot water. The coal allowance was dumped outside the coalhouse – at the bottom of the garden and usually adjoining the outside toilet – and it was up to the householder to shovel it inside through the 'bob-hole'. If a husband was on shift when the coal was delivered it was usual for the wife to shovel it in and she would rarely be short of help. Another day, she would help somebody else.

It was an offence to sell this concessionary coal – the penalty was loss of the allowance – and people rarely did. But they were always ready to help out with a bucket or two if somebody ran short. Buckets were important because they reduced the need to troop down the garden on cold nights to mend the fire; remember to fill three or four buckets early in the evening and you could sit by the fire all night without turning out. The outside lav was a different matter. It amazes me now to realise that I was twenty-five before we had an indoor toilet and proper bathroom. Friday night was bath night, when the old tin bath was filled from the copper in front of the fire. The routine was as predictable to us kids as the days of the week.

The back gardens of our terrace and of the one opposite were separated by a narrow lane – a 'ginnel' we called it – which met a slightly wider lane in a T-junction a few yards from our back gate. This was our playground, an area for football and marbles under the gaslight in winter, and for cricket, always cricket, in the summer. The thought that we might have played anything else never occurred to us. Tennis and golf were upper-middle-class games that needed fancy equipment, special clothes and preferably fancy accents. Cricket was simply organised, provided somebody had a bat and ball, though that was not as automatic as it sounds. A soft ball was pretty commonplace but a bat – that could be a very different matter, and the kid who had one wasn't short of a friend for as long as he was prepared to come out and play. The first bat I remember owning was called a Lambert and when it came it had the dark-brown sheen of something that had been regularly and lovingly oiled. I never looked after it, we were too busy playing to bother about things like that.

Stumps were chalked on the wall at the intersection of the T and a batsman took his stance on a manhole cover – it's still there – to face a bowler coming down the ginnel. Anyone who hit the ball into a garden was out, no argument allowed, so we were pretty selective in our strokemaking. If you wanted to stay in, you hit straight or played square on either side of the stumps, preferably along the ground. Psychologists can make of that what they will: I was simply playing cricket and enjoying every minute of it.

We played as long as it was light and as long as we were allowed. It was no good a mum standing at the bottom of her garden and shouting for little Willie to go in to bed. The first summons was ignored, then the second. Mum would finally arrive in person to drag Willie off despite his protestations that he hadn't heard her call in the first place. Everybody accepted the ritual, and a clip round the ear was small price to pay. There was always another innings to play and another over to bowl.

A livid scar some five inches long running vertically down my solar plexus is a vivid reminder – as if I needed one – of the day I came within an hour of dying. A freak accident put me in hospital for a fortnight and very nearly out of commission for good.

I was not quite eight when I fell off the railings separating our garden from next door and landed, by a million-to-one chance, on the upturned handle of an old mangle in the next-door garden. My chest took the full force of the impact and although there was nothing but a sore area to show for the accident, I felt terribly sick and vomited repeatedly. I spent the night stretched on the sofa in front of the fire, white as a sheet with shock and too ill to move. It was suggested that if I didn't improve, they would have to take me to the doctor in the morning.

Luckily for me, my grandmother came round early to see how I was getting on, took one look and immediately packed my dad off on his bicycle to fetch Dr Jackson before he began his morning surgery. The doctor examined me briefly and then sent for an ambulance, which whipped me off, sirens wailing, to Pontefract General Infirmary.

The impact on my chest had ruptured my spleen and I had been bleeding internally all night. An emergency operation was performed successfully but it was touch and go. Another hour, said the doctor, and I would have been a goner.

Dr Jackson probably didn't come across ruptured spleens every day but by an unlikely coincidence there had been a case only a little while before where a local rugby league player had injured his spleen, failed to have the injury properly diagnosed, and subsequently died. That might have alerted the doctor to the possibilities in my case. Either way it was a freak set of circumstances and I was fortunate to get away with it.

The injury pained me for a couple of years afterwards. It did not prevent me playing games but it was cruelly painful if I got a knock in the stomach. I was well into my teens before it healed well enough for me to forget about it. And the loss of my spleen meant I was vulnerable to every infection that was going. If there was a flu virus about I would be the first to catch it, even though I seemed to recover quickly enough and certainly could not be described as a sickly child. However, the risk of infection was always there and would have a significant effect on my career some years later when I had to weigh up the advisability of making a tour of India.

Oddly enough, the injury and its painful aftermath didn't stop me fighting. I have never quite worked out why schoolkids fight. I only know that we did and that I was involved as often as anyone. I was the Cock of the School at Fitzwilliam and there were always plenty of matchmakers ready to involve somebody else in a punch-up. We can't have gone in for a lot of body punching, because one jab anywhere in the region of the stomach and I would have collapsed in a heap.

I had one encounter with Frankie Kent which said something about the mood and attitudes of the times. Frankie was an adversary at primary school who annoyed me so much one day that I chased him into his kitchen and belted him before running off home. Mrs Kent came round and tore a strip off Mum, who naturally defended me stoutly while Mrs Kent was there and gave me a good hiding as soon as she had gone. Frankie had the last laugh: he claimed I had hit him on the throat, and that it affected his ability to sing in the school Christmas play. Since he was something of a star turn, that was serious, and Frankie threatened to take his story to the teachers. For a week or more, I poured all my sweet coupons and any others I could borrow into cough sweets to restore Frankie's vocal chords – which did not seem particularly strained to me. The point was that fighting would have put me in trouble with the teachers and that in turn would have filtered back to Mum and Dad, who would very probably have belted me on the assumption that I deserved it. Advance the clock to today and my parents would probably have descended on the school demanding to know why little Geoffrey was in trouble and why the teachers were picking on him. Discipline in those days began at school, was rarely questioned and was certainly not the source of sympathy from home. If a teacher clipped your ear the assumption was that you had earned it, and the assumption was usually right!

Life in a mining community can be warm and fulfilling and eventful despite the starkness and simplicity of the surroundings. But the community is also gnawed by a fear which is rarely acknowledged but which communicated itself to us as children, though we would not have been able to explain it. This was the fear of an accident in the pit, which, directly or indirectly, employs everyone in the area.

Our life was changed irreversibly by a knock on the door on 2 March 1950. We were having breakfast at the time and Mum went to the door. I never saw the man who called but I can hear his words as though it were yesterday: 'Jenny, I'm sorry but Tom's been hurt . . .'

My father worked at Hemsworth Colliery in Fitzwilliam as a roadlayer, responsible for laying and maintaining the tracks on which the coal tubs ran from the face to the pit shaft. It was hard work, often damp, always dark and dirty, and not well paid, but he accepted it cheerfully enough. It was a job and the work ethic in those days was much stronger than it is today.

Dad had had a terrible accident. He was working on the north level at Haigh Moor seam when, for some reason he never properly explained, a line of tubs began rolling down the track where he was kneeling. Dad sensed rather than saw or heard them and jumped backwards off the track, but he hit a pit prop which bounced him back into the path of the tubs.

He was dragged several yards along the seam until he managed, goodness knows how, to grab a safety lever and bring the tubs to a halt. By then he was a mess – a broken back, broken pelvis, both legs badly damaged, extensive internal injuries. He was just forty-two with three young kids.

The Coal Board report on the accident says that twelve tubs full of dirt were being taken for despatch at the pit bottom. It also records that two men went to Dad's help – W. Ellam and a Pole called S. Wolanin. Long after his accident, Dad always spoke warmly about the 'Polish chap' who went to his rescue.

Dad was on the danger list for ages. Mum used to visit him in hospital every day and there was no guarantee that he would pull through. It was two years before he worked again but he was never the same man. The accident ruined his health and his life, it ruined *him*: before the accident he was a straight, robust man of over six feet – now he could hardly bend one leg and stooped as he moved along with an awkward, rolling sort of gait.

The pit manager and some senior officials used to come to the house with a few apples, eggs and tomatoes. They were full of sympathy and promises. Indeed, there was plenty of goodwill but no financial compensation. Not in those days. The local union man, small and thick-set, made a lot of noise but that was as far as it went. They organised a pit-yard collection and concert on Dad's behalf in Hemsworth Working Men's Club. It was packed but I don't recall it producing a lot in the way of hard cash. There just wasn't the money around.

Dad had never been on a big wage. He had worked nights and done as much overtime as he could to bring in a bit of extra money but now, of course, the family situation became critical. I've never really understood how my Mum managed with three children – Peter, the youngest, was barely two years old – on the bit of sick pay she received. The neighbours rallied round and family helped when they could, but it must have been desperately tough for her. Times were different, of course – harder. People were more self-reliant. It went without saying that you lived within your means, however straitened they might be. If you could not afford something you simply went without. People had to manage and the women in the household usually handled the money. Most husbands would tip over their pay packet and get a bit back for a drink and a packet of cigarettes.

As soon as he was reasonably fit, and probably a bit before, Dad went back to work at the pit. Reassurances that he would be 'looked after' soon wore thin. Within a few weeks he was put back on roadlaying and the work was too tough for him. He could scarcely bend his knee and the hardships of the work meant he never regained his health – in fact it deteriorated. Years later he was given a sit-down job in the machine room, working the cages and the conveyors. It was a boring, repetitive job in dreadfully noisy surroundings where conversation was impossible, and Dad missed the company of his mates.

He used to go down to the club on Friday nights for a glass of beer – he wasn't a heavy or regular drinker – and for a game of dominoes, at which he had quite a reputation. He smoked a little but I don't remember him as a heavy smoker; probably he simply couldn't afford it.

Dad died in 1967. The official diagnosis was heart trouble but I have no doubt that it was his accident in the pit seventeen years earlier that really killed him. He was a broken man after it, but being a strong fellow he took a long time to die. His story could probably have been repeated a hundred times in the mining communities of the early post-war years.

I was conscious of the problems, of course, but kids are wonderfully resilient and we were probably too young to recognise tragedy then.

Fitzwilliam primary school was typical of countless state schools built by local authorities at the time – a square, red-brick building with some of the architectural overtones of a church. You can see them all around the country. It was not a big school, though of course it looked massive and very imposing when I first went there as a five-year-old – it might have been a cross between Dartmoor prison and St Paul's.

I played cricket in the tarmac playground, naturally enough, and when I was about nine I was selected for the school team in a nationwide competition to mark the Festival of Britain Year. The team was selected and coached by Mr Andrews and Mr Weaver, two remarkable men who devoted a lot of their energy and a great deal of their spare time to fostering in the boys a love of cricket and a genuine appreciation of its depth and charm. More than that, they taught us the rudiments of the game, chalking squares on the tarmac into which we had to bowl (straight) as part of a competition, with a prize for the most successful.

Cricket seems to be disappearing from schools now; it's certainly not as widespread as it was and that may be largely because it is a time-consuming game. The pace of modern life is much faster than it was when I was in junior school. Nowadays kids are fed an endless diet of razzamatazz; everything has to be instant. Moreover, schoolteachers are less inclined to give up their time to coach kids at cricket when they can more easily leave them to their own individual pursuits. We were lucky: Mr Andrews and Mr Weaver were always willing to put in time during and after school. They passed on their enthusiasm for the game and I shall always be grateful for the inspiration and encouragement they gave me.

That year we reached the semi-final in our area, which was played at Hemsworth Colliery, twenty overs a side – that means, I suppose, that my first big game was in limited-overs cricket! My dad made more impact than I did: in the knockabout before the game he threw the ball in too enthusiastically and hit me in the left eye. It swelled up in no time and I could barely see. I batted with a real shiner and didn't make double figures. We lost the match anyway.

The competition was so popular nationally that it was played again the following year. I was captain of the side, with a bit of a reputation as an all-rounder. We reached the final at Hemsworth Grammar School and lost again.

Most of us used to play in shorts in those days. But the final was a big event so I managed to find myself a pair of white flannels, goodness knows where. It was a mistake. I ran in to bowl and I felt positively dreadful with the trousers flapping round my legs. I simply couldn't bowl properly. I might have looked the part but I had no idea where my feet were or where the ball was going. I still squirm today when I remember the sheer discomfort of my first introduction to long flannels in cricket.

There was a consolation. A national newspaper ran a competition inviting schools to nominate outstanding performances as batsman, bowler or all-rounder. The prize was a Len Hutton bat. Against Cudworth I took seven wickets for nine runs and I felt sure that would qualify me for a prize – until some other player took seven for eight! I was heartbroken – the chance of a lifetime down the drain. Then I took six for ten and scored 45 not out in a match against Royston – and won the prize as an all-rounder. It was presented to me in front of the whole school. A Len Hutton bat, as white as snow with black writing on it. I can see it now. I don't recall with certainty what happened to it. There was no question of putting it away for safe-keeping – it was a practical prize, not a trophy. No doubt I used it until it fell to bits. It was the best thing I had ever had in my life. Nobody could have given me anything I wanted more.

Cricket was playing an increasingly important part in my life. I seemed to have some aptitude for it and I certainly took enormous pleasure in it. Uncle Algy took me under his wing.

Algy was on to a good thing, though I didn't give it a thought at the time. He used to take me with him to Ackworth, where he was a seam bowler, paying my bus fare from Fitzwilliam and back and making sure I got a sandwich and a piece of cake for my tea on match days. I used to knock up with the team and field for them in pre-match practice. I even learned to score.

After the game Algy would put on the most gorgeous cream gaberdine suit and call in at the Boot and Shoe, all dolled up and Brylcreemed and ready for a night out. I drank lemonade and ate crisps outside until the bus came, then I took Algy's bag and headed off home. The point was that Algy with no cricket bag to cramp his style was liberated and probably dangerous. All I knew was that I'd had a terrific day.

Algy used to practise on Tuesday and Thursday nights and I used to go with him, first there and last away and loving every minute of it. Because I was only a nipper I had to do a lot of fielding but that became a means to an end: if I did it long enough and uncomplainingly enough I could shame the older players into giving me a bat and a bowl before they went home. It might only be ten minutes but it was worth it as far as I was concerned.

Algy was a friend of Desmond Barrick, who had played county cricket for Northants and whose father now had a newsagent's shop in the area. Barrick's father had sent him for coaching to Johnny Lawrence some years earlier and Algy now decided that was the thing for me. Lawrence was a leg-spinner and batsman, Yorkshire-born, who had made a career with Somerset and had opened a coaching clinic at Rothwell, some twelve miles from Fitzwilliam.

We went off to assess the situation and found that cost was going to be a problem. The coaching sessions cost six shillings each, and the bus fare to and from Rothwell worked out at 3s 11d. That meant only a penny change from ten shillings for one Saturday morning session a week and my Mum and Dad simply couldn't afford it.

Algy agreed to pay 2s 6d, as did Aunty Annie and Uncle Jack, so my parents had to find five shillings. They could just about manage that, though there were no doubt plenty of other things they could have spent the money on. The money was paid uncomplainingly, until I was old enough to get a job and contribute myself. Saturday morning became a ritual I lived for.

Lawrence's cricket school was a pretty basic sort of a place, a converted greenhouse with makeshift floor coverings and very spartan changing facilities out the back. It was also the coldest place in the world on a winter's morning, heated only by an old coal-fired stove. I can still remember how we used to get there before the stove had taken the icicles out of the air, rushing to change our clothes and shivering uncontrollably.

I had to change buses at Wakefield, get off at the Halfway House pub and walk the best part of a mile to Lawrence's place. Rain or snow, I didn't mind a bit. Jack Birkenshaw, a young bowler later to play for Yorkshire, Leicestershire and England, lived next door to Johnny's school and I used to knock him up on the way past so I would have somebody to bowl at me as soon as I got there.

Birky developed the habit of blowing on his cupped hands to get back a bit of feeling in the icy cold of the indoor school. It stayed with him all his career. In the West Indies or on the hottest English day of the year, Jack would blow on his hands in unwitting memory of the mornings we spent with Johnny Lawrence in Rothwell.

Teaching cricket is an art as well as a science; there are plenty of people who know the game inside out, or fancy they do, but not that many who have the knack of passing on their expertise and experience in a way both interesting and intelligible to youngsters. Johnny Lawrence had that gift.

Johnny is a kindly, uncomplicated man with an enormous fund of knowledge and the paramount virtue – as far as coaching kids is concerned – of endless patience. Kids as young as I was when I first went to Johnny's coaching school simply do not have the ability to grasp more than one point at a time. The message has to be simple and the purpose has to be clear.

On top of that, Johnny had the knack of making everything we did enjoyable. He used to stress that cricket was primarily a relaxation and a pleasure. Playing well added to the enjoyment, but simply playing was the point of the exercise. Naturally, since we attended his coaching sessions voluntarily, he had some pretty receptive raw material but he still went out of his way to make sure that nothing became a chore. It's an attitude I try to recreate when I coach children today. My approach may be different from his but the underlying philosophy is the same.

Johnny was never negative with us. He would rarely tell us why we should not do something – rather he would emphasise what we should do to make the most of our ability. Youngsters, for instance, tend to want to hit the ball on the leg side all the time; it is the most natural stroke. 'That's fine,' Johnny would say, 'but that's the easy way. Let's see if you can do something a bit harder . . .'

We were learning all the time, stretching ourselves, trying to master a technique which, though difficult and in its own way manufactured, would make us better players in the long run. Johnny began with the premise that we should go forward and play straight. It sounds very basic and pretty obvious but it was not the natural reaction of a youngster.

Batting properly is not a natural thing. We grip the bat with two hands, which is instinctive enough. But the emphasis is on the weaker hand, usually the left, rather than the stronger right. For a righthanded batsman, the left is the skilful hand; the right hand imparts a bit of control and some extra power, but that is all. There is nothing basically natural about that. I know people like to talk about players being naturally gifted, having a flair for the game and so on. There is a suggestion that those who have to work at the game are one step down from genuine quality. Talent is a great asset in any activity, but cricket, like most worthwhile pursuits, has to be learned and some find that easier than others.

To encourage us to keep our left elbow up and hit straight with the left hand, Johnny devised a drill which I used for years and which I recommend to any youngster who wants to play the game well. It's simple enough: drill a hole in a composition ball, suspend it about knee height and concentrate on hitting it straight, stand sideways and control the stroke with the left hand. I spent hour after hour practising that at home and with a very important spin-off. It builds technique. It also improves patience, application and concentration. None of this was obvious or particularly important to us as kids, of course, but it paid handsome dividends in later years. When I went on the 1965 tour to Australia, Bobby Simpson saw my technique and wrote that I must have developed it practising in front of the mirror. It was a compliment but there was no truth in it – my ability to play straight was developed from hour after hour competing against a ball on a bit of string.

The fact that Johnny Lawrence was a leg-spinner was an enormous help to me, too. The rubberised batting surface at his indoor net was slow and 'turned' appreciably, not altogether surprising, and that made very early demands on judgement and concentration. It is impossible to hit through a slow, turning delivery with any safety; it forced us to choose the line much more carefully and judge the length more accurately. Right forward to kill the spin or right back to allow the ball to turn before playing it. Johnny used to stand shouting 'Wait for it, wait for it . . .' like a drill sergeant. No matter how early you see the ball you must take it late – that is the golden rule against spin.

Yorkshiremen have a traditional weakness against leg-spin. The county does not produce leg-spinners of its own and that naturally leads to an unfamiliarity with the style and so to a reputation for vulnerability. I grew up with leg-spin and it held no terrors for me. In fact I always enjoyed the particular challenge of facing leg-spinners and treated it as one of the pleasures of the game.

Leg-spin is not an exact science. It is a marvellous, unpredictable skill with many mysterious twists and turns. And I learned through trial and error a fundamental truth about playing it: you must never totally trust your eyes. You can learn to read the ball out of the bowler's hand but accept only 90 per cent of what you see – simply because the ball has to pitch and any sort of predictability ends there. A googly may be a googly while it is in the air – then it hits a couple of green blades of grass, shoots and becomes a top-spinner. The bowler tries to look as though he meant it; you try and look as though you expected it all the time . . .

Playing so much against spin gave me the confidence to face it with men round the bat. Unless you can stand up and belt the ball like Ian Botham, that takes a particular blend of technique and confidence. I found I could play the ball towards fielders with assurance whereas most batsmen try hard to keep the ball away from the clutching hands. Playing the ball with the spin in to the fielders takes technique but it quickly demoralises a spinner and the men who are supposed to be catching you out.

Johnny became, and still is, a personal friend, coach and private tutor. I went to him for advice and guidance long after I began playing for Yorkshire and England. He knows my game inside out and would quickly spot any creeping errors, which I probably could not pinpoint myself. Our coaching sessions together always had a purpose. There was never the air of a knockabout or half an hour to kill. Before I went overseas on tour, for instance, we would roll up the matting, polish the floorboards and practise on that. Naturally the ball did not turn much but it did bounce more and hurry through – the sort of conditions I was likely to encounter abroad. It was no coincidence that I often made big scores in the early tour matches: I was as well prepared as I could be.

I usually tried to stay in the net for about forty-five minutes, half an hour longer than most batsmen would stick at the county nets. There was a reason for this beyond some so-called gluttony for practice: it was a conscious effort to make myself concentrate for long periods of time in circumstances as close to the real thing as I could make them. Concentration does begin to wander in the nets after fifteen minutes or so – batsmen get sloppy and begin to play shots that would be fatal in the middle. I wanted to push my mental capacity that bit further and concentrate as hard on the last delivery of a practice session as I did on the first. For the same reason I insisted on three or four bowlers at the most, instead of a string who would come at you in rotation and give you no time to settle and think properly. I would not be rushed. Every ball had to be treated with respect and seriousness or the whole exercise was pointless. Batting that much longer also gets the hands used to gripping the bat for long periods. Big scores are not made in five minutes.

The legend has grown that I am some sort of a masochist, a workaholic who selfishly hogged the nets and drove saner people to distraction with my neurotic desire for practice. I love playing cricket and I make no apology for that. I enjoy practice and I think any professional worth a light should take it seriously. Larking about in the nets is dangerous, a waste of time and an insult to the people who bowl at you. The pursuit of excellence may be a bit old-fashioned in this sophisticated world but it made sense to me and still does.

Schooldays are supposed to be the happiest days of our lives. None of us is aware of it at the time, of course, and I suppose that as a schoolboy I was very much like any other – sometimes worried by the thought of the next, unfathomable lesson, sometimes totally oblivious, always in and out of trouble. We were fortunate in that we had masters of outstanding quality who took a real interest in what we did – and in some cases still do.

I failed the eleven-plus at Fitzwilliam and went to Kinsley Secondary Modern where, horror of horrors, the facilities for playing cricket were hopeless. The school was clearly more orientated towards soccer, and the so-called cricket pitch was a bumpy disaster area in the middle of the football field. I played a lot of soccer, enjoyed it and became pretty good at it under the guidance of the teacher Roy Schofield, a soccer nut from Normanton.

After little over a year at Kinsley I took the exam for late developers and passed to go to grammar school. It was no big deal to me and I told the headmaster so, all too aware of the financial strain that a new school would put on my already overstretched parents. The headmaster was furious. I suppose I must have appeared a typical feckless kid with no interest in getting a sound education and a start in life. He sent me home from school to break the news to my parents, who accepted the financial burden with good grace, more pleased for me than I was for myself.

I had expressed a wish, if successful in the exam, to go to Hemsworth Grammar, which was only a couple of miles away from home. Instead I was allocated to Barnsley Grammar School, which was ten miles away and which would – or so it seemed to me – add even greater expense to the already costly business of buying school uniform and specially coloured sports gear. The more I weighed up the cost, the less I imagined we could afford it.

We had already invested in a grey sleeveless sweater with the black and white trimming of Barnsley Grammar School when we were told that I would attend Hemsworth Grammar School after all. I don't know why the switch was made but the headmaster of Hemsworth, Russel Hamilton, was a very keen cricket man and I already had something of a reputation in the game locally. It may have been pure coincidence.

Hemsworth was beautiful, a converted manor house with sweeping staircases and high-ceilinged classrooms set in marvellous tree-studded grounds. And of course cricket was the game in the summer.

I went straight into the school Second XI, jumping the intermediate teams and playing alongside boys much older and considerably bigger than I was. My first match was against Ackworth School at Hemsworth on a Wednesday afternoon – Ackworth was a Quaker school and that was their day for cricket – and I scored a princely four runs. They must have been the best-looking four runs in the history of the game: I was summoned on Friday and told my next match would be in the First XI next day!

You can imagine my excitement. I went home in a dream, partly elated and partly scared stiff at the prospect, and packed my cricket gear. The following day I left home about 1 p.m. so as to be in good time for the afternoon start – we had started in the afternoon against Ackworth – and arrived at the school grounds with my heart thumping. But something was wrong – the playing fields were already dotted with people in whites. The awful realisation dawned that the match had started at 10 a.m. – I had been too excited to check the time. I was too scared and mortified to seek out the teachers then. I slipped away home and did my explaining on Monday morning, when I was predictably summoned to the staff room after assembly. It sounded like a feeble excuse and I'm not sure it was entirely believed but it did not cost me my place in the side. I played in the First XI, batting to begin with at number four, for the five years I spent at the school.

Mr Hamilton was an excellent headmaster, very supportive of all school activities and insistent that we should join in as many as possible, irrespective of our ability. I never learned to swim because swimming clashed with cricket on the timetable and in fact I can only swim a few puny strokes to this day, but I became pretty good at fives and even took to rugby union. As growing boys we had healthy appetites and I recall slipping away after a poor school lunch into the village for fish and chips. That was strictly against the rules and Mr Hamilton found out. With scrupulous fairness he gave us the cane and then went out of his way to see that the lunches in future improved in quality and quantity. He lives in retirement in Exeter now and still writes to me from time to time; it's always good to hear from him.

There was no soccer at Hemsworth Grammar School – it was traditionally a rugby school – but I continued to play soccer for local teams and did well enough to play a few matches at Under-18 for Leeds United. Raich Carter was manager then, John Charles was the top player before a move to Juventus and there was a red-headed wing-half called Billy Bremner who was about our age but already good enough to play in the second team. A wing-half myself, I played alongside Bremner in a night match at Doncaster Rovers.

Rugby union held no attraction for me. I had to play a bit during games periods, a second-row forward in constant danger of having his ears pulled off and invariably on the bottom layer of a collapsed pack, but I was perfectly happy to give school matches a miss and play soccer on Saturday.

Dudley Taylor and Les Tate were the masters in charge of the rugby teams and they used to needle me about not playing, suggesting that I was too frightened or not skilful enough, harping on subtly but incessantly until I became angry enough to turn up for a Second XV practice. I got into the side and played several matches for the school at stand-off or centre, not because I particularly liked the game but because it was a matter of pride to show them I could do it.

Pride satisfied, I faked an injury one day, cried off the school match on Saturday morning and was heading for Cudworth to play soccer in the afternoon when I walked straight into Taylor and Tate coming from the school match. They never said a word but I was back outside the staff room on Monday morning – and in the next Second XV practice match I was put at full-back battling into the teeth of a gale and a storm that would have finished off King Lear. Every kick was either a high punt with a giant forward on the end of it or a grubber kick that sent me sprawling about in the mud. A mixture of pride and self-preservation forced me to grab just about everything and the following Saturday I was full-back for the First XV. . .

Dudley Taylor is still closely involved with rugby at Wakefield's College Grove Sports Club. He was one of the Yorkshire members who seconded my nomination for the county cricket club committee. We still laugh about the way he turned a distinctly reluctant rugby union player into the school full-back, district schools full-back and rugby captain of his House.

Elections for house and games captains were held throughout the school and I was voted captain of Talbot House and captain of rugby and cricket. The voting was almost unanimous, which will come as a nasty shock to some. One way and another, I seem to have been involved in ballots for most of my sporting life . . .

2

Out of the Ordinary

The man with the most influence on my cricket as a schoolboy and therefore on my whole cricket career was undoubtedly Uncle Algy. He encouraged me to play – my father was a soccer player with no great talent for cricket – and made it possible for me to do so. He also planted the seed of many of the attitudes which I took with me throughout my career. We are all the product of many influences, especially early on in life. If any one man could be said to have moulded the young Boycott as a cricketer, it was Algy.

He tells me now that he encouraged me to play because he saw in me something out of the ordinary. I already had a passion for the game, I was a quick learner by all accounts and Algy would never allow me to show fear. 'If I see you back away, ever, you're finished . . .' I can hear him telling me that today. He made me dress properly and act properly. I once questioned an umpire's decision in a second-team match for Ackworth. Algy heard about it and gave me the biggest dressing-down I have ever had.

Algy had to push me a fair bit because there was a deep fund of parochialism in mining communities in those days. I played for Ackworth but lived in Fitzwilliam, which was all of three miles away. To that extent I was something of an interloper, an outsider taking a place in the team from a local player. There was a fair bit of backbiting but Algy kept his ear to the ground and headed it off. He was supported by the club's most elegant batsman, Arnold Norton, who insisted that since I had paid my subs I was as entitled as the next bloke to be considered for the teams.

There didn't seem much danger of my pinching somebody's place in the early 1950s. I was twelve and mad keen, but that didn't amount to much. Algy was shrewd enough to wangle me a place in the second team, chiefly by keeping his ears open. The teams were picked on Thursday, and on Friday night Algy invariably went for a pint with players from the club. Overtime in those days was precious, and anyone who was offered it rarely turned it down. So it was quite possible that a player picked in the side for Saturday would be unable to turn up. Nobody held that against him – it was part of the ritual of providing for a family in difficult times. Extra money was more important than a game of cricket. Algy made it his business to find out if anybody looked like crying off and if they did he would call in at our house on his way home from the pub. I would be in bed but Mum and Dad would be told to make sure I was ready in the morning, kit clean and packed, because there might be chance of a game.

I'd go with Algy to the Boot and Shoe, wait outside until it became obvious that somebody was not going to turn up and then volunteer. 'Here's our young 'un, tek him,' said Algy. It was a matter of being regarded as slightly better than nothing, but I didn't mind how I got a game as long as I got one. Algy went off with the first team, I made my way blissfully with the second.

The second team must have been short on 3 August 1953. It was Bank Holiday Monday so the chances are they were struggling to raise a side. I made my début in the local derby against Featherstone, batted at number eight and was lbw for a duck after playing for three minutes. The following Saturday I played against Castleford at Ackworth and was promoted to six, heaven knows why. A brawny fast bowler twice my size hit me over the right eye, the eyebrow opened like a split plum and I was rushed to Pontefract to have four stitches put in the wound. There was blood all over the place. I must have looked like Henry Cooper. The doctor at the hospital wanted to be sure I wasn't suffering from concussion. How many runs had I scored? What was the total? How many fours had I hit? I'd made 14, including one four, and I could have talked him through every stroke if he'd asked me. The possibility of concussion was ruled out.

Algy came round home to see me as soon as he got back from the first-team game. He was naturally concerned about the effect an injury like this might have on a twelve-year-old. It might have shattered my confidence and Algy worked on the principle that traditionally holds good when you fall off a bike: in no time at all I was back in the nets and he was bowling at me.

The first team must have been short on 5 September because I made my début for them in a match at Goole. I batted number seven and made nine in thirty-one minutes. Ackworth won the match by 54 runs.

The following year, on 24 April, I played my first home game for Ackworth first team and came to the notice of the press for the first time. Ackworth were 87 for 7 chasing 119 to win when I joined George Hepworth. He got out when the scores were level and I hit a cover-drive for four to win the game, with Algy at the other end. I was nine not out and that merited a little mention in the *Pontefract and Castleford Express*. The mentions have been getting bigger ever since.

George Hepworth was about five years older than me and quickly came to treat me like a younger brother. He became secretary of the Ackworth club and he still is – thoroughly steeped in cricket, the sort of chap who has been the backbone of club cricket for generations. We used the Ackworth club's ticket to watch Yorkshire play in the county championship and George took me to Headingley to watch the Test matches there, leaving Fitzwilliam on the 7.55 a.m. train and falling into the ground as soon as the gates opened at 9 a.m. I remember watching Fred Trueman take 4 for 27 against India in 1952; a chap near us in the crowd said when Fred took his third wicket that he would buy us all an ice cream if he took another. Fred did, of course, and we were suitably grateful, cheering the ice cream as much as the performance. They were marvellous times.

George also took me to watch Len Hutton. There is a myth in the game that I modelled my style on Leonard as a result of watching him at an impressionable age. It's a nice thought but there is no truth in it. We went to see Len twice and it rained each time, so not a ball was bowled. I did not actually see Len bat in the flesh until many years later, when he was over fifty and we found ourselves on opposite sides in a benefit match at Fenners of Hull. I volunteered to field at short leg so I could watch his footwork closely. I have an enormous admiration for Leonard and if anyone sees similarities in our styles I'm flattered. But there is no question of my having modelled myself on him.

George Hepworth also has a distinctive place in my memory because he was the first player to run me out. We were playing for the Ackworth second team against Stanley. I was sacrificed for 25 and George went on to make 52. When he got back to the pavilion, I was still sitting with my pads on unable to believe what had happened and thinking, no doubt, of the masses of runs I would have scored but for George's intervention. He fell about laughing, though it didn't seem a laughing matter to me as an earnest fourteen-year-old. He also confessed that it was his fault because he was trying to pinch the bowling. The absolute cad . . .

Things were moving pretty quickly as far as cricket milestones were concerned. I was good at the game and just as importantly I absolutely loved it. I find it hard even now to describe the pure pleasure I got from being involved with cricket at that time. Controversy was a long way away, of course. Nobody had developed entrenched views about Geoffrey Boycott and I was just a kid enjoying a game and striving hard to play it better and better. I cannot believe there was anything unhealthily obsessive or wrong in that. If there was, I was in pretty good company in 1950s England.

School cricket took me into the South Elmsall district team, eventually as captain. The South Elmsall district was not as fashionable as, say, Leeds or Barnsley and tended to be somewhat overlooked, but I went for Yorkshire schoolboy trials in 1954 – and was absolutely shattered by the experience. Suddenly, I realised how many talented boys there were in the county. There were dozens of kids, many of them from parts of Yorkshire that I had not even heard of. I was a little bloke from the sticks with very little appreciation of the world outside my own small universe. I was completely out of my depth and didn't get near the team in the first year, though I made 12th man the year after that and was finally picked to play for Yorkshire schoolboys against Derbyshire at Queen's Park, Chesterfield, on 1 June 1955.

The Yorkshire team included John Hampshire, Chris Balderstone, Jack Birkenshaw and Duncan Fearnley. Birkenshaw and Fearnley were quite exceptional schoolboy players – both were outstanding batsmen and Birkenshaw could bowl beautifully as well. They both scored over 50 and were then retired. I was batting at five and my instructions were to get runs as quickly as possible because we were heading for a declaration. I made 13 as fast as I could, got out and was promptly left out of the team – 12th man for the next match and nowhere after that. It left an impression which still annoys me today, a feeling of injustice which still burns. I did as I was told, tried to hit quick runs under orders and was judged, apparently, as though I had played that way through choice or lack of alternative. I felt as though I had been kicked in the teeth. Perhaps I suffered because I came from the South Elmsall district when most of the influential figures in schoolboy cricket at that time were based in the bigger, more fashionable areas. I don't know, but I still feel that being from the sticks certainly didn't help me or other talented young cricketers from my part of the world.

In July of 1955 I won my first competitive trophy, a canteen of cutlery as a member of H. Tibble's XI from the Plough Inn at South Kirby, which won the Hemsworth District Challenge Cup. It was hardly a competition for the purist – everybody bowled two overs and batsmen had to retire when they had made 25, so it was a fair old slog. Most of the team were current or former rugby players, big strapping lads who could belt the ball around, who could move quickly in the field and who had good ball sense. It was great to be in a winning side.

Later that year I opened the innings for the first time in league cricket. Ackworth were playing Featherstone, who included a big and fearsome fast bowler called Dick Bellfield – something of a bloodstained legend in his own area. We were short of an opener and there was no queue of volunteers. Algy would never have let me do it, so I waited until he was out of earshot and then offered to have a go. I don't really know why. Perhaps at fourteen I was too young to know any better. I just fancied giving it a go as an opener. By the time Algy knew what was going on I had my pads on and was all ready to go. I didn't score many but I do remember that the demon bowler said afterwards I had played very well. That was enough for me.

Although I probably didn't know it at the time, I played my last match for Ackworth on 1 September 1956 against Atlas and Norfolk. I was out first ball and Ackworth's Cyril Ecclestone, a medium pacer, took a double hat-trick – six wickets in seven balls!

Ackworth did a lot for my young cricket but there comes a time when you have to stretch yourself, aim for a higher standard to see how good you are or could be. Algy discussed my situation with Herbert Johnson, who had played for Barnsley in the Yorkshire League and reckoned I should move there. 'I've seen too many good young 'uns not make it because they weren't adventurous enough to move on,' said Herbert. That was not going to happen to me.

Herbert knew Clifford Hesketh, cricket chairman of Barnsley Cricket Club and a vice-president of Yorkshire, and arranged for me to have a trial at Shaw Lane. I arrived early at the indoor net – the tea room temporarily converted for the winter months – and batted against Eric Butcher, one of the club's leading bowlers. I was so engrossed in my practice that I didn't even notice Hesketh had arrived – I wouldn't have recognised him in any case. He must have been reasonably impressed because Barnsley said they would be happy to have me next season.

The Yorkshire League and Bradford League were easily the strongest in the county at that time, much stronger than they are today. The Yorkshire League even played on county grounds at Scarborough, Headingley and Sheffield's Bramall Lane. At sixteen, I wasn't likely to get in the first team and the second team played in the Yorkshire Council – the same competition as Ackworth's First XI. The surroundings would be familiar but the standard through the Barnsley club as a whole would be that much higher. In my early seasons there I practised alongside men like Dickie Bird, later to play for Yorkshire and Leicestershire and to become the world's leading Test umpire, Eddie Legard and Hubert Padgett, who had played for Yorkshire, and Peter Myers, a talented Yorkshire schoolboy player. They were good, they set high standards and I was a small fish in a big pond.

I was still playing for the grammar school First XI when I was picked for Barnsley seconds, so there was often quite a rush to finish one match in the morning and get to Barnsley's match in the afternoon. The Barnsley secretary George Northern used to pick me up in his car after the school game, or I would get a lift on the back of schoolfriend Eddie Hambleton's motorbike, clinging on for dear life. Sometimes it was impossible to make the Barnsley match in time, though they would keep a place open for me if they knew I was going to arrive late. George put his foot down or Eddie opened the throttle. We made it to as many games as we could.

School exams were beginning to play a bigger part in my life. I was getting very close to my GCE 'O' levels and doing a fair amount of swotting in the dim light at Milton Terrace. It was then that I came to the dreadful realisation that my eyesight was not 100 per cent, and with it the totally demoralising conviction that my ambitions to play cricket for Yorkshire were a waste of time.

I began to have difficulty picking out words on the blackboard and when I queried it with my mates at school they told me generously that I must be going blind. 'Get your ruddy eyes tested . . .' – so I did, at an optician in Hemsworth. The confirmation that I needed glasses was the most devastating news of my life.

It seems illogical and silly now, and of course it was. But it was very real to a boy of sixteen who loved sport, lived for cricket and was determined – like most of his contemporaries – to play for Yorkshire one day. Nobody, but nobody in top sport wore glasses; specs were for intellectuals and weeds, not sportsmen. There was as much chance of my playing for Yorkshire in glasses as there was of playing for them with one leg, or so it seemed.

The frames themselves didn't help. This was long before the days of fashion glasses. Spectacles were functional and not remotely decorative: two uncompromising glass discs plonked into a fragile frame and wired to the ears. Specky Four-Eyes to a T. I loathed my new glasses, hated them as I have rarely hated anything in my life, and became convinced, of course, that without them I couldn't actually see a thing. I used to take them off as soon as I got out of school and would catch my bus home on a colour-coding system, firmly persuaded that I couldn't read the number board or the destination. Pale blue and dark blue was my bus, the reds and greens were to be ignored. When I actually walked past my mother in the street and did not appear to recognise her, it was the last straw. She knew that something had to be done about a boy who cried in his room at night and was totally, illogically inconsolable.

A bouncer, aged eight months.

Portrait of Mum in 1933, sweet eighteen.

Smile please – Mum and Dad at the seaside, overdressed for the occasion.

In the backyard at Milton Terrace with Aunty Mary and baby Jane. Whatever happened to the curls . . . ?

Beach boys: with my younger brothers Tony (left) and Peter (centre).

Collars, ties and pullovers, even on the beach, with Tony.

On the front at Blackpool, aged ten, with Uncle Jack, Aunty Annie and Tony.

Likely lads at Fitzwilliam Primary School, sporting my first cricket bat and a basin haircut.

Earliest action pictures of the correct young batsman…

…and the stylish young bowler.

Mr Weaver, one of the earliest influences on my cricket, is extreme right of the Fitzwilliam Junior School group, 1952. The headmaster, Mr Perry, is extreme left and I am in the middle of the back row, aged eleven.

Junior School play, 1949. Watch out for the Wood Ogre with the moustache and beard, sixth from the right, middle row. The villain of the piece, even at nine years of age . . .

Hemsworth Grammar School Second XV, with the formidable Dudley Taylor (left) and Les Tate in the middle row. I am extreme left at the back.

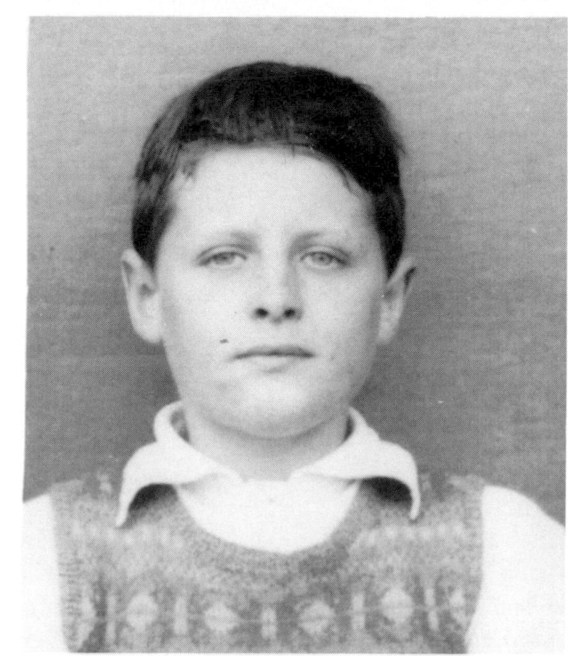

School portrait, 1951. A hint of strength in the ten-year-old face?

A handsome prize for a fourteen-year-old. My first cricket trophy, as a member of the Plough Inn team which won the Ackworth KO competition.

Grammar School cricket team, 1958, with me as captain sitting with folded arms. Les Tate is second from the right at the back; headmaster Russell Hamilton is in the middle. On the left in the front row is Eddie Hambleton.

Ackworth First XI pictured at Knaresborough, 1954. Uncle Algy is third player from the left on the back row, George Hepworth fifth from the left, Herbert Johnson extreme right. I am second left, front row.

The one man who probably knows my game better than I do. With my long-time friend, adviser and coach, Johnny Lawrence – inevitably, in the nets.

A gentle delivery from the greatest of fast bowlers: Fred Trueman helps me celebrate my first century for Yorkshire in the Roses match at Bramall Lane, 1963, with a drop of the not-so-hard stuff. Bryan Stott got a cuppa, and a century too.

Mum was right. She was at her wits' end and I was making life impossible for myself and everyone close to me. I bottled it all up inside, dwelt on the dreadful knowledge that my life was as good as finished and insisted that I was a failure. To myself, that is; I couldn't bring myself to discuss it with anybody.

Algy came to the rescue. He gave me a firm talking to, told me I was letting myself and my family down and pointed out that there were players in first-class cricket who wore glasses and did well – Roy Marshall at Hampshire and Warwickshire's M. J. K. Smith. I wrote to Mike about our supposed mutual problem and received a reply, handwritten on Warwickshire notepaper, pointing out that he wore rimless glasses with special shatterproof lenses for his cricket. Perhaps there was life after myopia after all.

My new spectacles fitted more snugly over the nose and behind the ears. They did not slip about and were a vast improvement on the National Health horrors, or so I thought. I probably looked like Himmler but the psychological effect was amazing – a huge flood of relief and a trickle of renewed self-confidence. I have always been grateful to Mike Smith for that.

Later I wore specially made spectacles for cricket and a more routine pair for everyday use. I eventually graduated to contact lenses and still wear them today. When I left Ackworth, an already venerable umpire, Ike Rudge, insisted that he had seen a future England player in the making. When I played my first game in glasses, for Hemsworth Grammar School against Wath, the local groundsman Mr Mansfield observed that there was no way I could play the game well in specs – I was finished at anything like top level. Ike Rudge was right; he lived to see me play for England, but I doubt that he knew how close I came to despair and to an emotional trauma that by itself very nearly proved Mr Mansfield right.

The first obvious and positive step towards playing for Yorkshire is to be invited to the winter nets, held at that time in Leeds, Bradford and Sheffield and the testing ground for the most promising youngsters in the county. They were nominated by a whole network of interested people – Clifford Hesketh put my name forward – and had the opportunity once a week to rub shoulders with their heroes from the county first and second teams while trying hard to make an impression of their own. Youngsters were coached and assessed then by Maurice Leyland, one of Yorkshire's great players, a kind and jovial man who was respected and popular, and by Arthur Mitchell, a stern and unyielding man who was respected and feared.

I think Arthur Mitchell thought I lived just down the road from the building at Headingley – a long, former refreshment hut roughly on the site of the present players' pavilion – where the nets were held in early 1957. I was usually there smack on time. After school I would dash home, grab a bit of tea and my kit, and catch the bus to Headingley, which was a good deal more tedious than it sounds. Nets started around 6 p.m. and by the time Arthur had finished with me (he would keep me bowling at the end) it would be well after 8.30. And that was a long day for somebody still at school who was up at 7.30 in the morning.

Then I had to catch a bus to Leeds city centre, change for Wakefield and change again for Fitzwilliam. Even if I managed to catch a train, it was usually gone 10.30 p.m. by the time I got home. I often fell asleep on the train and woke with a jolt as it started to pull out of Fitzwilliam station, bags and Boycott spilling out on to the platform as the train gathered speed. I missed Fitzwilliam altogether once and woke up just as the train was pulling out of South Elmsall on its way to Doncaster. Goodness knows how I would have got home from there at that time of night.

It never occurred to me to tell Arthur, or Mr Mitchell as I would then have called him, that I had a long way to go home. I enjoyed the nets too much and in any case he frightened me to death. He frightened everybody to death, including the first-teamers, who affected a certain familiarity but did just as they were told.

Arthur has always been known in Yorkshire as Ticker and I confess I still don't know why. I fancied it was because he was always ticking like a bomb ready to explode or because he was always ticking somebody off. Stories about Ticker's stony, autocratic attitude at the nets were legend. We were terrified of the man long before we set eyes on him and he did not disappoint us. A rebuke from Ticker could make you squirm and ruin your equilibrium for a week. There was no flannel, no soft soap – if Ticker had to make a point twice, you were in trouble. He would stop the whole net, make his point in a tone of voice that made it plain he was dealing with a lunatic and add with awful finality: 'Tha's no good to me if tha's not goin' to listen.' We quaked when he noticed us, but we lived in hope that he would, and that he would be impressed.

I remember reaching Headingley a little late one winter evening. We changed in what is now the old pavilion and it was pitch black as I hurried across to the net, homing in on a pinpoint of light from one of the windows. A shadowy figure passed me walking the other way and I thought for a moment that it was Ticker, but I dismissed the notion on the ground that he would already be hard at work in the nets.

When I got inside there was no sign of Ticker and no activity in his net.

Apparently a young celebrity by the name of Brian Close had been acting the goat in Ticker's net, banging the ball about and not taking the session altogether seriously. Ticker had gathered the balls from the bowlers, tossed one of them to Closey and said: 'Here's a ball, tha's got a bat, tha'd better play on thi own . . .' He went for a walk, which was when I passed him in the night. We could not imagine anything more ominous. We stood about like condemned men waiting for the appearance of the executioner and nobody messed about when Ticker finally returned.

Maurice Leyland had a totally different approach and would tell stories against himself – like the fact that in his career there were two bowlers he simply could not pick, so he just used to try and slog them around. It worked most of the time and they never imagined he was hitting them at random. Maurice thought that was a great joke – when he told the story he reminded me of the laughing sailor at the seaside: put in a penny and stand back for a predictable explosion. It was no wonder that a lot of youngsters tried hard to get into Maurice's net rather than Ticker's. I occasionally sought out Maurice's net for rest and recuperation but I was determined not to let Ticker demoralise me.

Ticker's idea of lavish praise was to mutter, 'Not bad, not bad.' It was like winning the pools or being given a knighthood to us. But I resolved that one day I would make him say 'Well played!' It became a matter of pride for me to play in his net and try to force him to compliment me on my ability. He never did, at least not until many years later when I had established myself as an England player.

I told him then – he mellowed a bit once his pupils had made the grade, and it became possible to talk to him – that I thought he was a hard and even cruel taskmaster when we were kids. We never got any praise. 'It paid off, didn't it?' said Ticker with a smile. 'I was hardest on those who had something. My job was to look for county cricketers.' Yorkshire at that time had a high and unrelenting expectation of success – an attitude still prevalent today despite many years of frustration and disappointments. If you could not take the pressure from Ticker at the nets you would never withstand the demands of the Yorkshire public. That was the theory and no doubt it helped to propagate the notion that Yorkshiremen were hard-bitten and single-minded, which is not a million miles from the truth.

Ticker's methods probably did destroy some youngsters over the years. His retort would probably have been to agree and point out that he had discovered and developed some pretty formidable cricketers too. But I doubt that he would get away with the same attitude these days. The present senior coach Doug Padgett has a sharp edge to his tongue when necessary but he's a dove compared to Ticker the hawk. Given Ticker's attitude today, parents would probably complain to the county committee and they would reprimand him for upsetting potential players of the future. It probably did not matter as much when half the eligible population of Yorkshire was queuing up to play for the county.

There was a side-effect of Ticker's coaching method that helped me enormously in later years, especially in Test matches against Australia. The Australians have a deserved reputation as the masters of 'sledging' in the international game. It's a fancy word which means simply that they try to anger and unsettle opposing batsmen by abusing them during an innings. It never bothered me. I can't even say it went in one ear and out of the other because it simply did not register, much to the surprise of umpires in Australia who asked me if I wanted them to take steps to stop the talking. After a few years of measured criticism from Ticker Mitchell, nothing an Australian could say would have any impact whatsoever.

Ticker played for Yorkshire for seventeen years and for England six times – a magnificent slip fielder and a dour opening batsman. There is a beautiful story that England were hit by the last-minute withdrawal of Maurice Leyland with lumbago before the 1935 Test against South Africa at Headingley and Yorkshire's captain Brian Sellers had to speed off in search of a replacement. He found Ticker cutting the privet hedge at his home in Baildon and bundled him off to Headingley where he scored 58 and 72 in the match.

After I scored my hundredth first-class century in the 1977 Test match against Australia at Headingley, Fred Trueman revealed how Ticker had once called him over in the nets and told him to bowl flat-out at the schoolboy Boycott. Fred was a bit taken aback but did as he was told, naturally enough, and was then asked what he thought of the young batsman. 'He's got a good defence,' said Fred. 'He doesn't play many shots but he's not going to be easy to get out . . .'

'You're right,' said Ticker with a distant look. 'He has got a good defence. Just think what we might have here if we could teach him to play a few shots . . .'

My Barnsley connection amounted to eight matches for the Second XI in 1957, a steady season in which I averaged 66 and bumped into a very good cricketer who has since made his reputation internationally but in a very different field. In a match against Monk Bretton at Barnsley I was relegated from opener because we had bowled out the opposition cheaply and there was a recruit from the first team who wanted the chance of a knock. He scored 46 not out before disappearing back to the First XI, with whom he had scored the first century in the league the previous year. 'A dazzling century,' said the local paper, scored against Harrogate (in the company of Dickie Bird) with three sixes and ten fours. The usurper's name was Mike Parkinson.

I broke into Barnsley's first team after the school term finished, made 19 not out in my first match and an unbeaten 43 in my second, leading Barnsley to victory at Castleford in an unfinished partnership with Parky, 15 not out.

Next year I had a very ordinary season with Barnsley but did well at school, where I was in my last term and captain of the First XI. I was still attending Johnny Lawrence's school and the Yorkshire nets, where Ticker and Maurice had a big say in recommending boys for the Yorkshire Federation Under-18 side. I was picked as vice-captain for what promised to be a full-week Midlands tour with matches against Leicestershire, Warwickshire, Worcestershire, Nottinghamshire, Derbyshire and Lancashire.

It should have been marvellous – the very thought of playing on famous county grounds was exciting enough. Instead it rained for practically the whole week, some matches were abandoned altogether and the whole atmosphere of the tour was ruined. I remember standing at Edgbaston, in pre-Brumbrella days, of course, and watching the pools of water get bigger and deeper.

School finished for me in July 1958 with seven 'O' levels, though I failed English Literature – I swear it was because I was too busy practising for an Under-18 match against Lancashire (which was rained off in any case). It was time to get a job. I leaned towards the sciences rather than the arts and there was talk of a career in metallurgy or draughtsmanship. The headmaster wanted me to stay on and aim for university but that was out of the question. My parents had subsidised me for long enough. They had never embarrassed me by making reference to financial difficulties but it was obvious that if I stayed on at school it would impose an intolerable strain on them. I never discussed it with them – I decided it was time to start bringing in a wage.

Like most school leavers, I had only the sketchiest idea of what I might actually do. An important consideration was that it should leave me free, if possible, to play cricket for Yorkshire. I was determined to get into the second team and I knew they played two-day matches in midweek. Where could I find a decent job that would release me when the time came? George Northern's wife Mildred suggested the civil service. I applied and was accepted as a trainee clerical officer at the Ministry of Pensions and National

Insurance in Barnsley. It was quite an eye-opener in more ways than one.

For a start, I was sent on a five-night course to London. I was eighteen and I hadn't really been anywhere, except on day trips to the seaside – Cleethorpes, Scarborough, Skegness, Blackpool – which represented the limit of the family budget and of relatives' generosity. A whole week in London was a fantastic experience. I was as much a tourist as anyone from overseas and spent hours just walking round Leicester Square and Piccadilly Circus marvelling at the lights and the bustle. There are those from the north of England who visit London and are glad to get away, annoyed and perhaps intimidated by the pace and clamour of the place. I loved it then and still do.

My new colleagues at the Ministry in Barnsley had advised me to go and see *West Side Story*, the newest stage musical in town and one which was receiving rave reviews from everyone who saw it. They knew that it was booked out for months and probably sniggered at the thought of me turning up at the theatre. I was naive enough to join the queue and ask for a ticket. 'When for?' asked the girl at the box office. 'Tonight please,' said the boy from the sticks. The extraordinary thing was that I got one – probably nobody else had the gall or the gullibility to ask – and found myself in the front stalls of Her Majesty's Theatre rubbing shoulders with black ties and sparkling diamonds. The show was marvellous. I have seen it three or four times since and still enjoy it as much as I did that first night.

I went to see *The Mousetrap*. It was the longest-running show in the world, so it had to be good; and I bought a ticket from a tout – a spiv he would be called then – to see *My Fair Lady* in Drury Lane. I ended up in the gods – I can't remember what I paid for the pleasure but it was worth it. After all, there was absolutely no guarantee that I would ever visit London again. I had to make the best of it while I could. When I got back to Barnsley my friends didn't actually believe what I had done. I had to recount all the details – except whodunnit in *The Mousetrap*, of course – and they listened suitably impressed. Looking back, I'm a little bit surprised by my own initiative.

Working at the Ministry of Pensions taught me a good deal about life and about people, but I can't pretend I enjoyed it. It opened my eyes to some of the raw realities of a working-class existence – I had never been protected from that but as a teenager I had never really confronted it either.

The building in Barnsley was about 500 yards from the bus station up a slight incline; you and I would not even call it a hill. But I lost count of the number of people who would arrive at the office in a state of near-collapse, coughing and wheezing through flecked lips, victims of chronic bronchitis or emphysema or some other awful illness directly related to the environment of pitheads and relative poverty. Many had struggled the 500 yards, stopping two or three times to catch their breath, just because their benefit money was a couple of days late and they had nothing to live on. Fine people reduced to wrecks through no fault of their own.

I was beginning to specialise in sickness, injury and maternity benefits, so I saw them all: shameless skivers, genuinely pathetic cases, those who imagined they were asking for charity and those who turned up at the front office determined to punch some busybody on the nose.

The forms were a nightmare for me, especially those dealing with maternity benefit, which required applicants to say whether they were married, divorced, separated and so on. Remember, we are talking about the standards of over a quarter of a century ago: there was an enormous social stigma associated with unmarried mothers and even divorcees. People would leave that part of the form blank on purpose. I had to press them for answers – it seemed very hurtful and personal, and I hated it. I felt awkward for them. It might have taught me the necessity of dealing with people as individuals and of not judging anybody at first sight, but it was a desperately sad way to learn.

That was experience, accelerated and invaluable, and so was my cricket with Barnsley, where the standards were higher and where I was doing reasonably well without creating any major sensations. I averaged 28 in 1959, finishing the season with a duck, which somehow summed it up, but I felt that I was steadily becoming a better player.

At that time I did not fancy batting against the new ball at all. It was not a question of physical fear – I have never been frightened by pace – rather a lack of confidence in my ability to play the ball when it swung or seamed. We developed a system which suited me and the team under which the wicketkeeper Eddie Legard would go in, see the shine off the new ball and enable me to play more easily later on. He and Dickie Bird set out against Hull in one match and didn't come back . . . Dickie scored 85 and Eddie 74, winning the match while I sat all afternoon with my pads on, chalking it up to experience.

Yorkshire finally picked me for the Second XI in a match against Cumberland at Penrith on 6 and 7 July 1959. I scored 5 and 15 batting at number five in the company of men like Brian Bolus, John Hampshire, Vic Wilson and the captain Ted Lester and we won by 91 runs. Oddly enough, the thing I remember most about the match was the performance of David Pickles, a Halifax youngster who had been hailed the previous season as an even faster bowler than Fred. Pickles was not expensive but he simply could

Boycott made his début for Yorkshire 2nd XI on 6 July 1959 against Cumberland at Penrith.

not find any sort of rhythm – the ball was bouncing three times to the wicketkeeper and the poor lad couldn't do anything about it. He gave his kit away at the end of the season and disappeared from the Yorkshire scene totally demoralised – so much promise so quickly evaporated. I felt sorry for him.

Yorkshire picked me for one more match in the seconds that season, against Nottinghamshire at Worksop, where I was run out for 1, and not out 2 in the second innings. Not the most auspicious of starts, perhaps, but at least I felt as though I was making progress. Playing only two matches for Yorkshire was infinitely preferable to no match at all. The club was strong then. The first team under Ronnie Burnet had just won the championship and the second team was littered with real prospects for the future like Hampshire, Birkenshaw, Fearnley and Phil Sharpe. I was a small part of it but a part nevertheless.

That is why the next year, 1960, was incredibly frustrating, a year when I should have been going forward and when instead I came to a dead halt. At least that's how it seemed to me. It started well enough – I played the first five matches of the season for Barnsley, was 12th man for Yorkshire's county championship side against Sussex at Middlesbrough and made top score of 36 for Barnsley against Scarborough, the best attack in the league. Ted Lester hinted strongly that I was about to be picked for Yorkshire Colts again, the world was my oyster – and I pulled a hamstring chasing a ball to the boundary in the same Scarborough match.

The injury refused to clear up, despite frequent visits to the physiotherapist and I missed the middle ten weeks of the season. The fact that Yorkshire kept expressing an interest in my progress was encouraging but probably counter-productive: I kept trying the injury out too soon and putting back my recovery for another interminable spell. Instead of chalking up more matches for Yorkshire seconds I ended up not playing for them at all that year – all the more maddening because I played well for Barnsley before and after the injury, putting together consistent scores and finishing with an average of 74, which suggested I was coming to terms with the demands of a tougher and more searching kind of cricket.

My experience as 12th man in Middlesbrough was quite a revelation. It was a privilege for me just to rub shoulders with the star names in their own environment. I probably tried to look blasé about it but I was tickled pink by the opportunity. The extra-mural activities were something else: Brian Close and Ted Dexter chipping golf balls into a large open umbrella until the hotel manager put his foot down in defence of a large and very expensive wall mirror; Close and Mike Cowan involved in a race round the hotel lawn which Close won largely because Cowan stopped chasing after a few strides and let Closey charge away as though the devil was on his heels. Close won his one-man race and could hardly stand up after it.

The fact that Yorkshire won the match against Sussex after twenty minutes' play the next day puts the night's revelry in context: Yorkshire were a very formidable team that played hard and then played hard . . . They could afford to let their hair down once they had a match by the throat, which was not uncommon in those days. Being involved as 12th man was an experience.

But that did not lessen the frustration of a season of injury and disappointment. I became very conscious of the fact that other young players, rivals if you like, had taken a year's start. John Hampshire played twenty-three innings for Yorkshire Colts that year, Chris Balderstone played twenty, Jack Birkenshaw played ten and moved into the first team, Duncan Fearnley left with a contract to Worcestershire. And I had done nothing, or so it seemed, but waste my time. I even watched the Colts play at Barnsley and saw then why everybody was talking in such glowing terms about Hampshire, a powerful shot-making opener with every prospect of a fine Yorkshire career. I didn't begrudge him his success but I fretted desperately at my own inability to get involved. They moved ahead while I was nursing a hamstring and a bad case of frustration. I had to catch up quickly – and the answer was a move from the Barnsley club to Leeds.

The move was made simply to improve my chances of progression, just as moving from Ackworth to Barnsley had promised me a better class of cricket and improved my game. The Leeds captain was Michael Crawford, already on the Yorkshire committee; their best player was Billy Sutcliffe, a former Yorkshire captain who would be elected to the committee in due course; Johnny Lawrence then played for Leeds, and it was the headquarters of Yorkshire county cricket. There was no doubt that it was a fashionable club and that if I played well there I would be noticed and my chances of playing for Yorkshire would improve. Only, of course, if I played well.

Billy Sutcliffe was keen that I join Leeds and promised to give me every bit of help he could. He wanted me to open the innings and although I was not all that keen we struck a bargain whereby I would give it a try and drop down the order if it didn't work out. Billy said he would teach me all he knew and he was as good as his word. We had our differences later but he was a tremendous help to me at that time.

If Barnsley were sorry to see me go – and I hope they were – I do not recall any hint of acrimony at my decision to join Leeds. Herbert Johnson's philosophy still applied – you had to move on to get on – and there was nothing dishonourable in a burning ambition to play for Yorkshire. I still practised with the Barnsley lads at Shaw Lane a couple of nights a week and captained local scratch team the Cuckoos to victory in a locally prestigious knockout competition for the Shaw Lane Open trophy. Further afield, things were looking up, too.

After a shaky start with Leeds I began to make runs as an opener and was selected for Yorkshire seconds' fourth match of the 1961 season at Worcester where I made an unbeaten 61 in the second innings. After that I played in most of the Colts' matches that season and felt as though I might just have arrived. Competition was fierce, Yorkshire had plenty of likely lads to choose from and it was part of their policy to run the rule over different players in the second team. I didn't get in every time but I didn't feel as though I was being rejected when I was left out. I began as a mid-order batsman and very soon was asked by Ted Lester to open the innings. The season developed just as I would have wanted it to and there was no doubt that my move to Leeds had paid off.

I was fifth in the league averages that season, topped the batting averages at Leeds, and, most significantly, headed the Yorkshire Colts' averages in my first full season: 688 runs at 38.2 with a top score of 156 not out against Cumberland at Bridlington. I felt that I had made up a lot of lost ground. After a year of stagnation and screaming frustration, I had played a great deal of demanding and important cricket and played it well enough to enjoy a feeling of real achievement. There was even a suggestion that I might be awarded my second-team cap but it appears that Brian Sellers, whose word at Yorkshire was law, decided I should prove myself for at least another season. Nothing was given easily at Yorkshire, which is precisely as it should be.

3

A Professional Man

At the beginning of the 1962 season Ted Lester gave me a bit of advice which has coloured my approach to batting for a living ever since: if you get the chance, said Ted, score centuries. Good scores are always valuable but centuries stick in the mind; there are influential people who might not notice a good innings of 60 or 70 but they will react if you get a hundred. I hadn't thought about it in quite those terms but Ted was obviously right. The difference between a score in the 90s and a century is often reflected as the difference between failure and success. It may be illogical but a century in cricket has its own magic.

The season began well when I scored 126 not out for the Colts against Cumberland at Gargrave in front of Sellers and was given my second-team cap. I remember an incident which followed that may have had a profound influence on my attitude, though I was not conscious of it at the time. We went into a local pub and Sellers offered to buy a round. When it came to my turn and I told him I would like an orange juice he snorted with contempt. 'You can buy your own bloody orange juice. Fancy drinking orange juice . . .' I didn't know Sellers well at the time, though his power at Yorkshire was legendary and he was obviously a man used to giving orders and having his own way. There was no need for him to try and belittle a young man who quite simply did not like the taste of beer. I felt small and humiliated.

But the runs continued to come – 39 and 87 not out against Northumberland, which prompted the new Colts captain Robin Feather to suggest I was very close to being picked for the first team. The second-team match against Lancashire was coming up, a much bigger occasion in those days than it is now and one fought implacably by the committees on both sides. Do well in the junior Roses match and the committee really will sit up and take notice, said Feather. I scored 39 and 104 not out against Ken Higgs and Peter Lever bowling well, followed by 56 in the next match against Cumberland.

Boycott's first-class début for Yorkshire was against Pakistan at Bradford on 16 June 1962.

At last, at the age of twenty-one, I was picked for the first team, to play against Pakistan at Bradford. It was another challenge, another hurdle to overcome, and I do not honestly remember any exceptional sense of delight. No doubt I was pleased with my progress but the important thing was not just being selected for the first team, it was finding out if I was good enough to make it. The signs weren't all that promising.

I hit the first ball I received from medium-pacer D'Souza for four; so far so good. But he bowled me soon afterwards and got me out for four again in the second innings. England's Test players were queuing up at the time to smash D'Souza all over the place and here was I making a mess of two important innings against him. I obviously still had a lot to learn, and George Hepworth who watched the match admits that for the first time he had doubts about my ability at the highest level. 'I hope he's going to make it,' said George.

I was disappointed but I still had some faith in my own ability and I didn't think that failure against Pakistan was the end of the world. Yorkshire picked me for the first team for the next two matches, batting down the order at Northampton and opening the innings at Chesterfield. Two incidents overshadowed any runs I made and became the breeding ground for a new and gruesome reputation.

Phil Sharpe was run out for 18 at Northampton. He played the ball to cover, saw there was a misfield and called for a run; I sent him back. I cannot recall to this day if it was my fault – it all happened very quickly and I may have been responding to the old rule of thumb about never running to a misfield. I really don't know. What I do remember is that Sharpe was very annoyed and that the captain Vic Wilson gave me a dressing-down. Sharpe was in form at the time and was anxious to press his claim for a place on the winter tour to Australia. Wilson's message was loud and clear: as a very junior player it was up to me to run when Sharpe called, it was not up to me to doubt his judgement. Quite simply, I should do as I was told and no more.

I couldn't accept the logic of that. If I was at fault I was more than willing to apologise. I was sorry if I had made a mistake. But cricket is a thinking game and I was being asked not to think. I accepted the seniority and extra experience of the other players but blind obedience really was not my style. It may have been a mistake to stick up for myself quite so forcibly in the circumstances; it may be that Vic had not made his point very well or that I had misunderstood him. Either way, we agreed to differ.

That was bad enough. But at Chesterfield Ken Taylor was run out for

36. He played the ball to mid-on, set off for a quick single and was hopelessly run out when I sent him back. I was already in bad odour after the Sharpe incident and now my name was mud, even though I was carrying an injury which restricted my mobility and which the team knew about. I had bruised my hip-bone fielding earlier in the match and there was some question of whether I was fit enough to open the innings. No matter, run-outs are annoying and emotive. There is no more aggravating way of getting out at cricket than being run out. Cricket is all about mistakes, or avoiding them, and run-outs involve two members of the same team who briefly do the opposition's job for them. There is an immediate and natural desire to apportion blame, especially on the part of the batsman who is out. He has time to reflect on the foolishness of the dismissal, the waste of an opportunity, the growing sense of annoyance and injustice which isn't exactly soothed if his former partner goes on to make runs. That is human nature. It may not be an entirely Corinthian response but professional cricket is a living as well as a game. The first emotion of a batsman who has been run out is probably resentment and as a professional I find that totally understandable.

What began to happen to me, even this early in my career, was considerably more sinister. It was the suggestion that I did not actually care if I ran somebody out, the muttered accusation that I was ready to look after myself and to hell with my team-mates. A belief took root and grew out of all sense and proportion that I was a lone and selfish individual, interested only in looking after number one. Thinking back, I am convinced that the legend grew as a result of what I did not do rather than because of anything I actually did.

Specifically, I did not go in the bar. Social drinking and sometimes serious drinking is an implicit part of cricket, whether it follows a game on the village green or a Test match. It has come to be accepted as part of the fellowship of the game and as a genuine opportunity to foster team spirit. I have no criticism whatsoever of those who get together for a drink. I do not like beer so I didn't go in the bar – and I'm convinced that if I had, I would have stifled my reputation for selfishness before it had a chance to become folklore.

Because I was not in the bar, mulling over the run-outs, talking them through, probably apologising for the umpteenth time, there was no opportunity for the other players to see that I cared about what had happened. Once you have apologised, as I did, what more do you have to do? Burst into tears? Go on bended knee? The obvious answer would have been to go into the bar, buy a few drinks and let beery bonhomie take its course. Instead I was conspicuous by my absence.

The fact that I didn't and still don't actually like the taste of beer was only a basic reason for not joining the boys at the bar. Sellers had tried those months earlier to embarrass me into drinking beer and had failed. I didn't really consider there was anything remarkable in beer – I was more interested in playing cricket.

The suggestion follows that I might have gone to the bar and socialised without drinking a great deal, just shown a willingness to be with the boys because my absence could be construed as a reluctance to join in. I can understand the argument.

But the fact is that being at the bar talking about cricket as we inevitably were did not help me unwind. On the contrary it filled my head with all sorts of theories and suggestions until I found it quite impossible to sleep. Most cricketers find that a couple of hours round the bar and a few pints actually help them to relax. In my case it had the opposite effect. That had nothing to do with alcohol – it was the same on orange juice. My mind would be racing with all kinds of ideas and I simply could not get off to sleep, which is hopeless as far as I am concerned. Throughout my career I have always needed my sleep, at least eight and a half hours if I was going to be fit company and fit to play. Not everybody needs that but I do. I recognised the fact and planned my relaxation accordingly.

Boycott's first ball in first-class cricket was despatched for 4.

I found it far more beneficial to go to my room, do some reading, watch a bit of television, write a few letters, have an evening meal and relax. That is a habit which has stayed with me more or less all my professional life. It might not suit everybody but it suits me. I didn't realise as a young man trying to make my way that it would create a particular image for being anti-social or uncaring – if I had, I might have made a conscious effort to change, though somehow I doubt it. Brian Close spotted a non-drinker and non-smoker in the team and forecast that I would end up doing both before long. I bet him that I wouldn't and I won my bet.

I played only two more matches for the First XI that season and acted as 12th man several times, which was good as far as the experience and involvement went but did not give me much opportunity actually to play cricket. My batting suffered through lack of practice and eventually I couldn't even make runs in the second team; the year just seemed to tail away. One oddity remained: on 14 July I made an unbeaten 139 for Leeds against Rotherham, the highest score in the league that season. John Hampshire scored 104 in the same match and helped Rotherham to victory. Our fortunes already seemed to be interwoven.

Close became captain in 1963 when Vic Wilson retired, which was probably a good thing as far as my future with Yorkshire was concerned! Wilson was apparently adamant that I shouldn't have one. He told Sellers at the end of the '62 season that Boycott was not a good enough player to be persevered with and, in any case, was not the right sort of person for Yorkshire – whatever that meant. Sellers asked Close for his opinion. Close said he had not seen enough of me as a player to make a firm judgement but had always found me helpful and co-operative. Instead of releasing me, Yorkshire named me in the squad for the first two matches of the season with the proviso that I would be 12th man against the MCC. I remember the match because Graham Atkinson scored 176 for MCC, the same Atkinson who used to stoke the fire at Johnny Lawrence's icy indoor school; I remember it too because Fred Trueman ran out Jimmy Binks.

Binks had a long and distinguished career with Yorkshire. He was a very durable individual and a magnificent wicketkeeper, but he never scored a first-class century. It looked as though he would crack it at Lord's, 88 not out, when Fred ran him out. Binks was furious, predictably enough. The language and the drift of his remarks to Fred were much the same as had been directed at me or would be hurled at anybody involved in one of these infernal run-outs. That incident cropped up repeatedly during my career alongside Binks at Yorkshire. Others may have forgotten it but I don't think he ever did.

Ironically enough, Fred scored his own maiden century not long afterwards in a match against Northants, a game in which Colin Milburn – bigger and fatter than ever – bowled me out for 8 and is still determined never to let me forget the fact.

Fred's century was a real eye-opener, a genuine innings full of fine strokes and authority: I would have been more than proud of it myself. I batted with him for a while and marvelled at his confidence and presence. The thought occurred that if he could bat like that as a tail-ender, what possible hope was there for me trying to get on as a recognised batsman? I certainly wasn't finding professional cricket easy at the time. Fred that day made batting look like a piece of cake which, relatively speaking, he probably always thought it was.

We were bedevilled by injuries that season, which probably helped to keep me in the side, and after I'd been rushed by plane down to Gravesend to play against Kent I was picked for the Roses match at Sheffield's Bramall Lane. As a ground it had an enormous amount of character, and Roses matches being what they were in those days it was packed for a Whit Saturday start. We fielded first and bowled Lancashire out for 151, so we had to bat at the end of the first day. I was supposed to bat at six and went off into the nets for a spot of practice, never dreaming that I would be needed until Monday, but we lost three wickets fairly quickly to Brian Statham and Peter Lever. Close was due to bat at five but he had put in a big effort earlier in the day, three wickets off twenty-five overs, and he was a bit drained, so I was called from the nets to go in early. I got through the last twenty-five minutes or so and was 17 not out overnight.

Dad was ill in hospital and because we had Sundays off in those civilised days I went to see him. He was naturally interested in the Roses match and I knew it would be live on television the following afternoon, so I arranged for him to have a TV set near his bed. 'I'll try to stay in until the afternoon so you can watch me,' I said. It worked out far better than I could ever have imagined: my first century for Yorkshire, 145 before I was bowled by Tommy Greenhough, made in a Roses match in front of 20,000 at Sheffield.

On 3 June 1963 Boycott scored his first first-class century, 145 for Yorkshire against Lancashire at Sheffield, and took part in his first century partnership, 249 for the 4th wicket with W. B. Stott (which remains Yorkshire's record 4th-wicket partnership against Lancashire).

It was the stuff dreams and newspaper headlines are made of, especially since I helped put on 249 with Bryan Stott. But I'm bound to confess I don't recall too many details of the innings. I know it was as hot as hell and I well remember the sportsmanship shown by Statham, who bowled fiercely but wasn't above telling me I'd done well from time to time. Statham bowled one chin-high bouncer which I cut for four – I was a willing cutter and hooker in those days – and Statham acknowledged the shot with a little applause of his own. It meant an enormous amount to me then. I also remember a standing ovation when I got out, a long and tired walk back to the pavilion with people standing and cheering like mad, cushions being thrown in the air. Everybody seemed to have a huge grin on his face and the noise was deafening. I don't remember ever feeling intimidated by playing in front of a big crowd but I can still feel the warmth and sense of achievement of that day in Sheffield, 3 June 1963. Stotty made 143 and Yorkshire won the match by 110 runs, which made the whole thing just about perfect.

Close made a wonderful piece of history himself that season when, batting for England, he stood up to the West Indians Wes Hall and Charlie Griffith and let the fastest bowlers in the world drill the ball into his chest and side. Even knowing that Close had an extraordinary resistance to pain – a philosophy of mind over matter that said if you didn't think about pain you didn't feel it – we could hardly believe it and I don't think Charlie Griffith ever recovered completely from the experience either. Close arrived back in the Yorkshire dressing room sporting the lurid bruises that had been photographed for the front page of just about every newspaper in the country. I was curious and misguided enough to poke them inquisitively with a forefinger. Closey nearly went through the roof and I was lucky to escape without being throttled. Facing Griffith was one thing – being tampered with by a callow Colt was a different thing altogether.

Being a Colt, without a first-team cap, meant I did not have any security at Yorkshire and lived literally from one performance to the next. There was nothing unusual in that – uncapped players received only match fees – but naturally enough it put a strain on me. I had been fortunate in that working for the civil service gave me the chance to organise my holidays and spare time a bit but it couldn't last for ever. Sooner or later I was likely to be faced with a decision.

Part of the job at the Ministry involved working Saturday mornings, not every Saturday but as part of a roster. Working on Saturday morning entitled you to half a day off in lieu so it made sense for me to work as many Saturday mornings as I could in the winter and build up a backlog of time owing. I used to ring round the married women – they weren't too keen to work on Saturdays – and volunteer to do their Saturday shift. I planned it like a military operation and knew weeks in advance who was due to work on which Saturday, so I could get in early with my offer to take their place. They quickly saw how important it was for me to do the Saturday shift so they took advantage as far as they could. I was forever running errands and playing the office boy just for the privilege of doing extra work. But the fact is that a Yorkshire match played over three days ate quickly into any half-days I could accrue. When my leave was just about exhausted I wrote a letter with the help of the manager asking for leave without pay to enable me to continue playing for Yorkshire. The Controller of my (Leeds) area had suggested privately that leave without pay should be no problem, so it came as a severe shock when my application was turned down.

I was out of the office playing for Yorkshire at the time so I didn't get the official reply for five days, by which time I knew I had been picked for the next Yorkshire match. I had three days to decide between my job at the Ministry of Pensions – secure, frankly cushy, with a well-defined future which included a pension unless I tried to set fire to the place – and a possible future in county cricket. There was no guarantee I would make it for Yorkshire but emotionally the die was cast: I could live with the possible disappointment of not making it in cricket, but I would have been plagued by regrets and unanswered questions for the rest of my life if I hadn't tried.

I knew full well that if I packed in my job with the civil service I could not go back, and my responsibility to my family after so many years of making ends meet without a financial contribution from me weighed on my mind. But at twenty-two I felt I had to discover whether I was good enough to make a career with Yorkshire. I put in my notice with immediate effect on 12 July 1963. Next day I went to the Oval with Yorkshire and made an unbeaten 50.

When it became known at Yorkshire that I had thrown in my job the secretary John Nash took time out to discuss my future. John was a member of the old school, very straitlaced and utterly professional, and I always got on with him very well. He took an interest in what I was doing; unlike most club secretaries, his desk always seemed to be clear and he invariably seemed to be able to find the time to talk and advise. His chief aide then was Esmee Coates, as formidable a lady as you would ever wish to meet, and she too found time to discuss my hopes and ambitions. Quite simply, I wanted to captain Yorkshire and play for England. It seemed reasonable enough if a little high-falutin' for a player not yet sure of his place in the side. There was and still is nothing wrong with ambition and the pursuit of excellence.

Sellers then told me that, since I had given up my job, the club was prepared to guarantee me £16 a week in the summer and £8 in the winter. I didn't know much about contracts then but it seemed that the offer was unusual if not unique. Yorkshire's capped players had a modicum of security but even they were offered an agreement, not a contract, which the club would renew or not as it thought fit by the end of July each year. As an uncapped player I did not have any sort of security but at least I now had the offer of regular payment from Yorkshire whether I got into the side or not.

Naturally, I was desperate to do well in the first team and found to my horror that Close wanted me to open the innings. Against Sussex at Bradford and Surrey at Sheffield I had amassed the princely scores of 2, 5 not out, 0 and 2. As a mid-order batsman I seemed to have some prospects and some contribution to make; as an opener I was a disaster, and I asked Close if I could drop down the order again. He agreed that I could while he was away on Test duty but insisted I should open the innings again when he returned. After scores of 80, 32 and 37 from mid-order I thought he might relent but he said simply that if I didn't open the innings I would not play at all. As conversations go it was pretty one-sided and I got the message all too clearly: opening the innings certainly wasn't my preference but it was that or goodbye Yorkshire. Having given up my job, I didn't have a lot of choice.

On 29 August 1963 Boycott and Ken Taylor completed century partnerships in both innings, 105 and 105, against Leicestershire at Leicester.

Opening the innings, I made 62 and 28 against Warwickshire and then went to the Roses match at Old Trafford and scored 113. Not many Yorkshire players score two centuries in a season against Lancashire and I was the first Colt to score his first two first-class hundreds in Roses cricket. Without Close's insistence on my going in first it might not have happened –

who knows? Perhaps Close recognised that I would respond to the responsibility of opening the innings – and putting my future at stake – even if I didn't particularly enjoy it at the outset. It obviously served his purpose but I'm the first to admit that there have been times in my career when I've needed direction and have not always been the best judge of my own salvation. That was especially true when I was learning the ropes and desperate to do well.

I applied myself to opening the innings and was pleased with a score of 90 out of 144 on a difficult pitch at Lord's. We played the West Indies at Sheffield – as champion county we had the dubious distinction of playing them twice that season – and I made 71. Hall and Griffith were in full cry and there was a lot of talk in the newspapers and around the counties about Griffith's yorkers and bouncers. Richard Hutton got stuck at Griffith's end and clearly didn't relish the thought. He liked to lunge well forward and Charlie's short delivery wasn't exactly conducive to that. Hutton was hit on the arm and came down the pitch. 'I say, Boycott, why don't we swop ends?' I told him jokingly it was simple enough – all he had to do was get a single . . . Another century opening the innings against Leicestershire late in the season helped Yorkshire to an innings victory. We won the championship and I topped the county averages with 1628 runs. In the national averages I was second to Mike Smith, whose advice about the feasibility of playing first-class cricket in spectacles certainly seemed to be paying off.

It is odd how certain matches which probably should make a big impression leave very few lasting memories while some others stick in the mind for no obvious reason. I particularly remember the match we played in June of 1963 against Somerset at Taunton. The ball seamed about all over the place and batting was especially difficult against Fred Rumsey, Kenny Palmer and Bill Alley. I batted for a while with Fred Trueman, who was particularly solicitous when Rumsey began bowling a spate of bouncers. Rumsey, it seemed, had gone completely off his head: he bowled a series of bouncers at Fred! Not just one or two, but four an over, grinning all the time and clearly enjoying himself. Fred gave me lots of advice but didn't actually follow any of it himself. He stood like a statue while Rumsey piled into him with the ball whistling horribly close to the peak of his cap.

Finally he was hit on the bicep and he walked slowly, purposefully down the pitch. 'Do you want to die?' It was an invitation, not a question. Fred looked as though he was thinking a lot, and that was ominous for Rumsey. Somerset declared their first innings, with eight wickets down so Rumsey did not have to bat, but as soon as he emerged in the second innings Fred demanded the ball.

Close wouldn't let him have it and Fred was on the verge of apoplexy. By all the written and accepted rules, from the Geneva Convention to the Articles of the Fast Bowlers Union, Fred insisted he had every right to bowl at Rumsey and – the implication was obvious though unstated – very probably dismember him. Several of the senior players agreed and there was an extraordinary mid-wicket conference discussing the pros and cons of the situation while Fred fumed and Rumsey waited, knowing that he was perilously close to attending his own funeral. Close stood his ground. He was not a squeamish man and there was nothing altruistic about his refusal to let Fred loose. Rather he acted on the simple conviction that Fred would do murder, and that would lead to all kinds of irritating complications. You'll probably kill him, Fred, and we can do without that sort of publicity. . . . So Rumsey lived to tell the tale.

Boycott was awarded his county cap on 2 October 1963.

In the close season, I was awarded my county cap alongside John Hampshire, who had scored 1236 runs, and Tony Nicholson, with 66 wickets. I was staying with friends in Doncaster when they brought me a cup of tea in bed and said they had just heard the news on the wireless. A letter from the club dated 3 October 1963 informed me that as from 1 September I would receive a salary of £624 per annum as well as my usual match fees and a special bonus of £100 for winning the county championship. Things were looking up. Match fees at the time were £11 for games in Yorkshire and £20 for away matches. If I played regularly I would certainly be better off financially than I had been in the civil service – and, infinitely more important than that, I was doing what I really wanted to do with my life.

4

The Learner

The inconvenience of not having a regular job was solved in the winter when I took on a temporary clerical position with the Yorkshire Electricity Board in Wakefield. It sounds terribly humdrum and I'm bound to say it wasn't Hollywood, but I am not easily bored – perhaps just as well – and I found new friends who introduced me to golf. We played on Sunday mornings and I became hooked on the game to the point where we would venture out in the snow and lose a few balls before we gave it up as a bad job. A familiar syndrome to the developing golf addict.

I was able to wear my Yorkshire First XI sweater for the first time at the winter nets. It felt distinctly odd and was a constant reminder of new responsibilities. The previous year had been a dramatically good one for me and I was determined that it would not turn out to be a flash in the pan. The Cricket Writers' Club had voted me Young Cricketer of the Year and I realised with a thrill and some apprehension that players who received that honour usually went on to play for England. I received my award from the Cricket Writers' chairman Brian Chapman at a dinner given for the Australian touring team at the Fishmongers' Hall in London. It was a grand occasion for me, rubbing shoulders with many leading personalities in the cricket world and meeting the Australians for the first time, albeit over a knife and fork.

My preoccupation at the start of 1964 was not to let anybody down, myself or anybody else. But I became aware of an attitude in the Yorkshire dressing room which I could not entirely rationalise or understand but which made a growing impression on me. It became obvious that Yorkshire's preference was to put me down rather than build me up.

The talk was always about John Hampshire, his power and the range of his shots. With me, it was always a matter of what I could not do rather than what I was reasonably good at, as though the dressing room preferred to nit-pick and find fault. I was told sternly, for instance, that I would have to learn to hit over the top. It was clearly not my strength but I thought I ought to give it a go. I tried it for Leeds and made a mess of it; I tried it for Yorkshire on a slow pitch at Hull – hardly the right place or time, but that shows how the criticism was preying on my mind – and I was caught for 19. It did not make any sense to me. I could not see how anybody could benefit from my being asked to play in a way foreign to my nature and not making a success of it. I determined to accentuate the positive, to try and play my natural game, and I scored 151 not out against Middlesex and my third successive Roses century – 131 at Old Trafford.

On 16 May 1964 Boycott completed his third consecutive century against Lancashire.

I remember in that match that Ken Taylor was 99 not out in the last over before tea and was desperate to get his century rather than go in and worry through the interval. I have rarely seen a good player so nervous. 'If it comes to the last ball and I'm still 99, run like hell wherever I hit it,' said Ken. Fair enough, but what if a run-out resulted? I could just see the headlines: Taylor 99, Boycott involved, in a Roses match! It didn't bear thinking about. Luckily, we duly scrambled his single and Ken had his century at tea.

I was struck at the time by the fact that Taylor was so nervous. A very experienced and very capable player, yet there he was, worried to death. I'm bound to say that in his position I don't think I would have been too bothered. It certainly would not have affected me the way it did Ken. That is not to say his reaction was wrong or unworthy – it just reminded me at the time that we are all different and we all deal with situations in a different way.

My Roses century had one delightful consequence: Sir Leary Constantine, whom I had never met, asked to see me and told me he thought I had a real future in the game. It would be hard to over-emphasise the pleasure I took in a compliment like that.

The MCC match against the tourists had in those days the importance and significance of a generation of Test trials that were to follow. Being selected for the MCC side was significant, and doing well in the match itself was a pretty solid step towards being selected for the Test teams. I was picked for the MCC match against the Australians and was narked by the fact that I made 0 and 7 against Worcestershire in the game immediately before it. 'A good thing,' said Ray Illingworth. 'You have been putting together some big scores and failing here won't do you any harm. It will guard against complacency and over-confidence.' Good advice.

Brian Bolus made 72 and John Edrich, batting at number three, made

32; I made 63 but I really did not think I had done enough to get in the first Test at Trent Bridge. I considered that, as the challenger, it was up to me to do considerably better than anybody else to press my claim and I couldn't honestly believe I had done that. Yorkshire were at Leicester in late May when the Test team was due to be announced. Fred had taken 5 for 53 and I was about 70 not out at stumps on the Saturday night. The Test team was to be announced around noon on Sunday.

Alan Thompson, the northern cricket correspondent of the *Daily Express*, enquired solicitously if I would care to have lunch with him and his family at Wetherby. It was to be a typical Sunday lunch, roast beef and Yorkshire pudding, better than anything I would get in Leicester, and he would return me to the team hotel in good time on Sunday evening. It seemed a kind thought and I was happy to accept. In 1964 I had absolutely no conception of the wiles of the press and the fact that Thompson's offer might be (ever so slightly) calculated never entered my head.

So there I was next day, playing cricket on Thompson's lawn with his son Ian while an *Express* photographer took an exclusive picture and the rest of the country's cricket writers went spare trying to track down the Yorkshireman who had just been picked to make his England début against Australia. It was a great coup for Thommo, not that I had the faintest appreciation of it at the time. All I remember was that the surroundings were relaxing and the Sunday lunch was great.

Phil Sharpe and Fred were also picked in the squad for the first Test, but Brian Close was not, despite his heroics the previous season against the West Indies. I was surprised to be picked, though naturally delighted, which probably sounds corny but was real enough at the time. I did not think I had done enough – I had played first-class cricket for only one season plus one month and I knew I still had a lot to learn. The Australians are good teachers . . .

Bob Simpson thought that as a Yorkshireman I played cricket the Australian way. There may be some truth in that. Certainly, I was soon to discover that the Aussies have a very down-to-earth philosophy about playing the game to win.

It had already been well documented in the press that I liked to keep to myself before an innings, sit quietly without any interruption and concentrate. It was exaggerated. The fact that I would sit and ponder on my dismissals – how, why and could I avoid it happening again? – was recorded and exaggerated even more. This all developed the image of the introverted, aloof young man whose commitment to the game was somehow unnatural, and like most images – flattering and otherwise – it was only true in part. But the Australians can read.

Before I was due to bat, there would be a veritable procession of Aussie players through the dressing room just wanting to have a word, enquire about my health or wonder if it was true what they had read in the press about me needing peace and quiet. Some hope! It was done on purpose to put me off and disrupt my preferred routine, of course. It says something for my naivety at the time that I didn't really know what was going on. The whole Test scene was fascinatingly new, not totally intimidating but unexplored and unfolding. The team's eve-of-Test dinner was a case in point.

Boycott made his Test début against Australia at Nottingham on 4 June 1964.

As a total newcomer I had very little to offer except an open mouth and a pair of flapping ears. The captain Ted Dexter ran through the Australian batting line-up and offered a few remarks about how we might handle each player. That was a routine which survives to this day. The Australian line-up was formidable to say the least: Lawry, Redpath, O'Neill, Burge, Booth, Simpson. It was a world-class batting order and not to be taken lightly. But F. S. Trueman had the answer, all the answers, in fact. As each name cropped up, Fred mapped out his immediate and very brief future in a few well-chosen grunts. 'Oh, 'im . . . a couple short of a length, a yorker, he's gone. That feller . . . a couple in the ribs, then the old outswinger, goodnight vicar . . .' In twenty minutes the whole Australian team had been dismissed, Fred had bowled every conceivable delivery in the book to order and taken something like 7 for 11! It was marvellous to listen to and I swear I believed every word. Those who had experienced Fred's indomitable optimism before were less gullible if no less impressed. The Test might last more than a couple of days after all.

John Edrich injured himself at practice the day before the Test and I went out to open the innings with Fred Titmus – something of a novelty and a twist of circumstances that very nearly landed us in the middle of a run-out controversy. As it was, the incident was illuminating enough.

I pushed a delivery from Neil Hawke out on the on-side, called and set off. Titmus is not the fastest thing on two legs and is a little deaf in one ear. He was slow to set off and by the time he got into his stride, so had Hawke, charging down on the ball with all the athletic determination of a well-built Aussie Rules player. The collision was fearsome and very one-sided. Titmus was lying prostrate and nowhere near safety when Hawke lobbed the ball back to Wally Grout standing over the stumps. A long pause – and then Wally lobbed the ball back to Hawke and Titmus groggily made his ground. It was a great gesture and one not entirely in keeping with the manufactured

Australian reputation for being hard, ruthless competitors. Those who imagine the Australians are interested only in winning and take that to the point of fixation do not know their sportsmen. They unquestionably fight tough but they generally play fair too. Their image sticks, like the assumption that every kid with a Mohican haircut must be a waster and a rogue. Labels are dangerous.

I remember being nervous at first, so nervous that I picked up my bat to play the opening delivery from Graham McKenzie and it was in Grout's gloves before I had time to play a shot! McKenzie chipped a bone in my finger and I couldn't bat in the second innings but I made 48 top score in the first innings before being caught by Simpson off Grahame Corling, a combination that was soon to force me into a fundamental change in my batting style.

Before that, I discovered in no uncertain terms that my fielding was simply not good enough if I wanted to carve a lasting career with England. My informant was Willie Watson, an England selector at the time, who pointed out my deficiencies as he gave me a lift home in his car after the Test match. I was astounded, not because I wasn't ready to accept that Willie was right but simply because he was the first person who had ever drawn attention to my fielding ability, or lack of it. I had simply not given it a thought.

That is probably an indictment of me but it also reflects very little credit on Yorkshire. It seems ludicrous now, with the modern emphasis on fielding sharpened by the demands of one-day cricket, but when I was a youngster at Yorkshire there was absolutely no thought paid to fielding – unless it went wrong. Fielding practice, such as it was, was optional and desultory. We worked very hard on batting and bowling but paid no attention, as far as coaching went, to fielding skills. Lord Hawke himself had written: 'I do not care how good a bat, how good a bowler, a man may be, he is not worth his place in a county team unless he can field. The crying need of cricket today is that more attention should be paid to fielding.' His lordship must have been spinning in the family vault at Yorkshire's attitude sixty years later – not that he would have complained about the standard. Blessed with natural individual talent, Yorkshire were an excellent fielding side.

There was no finer outfielder in the country than Ken Taylor. I still rate him with Clive Lloyd and Colin Bland as the best fieldsmen I have ever seen, and Willie Watson suggested I should seek Ken's advice to improve my own fielding. Ken, a thorough gentleman, was only too happy to help and we used to travel together while he told me how to practise, how to throw, how to judge from the movement of a batsman's feet whether the ball was likely to be played to a fieldsman's right or left. All this was a revelation. Yorkshire talked about the importance of being tight in the field and were sometimes given extra practice – significantly enough as punishment – if we had a particularly bad day but there was no attempt to make the art and science of fielding part of the coaching process. Ken even taught me how to throw properly. He had a powerful arm and could throw from unlikely positions but he never suffered a related injury in his life. Gradually my fielding improved. It's obvious to me now that every professional cricketer should be at least a competent fielder, but I was playing for England before I gave it a thought and my only excuse is that nobody pointed out the deficiency earlier.

In the Trent Bridge Test, I snicked the ball and Simpson had thrown himself headlong to take a brilliant right-handed catch behind Ian Redpath at second slip. It was a superb effort, faithfully caught by the camera and reprinted, it seemed, in every cricket publication for the rest of that season. Not least because I had just had my own weakness as a fielder revealed to me, I got sick and tired of having it thrust under my nose – and being asked to sign!

My finger injury ruled me out of the second Test, though I noticed that England opened with Dexter rather than picking a specialist opening batsman in my place. That seemed significant: my place was being kept open, which was good for my confidence. My Mum and Dad went to watch me in the third Test at Headingley, where I played pretty well in the first innings and was out for 4 in the second. The weather was gorgeous and the pitch was perfect; I made 38 in the first innings and apparently told my Mum, 'I could have batted all day, it was that nice.' The fact is, of course, that I didn't and couldn't. The combination of Simpson and Corling was becoming a real worry.

Corling had got me out at Trent Bridge; he did so again in the first innings at Headingley and yet again in the second, caught by Simpson every time. It was not surprising but ominous when Corling opened the bowling against me in the second innings at Headingley – Australia clearly thought they had found my weakness, and I could not be sure they weren't right.

Corling bowled at a lively medium pace and moved the ball away around the off stump. Simpson had a pretty close view of proceedings and came to the conclusion that I had schooled myself into a mechanical sort of straightness and could not adjust to the ball that moved away. It was a sobering thought.

Nobody had to tell me I was in trouble – the signs were obvious, and so was the fact that I would have to do something about it pretty quickly. The team for the winter tour to South Africa was to be announced fairly soon and if I didn't win a place on that I might drift into obscurity before I had chance to establish myself. There was nothing to be gained from making a song and dance about it – that would have cheered up the Australians no end – but I needed some good advice. I got it in discussion with Bill Bowes, the former Yorkshire and England bowler who was now cricket writer with the evening newspaper in Yorkshire.

Bill drew a parallel between my batting and Herbert Sutcliffe's. In Herbert's era, a batsman could not be given out lbw unless the ball pitched on the stumps, so the first deliberate movement was back and across. If the ball swung away, Herbert let it go; if it nipped back he could not be lbw because it had pitched outside. The rule had changed, so I could, of course, be out in those circumstances, but my worry at the time was not lbw – it was how to deal with the ball that moved away outside the off stump. I had to learn which balls to play and which to leave. I practised this in the nets, but only the fourth Test at Old Trafford and another meeting with Corling would tell me for sure if I'd got it right.

As it turned out, I thought I was never going to get in. Bill Lawry scored a century, Brian Booth made 98 and Simpson scored a marvellous 311 in Australia's first innings; I had plenty of time to ponder my confrontation with Corling because it was almost lunch on the third day before England went in to bat. Sure enough, Australia opened with Corling but this time there was no quick execution. I got out just after tea, bowled by McKenzie for 58. With Bill Bowes's help, I had mastered my problem outside the off stump.

Dexter made 174 and Kenny Barrington 256 in England's only innings; I had plenty of time to kill so I slipped away – with permission – to meet a sportsman I had idolised. Denis Law had returned from Italy and was back with Manchester United at Old Trafford. It was a privilege to meet him in the flesh.

On 25 July 1964 Boycott shared his first century partnership for England, 111 for the 2nd wicket, with Ted Dexter, against Australia at Manchester.

The following Saturday, on the morning of the August Roses match, MCC named eleven players to tour South Africa, with the rider that five more would be added after the last Test. Two omissions were interesting. Ted Dexter was standing as Conservative candidate for Cardiff South-east (assuming he actually knew where it was) and would join the South Africa tour only if he did not get in at the autumn election. He duly lost and turned up. And Colin Cowdrey was unavailable 'for family reasons', which seemed perfectly reasonable to me and was accepted without fuss at the time. The same cannot quite be said for the reaction, some time later, when I declined to go on an England tour . . .

The fact that I had made the tour party to South Africa was a big relief. Rather more pressing was the possibility of a fourth consecutive hundred in a Roses match, which was not to be sniffed at. A. A. Thomson, a fine cricket writer with a particular affection for Yorkshire and Lancashire, was working on a history of Roses matches and told me he had suspended it until he knew whether I would make it four centuries in a row. Thomson was a very genuine old chap who took a particular liking to myself and John Hampshire. But I couldn't make his book-writing delay altogether worthwhile. I fell lbw to Sonny Ramadhin for 62 and took consolation from the fact that we won the match easily thanks to marvellous bowling from Tony Nicholson in the second innings.

Soon afterwards Yorkshire played the Australians at Bradford and Simpson left us 323 to win in less than a day. We didn't have a ghost of a chance and I wasn't exactly smashing the ball around. Simpson deliberately and very publicly brought all nine fielders round the bat to reprove my slowness – an odd rebuke considering he had already killed any hope we had of winning, but another example of the tough Australian way of cricket. As psychological warfare went it did not succeed completely because I made a century, but Simmo had the satisfaction of winning the match by 81 runs.

John Edrich was dropped for the last Test at the Oval, a strange-looking decision since he had made a fine century in the series and batted pretty well throughout. But I remembered that he had made a point at Old Trafford of telling the selectors about his self-doubts, his lack of self-satisfying form, the fact that he was not going as well as he would have liked and so on. That sort of talk after being picked for a Test, as opposed to admitting that you did not feel in good enough form to be picked in the first place, seemed very odd to me. I put it on a par with telling the opposition bowlers, and it did not make sense.

I opened the innings with Bob Barber on an overcast first morning and made 30 before Neil Hawke knocked my middle stump out of the ground. It flew many a mile, at least that is what Neil always tells me and he ought to know since he has a picture of the dismissal hanging on his wall in Adelaide. Neil was just the sort of Australian it is impossible not to like – physically strong and with a bold, brash exterior but a humorous, warm and decent man. I don't think he had too many pictures of my second innings: 113 and my first century for England before Simpson had me caught by Redpath to record his only wicket of the series. We had been to see the musical *Pickwick* on the Saturday evening and met the cast at a small party afterwards. When I completed my century on Monday Harry Secombe sent me a case of

Boycott made his first century for England, 113 against Australia at the Oval, on 17 August 1964.

champagne, which was a happy gesture appreciated by more than just myself.

I learned a lot that season. I learned more about the game, about the problems and the pleasures of playing in Test cricket, a little bit more about myself. And I learned something else about playing for Yorkshire under Close, a lesson that registered forcibly at the time and still leaves me a bit confused today.

Early in September we played Gloucestershire at Bristol on a pitch which was obviously going to turn square. It looked suspect before a ball was bowled and Close went so far as to announce that if we won the toss and made 250 we would win the match by an innings! We won the toss, batted and I attacked just about everything on the assumption that getting out was only a matter of time. I had made 150 with a mixture of good luck and reasonable management – and there was Close on the balcony, waving his arms about like a man demented and gesticulating that I should get on with it, as though I had been hanging about. I was furious. This was the same Close, remember, who had forecast that a first innings score of 250 would be enough to win the match. The more excitable Close became the more it annoyed me. I got out slogging on 177 and we had a fair old row in the dressing room. I respected Close, there was no question of that, but I was not prepared to sit quietly while he tore a strip off me when I didn't think I was in the wrong. Close declared at 425 for 7, Gloucestershire scored 47 and 84 and Yorkshire won the game by an innings and 294 runs at 3.50 p.m. on the second day!

Why on earth Close felt it necessary to carry on about my batting was a complete mystery – except for that tendency I had already noted for no one in the dressing room to offer praise for long. It seemed that nothing was ever good enough, no matter how hard you tried – you had fallen short in some respect. I found out later that Close had been singing my praises at the bar, but he could not find it in himself to do it to my face. I found that quite extraordinary – educational, perhaps, but not a pattern of behaviour which I could agree with or understand.

5

New Horizons

The most beautiful cricket ground in the world is not, as many might imagine, in one of the great cricket-playing nations. It is not in the sun-kissed West Indies or even in breathtaking South Africa. My nomination goes unhesitatingly to the Brockton Point cricket ground in Vancouver. If that sounds strange, I can only say I'm in good company: Sir Donald Bradman referred to it as the most beautiful ground in the world in his autobiography – the first time I heard the name – and I certainly wasn't disappointed when I actually played there in 1964.

Newlands in Cape Town and Queen's Park Oval at Port of Spain in Trinidad are generally accepted as the most memorable Test arenas in the world, but for sheer scenic impact they can't hold a candle to the Brockton Point ground. It is set on a small peninsula surrounded on three sides by water, with distant views of the Vancouver city skyline on one side and the snowcapped Rocky Mountains on the other. The water is an arm of the harbour and it is not uncommon, though pretty unnerving, to see huge ships passing slowly behind the bowler's arm, so close that you feel they are going to plough across the pitch. The playing area, once an Indian reservation, is bordered by woodlands and totem poles, an absolutely stunning sight and one I shall never forget. We arrived there as part of an end-of-season tour for the Yorkshire players and I was billeted out with a chap from Oldham who informed me that there were enough expatriate Yorkshiremen and Lancastrians in the area to play an annual Roses match. Lancashire, he added, always won . . .

That tour, which took in the United States, Canada and Bermuda, was my first trip abroad, at the age of almost twenty-four. I suppose most young people of the modern generation have been on a package holiday to Europe at the very least by that age, but international travel was certainly not as cheap or common twenty years ago. It was a wonderful experience, even though it started badly. We had the customary course of injections before the trip and I reacted badly to the smallpox jab. The first one would not take and the second brought me out in a shivering fever on the plane, as I sat swathed in blankets and alternating between breathlessly hot and abominably cold. I tried to play in the first match in New York but became so ill that I had to be rushed back to the hotel – by a local cop all the way from Yorkshire! His name was Frank Harte, he was born in Wombwell a few miles from Fitzwilliam and he had heard about the match on the radio. His chief job now was as an outrider for important state visits, clearing the way for VIPs such as Churchill, General de Gaulle, Eisenhower and Queen Frederika; suddenly, he was looking after a little-known and distinctly sickly Geoff Boycott. We raced through the New York streets in his patrol car, sirens wailing and lights flashing like something out of Kojak, except that he had not been invented at the time. When we reached the local hospital it was discovered that my legs and ankles were swollen and I had a temperature of 101 degrees – a reaction, apparently, to the smallpox vaccine. Although I did not dwell on it at the time, it was ominous that my body could react so violently to this sort of preventive medication – perhaps a consequence of the removal of my spleen.

Once recovered, I was the typical innocent abroad, visiting as many places as I could and smitten with that sense of wonder which grabs the first-time traveller and which has dimmed through familiarity but never quite disappeared. Washington in the fall, as they say; George Washington house, the Capitol buildings, the Kennedy Memorial and the Eternal Flame at Arlington cemetery, a meeting with the Speaker of the House of Representatives and a spell in a log cabin at Calgary where the snow made it impossible to stampede, let alone play cricket. Beautiful Toronto, where I was struck by the marvellous facilities at the clubhouse where we played cricket: it incorporated a curling rink, an ice-skating rink and a bowling rink, four squash courts and eight tennis courts – a million pounds' worth of sporting investment, which was a hell of a lot of money in those days. Boycott went to Hollywood and played on the Sir C. Aubrey Smith Memorial Ground, founded in the 1930s and trod in its time by other dashing characters like Ronald Colman, Errol Flynn and David Niven . . . The ground was next to a riding school and, inevitably, Brian Close was soon in the saddle and galloping round the ground. The smog was bad even then. It cleared only slowly and I remember batting in a strange sort of haze as the sun tried to break through. No visit to Los Angeles would be complete without a trip to Dodger Stadium for the pro baseball. Los Angeles Dodgers versus Chicago Cubs – I was particularly impressed with the fielding, the speed and sureness of the throwing. Even with the help of a webbed mit, the catching was remarkable.

Bermuda was brilliant, the living image of everyone's dream of a coral island. Houses in pastel shades of pink, blue, green and cream; a quaint little place where residents were restricted to one small car per household and most people negotiated what roads there were on buzzing scooters. John Hampshire and I explored several beaches by moped, a fantastic blur of sun, sea and sand. But when I got back to the hotel, Mel Ryan remarked that I was a rather livid shade of pink. Naive as I was, it hadn't occurred to me to use any sort of suncream and as the evening wore on I began to pay the price. I was badly sunburned and the doctor had to be called in; the local view was that the best way to take the fire out of the burn – and they should know – was to pickle the victim in vinegar. For several days I lay in agony, thoroughly miserable and totally pickled, smelling to high heaven. It was not an experience I intended to repeat and from that day to this, I have never been one to sit out in the sun on tour. Others do and my reluctance to conform has taken on all kinds of overtones, more evidence for those who want it that I am some sort of an oddball who thinks that sunbathing weakens the body, if not the mind. I happen to think that too much sunbathing does tend to create a sort of lethargy but there is no deep psychological reason for my keeping out of the sun; it's just that I was painfully burned once and realised that a lot of exposure does not agree with me. Simple as that.

Bermuda also offered me one of the treasured memories of my life – the opportunity to bat in the same team as the great Garry Sobers. As uncrowned King of the Caribbean Sobers guested for Yorkshire in a match against St George's: 'Name the modern overseas player who played for Yorkshire' became a favourite trick question.

Thousands of locals filled the tiny ground and it looked at one stage as though they might see a slaughter rather than a cricket match. The pitch was matting on top of concrete, lightning fast and frankly dangerous if somebody decided he wanted to make a name for himself. Fred and Garry did not have to: St George's were put in and bowled out for 48, Trueman taking 4–23 and Sobers 4–11. But the local bowlers weren't exactly friendly. In no time at all Yorkshire lost five men for single figures and there was a real possibility we might lose the match. I was due to tour South Africa with England and there was no way I was going to jeopardise my fitness for that, so I used a long-handled bat for the only time in my life – better that than a broken finger. There was an enormous amount of short stuff, potentially lethal on a hard, bouncy pitch, and Sobers came to the rescue in more ways than one. He scored a fabulous 117 and he insisted on some sanity from the bowlers. 'Cut that out, man, bowl properly,' he insisted when he wasn't getting one in his half, and of course they did as the Great Man said. At the end of the over I ventured the thought that I was liable to be beheaded, too. 'Same goes for him,' Sobers told the captain. 'You bowl properly at him.' I survived and scored 108. All in all a memorable match and a huge thrill for me to bat with a very great player.

Boycott's first first-class match overseas, for the MCC against Rhodesia at Salisbury, was on 24 October 1964.

The South African tour of 1964–5 was an enormous adventure for me, a chance to develop my game and an opportunity to visit places I had only read about or sketched in coloured crayons during geography lessons at school. It also brought me into close contact with two men for whom I have always had the utmost respect and admiration, Bob Barber and Mike Smith.

Touring was more relaxed in those days. There was time to stand and stare, to visit beauty spots and even to develop a feeling that you might be in the same hotel bed for more than a couple of nights on end. We had the afternoons off for the two days immediately before a match and of course we never played on Sunday, so there was a fair amount of leisure time available for those who wanted to use it profitably. I was interested in making a home movie of my visit and Roy Castle suggested I ask the advice of Harry Secombe, an accomplished photographer in his own right. Harry loaned me a 16mm movie camera and I made a film which formed the basis of a modest lecture tour in later years. Victoria Falls, a cable-car ride up Table Mountain and tea at the top while contemplating what Sir Francis Drake had called 'the fairest cape in the whole circumference of the world'. The view is certainly stunning. Kruger National Park, the Wankie Game Reserve in Rhodesia, the Hluhluwe Game Park – I still have the movie shots, rather outdated in this age of ultra-professional colour films but real and evocative nonetheless.

My regular companion on these adventures was Bob Barber, a splendid left-handed opener and one of the most genuine men you could ever wish to meet. Bob was a little older than me, more sophisticated and more mature: he looked after me like an older brother and we had some marvellous times together. In Natal, I recall, we went off on foot in search of the white rhinoceros under the guidance of the Ranger, Gary Player's younger brother Ian. We may have looked and certainly felt very professional, stalking about in the bush and hot on the trail of a white rhino which we would recognise, apparently, because it weighs two tons whereas the black rhino merely weighs one. In the event we came upon a black one and slid confidently closer until we were about fifteen yards away. Then it turned and looked at us; I can still see its piggy little eyes. We were terrified, rooted to the spot for the longest fifteen seconds of my life. I could not have moved if I'd wanted to and Bob had wrapped his arms round a tree ready to shin for dear life if it advanced. Ian motioned to us to keep still and say nothing, which was a little superfluous in the circumstances. We slowly backed off and then fled for safety. Great white rhino hunters we were!

Gary Player called in to see us during the tour and played a round of golf in Johannesburg with Ted Dexter, whom he described as the best genuine amateur golfer he had ever seen. As the worst golfer in the party I usually ended up partnering Ted, the best; we never lost, which was not entirely thanks to me.

Boycott's first Test match overseas, started on 4 December 1964, was England against South Africa at Durban.

Bob Barber was a revelation to me. Having learned my cricket in a fairly tough environment and developed it professionally in an even tougher school with Yorkshire, I was amazed at Bob's apparently cavalier approach to the game, even at Test-match level. That is not to suggest for a minute that he did not take the game seriously – he was a thorough professional. But he rarely played cricket with a long face. It was obviously a source of pleasure and entertainment to him, as it was supposed to be to other people. The South Africans, some of them pretty humourless Boers, really didn't know what to make of him. In the first Test in Durban, for instance, the pitch was receptive to spin and England eventually won after Titmus and Allan bowled SA out. Before that, Bob and I put on 120 for the first wicket, a partnership enlivened somewhat by the fact that Bob insisted on giving their off-spinner Kelly Seymour the benefit of his experience and advice. 'You can't bowl at me without a man down there,' said Bob, pointing to some distant part of the field, and when he was predictably ignored he peppered the target area until Seymour put a man there in sheer exasperation. 'You'll need one down there, too,' said Bob, indicating some quite different point of the compass. Again he was ignored and again he slogged the bowling in the nominated area until the field was moved to plug the danger. This seemed to go on for ages – the ball disappearing into the distance, Bob chatting and laughing away and the South Africans totally bemused by the whole business. I was pretty surprised myself – this was a Test match after all – but Bob scored 74 to prove the effectiveness of his philosophy. In the second Test at Johannesburg, Peter Pollock bowled at genuine pace and Bob would duck the bouncer before pretending to play a sweep-shot, with the ball in the wicketkeeper's gloves. When Pollock pitched it up, Bob drove superbly and played a glorious innings before he was bowled off an inside edge for 97. He was very, very disappointed and made little effort to disguise the fact in the dressing room, one of the few times I saw him actually acknowledge the fact that there was a committed attitude beneath the casual exterior. He really was a priceless team-mate and a lovely bloke.

I struggled for form, trying desperately to come to terms with the unfamiliar conditions. I had never met pitches as firm and fast before, the light was dazzlingly bright and the ball seemed to come through the air so much quicker. My favourite back-foot forcing shots were getting me out to catches at gully and point. By the time we came to play against Eastern Province at Port Elizabeth I had scored fewer than 200 runs in ten innings, but I redeemed myself there with an unbeaten 197. There was a little story behind that, as I discovered later.

Mike Smith had sent out a message saying he was going to declare at lunch, and that I should bear that in mind if I wanted to try for 200. Pollock probably guessed the situation. In any event he took absolutely ages to bowl the last over before lunch, whipped in a couple of bouncers that I couldn't have reached with a stepladder and included two beamers which didn't miss me by much. Barber was not playing in the match but he was in the bar later that evening when Pollock remarked that Boycott hadn't liked his beamers. Bob stopped him short. 'Do you actually mean to say you bowled those on purpose? If you bowl any of those at me you'd better not miss because I'm coming straight for you with the bat. And you had better not bowl any more at Geoff while I'm at the other end . . .' They don't come any straighter than Bob.

I was fortunate on that tour to have a superb captain in Mike Smith. If he lacked anything tactically compared to men like Close and Illingworth, he more than compensated for that in terms of his personality and attitude – very important to a young man like me on his first tour. Mike took everything in his stride, and was always willing to talk about problems rather than apportion blame. And he didn't do his talking at the bar. When I was struggling for runs before the match in Port Elizabeth he took time out to discuss the problem with me, to offer advice and reassurance. I would have done anything for him and when the team was bedevilled by injuries I was only too willing when he asked me to help out as a bowler. I even took five Test wickets. I wasn't quite as quick as John Price and Tom Cartwright, who were both injured, but I picked up 3–47 in the third Test at Cape Town – Graeme Pollock, Colin Bland and Sid Burke out to the demon bowler. In the fifth Test at Port Elizabeth Eddie Barlow was caught off my bowling by Peter Parfitt at slip. 'I may not be as good a slipper as Sharpey but I got that one, Fiery,' called Parfitt – and I came to realise I had a new nickname which was likely to stick. I have since heard lots of stories about the nickname Fiery. Many people have naturally insisted that it is an ironic reference to

On 6 January 1965 Boycott took his first wickets in first-class cricket, 3 for 47 for England against South Africa at Cape Town.

my speed and demeanour with the bat! But the name first came into currency on that South Africa tour and was derived from the fact that Fred was Fiery Fred to the public and just about every headline writer in the newspapers. It followed that since I was from Yorkshire, I would be GeofFiery – and the name was shortened to Fiery when Fred was no longer on the England scene.

It is impossible, given any sort of willingness to learn, to play alongside men like Dexter and Ken Barrington and not improve your own game. I watched them a lot and marvelled at their ability – Dexter's fabulous 172 in the second Test and Barrington's amazingly consistent big scores. Ken had a set routine in his bustling, busy way: practice in the morning and golf in the afternoon. There was not the slightest doubt that it worked for him.

On 15 February 1965 Boycott scored his first Test century overseas, 117 against South Africa at Port Elizabeth.

My own batting improved to the point where I was able to help save the fourth Test in Johannesburg – 76 not out in an England second-innings total of 153–6. Unfortunately, Bob Barber broke a finger, which forced him to return home from the tour. In the fifth Test at Port Elizabeth I made 117, my first Test century abroad, and helped save the match with Barrington, who scored 72. Ted Dexter was run out in that match: we both finished up at the same end after I had tried to send him back. There was not the slightest suggestion at the time that it was my fault and many reports went as far as to stress that Dexter had failed to respond to a clear call. But I have seen reference to it since, with the predictable insinuation that Dexter was another of my 'victims'. The reputation was clearly impossible to live down, whatever the circumstances.

It is strange, looking back over the years, to reflect that this was the last official Test tour to South Africa. We were all involved in a piece of history, though we never imagined it at the time and would not have relished it too much if we had. The fashion for dissecting and intellectualising the situation in South Africa had not become popular then. In fact nobody in cricket gave it much thought until South African politicians stirred a hornets' nest in the infamous D'Oliveira affair. As players, we went out and played cricket with the blessing of the MCC, the South African cricket authorities and, as far as we knew, the entire world. The MCC president warned us before we left England not to involve ourselves in the politics of the country, but the caution was hardly necessary since politics had no interest for most of us. Yet it quickly became clear that South Africans themselves had a pressing, almost neurotic interest in how they were seen by the rest of the world. The question in company was never 'Are you having a good time?' but always 'What do you think of South Africa?', as though they needed some sort of reassurance.

Cricket was not integrated then. There were no coloured or black players in the white teams we met and we played matches in front of strictly segregated crowds. The largest areas were reserved for whites; a smaller section, usually pretty well patronised, for coloureds; and a very small area, generally almost empty, for blacks. The blacks themselves seemed to have very little interest in the game.

Twenty years later I returned to South Africa with a 'rebel' team of white cricketers. The segregation of the crowds had disappeared and there were coloured players in some of the teams we played. When we played before segregated crowds we were legitimate; when we played before integrated crowds we were not. The arguments were and still are raging but the irony was lost on nobody who took part in the 'rebel' tour.

6

Gillette

Boycott the Bore became Boycott the Whizz-Kid – for a while at least – on the strength of one innings in 1965. An innings which many good judges still regard as the best I ever played and I wouldn't take them to task on that, certainly as far as one-day cricket is concerned. Yorkshire won the Gillette Cup at Lord's by 175 runs and I made 146 – still, and remarkably after all these years, the highest individual score in a limited-overs final. It has overshadowed everything else that year in most people's memory, but there was a lot more to 1965 than the Gillette Cup final. It was a year of extraordinary ups and downs for me.

Wisden began it on a high note by naming me as one of the Five Cricketers of the Year along with Graham McKenzie, Peter Burge, Jack Flavell and Bob Simpson – exalted company considering that I had played cricket professionally for only two years. I had crammed a fair bit into that period and Bill Bowes strengthened the popular image when he wrote in Wisden that the young Boycott 'had four sessions of net practice each day and regretted he could not get more'. Bill also referred to the phase of every cricketer's life when he has to battle against a string of low scores – he did not know it then but his words were all too prophetic. First of all I missed two early Yorkshire matches with a pulled muscle, then Yorkshire were shot out for 23 in an amazing match at Middlesbrough, I was run out twice in a match against New Zealand (which may be something of a record) and I missed another two weeks because of an injured shoulder. On top of all that, pitches throughout the country were poor that season and I struggled desperately for rhythm and runs, though I did score 76 as England beat New Zealand by seven wickets at Lord's. I did not make a first-class century that season and I was dropped from the Test team. Perhaps it's just as well that 1965 tends to be remembered for the Gillette final!

The Middlesbrough match against Hampshire was a gruesome affair.

We lost by ten wickets before lunch on the second day, which hasn't happened to Yorkshire too often before or since. Close had a brainwave that we ought to use a new kind of ball with extra circles of stitching round the seam: just the thing for our formidable seamers, Fred and Tony Nicholson. The theory might have been sound but Hampshire's seam attack wasn't the worst in the world – Derek Shackleton, Butch White and Bob Cottam – and we fell in a terrible heap. Fred rescued us in the first innings with a big-hitting 55 but nobody made double figures in the second innings – all out 23 with White taking 6–10. I was on a pair facing Shackleton, who bowled a half volley about twice a season, and I didn't fancy my chances too highly in the circumstances. As he walked back to his mark I stepped a yard out of my crease and took block there. Shack bowled his usual good length and I was able to drive it for four, so the dreaded pair was avoided – not that it extended my life expectancy all that dramatically. Our top scorer was Don Wilson with 7; as far as I remember we did not repeat Close's experiment with heavily stitched cricket balls . . .

South Africa toured after New Zealand, and England got its first look at Graeme Pollock, a wonderfully talented batsman, and the extraordinary fielder Colin Bland. He really was a phenomenon – strong, athletic and with amazing balance that enabled him to throw the ball in at great speed from impossible positions with deadly accuracy. He finished second in South Africa's Test averages for that tour but I reckon people will always remember him for his fielding rather than as a very capable batsman. My own batting was a torment; I could not develop any rhythm or groove myself into a sequence of decent scores. I was desperate to go on playing for England and I put myself under enormous extra pressure. I know the word 'pressure' is overused these days and I don't necessarily subscribe to the theories about pressure on sportsmen, but I do know that I became more and more tense and therefore predictably less likely to do well. The sorry sequence came to a head in the second Test against South Africa at Trent Bridge.

I was out for a duck in the first innings, all tightness and hesitancy, and I was so desperate to do well in the second innings that I froze solid. It was the most obvious arm-ball you could imagine, bowled by the left-arm spinner Athol McKinnon. I read the delivery from the moment he began his run; his approach was different, his arm action was different, he even delivered the ball from a different spot on the crease. The arm-ball could not have been clearer if he had announced it over the loudspeaker – and I watched it bowl me, the classic sucker punch. We lost the Test match, the first time South Africa had won on English soil, and long after the end a deserted Trent Bridge echoed to the sound of scantily clad South African players celebrating their victory with another drink and a boozy dance round the square. I drove home in silence, totally deflated and fighting back tears because I knew I would be dropped from the team. And rightly so.

By early August it was clear that Yorkshire were not going to win the championship. Brian Sellers, the Yorkshire chairman, thrust his head round the dressing-room door at Headingley and told everyone he would see them individually next morning. It was like a summons to appear before Judge Jeffreys. Sellers in a bad mood would have frightened the devil himself, and Yorkshire's performances were not likely to have put him in a good one. His words were frequently undiluted Anglo-Saxon, straight to the point and – as near as made absolutely no difference – the law of the club. One by one the victims were summoned into the presence, one by one they returned with long faces and a distinct trace of scorch-marks round the ears. Sellers was clearly not in the mood for a cosy chat.

Richard Hutton looked especially crestfallen. Sellers kept him standing while he crouched over the desk, writing mysteriously for what seemed like half an hour, though it was more probably half a minute. Sellers finally looked up and made a few pungent remarks about Hutton's bowling. 'There are three things a bowler needs,' Sellers concluded. 'Line, length and pace. And you've got f— all.' Hutton retired hurt.

I was the last to be called in and had begun to imagine that I'd been forgotten. No man in a condemned cell ever created more fantasies of escape than I did that morning at Headingley. But Sellers was efficient and remorseless. I eventually found myself quaking in front of him, mesmerised by his gaze over the half-glasses that made him look like a Dickensian headmaster. I expected a volley, but Sellers simply said, 'Now then, what's the matter?' It was clear from the question and his tone that Sellers knew I was suffering. I had steeled myself for an ear-bashing and here was the fearsome Yorkshire chairman offering sympathy and advice. I told him I couldn't work it out myself: I had tried harder and harder, practised conscientiously and still couldn't get it together. After the success of the previous season it all seemed like a nightmare. Sellers was understanding personified. He suggested I was trying too hard and had become too tense, and told me to go out in every innings to the end of the season and concentrate on relaxing and taking my time. Take an hour to get used to the pitch and the bowlers and then just play naturally – and don't worry if you get out. It wasn't what I expected but it was certainly what I needed. I went out that day and scored 84 against Leicestershire, my best score of the season. The whole team had taken Sellers' advice to heart, and we beat Leicestershire by 148 runs just before 4.30 p.m. on the third day.

Gillette

The myths of the 1965 Gillette Cup final have been repeated, embellished and inevitably accepted as part of the folklore of cricket over the years. As recently as 1978, Brian Close told a version of the final in his autobiography which did not quite reinforce the most popular myth but which did not seek to dispel it either. The suggestion is, of course, that I was piddling along until Close arrived and told me to get on with it or else, thus forcing me to play a memorable innings which would not have been possible without his rugged intervention. It makes good reading, especially for Close, but it is not the way I remember it at all.

Boycott's 146 not out against Surrey in the 1965 Gillette Cup final is a record for the competition and won him the Man of the Match award.

Let me put the match in context. It rained torrentially the night before the final and Surrey's captain Mickey Stewart had little hesitation putting Yorkshire in after winning the toss. 'I consulted my lieutenants and we agreed that as the Lord's wicket was similar to the Oval it would help the quick bowlers as it dried out,' said Stewart. 'I thought the ball would fly, that scoring conditions would be much slower than when the outfield had dried. We bowled badly and they batted superbly, so we came unstuck.'

There was a long discussion in the Yorkshire dressing room as to who should be 12th man and naturally everybody was keen to play in the final. My form had been poor to indifferent all season and although it had improved of late I realised it still wasn't anything to write home about. I made a half-hearted offer to stand down which, thank goodness, was ignored. The losers of the final were due to play in the Scarborough Festival and when we lost the toss, John Edrich said cheekily: 'Good luck when you get to Scarborough . . .' The ground was so wet that the start was delayed for ninety minutes and even then the outfield was saturated: we expected it to be hard work and it certainly was – 22 runs in the first twelve overs before Ken Taylor got out.

Close came in, we exchanged the usual brief observations and then I straight-drove Geoff Arnold for two boundaries and pulled him for three. David Sydenham, the left-arm medium pacer, was predictably difficult to get away because he swings the ball into the righthander's pads but I took a risk and swept him, then picked him up with the swing. Both shots were mistimed on a pudding of a pitch and I nearly holed out each time, but they got me moving and laid the foundation for the innings to follow. It was obvious that we had to pick up the pace of our innings and, at risk of belabouring the point to death, let me make it perfectly clear: so far as I am concerned, at no time did Close tell me to get on with it, or anything remotely similar. The myth about my attitude and motivation that day supports the image of a bold, decisive captain dominating a reluctant subordinate by the force of his personality – a useful adornment to Close's image if it were true – but not once did he threaten or cajole me into playing the strokes I played.

Another impression to emerge from the final was that Close had recognised we were struggling and had promoted himself in the batting order to put matters right. He did bat at three and scored 79 very precious runs, but it was no last-minute inspiration. At Bradford earlier in the season and more recently at the Oval – after we knew Surrey were to be our opponents in the final – we had struggled against Sydenham. It was obvious that he would be a real nuisance in a limited-overs game, especially to the righthanded batsmen – and Close was the only recognised batsman in the team who was lefthanded. He made a pretty brisk and unbeaten 30 against Sydenham in the championship match and several of us floated the idea that he should go in early in the final. I discussed it with Illingworth, the power behind the throne as far as Close was concerned, so the plan to push Close up the order to prevent Sydenham bogging us down had been formulated at least a fortnight before the final.

The main thing is that it worked and we won – by a comfortable 175 runs as it turned out. Close and I put on 192 in thirty-five overs for the second wicket, Yorkshire made 317–4 and Illingworth took 5–29 as Surrey were dismissed for 142. Once I got into my stride I didn't seem able to put a foot wrong that day. I hit three sixes and fifteen fours, and only Stuart Storey gave me any sort of trouble. I still remember moving down the pitch to Arnold and lifting him straight for six, with the Yorkshire players trying to catch the ball on the pavilion balcony. I grabbed a stump at the end of the game and still have it, suitably engraved. The crowd was marvellous and there was a fair bit of good-natured ribbing for Doug Insole, chairman of the selectors, who had dropped me from the Test side and was now presenting me with the Man of the Match award. It was a tremendous climax to a chequered season for Yorkshire and for me. I told the press at the time that 'I was beginning to wonder if I'd ever hit another hundred,' and I meant it.

There was one abiding disappointment – the fact that the game was not recorded by television. Quite apart from its statistical significance as the highest score in a Lord's final, my innings did disprove the theory that I was technically and temperamentally incapable of scoring at a brisk pace. It was one of the best innings I ever played, different in character from many that people choose to remember but with a context and a significance all of its own. For the sake of balance and the sheer thrill of it, I would like that innings to have been recorded for posterity.

7

Downunder

Australia and a pain in the backside will always be closely associated for me. Actually, I love the place. I have spent a fair bit of time out there over the years and I always look forward to going back. Sydney was once described as the best-kept secret in the world and I have no hesitation in electing it the most beautiful city I have seen – I've seen a fair few. But my first experiences of Australia were physically painful and excruciatingly frustrating – a long-drawn-out struggle on the 1965–6 tour under Mike Smith. He was the captain but the tour manager was Billy Griffith, then secretary of MCC, and it was announced for the first time that the manager, not the captain, would be 'responsible for overall tactics'. That was an extraordinary state of affairs and may have stemmed to some extent from a suspicion that Mike Smith was too defensive as a captain. If so, it was an impression which did not take into account the circumstances of Mike's captaincy and the fact that he had been confronted by an unusual number of injuries to bowlers – the fact that I had bowled fairly regularly in Test matches was evidence of that. England under Mike had beaten South Africa in South Africa and New Zealand in England before losing the home series against South Africa, when Tom Cartwright had been injured. Whatever the thinking, Griffith was in charge and that meant a stated policy of positive, attacking cricket – always a popular slogan.

Nobody had advised us what we should or should not eat when we stopped off to play two one-day matches in Ceylon, now Sri Lanka. By the time we boarded the plane for Australia I was ill and by the time we stopped off at Singapore I felt as though I was at death's door. I was rushed to hospital and kept in for eight days while the rest of the party pushed on to Perth. The official diagnosis was a severe attack of gastro-enteritis and I spent my twenty-fifth birthday fighting it off. When I did get to Perth I was nowhere near fit enough to play immediately and the medical advice was that I should recuperate slowly. I missed the practices and two first-class matches in Western Australia but felt I would be okay for the upcoming match in

Adelaide – except that now I had developed a nagging pain in my backside and down the back of the left thigh. It was diagnosed as a touch of sciatica and the theory was that exercise plus South Australia's pleasant climate would put it right.

Since my innings in the Gillette Cup final, the press had come round to the view that there was no earthly reason why I should not take attacks apart every time I batted. I had all the shots, all the power, I could never again hide behind the theory that I had a limited range of strokes, and so on. I was conscious of their expectations and also aware that a lot of their observations were veiled criticisms of my usual way of batting. Griffith's call for 'positive' cricket added further fuel, and I made an aggressive 94 in Adelaide after South Australia were bowled out for 103 on a decidedly sticky pitch. The surface got better to bat on after South Australia were all out, just after lunch, and I was mindful of what was expected. But I had another incentive to try and hit boundaries: the pain in my backside made it very difficult to run.

By the time we came to field on the second day I was in real trouble. The pain down my leg was excruciating and even out on the boundary I couldn't get near anything which was more than a few feet away. Finally I was practically carried off the field and sent to a specialist, Don Beard, who looked after many of the South Australian players. I spent another two weeks in hospital while Dr Beard ran tests, made examinations and concluded that my problem stemmed from the time I spent in hospital in Singapore. There I had been given an injection in the backside – by a doctor, rather than a nurse who would probably have done mundane jobs like that more often – and the needle had just missed the sciatic nerve. That had set up an inflammation aggravated by the exercises I had undertaken in the belief they would do me good. I had time to ponder the irony of that, flat on my back in Adelaide's Queen Elizabeth Hospital when I should have been playing for England. There was one quite amazing consolation – I received a visit from Sir Donald Bradman.

He arrived unannounced and totally unexpected, bringing with him a signed copy of a book written by his friend A. G. 'Johnnie' Moyes called *The Changing Face of Cricket*. I still have it. We must have chatted for about twenty minutes and the extraordinary thing is that I totally forgot to ask the Don any of the questions I had always wanted him to answer. Here was a man normally inaccessible simply because of his fame and status, naturally reticent and not given to making speeches about himself, and I had him completely to myself for the best part of half an hour – too dumbfounded to ask him anything sensible. The more I think about it the more I regret it.

Bradman was and remains the idol of my professional life.

After leaving hospital I stayed for a short time with Doc Beard and had net practices at which he would bowl. He was the most blatant chucker I have ever seen, though it says a great deal for his popularity – and perhaps not much for his effectiveness – that nobody drew attention to this in his club cricket. 'I just get a little nip off the pitch when I bend my back,' he explained. It was the bent arm that intrigued me . . . By the time I rejoined the tour party and went into the match against Queensland in Brisbane I had played only one first-class innings in twelve weeks. Hardly the stuff Test places are made of, but I cobbled together some runs in Queensland and was picked for the first Test – to bat at number six and bowl a bit if required. Peter Parfitt was out of form and Eric Russell was due to open the batting with Barber. In the event, Russell injured his thumb fielding as Australia made 443–6, so I opened with Bob and made 45 out of a total of 280. We followed on, though not in much danger of defeat since there were only three hours left in the match, and Bob sprung another of his little surprises. 'I fancy a bit of sunbathing today,' he confided – and immediately set about the bowling as though it was a one-day match on the local park. He slogged everything. He even swung himself off his feet clobbering one huge six, and sure enough he was caught when he'd made 34 in absolutely no time. I batted rather more circumspectly for 63 not out, conscious for most of the innings that Bob was stretched out and soaking up the Brisbane sunshine.

One incident during that Test said a lot for the Australian character and the spirit in which matches were played between the countries in those days. During the Australian innings, we were convinced that Bill Lawry was caught behind for a duck. We claimed it confidently, but the umpire was unmoved and Lawry showed no inclination to go. The fact that he went on to make over 150 did not exactly endear him to us and we made little secret of the fact that we thought he should have walked. In my first innings I played and missed at the second delivery and immediately the wicketkeeper and the entire slip cordon went up for a catch. I was nowhere near it. The appeal was obviously premeditated, a deliberate attempt to pressure the umpire. It was probably the Aussies' way of telling me I should walk when they appealed, too! In the second innings I had made 23 when I played a delivery from the leg-spinner Peter Philpott defensively off the back foot, then tapped it gently with my bat and brushed it away with my glove as it bobbed round my shins. The unmistakable voice of Wally Grout said quietly, 'We're not appealing this time, mate, but do that again and you're out.' Quite simply, and with a self-confessed ignorance that would probably have given them apoplexy at Lord's or Headingley, I did not understand the law relating to handling the ball. I thought it applied only if the ball was actually going to hit the stumps, which it was clearly not going to do on this occasion. The Australians had only to mutter 'How's that?' and I would have been a goner. I have looked up the law since, of course, and wonder how many modern players know its full implications. We see so many batsmen tossing the ball to fielders these days, though the law says that, unless the fielding side specifically asks them to do so, they can be given out. Perhaps they all know the law, perhaps they aren't as daft as I was. I apologised to the bowler, the umpire and the Australian captain Brian Booth afterwards; Wally Grout apologised to me for the premeditated appeal. The Australians were like that and I hope still are: absolutely intent on winning but never malicious or unsporting. It was a chastening lesson, but a reassuring one at the same time.

Christmas 1965 was one I shall never forget, though I would prefer to. I fielded for two days while South Australia made 459–7 declared, then I went in to face a few overs before the close and was out first ball – caught at first slip by Ian Chappell off a bowler playing in his first State match and blessed with the name of Jack Frost. Imagine that – 80 degrees in the shade and I'm a victim of Frost. Just as bad, I spent Christmas Day and Boxing Day sweating on a king pair before the match resumed.

A score of 58 in the second innings eased the pain, then I made 99 against a South Australia Country XI and 95 against the Prime Minister's XI, which suggested that the strength was returning to my legs and my rhythm was improving. So I was mortified to learn I had been left out of the team for the second Test in Melbourne.

Griffith told me that I was in the 13 but that Eric Russell would play. Russell had not batted since the State game against Queensland, nursing an injured thumb, but he tested it in the nets the day before the Test began and said he was fit to play. The only doubt in the make-up of the side concerned Ken Higgs, my room-mate at the time, who was suffering with a stomach bug. If he could not play, then David Allen would move into the side and I would replace Russell because I could bowl! I was livid, so annoyed in fact that I made noises about pushing Eric Russell downstairs if I had to! Griffith was due to check on Higgs's fitness on the morning of the match. I didn't wish him – or Russell – any harm but I wanted to play. 'Ken, you don't look all that well. Stay in bed for your own good . . . It's as hot as hell out there – you'll be bound to collapse, you might even die . . . Don't you *dare* get out of that bed!' Higgs stayed in bed, I played – and figured in an extraordinary opening stand with Bob Barber. We had fielded for a day and a half, and Bob was apparently feeling a bit tired. In any event he announced as we walked out to open the innings, 'We're not running any singles today.' It was always difficult to take him completely seriously but he insisted: 'If you run any singles, you'll run 'em on your own.' And sure enough he set about the bowling. I was dropped by Peter Philpott off Graham McKenzie at third slip in the first over and then galloped off to 51 before I got out. We had put on 98 in seventy-seven minutes, scoring at six an over. Mr Griffith must have been delighted, even if the match was unavoidably drawn.

The third Test at Sydney was memorable for a big England win, by an innings and 93 runs, and for an absolutely brilliant innings from Bob Barber. The pitch was quite lively – McKenzie flicked my left ear with one delivery – but Bob and I put on 234 before tea, the third-highest opening partnership for England against Australia. I went for 84 but Bob pressed on to 185 with what must be one of the truly great displays of batting in Test cricket. His driving on the off-side was a joy and it did not seem to matter what they bowled at him; the half-volleys disappeared inevitably, but he was just as fluent driving on the up. The only time I reckoned he slogged a bit was when he was facing David Sincock. Nicknamed Evil Dick, Sincock was a left-arm bowler of googlies and chinamen who spun the ball prodigiously and had a habit of fixing you with a murderous stare if you read him wrongly and got away with it. Bob didn't worry too much about picking the delivery – he subscribed to Maurice Leyland's theory and laid into practically every delivery. It was a marvellous, memorable innings.

A damaged finger put me on the sidelines for ten days but I was fit enough to bat with the help of a finger-splint against a Combined XI in Hobart. And that paved the way for one of the celebrated mickey-taking stories of the tour. MCC batted second and I made 156, not against the most formidable opposition, true, but especially valuable to me because I had not scored a first-class century for eleven months. My last had been against South Africa in Port Elizabeth.

It was an enormous relief to me, and the rest of the party knew that well enough. Subtly and with many a knowing wink among themselves, they introduced the suggestion that the match might not be first class. It still had to be decided at Lord's, they said, and a lot would depend on the views of Colin Cowdrey, captain for the match while Mike Smith had a rest. I quizzed Cowdrey about it – desperately keen, of course, that the match should have first-class status – and he said he would do what he could – it might help if I were to bowl a few overs in the second innings. In the circumstances, I would probably have bowled at both ends; as it was I bowled seven overs for 39 runs, anxious to stay in Colin's good books, while the regular bowlers had a rest in preparation for the forthcoming Test at Adelaide. As soon as the game was over the lads let me into the secret that the match was, and always had been, first class: they fell about laughing. I had fallen for the ruse hook, line and sinker.

There was very little to laugh about in Adelaide, where we were never in with a chance and lost the fourth Test by an innings and nine runs. Bob Simpson returned as captain after a bout of chickenpox and thumped 225, Bill Lawry made 119, Graham McKenzie roared back with 6–48, and the whole thing was over in four days. A massacre – and the annoying thing was that we had contributed to our own defeat. The clarion call was still for bright, attacking cricket and that sounds fine until it becomes a fixation and a form of suicide. We played so attractively that we were all out before the close on the first day and the match was already as good as lost. Ken Barrington was furious. He reckoned that we had only to play solid, sensible cricket to preserve our one–nil lead in the series and instead we were being encouraged to play like Flash Harrys. I was nowhere near senior enough to say much but I agreed with him wholeheartedly. After all, we were there to win the series. We got the worst of a draw in Melbourne and the series was drawn 1–1, so Australia retained the Ashes.

Bob Barber, Jim Parks and Fred Titmus were allowed to return to England when we pushed on for a three-Test tour of New Zealand. My illness early on in the tour may have caught up with me, perhaps I was just plain tired, but my batting deteriorated like the England team. New Zealand was damp, dull and cool, rather like England in early April, and I could not put any runs together – 4, 4 and 5 before I was predictably left out of the third Test. On the way home we stopped off in Hong Kong where I made 108 in a match at Kowloon and, more significantly, discovered an extraordinary city which has drawn me back many times since – I love the lights, the bustle and the atmosphere of the place.

Peter West will probably remember the climax to the 1966 season as vividly as anyone who packed into the St George's Road ground at Harrogate to see Yorkshire clinch the championship by beating Kent. In his radio reports, West gave the distinct impression that he fancied a Kent victory and he was not too complimentary about Yorkshire cricket in general, a view which did not go down too well with the customers at the last match. The ground was full and to reach his position West had to walk the length of the old 'scratching shed' along one side of the ground. He was stepping it out smartly – as the compère of TV's *Come Dancing* might – when one wit bellowed 'Slow, slow, quick, quick, slow!' The crowd took it up and West had to walk the gauntlet, trying not to fall into step with the crowd's refrain and trying even harder to look as though he was enjoying it. He spent the next two days trying to cadge a lift into the ground in one of the players' cars but we weren't having any of that. We used to wait for him to arrive as we knocked up. 'Slow, slow, quick, quick, slow . . .', here he comes again.

A new rule that season enforced a declaration after sixty-five overs in the first innings. It was designed to produce more results but it was not necessarily beneficial to the game as a whole. Mid-order batsmen, in particular, rarely met a situation where they did not have to slog in the first innings. But it suited the make-up of Yorkshire's team, with mean bowlers and solid hitters in the middle order, and we won fifteen of our twenty-eight championship matches. I made six hundreds that season and made two hundreds in a match for the first time – 103 and 105 against Nottinghamshire at Sheffield, where we won by 229 runs. The pitch for the last match against Kent was damp and awkward, especially against the young Derek Underwood, who finished the match with eleven wickets. I top-scored with 80 in the first innings, which I considered was a very professional innings in the circumstances.

Boycott completed centuries in both innings of a match for the first time on 18 July 1966, 103 and 105 for Yorkshire against Nottinghamshire at Sheffield.

The Test series that season was against the West Indies and after being left out at Old Trafford I was picked to partner Colin Milburn at Lord's. 'Ollie' Milburn was considerably larger than life, a marvellously expressive player and a great character, but decidedly not the fastest thing on two legs. He had been run out for a duck in the first Test and as we were padding up at Lord's, selector Peter May came over. 'You won't be trying any quick singles will you, Geoff?' he enquired. 'Why's that?' 'Because I don't think Colin will make it . . .' The point was well taken. Ollie promised me a night on the town and took me off to Raymond's Revue bar: strippers (very tasteful, of course), near-naked dancers and near-nudes swimming in what looked like a large fish tank. They all seemed to know Ollie, so I assumed he was a frequent customer.

That series marked the return to Test cricket of Tom Graveney, the batsman I had most admired as a youngster. Tom was thirty-nine then; he'd been out of Test cricket for three and a half years and missed thirty-eight Tests, but he could still play, there was no mistaking that. Ollie got out early at Lord's and Tom and I shared a century partnership. It was a privilege and a great thrill to play with a man I had admired for so long. Tom finished up heading the batting averages for the series with 459 runs at 76.50, a great achievement. The third Test at Trent Bridge was memorable for me because I very nearly bagged a pair. Garry Sobers did me all ends up in the first innings, trapped lbw by a delivery that swung prodigiously – the best delivery I have ever faced in cricket. I sweated on a pair and in the second innings he produced another wicked delivery that swung very late. I got a faint inside edge on to my pad or I would have been a goner. As it was, I went on to make 71 – that's the way it goes.

8

Labelled for Life

I have been accused of many things in my career. Cricket can be a cruel as well as a wonderfully rewarding game and that may be part of its fascination. But the barbs still hurt, and the deepest wound of my professional life was inflicted by the England selectors on 18 June 1967, when I was dropped from the England team as a 'disciplinary measure'. I had just scored 246 not out in an England Test victory over India.

Boycott's highest score in Test matches was his 246 not out against India at Leeds on 8–9 June 1967.

The decision stunned me at the time, though looking back I now see that it had become inevitable. I was mortified with embarrassment and filled with an angry, burning sense of injustice which I can remember clearly and painfully to this day. Even after twenty years and with plenty of opportunity to ponder all the aspects of the affair, I still feel the selectors were wrong. They inflicted upon me a stigma which I cannot believe I deserved but one which I will take with me to my grave. Being dropped by England then was an indelible stain on my record; more, it was a stain on my character which has been used as an official endorsement of the accusation that I played the game selfishly and with total disregard for others. When the circumstances have long been forgotten, the fact that I was dropped for slow scoring – and the inference that it was wilfully slow scoring – will remain. I still believe I was the victim of a miscarriage of justice.

It is important to ink in the background. The 1967 season began badly as far as the weather was concerned, several matches were rain-affected and two Yorkshire matches, against Leicestershire at Leeds and Lancashire at Old Trafford, were abandoned altogether. That is the sort of situation I hate – continuity and rhythm have always been important to my cricket. I recorded my only pair in county cricket, against Kent at Bradford, where Norman Graham bowled out Yorkshire for 40. The ball reared, hit my arm and dropped on to the stumps in the first innings; in the second I fended it off a glove in front of my nose and was caught by Alan Knott. David

Swallow, cricket writer for the *Bradford Telegraph and Argus*, had the job of coming into the dressing room to ask if it was the first time I had bagged a pair. I can't remember what I said to him but I suspect it was rather more than a simple yes! By the time the first Test against India came round at Headingley I was in no sort of form and a near-desperate frame of mind. In twelve innings I had made a grand total of 280 runs and 162 of those had come in two knocks. It might not have been an enormous surprise, though certainly it would have been a big disappointment, if I had been left out of the Test side. I can only assume that the captain Brian Close wanted players whom he know would graft, whatever their form, and it was not insignificant that Ray Illingworth and John Edrich were back in the side.

My run of scores leading to the Test made macabre reading: 45, 9, 102, 0, 0, 6, 4, 0, 24, 60, 24 and 6. Of course I was worried about my form and by the fact that I had not spent much time in the middle. I was very conscious, when Close won the toss and we batted, that I was going into a Test match very poorly prepared.

At the end of the first day England were 281–3 and I had scored 106 not out in six hours. My rate of progress – or lack of progress – was faithfully recorded at the time and still looks dreadful: 17 runs in the first hour, then 8 in the second, 15 in the third, then 23, 21 and 22. What made it worse was the fact that India's bowling attack was eventually depleted by injuries to Surti and Bedi, and it was not the most fearsome-looking Test attack in the world to start with. Next day I added 140 runs in three and a half hours and England declared at 550–4, by which time the controversy had broken with a vengeance.

The press pilloried me for my slow scoring on the first day and the call grew almost unanimously for me to be dropped from the second Test as a punishment. It was pointed out that Ken Barrington had been dropped in similar circumstances after scoring 137 against New Zealand two years earlier. The selectors – chairman Doug Insole, Peter May, Alec Bedser and Don Kenyon – had only to read the newspapers to know that they would be hailed as strong and far-sighted if they left me out of the next Test and criticised as gutless if they did not. The England establishment was still trying to lead the world in a verbal crusade for 'brighter cricket' and Billy Griffith – described by one newspaper as 'the hot gospeller of livelier cricket' – was at the ground talking to Insole. If ever there was an opportunity for the press to pontificate and the selectors to show their Corinthian mettle to the world, this was it. The analyses of my innings even suggested that by scoring more quickly on the second day I had condemned myself, because it proved I could do it if I wanted to.

The fact is that most of the men writing that sort of stuff had never experienced the horror of being out of form in a Test match. I did not expect praise for my first day – it was a grim-looking innings and I did not need anybody to tell me that – but I was satisfied that I had at least shown the character to stick with it. The alternative would have been to give my wicket away and retire to the anonymity of the dressing room. That would have left the press to write about somebody else and would probably have assured me of a place in the second Test. Nobody regretted my inability to score quickly more than I did, but I did not consider I was picked by England in order to surrender my wicket when things got tough for me. As I said at the time: 'I was never conscious of the time factor . . . but when you are in bad nick you never seem to get the half-volleys. And when you do play a shot the ball always seems to hit the fielders.' That was the way it was. It happens to anyone who plays cricket, whatever the level.

Close himself put my predicament very well when he later wrote: 'Anyone who has played a long innings will well understand Boycott's problem. The sheer effort makes one like an automaton; very often you don't even hear the crowd; all you are concerned with is that ball, which must not beat your bat. One needs to understand Boycott's frame of mind as an out-of-form batsman trying to prove himself good enough for England; and to study the innings in this context to reach a charitable understanding of why he played as he did. Such tenacity, in different conditions, would have been hailed as a masterly exhibition of the bulldog spirit; but on this first day of a Test it was being viewed in a different light.'

So what about the contrast on the second day, when I doubled my scoring rate and outstripped as strong a strokemaker as Basil D'Oliveira? Proof positive, surely, that I had been goaded into action by the press and wanted to redeem myself? Plausible, a handy enough argument, but it wasn't true. The undramatic fact is that I was relieved to have got through the first day, I'd had a good night's sleep and I felt considerably more relaxed in the knowledge that runs were on the board. I had worked very hard and unglamorously for them but they were there, and if the critics weren't best pleased, neither were the Indians. It is a fact, too, that when you limit your strokeplay through lack of form and lack of confidence, you fall into a routine that is very hard to break. Grafting one minute and glittering the next is a great deal harder than it sounds.

As the press comment took on the proportions of a campaign, there was the suggestion, no less tiresome for being familiar, that I had wilfully disregarded instructions to speed up my scoring on the first day. The day after I was dropped, Ian Wooldridge in the *Daily Mail* reported the selectors as saying: 'At tea-time on the first day Boycott was ordered by his captain, Brian Close, to step up his scoring rate. He didn't do so. We are dropping him as a disciplinary measure.' Somebody was very badly informed – Wooldridge or the selectors or both. At no time did Close tell me to get on with it and he had plenty of opportunity. He could have told me at tea or when D'Oliveira came in to bat during the last session. He has revealed that he tried to catch my attention from the balcony with the order to speed up but, as he accepts, I never saw him. At the end of the innings Close was pictured with an arm round my shoulders – hardly the reaction of an annoyed man; and to be seen supporting a man who had ignored the philosophy of 'brighter cricket' was a gesture that might not have done him any good. Clive Taylor said in the *Sun*: 'Close made it obvious at the end of the day – and again at the end of Boycott's innings when he posed with an arm round his shoulder – that he was not dissatisfied with either his side or his number-one batsman.'

I learned later that the selectors had spoken to Close on the afternoon of the first day and had suggested he should hurry me up. The fact that he never did – but that it was later reported he had – is interesting. The selectors met on Friday to choose a second Test team that would be announced on Sunday and it is perfectly clear to me now that I did not have a chance – not with the selectors keen to prove their strength and their commitment to 'brighter cricket'. Not with the press full of indignant outrage. But at the time I thought that logic would win through. The captain had not said a word of criticism about my innings and no doubt he would speak up on my behalf at the selection meeting. My slow innings was unfortunate, agreed, but I did not consider it was treasonable. Without it, in view of a much improved India batting performance in the second innings, England would not have won the match.

Yorkshire were at Bristol over that weekend and on Sunday morning, before the team was officially released, Close broke the news that I had been left out. I was shattered. Despite all the furore in the press, Close had never once criticised my innings: he had not admonished me during it nor reproached me after it. And here he was telling me that the selectors had decided to leave me out. I went to Abergavenny and played for the International Cavaliers, which was probably worth a smirk or two at the time. Hardly anybody spoke to me and I felt a bit like a leper until Lance Gibbs took me aside and commiserated. 'The selectors must be crazy: if you made those sort of runs for the West Indies you'd be a hero.' It was good of him to try. I felt too disappointed and too confused to say much to anyone.

I have thought about it a lot since. I know rather more about the power of the media and I read situations a lot clearer than I did then, when I imagined that getting on with the job in hand was what mattered. It seems obvious now that Close did not go in to bat for me at the selection meeting. He was probably faced with the choice between sacrificing me or putting his job as captain on the line, and he made the choice in hard, professional terms. Maybe the selectors thought that he had carried out their wishes by instructing me to speed up and that I had ignored him.

Close wrote later that he had defended me at the selection meeting but that the vote went against me for two reasons: 'The first was the fact that he had – even though unwittingly – prevented Basil D'Oliveira from pushing the score along by retaining too much of the bowling. And the second was that a precedent had been set by the dropping of Barrington in similar circumstances in 1965.' As I read that it struck me that Bill Athey had just taken 72 overs to score 76 for England in Brisbane this winter. 'I suppose England will drop him now,' I said to myself, 'not because he deserves it but because there are precedents . . .' The first part of the argument is even more ridiculous. Basil D'Oliveira came in to bat at eight minutes past six on the first day: simple arithmetic says he batted for twenty-two minutes that night. Perhaps the intention was that he should launch a stinging attack before stumps, perhaps he was supposed to knock up a quick 50 in the interest of 'brighter cricket'. As it was, he made 19 before the close and I outscored him next day. Where the notion comes from that I prevented him pushing the score along is quite beyond me.

The fact is that I played poorly because I was out of form. I improved next day and atoned for that to some extent. And I was the victim of a pretentious press campaign backing the selectors' new policy. I am not against 'brighter cricket', assuming that anybody knows what it means – it is one of those marvellously imprecise mottoes that everybody agrees with and nobody can quite define, the sort of thing politicians love. It has become less fashionable to talk about 'brighter cricket' now but it was very much in vogue then. What we needed was not so much brighter cricket as brighter selectors.

What still upsets and angers me is the suggestion that I disobeyed captain's orders in playing the way I did. It opens a vast and fertile area wherein Geoff Boycott plays for himself and to hell with the team, the game and the spectators. England's decision more or less confirmed that that was the official view. Let me say again that Brian Close never instructed me to quicken the pace. If the selectors thought he had and he needed to pretend as much to save his face and the captaincy, that is a matter for his conscience. I had enough esteem for Close to try my damnedest to speed up if he said so;

and I had enough respect for him to know that if I wilfully disobeyed an order he would probably put me through the dressing-room window. Close himself was in favour of dressing-room discussion, debate, even argument. As a professional I would put my ideas forcibly when I felt strongly about an issue. But the idea that I would refuse to carry out a captain's orders, especially when that captain was Brian Close, is hurtful nonsense.

Strangely enough, I still believe that it was felt at the time that a one-match suspension would wipe the slate clean and soon be forgotten. Close himself said: 'The selectors felt that Geoff's performance on the first day was not in the interests of cricket in general and the team in particular. But I know him well enough to say that he is a good enough player to take it and bounce back to become an even better player . . .' The implication was that being dropped would prove a point and wouldn't really do me any harm. How misguided could anybody be? The stigma of being dropped by England, apparently for selfishness, was to mark the rest of my career and hangs round my neck like a millstone to this day. My conscience is clear but the blot on my record and on my integrity will never go away.

It certainly stalked me for the rest of that season. Whatever anyone else may have thought about it, I could not come to terms with the fact that I had battled hard to help England win a Test match – a Test match, not an exhibition game – and had been dropped for my pains. Close made some complimentary remarks about the composure I had shown and the way I had accepted the decision. I made the right noises to the press but frankly I was devastated. I simply did not know how to handle the pressure that came from outside the game. If I looked cool I certainly did not feel it.

Yorkshire completed the match at Bristol, where we were left two hours to score 193 for victory. With only a few runs needed, Phil Sharpe offered to give me the strike so I could complete a century but I was so anxious not to look as though I was putting self before team that I told him just to play normally. Sharpe finished with 71 not out and I made an unbeaten 98. In the next match against Northamptonshire at Sheffield I made 220 not out. That brought my aggregate of runs since the double Test hundred to 584 in four innings, and for once out I had doubled the output of the dozen innings before being picked for the first Test. Things might have turned out very differently had I just been setting off for Headingley now.

Having served my one-match suspension – and the beginning of a life sentence – I was chosen for the third Test at Edgbaston. The atmosphere was strained, to say the least, when the selectors joined us for drinks and dinner the day before the game. I did not know them personally and making small talk was never my forte. Doug Insole tried hard to be 'natural' and put me at my ease, but his eyes wandered as we spoke and it was so obvious he was ill at ease that it put me on edge too; they were among the most uncomfortable moments of my life. When we batted next morning, the pressure was awful. Even before the match started, my mind was in a whirl. I was terrified in case I played a maiden over and was accused of not trying to get on with it – and the fact that I was opening with Colin Milburn wasn't likely to help! The way he bats can make anybody look stolid by comparison.

Instead of batting properly, taking the shine off the new ball and filling the role of an opening batsman in a Test match, I was going to ping the ball about like nobody's business. And that feller Milburn wasn't going to outscore me . . . I made a conscious effort to hit every ball and to keep up with Milburn – it was the most elementary nonsense and, not surprisingly, I didn't last long. Milburn was 40 not out when I sallied down the pitch to Bedi and was stumped by Engineer. Stumped – I was so far down it could have counted as a run-out! And fancy a Test opener, especially me, being stumped before lunch. Still, I had made 25, a significant blow for 'brighter cricket'.

India must have been hooked on 'brighter cricket' too because they were bowled out for only 92 facing an England first-innings total of 298. Close should have enforced the follow-on but he didn't – it was a decision which did not make sense professionally and which he has struggled to justify since. He said at first that his bowlers were tired, which was a joke considering that John Snow had bowled 12 overs, David Brown 11, Ray Illingworth 7 and Robin Hobbs 6.3. Then he said he thought the selectors would want to see England bat again, to finalise their plans for the forthcoming West Indies tour, and he pointed out that another day's play brought in a bonus £6000. That, I think, was closer to the truth than any cricket consideration; Close putting himself in the good books of the selectors and the administrators. It was certainly out of character for a man whose attitude towards cricket, and especially Test cricket, had always been professional and ruthless. I was still in a state about my batting and the need to be seen to score quickly. Now I felt that the entire press box was waiting with pens poised for me to play a defensive stroke. An over-reaction? Not to someone who has had his attitude and character plastered over every back page in the land for the best part of a week and found that desperately hard to handle. England made 203 in the second innings, a poor effort but our hearts weren't really in it, and then bowled out India for 277 to win by 132. I was bowled for 6 by Subramanya, a piddling medium-pacer who was about half as formidable a bowler as I was. The stroke was a dreadful attempt to force through midwicket – it was never on, but that says it all about my frame of mind.

My father died soon afterwards. He had been ill in Gateforth hospital near Selby for some time and I was at the Oval with Yorkshire when the secretary John Nash rang with the news. Close suggested I stayed and played the match. There was, after all, very little I could do until the funeral. He was probably right. The end of the season could not really come quickly enough for me, though there was plenty of cricket left to be played and Yorkshire finished on a high note by beating Gloucestershire at Harrogatc to win the championship again. The pitch was damp and difficult, but Sharpe and I put on 127 for the first wicket and left the rest to Illingworth, who scored 46 and then took 7–58 and 7–6! A truly magnificent performance.

By the end of the season I was shattered, mentally and physically. The difficulty of playing well, the incalculable strain of being dropped by England and the worsening illness and death of my father – it all mounted and overcame me until I was physically affected. I was on edge, I had no appetite for food or cricket, I felt totally lethargic. A local doctor prescribed not pills or potions but golf, and I found it wonderfully therapeutic. By the end of November the mood had passed and I felt human and optimistic again.

9

Mr Runs

It may have been the trauma of the 1967 season that encouraged me to work extra hard in preparation for the tour to West Indies early the following year and I also felt that I hadn't done myself full justice on my previous tours with England. I might be considered a fairly obvious choice – I had established myself to that extent – but I did not feel I had done anything out of the ordinary on tour. It was up to me to put that right and I sought the advice of Fred and Ray Illingworth about the pitches and conditions in the Caribbean. Their overriding message was that it was important to get to terms with West Indian conditions as quickly as possible. Remembering the shaky starts I had made to tours in South Africa and Australia, for one reason or another, that was obviously good advice. The tour itinerary, designed to give us Christmas lunch at home, also left us with only two first-class matches before the first Test, so there would be no time to spare. I pushed myself hard physically, running in gloves through a bitterly cold December when the frost clamped itself to my eyebrows, and practised for all I was worth with Johnny Lawrence at Rothwell.

The practice routine was designed specifically to reproduce West Indian conditions, which is not exactly easy at Rothwell in an icy English winter. The artificial surface was rolled back and the wooden floor beneath was polished until it shone – any housewife would have been proud of it. We used composition balls, much harder than leather and therefore likely to bounce more, and the local fast bowlers – fast-medium to me – were asked to go through the crease and bowl off twenty yards to simulate the West Indians' extra speed. I practised every day for a solid month, batting for forty or fifty minutes at a time so that I became hot and tired and saturated with sweat, which was how it was going to be on tour. Johnny bowled over after over of leg-spin, top-spin and googlies which bounced and hurried on off the wooden floor. It was hard work but it was imperative that I should have sharp reflexes and a good touch right from the moment we landed in the Caribbean. Two first-class matches was precious little preparation for a Test if we came cold out of an English winter.

The tour captain, Colin Cowdrey, took me on one side and told me he wanted me to play in my natural way throughout the tour irrespective of any instructions he might issue to the team as a whole. 'If I want you to bat outside your normal style,' said Cowdrey, 'I'll make a point of telling you personally.' I discovered later that Cowdrey's attitude, which I appreciated, had been suggested by Brian Close. The runs came steadily enough early on, although things looked ominous for me after MCC's match against Trinidad: Wes Hall broke the top knuckle on the ring finger of my right hand. The tendon was damaged and the finger suddenly bent at an impossible angle. It is still crooked to this day, one of many distinct impressions Wes left during his career.

The finger mended quite quickly with the help of an aluminium splint, which also offered a fair measure of protection and enabled me to bat during the rest of the tour. It was not ideal but it was not hopelessly uncomfortable either. The second Test at Jamaica was memorable on two accounts – riot stopped play, and we almost talked ourselves into enough extra time to lose the match. The riot was sparked off when Jim Parks flung himself headlong to take a leg glance by Basil Butcher in West Indies' second innings. They had followed on after John Snow took 7–49 to dismiss them for 143 against our 376, and the West Indian crowd sensed an unusual and quite unacceptable possibility of defeat. Butcher stood his ground when Parks claimed the catch – quite rightly since he could not be certain that the catch had been taken cleanly – and that few seconds of enquiry was interpreted by the crowd as disbelief at the decision. The bottles came over in an ever developing shower; we galloped from the field and passed the riot police going the other way. The ritual tear-gas attack did its job until the wind changed and wafted it into our dressing room. I had never realised what a dreadful experience it is to be caught by tear-gas. It was unbearable and, since we couldn't go anywhere to escape, I sat with my head in the sink to try and keep the stuff out of my eyes.

Being in a strong position and not wanting to allow a fashion for mob rule to develop on the tour, England pressed strongly to have the time lost because of the riot restored in the form of an extra day. It was agreed – and it almost cost us the game. Garry Sobers played a magnificent innings on a difficult pitch to save West Indies, then he suddenly declared 158 in front. The pitch was criss-crossed by extraordinary cracks, wide enough and deep enough to accept a hand as far as the base of the thumb. When the ball hit the edge closer to the bowler it shot; when it hit the edge further away it lifted. Batting was murder and England clung on desperately, 68–8 at the close and glad to escape with a draw. The tension was terrific and clearly communicated itself to the umpire Douglas Sang Hue. He was standing at point as West Indies crowded the bat and rushed through the overs in a bid to force a win. Fred Titmus played a delivery which squirted off his pad and ran through the fielders to point – where Sang Hue picked up the ball and tossed it quickly back to Lance Gibbs the bowler! We laughed about it later but I don't recall it causing too much merriment at the time.

The humour on the tour was provided, inevitably and inexhaustibly, by Colin Milburn. His rendering of Tom Jones hits, especially 'The Green, Green Grass of Home', was enough to reduce strong men to tears – especially if they happened to be music lovers. His sheer size was enough to make him a favourite with the West Indian crowds, who loved to see him waddling after the ball with a formidable backside and near-voluptuous breasts wobbling in disharmony.

The selectors had been worried about Ollie's girth and had suggested he should make an effort to get his weight down. His Northants captain Keith Andrew was told to pass on the hard word. When Ollie admitted to a passion for fish and chips and pints, Andrew suggested he should drink halves. Ollie went to the bar and ordered himself two halves . . . What can you do? His tour had been most disappointing by the time we got to Antigua – only two first-class matches in seven weeks and not many runs in those – and nobody felt it more keenly than Ollie himself. He was very anxious to do well and the crowd was anxious that he should, since they had heard a lot about his attractive batting and wanted a full display. Convicts from the local prison rolled the pitch – they had the time to make a really good job of it – and when Ollie and I opened I went to the non-striker's end. The umpire at my end greeted Ollie like a long-lost brother – a big smile, a cheery greeting, 'Very pleased to see you, Mr Milburn,' that sort of thing. With the crowd and at least one umpire on his side, how could Ollie fail? Milburn got a very thick edge on to his pad in the first over, the bowler let out a strangled appeal and the umpire's finger shot up like a rocket! Ollie could not believe it; not only was it a dreadful decision, it came from his new-found mate who had only just finished telling him how popular he was. 'I hit it, I hit it,' said Ollie, totally exasperated and suddenly living in the forlorn hope that his 'mate' might change his mind. Some hope – and poor Colin Milburn's hope of breaking into the Test side on that tour was gone for good.

I scored 168 in that match and 243 when we moved on to play Barbados, the best of the Caribbean island teams. Tom Graveney captained

MCC in that game and was very anxious that we should do well to take a psychological advantage into the third Test immediately to follow. The long innings took a lot out of me. I felt tired and extremely weak and was put on a course of extra vitamins, resting up for a couple of days before the Test. Even with my intensive winter training, the exhausting effects of dust and West Indian heat took their toll.

After three drawn matches, we won the series with a win in the fourth Test in Trinidad, where what I still believe was a serious miscalculation by Sobers gave us the chance to snatch victory. Sobers declared and left England to make 215 in 165 minutes: he said then and has repeated since that it was a sporting declaration that misfired. It certainly misfired but I don't think Sobers was being entirely generous when he made it. The fact is that West Indies expected to win or draw, and certainly did not believe they could lose the match. It was obvious from remarks our non-players overheard from the West Indies dressing room that they did not think we had the ability to chase runs intelligently and win. They were over-confident. The theory was that we would lose three or four wickets chasing runs and that wrist-spinner Willie Rodriguez, Sobers, Gibbs and even Butcher would then be able to polish us off, even if we tried to dig in. Why not? England had collapsed from 373–5 to 404 all out in the first innings and Butcher had taken 5–15 in eight overs! It didn't turn out that way.

Cowdrey was inclined to be cautious, no doubt about that, and his instruction to John Edrich and me was to play steadily to tea and reappraise the situation then. Several players thought we should be more positive from the outset and said so. There was obviously a clash of philosophies which did not help the pair at the wicket. Edrich got out, and we were 73–1 at tea, needing 142 to win in ninety minutes. Cowdrey was still inclined to bat for a draw. Tom Graveney agreed with him but Edrich, Ken Barrington and I thought we should go for the runs – and Ken said so in no uncertain terms. The conversation was a little heated and I went outside to put my pads on. Cowdrey came out and told me to play my normal game and he would see if he could push it along – and he was as good as his word. I pushed for singles, gave him the strike and saw him score a beautiful 71 before he got out. When Sobers had made his declaration, Brian Close had said in the press box: 'We'll win this if GB stays in. He'll take his time and win it with a few minutes to spare, not before he has to.' Close knew me well enough. I finished with 80 not out and we won the Test with three minutes to go. Sobers could only put a brave face on it. 'You are great when your gambles come off but an idiot when they fail. We bowled quite badly, including myself, while the English batsmen played well,' he said. Not untrue, but no mention of the over-confidence and professional misjudgement which had led to his decision.

The last Test in Guyana was drawn after I had made 116, an overdue Test century, and we clung on, still 100 behind with our last pair at the wicket. Alan Knott made a splendid 73 not out and Jeff Jones pushed and prodded for ages to save the day with a memorable unbeaten nought. Men round the bat, the spinners on and Jones playing as many with his pad as he did with his bat – we thought it was only a matter of time before he made a fatal misjudgement or an umpire cracked under the strain, but Jeff held on bravely. Les Ames and I watched nervously from the pavilion balcony – the rest of the players were too anxious to watch the closing minutes.

I felt I had come of age on the tour. My performances had been sound under pressure and I had made 1154 runs – the most on a West Indies tour since Patsy Hendren and Andy Sandham and against a much better West Indian side than they had encountered. Somebody had chalked 'Mister Runs' on my luggage and wherever I went, in the street or in the hotel foyer, the locals – friendly, smiling and very knowledgeable – were anxious to talk about me and the game. I had a chance to talk to Clyde Walcott and Everton Weekes, and I remember Walcott saying how much I reminded him in style and attitude of Leonard Hutton. When I told him I had never seen Hutton play, he was amazed.

I also learned a little more about the eccentricity of Ken Barrington. We roomed together in Guyana and the usual practice was to use the air conditioning to keep down the room temperature during the day and switch it off at night. It often made an unholy din and in any case it was regarded as none too healthy to sleep with the conditioning on. I would wake up in the small hours covered only by a sheet and find I was freezing to death in the icy blast of an air conditioner which Ken had turned on full. And he would be laid in bed under extra sheets and blankets wearing a woollen sweater and a cricket sweater for good measure! I couldn't make sense of it but Ken refused to depart from his routine. In the end I used to room with Ken during the day and disappear down the corridor to room with the captain at night, leaving Ken muffled up against the self-inflicted elements.

A forcing shot off the back foot, already characteristic of a twenty-two-year-old in spectacles and a Yorkshire second-team sweater.

Mum and brother Tony play the role of fielders, naturally, when we have a knock-up in the backyard.

Just room in the front room of 45 Milton Terrace, Fitzwilliam, for the paraphernalia of my first MCC tour, to South Africa, October 1964.

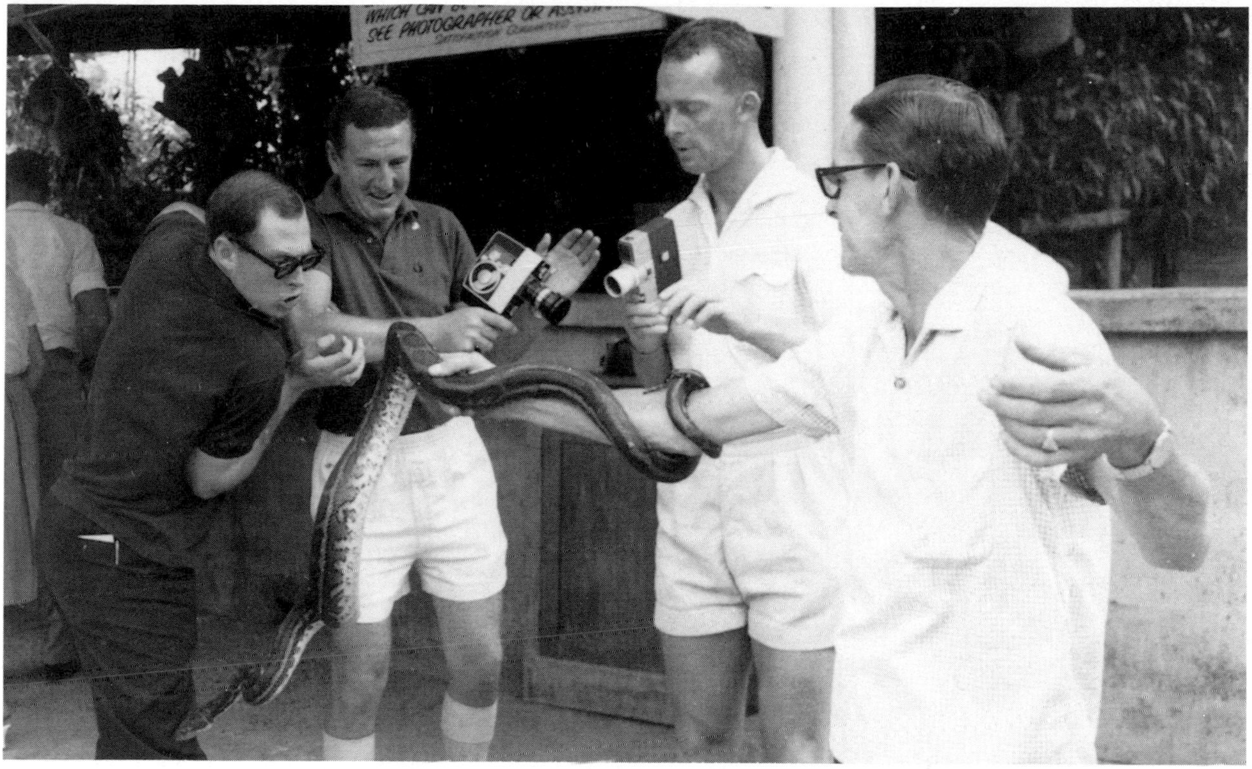

Charming . . . Good action pictures for Jim Parks (left) and Bob Barber, but no great fun for a bloke who is not fond of snakes to begin with. Brisbane, 1965.

'No singles today. . .' Walking out with Bob Barber to open the first innings in the second Test match at Melbourne, 1965. There are times when it pays to bite your tongue.

Tempting fate – and winning. A pick-up high on the leg-side off David Sydenham during the Gillette Cup final against Surrey, 1965.

He should be telling me to get a move on or else . . . In fact, Brian Close congratulates me on a century in the Gillette Cup final against Surrey, 1965.

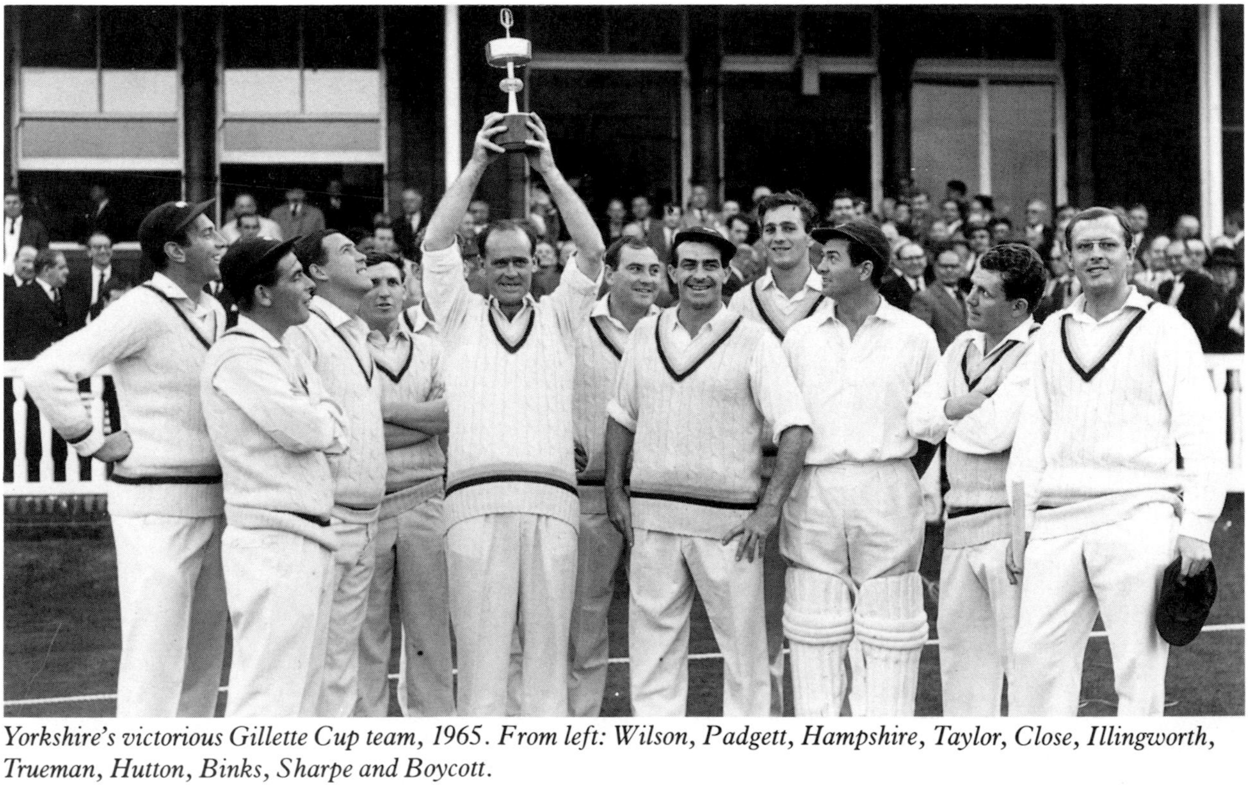

Yorkshire's victorious Gillette Cup team, 1965. From left: Wilson, Padgett, Hampshire, Taylor, Close, Illingworth, Trueman, Hutton, Binks, Sharpe and Boycott.

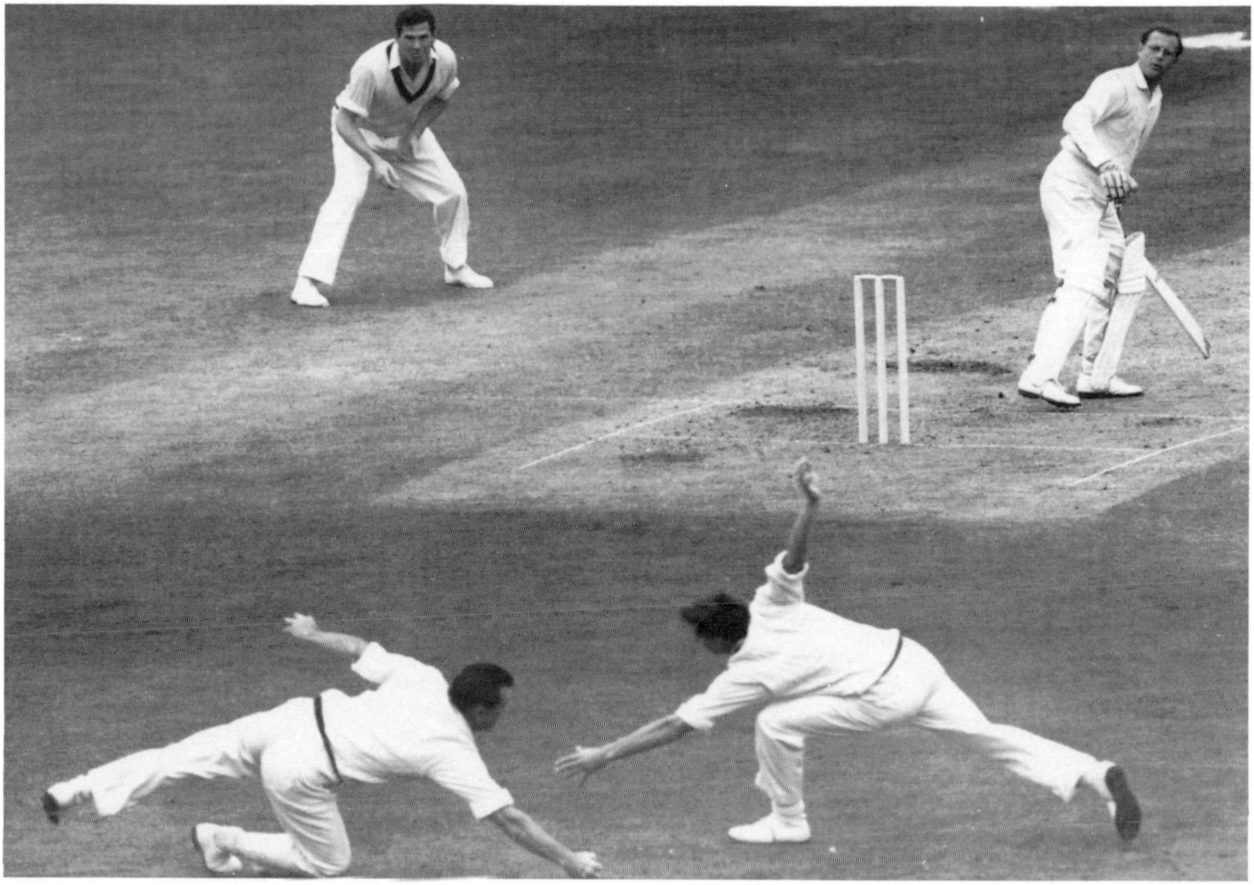

A picture to haunt me – again. Australian captain Bobby Simpson dives at first slip to take a superb catch off the bowling of Grahame Corling and end my first Test innings for 48, Trent Bridge, 1964. Ian Redpath is at second slip and Neil Hawke watches from short square leg.

Airborne David Hughes makes a desperate attempt to get rid of me in a John Player match before a packed Old Trafford in 1970. Farokh Engineer's reaction suggests he did not fail by far.

As a young Yorkshire player practising in the nets at Bradford Park Avenue, 1965.

The bowling style did not change over much, even if the circumstances did. Bowling for England – cap and all – against West Indies, 1980 at Lord's. Clive Lloyd looks suitably apprehensive; Peter Willey strangely concerned himself . . .

get

10

Exit Close

Injuries – chronic, unresponsive, irreparable injuries – are the biggest fear of any professional sportsman's life. Problems of form, mood and general fitness are bound to crop up from to time, but they can be overcome; chronic injury is feared because it can end a career, however committed the individual. I went close to losing my career through a back problem in 1968.

The county season started well enough. Having just returned from tour I was in good form and the ball looked like a football. I should have been tired but I never noticed that as the runs flowed with centuries against Sussex, Leicestershire, Warwickshire, Gloucestershire, an International XI and Leicestershire again, all within the first few weeks of the season. Tom Cartwright got a bit moody when I lifted him on to the tents at Middlesbrough on my way to 180: 'A poor man's Compton,' he called me. It wasn't meant as a compliment, not the way he stalked down the pitch to deliver it, but I'd accept the association any day, even from 'the poor man's Shackleton,' as I called Cartwright. The runs were coming, but I was having increasing trouble with my back – a twinge at first, then a dull ache, then genuine pain. I assumed that I had probably let the chill of an English summer get through to me after a spell in the Caribbean and expected it to put itself right, but it reached a point where I could hardly get out of bed in the morning and it was impossible to bend down and tie a shoelace. During the third Test against Australia in Birmingham, Ray Illingworth and I went off to the local cinema and after sitting in the same spot for a couple of hours my back was so painful I had to go and stretch out in my room. Two days later I was in absolute agony: my back seized up while I was batting and it was quite a performance just to bend enough to squeeze into a car with the passenger seat reclined.

Boycott carried his bat through a completed innings for the first time, 114 not out, out of 297 for Yorkshire against Leicestershire at Sheffield on 15 June 1968. He has achieved this feat 8 times for Yorkshire and once for England.

The England physiotherapist Bernard Thomas recommended I consult Paddy Armour in Wakefield – the beginning of a painful but pleasurable association with a man whom I consider an absolute genius when it comes to treating sports injuries. Paddy used to be the head remedial physio at Wakefield's Pinderfields Hospital and is now in private practice. He's had more live meat on his table than any man I know – the Butcher of Agbrigg Lane I call him, and I really could not have done without him over the years. He came to my rescue in 1968 and I never hesitated to see him after that whenever I needed treatment. Paddy gives you no flannel. He gets down to brass tacks, finds out what's wrong and puts you right – fast. On this occasion he diagnosed disc trouble and recommended to Yorkshire that I see an orthopaedic surgeon, Reg Broomhead, who was a huge help when I seriously feared that my career might be in danger. Reg admitted quietly to Paddy that the problem was very serious, a swollen and damaged disc, and that I would need very careful treatment if I was to continue playing for a living. He told me to my face that I would play again provided I was patient and did exactly as I was told.

His optimism was reassuring and I felt I had some control over my future, albeit in a literally passive sense. By now I could barely move without help and the very thought of playing cricket seemed laughable. There were two options open to me: wear a plaster cast for about three months and spend another three months re-educating my back to work properly or try a specially made corset and see if three weeks' total rest would reduce the swelling in the disc. The corset enveloped me from armpits to abdomen and was my closest companion for the next few weeks as I lay completely motionless on a bed of boards. Mum washed and looked after me, even to serving meals which I could balance on my chest and eat with the minimum of movement. I got up to go to the toilet but that was absolutely all. The less I moved the sooner my back would mend and Paddy Armour used to call in – usually unannounced – to make sure I was behaving myself and that the boards were properly positioned. Paddy eventually worked out a course of special exercises which accelerated my recovery, though there was not the slightest question of hurrying. Quite literally, I had to sit before I could stand and walk before I could run. Paddy supervised every inch of the way and I will always be grateful for his concern and his expertise.

I was out from early July to the first week of September, when I played in an England XI against a Rest of the World XI at Scarborough, mainly to prove my fitness with a winter tour of South Africa in prospect. I made 93 and 131, which was a considerable reassurance. In the event the world of cricket was taken over by the infamous Basil D'Oliveira affair and the tour to South Africa was cancelled. A short tour to Pakistan was arranged in its place but I expressed a desire not to go. It was obvious my back could do with a bit more rest and I was still nagged by doubts about my health in the underdeveloped countries. I had reacted so badly in the past to what might otherwise have been minor ailments that I still did not fancy the thought of touring the Indian subcontinent.

Boycott finished top of the national batting averages for the first time in the 1968 season with 64.65.

Before all that, there was the small matter of 25 and 102 not out for Yorkshire against MCC at the end of the season – and the first and only time that I have batted under the influence of a monumental hangover. Hardly disorderly or incapable but definitely a bit on the fragile side.

Yorkshire had beaten Surrey to win the county championship, and the MCC match, part of the Scarborough Festival, was an obvious end-of-season opportunity to celebrate. There was plenty of raw material – a championship-winning Yorkshire side could be sure of several cases of champagne from well-wishers. Closey had slipped a magnum in his bag to take home for future reference; I slipped it out while he wasn't looking and tried to get it open while he chased me round the dressing room with a string of threats and curses, tripping over bags and bodies. The cork eventually came out in a great, wasteful shower and I dispensed his champagne to wives and girlfriends, as well as having a drop or two myself.

The fact is that I had more than a drop. The whiff of a barmaid's apron would have knocked me over then and still does, but here I was getting more and more tipsy, more and more talkative. The MCC players were invited to the celebration and when their captain Roger Prideaux wandered past I waffled: 'Get some champagne down you' – an evangelical drinker already – 'You'll never get me out tomorrow . . .' The night disappeared in a bubbling blur. I had a bagful of fish and chips and was put to bed at 9 p.m., distinctly the worse for wear. The night was hideous, the only time in my life I have been the worse for drink, and the morning after was no better. There are supposed to be many good reasons for not drinking; the hangover will do quite nicely for me. I felt as though I had drunk ten gallons, though the truth of the matter is probably that I'd barely had enough to quench most drinkers' thirst; I simply couldn't take it. My boast of the previous night came back to haunt me. Feeling dreadful or not I simply couldn't let MCC get me out cheaply and I made a distinctly painful 102 before Yorkshire declared. Never again – the man who asked Geoff Boycott to drink and drive, or cut, or play any sort of stroke from that day on was wasting his time.

MCC just squeezed a draw with nine wickets down. Ray Illingworth took 7–73 and although nobody knew it for certain at the time it would have been especially fitting if he had won the match. It was his last with Yorkshire for fourteen years. Illingworth wanted a contract – and, as I have mentioned before, Yorkshire at the time was the only first-class county in the country which did not have a contracts system. The club's system would bear comparison with any, certainly as far as finances went, but it did not offer much security and, at thirty-six, Illingworth not unnaturally believed that security was important. It may well be that after seventeen years at Yorkshire Illingworth felt in need of a new challenge. In any case an offer from Leicestershire held out the prospect of real security, plus the captaincy of the side. As it turned out, Cowdrey tore an Achilles tendon and Illingworth was captain of England within weeks of taking over at Leicestershire. Kismet may have had a hand in it – Brian Sellers obviously did. 'He can f— go and so can anyone else who wants to,' said Sellers, which was poor reward for the years of loyalty and service Illingworth had given the club. He was a very fine bowler, a great tactical brain, a player who would be welcomed by any county side in the land, and Sellers was treating him like a chattel. There was already a stage whisper that Geoff Cope was ready and able to take over Illingworth's mantle as Yorkshire's off-spinner and that sort of dismissive attitude from Sellers could only have confirmed Illingworth's suspicions. I had and still have the highest regard for Illingworth as a player and I did my best to persuade him to stay at Yorkshire. I telephoned him and went to see him at his home – he was clearly too good a player to lose, even if Yorkshire seemed to regard his request for a contract as something approaching heresy.

There was a feeling, even among the rank-and-file Yorkshire membership, that Illingworth's decision to move to Leicestershire amounted to disloyalty. He had been given a benefit three years earlier which had raised £6604 – a tidy sum then even if it does not look like a lot now – and there were those ready to see his decision purely in financial terms. The pull of Yorkshire cricket has always been strong, and many supporters could not understand how Illingworth could turn his back on the county (especially their county) that had given him a chance, helped establish his reputation in the game and so on. It is an emotive subject and individuals must make their own choice, but I cannot really see how any man can be condemned for looking after his professional interests in a professional world. Loyalty has to be reciprocal.

What concerned me infinitely more was the effect Illingworth's departure, plus the retirement of Fred and Ken Taylor in the winter, was going to have on Yorkshire. It did not take long to find out. In their absence and despite the contribution of the stars (some of them self-styled) who were left, Yorkshire plummeted to thirteenth place in the championship. The value of Fred and Illingworth as match-winning bowlers was never more obvious than when they were no longer there.

The controversy surrounding Illingworth's departure had one beneficial side-effect as far as the remaining players were concerned. A meeting was held with the finance committee and new agreements were drawn up regarding salaries and match fees for the 1969 season. In common with the other capped players I received a generous increase in my salary. No doubt Yorkshire would deny that it had anything to do with Illingworth's stance, but if it didn't, it was a very happy coincidence. My new salary was £1500, the home championship match fee was £6 and the away fee £11. Significantly, perhaps, the fee for a home match in the Sunday League was £6 10s and the away fee £11. Win bonus was £5 a match and the overall effect was that if I played in all Yorkshire's matches throughout the season I would earn £1878 plus bonuses – a decent income for playing cricket in those days. On top of that, there was a figure on the horizon who, at least according to the press, was going to make me a millionaire . . .

Mark McCormack's International Financial Management had done financial wonders for the likes of Arnold Palmer, Gary Player and Jack Nicklaus. Now it was about to turn its Midas touch on Boycott and make him the highest-paid cricketer in the universe, or something like that. I signed for IFM midway through the 1969 season amid a blaze of hype and publicity which probably did McCormack more good than it did me. From then on, my cricket and the publicity fell away fast. The basic problem, I think, was that IFM's young executives were very slick, high-powered and committed but also very American in attitude, with precious little idea about cricket or the way it was run. They wanted to handle negotiations on all my contracts, including those with Yorkshire and England, and it obviously came as a shock to men brought up in a fierce meritocracy to discover that, where contracts or at least agreements existed, they were the same for me as for the other players in the team. They couldn't believe it. After all, baseball and American football players were part of a team but they still negotiated individual contracts and the most successful demanded the most money. There was no way IFM was going to descend on Headingley or Lord's and negotiate massive sums of money for me – and that hit at the very heart of their system.

Normally IFM took one-third of a client's direct income as their cut for handling his affairs and putting the opportunity to earn more money his way. When a celebrity was earning large sums of money that was fine but it did not make sense for me to turn over one-third of my cricket salary – I simply could not afford it! We compromised: I was to pay IFM 20 per cent of everything they earned for me, but even that had its pitfalls. I had a contract with Mitre Sports, who manufacture and supply soft leather goods as well as cricket pads, thigh pads and gloves. Their managing director went off to a meeting with IFM representatives in a plush London hotel and was told what they were going to do for me, what great plans they had and so on. But he had to point out to them that he had only recently seen that an invitation for me to appear on a TV programme had been withdrawn because I demanded 'such a phenomenal fee'. He considered that was bad publicity for me and by association bad publicity for Mitre Sports, and I had to agree with him. In the two uneasy years I was with IFM I never met McCormack personally, which struck me as being distinctly odd. My association with his company didn't do much for either of us financially but it was an experience.

When I was picked for the first Test at Old Trafford against the West Indies in the 1969 series I had been out of Test cricket for eleven months. The back problem seemed to have settled down okay and I was in the process of coming to terms with contact lenses, an innovation which caused a great deal of comment and speculation in the press. I scored 128 from 316 deliveries and England won. The statistics may be relevant because two years earlier I had scored 106 in a Test match from exactly the same number of deliveries – and had subsequently been dropped for slow scoring. John Hampshire scored a splendid maiden Test century in the second Test at Lord's, I made another century and the match was drawn. But the season fell away badly for me after that. I could not make runs in the Test matches and there was the now-familiar overexposure in the press. Some blamed my contact lenses – I'm convinced they were quite wrong in that, and I'm still a big fan of lenses – and some made uncomplimentary remarks about my association with the McCormack empire.

That sort of public inquisition may have had some effect on my form; perhaps I was still a bit rusty after my long lay-off. Whatever the root causes I felt tenseness creeping into my game and it was reflected in my low scores. The pitch for the first Test against New Zealand at Lord's was green at the Nursery end – ridge and all – and dry and patchy at the Pavilion end, so none of the batsmen fancied batting first. Illingworth, still captaining in place of Cowdrey, asked me what I thought and I told him that I hoped he would put New Zealand in if he won the toss – but that if I were making the decision I would bat because Underwood would bowl them out in the second innings. Illingworth won the toss and batted. I was caught at gully second ball for a duck and England won the Test after Underwood took 7–32 in the second innings. Illingworth thanked me for my advice and acknowledged that there was an element of self-sacrifice involved – which is more than can be said for an irate gentleman on the stairs leading to the England dressing room. I was plodding back there after getting out in the first innings when he barred my path. 'What do you mean by it? I've come all the way from South Africa to see you bat, all the way from Johannesburg. And you go and get out. What do you think you're playing at?' He was livid. Perhaps I should have rubbed it in by telling him I got out on purpose.

Exit Close

When Dick Motz got me out for a duck in the second Test I had recorded three ducks in four Test innings and I felt really low. Fate being what it is at times like these, I went to hook Motz and the ball hit me on the right arm, thumped me on the chest and then fell on the stumps, just dislodging a bail. A freak dismissal, perhaps, but that's what happens when you are in a bad seam. Things didn't get a lot better after the Test series finished. Illingworth had asked me during the Tests to ginger up John Snow a bit, get him to bowl really quick and think about what he was doing. Most batsmen are a bit reluctant to get on the wrong side of bowlers as fast and fiery as Snow but I gave him quite a bit of stick and, since it made him angry, I suppose it achieved its purpose. Snow promised what he would do to me when he got me in his sights on a quick pitch and, sure enough, Yorkshire arrived at Hove to play Sussex with Snow coming down the hill like a runaway train. I knocked him off for two and as I turned at the bowler's end he stood in my path. I tapped him lightly – playfully, I thought – on the shin with my bat. And Snow promptly kicked me off my feet! I made my ground, we exchanged heated words and the umpires intervened. So much for goading a fast bowler. Then Snow raced in, smacked me on the side of my left hand and broke a bone, which put me out of Yorkshire's Gillette Cup final victory against Derbyshire at Lord's. One way and another, I was not sorry to see the 1969 season end.

Yorkshire, in making 450 for 4 wickets declared against Essex at Colchester in 1970 (Boycott 260*), scored their runs at 57.47 runs per hundred balls – *faster* than Holmes's and Sutcliffe's 555 against Essex at Leyton in 1932!

As I have said, 'pressure' is not a word I like to use too often. It's an easy word, something of a cliché in sporting terms. It is rarely defined and it suggests that sportsmen experience greater burdens in their job than other people. The guy who goes down the pit is under pressure to do his job properly, he has the bills to pay, the everyday problems of home life. Pressure is as familiar and as real to him as it is to any sportsman. Having said that, I do feel that the stresses of life in the public eye can be extreme and sometimes rather overpowering. When we fail we fail very publicly, a phenomenon which most people rarely experience.

England were due to play a series against the Rest of the World in 1970, a stop-gap imposed by the cancellation of South Africa's tour – another casualty of the D'Oliveira affair. I was playing indifferently and I did not see much prospect of an immediate improvement, so I asked to be left out until I found some form. That can be interpreted as a fear of failure – I regarded it then and now as a professional appraisal of my fitness to do the job well. I could take the pressures of the job, but I was stressed and anxious. 'Too much anxiety can paralyse you,' said a university professor discussing stress in sport at the time. I knew what he meant. The selectors were very understanding and the chairman Alec Bedser wrote me a letter reiterating their faith in my ability. He offered consolation and advice, which I appreciated. I worked hard at getting my game together and returned to the side for the fourth Test at Leeds.

The season had begun uncomfortably. I had developed a muscle spasm in the neck soon after returning from an MCC tour of the Far East. I had to wear a surgical collar and missed the pre-season practices with Yorkshire which was a genuine pain in the neck. Jimmy Binks had retired so there was an obvious vacancy for a wicketkeeper. At Bradford early in June a young lad offered to carry my bag to the dressing room, which was common enough, and then hung around after delivering it. I thanked him and expected him to leave but he said, 'I'm playing.' Hello, David Bairstow.

Boycott's highest score in England was his 260 not out for Yorkshire against Essex at Colchester, completed on 27 July 1970.

Phil Carrick, Yorkshire's latest captain, made his début the same year and still tells the story of his first match, at Bristol. Apparently he got off the mark in the second innings, not having batted in the first, and was summoned for a single when I was on 49. As we passed, I said, 'Good luck, Phil,' which was something of a parting shot since he was run out by a distance and carried on towards the dressing room. That's the way he tells it. I can honestly say that I cannot remember the incident at all.

My association with England that season was relatively brief but not entirely uneventful. During the Leeds Test, Illingworth asked me who I thought were the best fast bowlers to take with John Snow to Australia for the Ashes tour that winter. We agreed that Alan Ward was a prime candidate, but who else? I plumped for Lancashire's Peter Lever, who was bowling at a lively pace and could swing the ball out very dangerously.

Peter was the sort of bowler who responded to a big occasion, and he always bowled at a very respectable pace in Roses matches when the crowds were large and demanding. He played in the fifth Test at the Oval and took 7–83 in the first innings, which justified my faith in him and booked him a place on the Ashes tour. After Lever I recommended Ken Shuttleworth, a singular personality in some ways but a strong and lively bowler who could be quite a handful on his day. I reckoned he was worth the risk and he made it to Australia, too.

The Rest of the World won the fifth Test by four wickets, but not before I played what I still regard as one of my finest innings. The pitch was wearing, the odd delivery went through the top and the ball turned, sometimes prodigiously. It was not a dangerous pitch, in fact it was an excellent result pitch, but that did not make batting any easier against an attack which comprised Mike Procter, Graham McKenzie, Garry Sobers, Eddie Barlow, Intikhab and Clive Lloyd. I made 157 before I edged a delivery from Lloyd to Barlow at slip, an innings which earned me £250 and the Lawrence Trophy for 'the most valuable innings by an English batsman in the 1970 series'. I'm still proud of that knock.

Yorkshire finished fourth in the championship that season but won only five out of sixteen matches in the Sunday League. On top of that, we were beaten in the first round of the Gillette Cup by Surrey after wintry weather at Harrogate in April had delayed the tie for a day. The storm clouds were gathering around Brian Close, who had missed six championship and seven Sunday League matches with an injured shoulder and who – perhaps more damagingly – had made no secret of his dislike for one-day cricket. The season was a financial disaster for Yorkshire – 'the most disastrous in the history of the club' according to the annual report – and stood in stark contrast to events over the Pennines, where Lancashire's success in the limited-overs game was pulling in the crowds. The committee was disturbed at Close's criticisms of the one-day game (most of them since vindicated) and was probably miffed by the sight of an £8000 loss on the season while Lancashire were doing so well. There was talk of Close not continuing with the club in 1971.

I was appalled at the idea. Close's vice-captain and the man apparently most likely to succeed him was Phil Sharpe – and he was definitely not my idea of a Yorkshire captain. Close, for all his idiosyncrasies, was the epitome of the way Yorkshire played cricket: he was strong and positive, a bit bloody-minded, perhaps, but a man who left nobody in any doubt that our job was to win matches. Sharpe was nowhere near as strong or as vibrant a character; his tactical skills were very limited and he had no leadership qualities to speak of. If Close represented a win and a pint of beer, Sharpe was a jolly good game and a gin and tonic, preferably accompanied by a sing-song round the piano. Close welcomed discussion off the field and led the side on it; Sharpe seemed to have little to offer in discussion himself and led the side as though it were a debating society. I was afraid that if Close left and Sharpe became captain, the team would reflect his social, rather weak and insipid attitude to cricket. I couldn't see myself putting up with that: if Close left, I would leave Yorkshire myself before I would play under Sharpe – and I visited Close at his home in Shipley seeking a reassurance that he did not intend to pack it in. Close assured me that he had no intention of retiring – his shoulder should respond to a winter's rest and I could go off to Australia with an easy mind in the knowledge that he would be back leading Yorkshire the following season. If only we had known.

Brian Close's sacking by Yorkshire in November of 1970 must still rank as one of the cruellest incidents in the history of sport. I doubt that Yorkshire will ever quite live it down. Close had given the club twenty-two years' service, eight as captain, when he was called into the presence of Brian Sellers and given an ultimatum: resign or be sacked. Close was so taken aback he more or less resigned, a decision he tried to withdraw before the club made an official announcement only a couple of hours later. The club's official reason for sacking Close was 'his often-stated dislike of one-day cricket, a form of the game which becomes increasingly important as the years go by' – and there was some truth in that. But the way in which Yorkshire dismissed him said a great deal for their view of the people they employed; it was revealingly hideous. A members' Action Group was formed and the committee was given a dreadful mauling, the only obvious result of which was the eventual resignation of Sellers as chairman of the cricket sub-committee. He really must have valued his friends on the committee then.

I was in Australia with England, blithely unaware of the seriousness of the situation back in Yorkshire and never imagining that I was anywhere near the captaincy. I had Close's word that he would be carrying on and that was good enough for me – until the Yorkshire secretary John Nash rang with the news. Close had resigned and I was the new Yorkshire captain – that was the message Mr Nash relayed, with the additional information that Don Wilson was to be vice-captain. I had barely put the phone down when the touring press were on the doorstep asking for my reaction – and it must have seemed a bit heartless at the time. 'The greatest thing that has ever happened to me,' I said with a glass of champagne in my hand. I did not know then, of course, that Closey had been forced to resign; I just assumed he had made his own decision and left of his own accord. I was delighted to be offered the captaincy of Yorkshire but there was no way I was gloating over Close's departure. As I wrote to him at the time:

> I am sorry I have to write to you and am not able to speak to you personally in this situation.
>
> After playing with you for eight years I would like to say how sorry I am that you will no longer be a part of the Yorkshire scene. I think I understand how much Yorkshire has meant to you Brian and how

much of you personally has gone into Yorkshire cricket in the last 20 years. Because of this, you must feel very sad to be leaving the county.

I had no idea that you would be leaving the county and that I would be asked to be captain in your place.

I am honoured to be made captain but, in a way it is a very sad occasion. To me, cricket has lost the best tactical captain I have known. I only hope that next year I can put into practice some of the ideas I have learned from watching you. And Brian, whatever happens, I know that I am following in the footsteps of one of the greats.

Close has often said that, given the opportunity, he would have groomed me for the captaincy in another couple of years' time. He thought the choice was right but the timing was premature – and all things considered I would not disagree with him. Another couple of years learning under Close would have done me no harm whatsoever and I certainly would not have objected to his continuing at the time. But the Yorkshire committee, in their wisdom, had made a choice and you do not turn down the captaincy of Yorkshire. I hovered somewhere between delight and a state of shock, very proud and also very conscious of my new responsibilities. But they would have to wait for a while at least. We had a Test series to play against Australia – as it turned out, one of the toughest and most eventful in modern times.

11

Adelaide

The mix of the 1970–1 tour party to Australia was difficult from England's point of view. Ray Illingworth was captain, quite rightly, with Colin Cowdrey as his vice-captain and David Clark as tour manager. Clark was obviously closer philosophically to Cowdrey than to Illingworth and they never really looked like getting on; Cowdrey and Illingworth didn't exactly get on like a house on fire either. It had all the makings of friction and, perhaps with my new role at Yorkshire at the back of my mind, I hoped I would be co-opted as a tour selector since Illingworth often asked my advice in the home series. John Edrich got the job and I was not best pleased.

Attitudes in the opening State match of the tour against South Australia in Adelaide did not help. We were 326–2 overnight: I was 173 not out and very pleased with my form, and Keith Fletcher was 67. Five minutes before I went out to bat next day Illingworth and Clark announced that they wanted me to get 200 and Fletcher to get a century, then we should get out to allow others opportunity for practise. I was very annoyed, a few heated words were exchanged, and I was out to the third ball of the day, which gave me an early opportunity to press my point again. I pointed out forcibly that this was the first meaningful match of the tour, that there were twelve innings to come before the first Test which would give everybody time to find form, and that it was ludicrous to start asking players to give their wickets away so early on tour. It might make sense nearer the first Test but so early in the tour it was folly. Edrich tried to mollify me and I snapped at him. I knew of old how important it was to find form early on tour and here I was being cut off in mid-flow by some half-baked theory. I was like a bear with a sore head and it took a while before I got together with Illingworth and then Edrich to put things back in perspective. A flash of temper, an angry remark in the heat of the situation: these things happen in any cricket dressing room. But I felt the responsibility of batting for England very heavily: Richie Benaud wrote that 'as far as England is concerned, Geoffrey Boycott is the batting key to the tour,' and if that was going to be so I would need all the form I could get.

Our bowlers were plundered quite mercilessly by Barry Richards and Ian Chappell and the match against South Australia finished in a high-scoring draw. Then we lost by six wickets to Victoria, spearheaded by Alan 'Froggy' Thomson. He was a big, wild-looking customer who appeared to bowl off the wrong foot à la Mike Procter and his nine wickets in the match were to win him a place later in the Test series. My first impression of Thomson was memorable because when he got me out, he continued running down the pitch waving his arms in jubilation. I passed him going the other way towards the pavilion. It happens all the time now, of course, but it was certainly out of the ordinary in 1970. We drew the match against New South Wales after being made to follow on, a chastening experience but one which Illingworth thought we might use to our advantage.

Most of the damage in our first innings was inflicted by the NSW spinners, Kerry O'Keeffe and John Gleeson. Illingworth reckoned we would face at least one wrist-spinner in the Tests so it wouldn't do us too much harm to have a long look at them. Gleeson was awkward and terribly difficult to get away. Nobody could read him and you had all on just to play for your stumps. I made 129 not out as we saved the game but I wasn't much wiser about Gleeson when I finished than when I started. It was the devil's own job trying to work out which way the ball would turn.

But the runs were on the board. By the end of the match against Queensland I had made 535 at an average of over 100 and the stories were beginning to develop about my appetite for batting – not always accurate or complimentary ones. Against Queensland, for instance, I made 124 and elected to retire hurt at lunch, knowing that men like Fletcher, D'Oliveira, Edrich and Illingworth needed the batting practice more than I did at that time. I had a very slight leg strain which a little rest would not harm. A story immediately appeared in one newspaper claiming that Illingworth had virtually had to instruct me not to bat on and that it had developed into a stand-up fight. Pure imagination on somebody's part and Ray and the manager issued a statement to that effect, but the accusation tends to stick after the denial has been forgotten. I was quoted in Melbourne, and I remember it vaguely, as saying: 'I'd tax the devil, I'd bat longer than he'd bowl,' which no doubt added to the reputation. 'Runs are my business. The more I get the better it is for my captain and my team' is another quote from the time which summed up my attitude.

The first Test in Brisbane was drawn, but not without incident. For a start, Keith Stackpole was clearly run out when I hit the stumps with a throw from mid-off. He was on 18 at the time and newspaper photographs showed him well out of his ground with the bails in the air – but he was given not out and went on to make 207! 'Generally you know whether you are out and I was so confident that I didn't bother to look round for the decision,' said Stackpole. 'It became close when Boycott's throw hit the wicket but I was sure I was in.' How wrong can you be.

Then there was the problem of John Snow's bowling. It was especially important he fired because Alan Ward had returned home with leg trouble – to be replaced, incidentally, by a promising young man called Bob Willis. John Edrich recommended him strongly and it was obvious even then that Willis was bright, eager to learn and had a genuine turn of speed. Snow had been allowed to plough his own furrow in getting ready for the Test series; Illingworth more or less gave him a free hand on the understanding that when it came to the Tests he would be ready to bowl accurately and really fast. At Brisbane he looked hopelessly underprepared – the legacy of having bowled only sixty-seven eight-ball overs on the tour so far. The Australian media were already trumpeting the suggestion that our attack was 'powder-puff', and Neil Harvey thought we were 'rubbish'.

Snow took six wickets in Australia's first innings but it was not until the second innings of the second Test in Perth that he really began to look like a spearhead fast bowler. Then he bowled at his true pace, making the ball cut and snake at batsmen off a length, and looked as though he could take a wicket at any moment. There have been quicker bowlers than Snow but at his best he was a marvellous performer.

The intervening match against Western Australia at Perth brought me another century, an opening stand of 215 in 195 minutes with Brian Luckhurst and my first sight of a new fast bowler. The first delivery of the match was quick on a very quick pitch, short of a length and on a collision course with my forehead. I jerked my head out of the way and my cap fell off as the ball whizzed over Rodney Marsh's head and clattered into the fence. Trying to look as nonchalant as possible, I bent down and retrieved my cap without looking at the bowler or any of the fielders, but out of the corner of my eye I could see the England balcony filling up fast. Nobody wanted to miss this new firebrand who had knocked Boycott's cap off and cleared the wicketkeeper for four byes – and was even now standing only a few yards from me at the end of his follow-through, snorting aggression. Dennis Keith Lillee had arrived.

The second Test was drawn. Luckhurst made 131, Ian Redpath 171 –

and Greg Chappell, batting at number seven, scored 108 in his first Test match. England clearly needed to win matches to regain the Ashes and we came in for some stick about our slow batting. Since I was the man in form and in the public eye, much of it was aimed at me. But the fact is that it was extremely difficult to score, let alone score quickly, against the leg-spinners, Terry Jenner and John Gleeson. They had got me out four times in four Test innings and as a batsman who prided himself on a reasonable expertise against leg-spin – courtesy of hours spent facing Johnny Lawrence – that was particularly galling. Gleeson was the major problem, so unorthodox that it was virtually impossible to pick him. He bowled the ball a bit faster than most leg-spinners, there was little loop and it was on to you quickly, giving less time to read which way the ball might turn. On top of that, he bowled with very little wrist action – the spin on the ball was imparted by very strong fingers – so there were few clues for a batsman. The one that looked like a leg-spinner turned out to be an off-spinner, the off-spinner was a leggie and from time to time the ball ran on into you very quickly and for no discernible reason. So we struggled, we all did, unable to read him and forced to play from a position of near-total uncertainty and from the crease, protecting our stumps. The only way to attack him was to predetermine an aggressive stroke and hope you got it right. We scored slowly because Gleeson would not let us score any quicker.

David Clark did not help matters by announcing that 'positive and challenging tactics' were needed from both sides, the sort of ra-ra sentiment much loved of tour managers in the knowledge that nobody is likely to disagree. Illingworth and Bill Lawry – similar men in their down-to-earth, professional way – weren't exactly the laughing cavaliers of the game, and Illy did not take kindly to Clark's interference. Shades of Billy Griffith and the parrot cry for 'brighter cricket'. It sounds fine and nobody challenges it as a philosophy until the 'brighter' team collapses in a strangled heap and loses a Test series. Neither Illingworth nor Lawry was the sort of captain to be seduced by slogans.

I received a letter from Uncle Algy about my batting against Gleeson in the second Test. 'You looked hesitant and cramped and a long way below your best,' he wrote. 'Remember you are the batsman they fear most; get in and then go for your shots, you can do it.' I accepted his philosophy but it was very hard to put it into practice. It was difficult to get down the pitch to Gleeson and when you thought you had begun to work him out, he produced a delivery which totally deceived you. Illingworth and I watched some film of him – largely, I confess, because we wanted to see whether he threw his off-spinner – but even that did not help us much. Yet we had to work him out if we could and I spent hours discussing his action with Alan Knott. We came to a sort of conclusion that he spun the off-spinner off his first finger and the leg-spinner off his second finger – with very little wrist action, which meant that his fingers must have been immensely strong. Knotty used to throw the ball to me as near as he could manage to Gleeson's style – 'Watch the fingers, watch the fingers' – sometimes with his arm coming over like a bowler in slow motion. But even when we had developed the theory, there was nobody – apart from Gleeson himself, of course – who could give us any practice against it. Knotty tried one day when I thought it would be a good idea to see what I could pick up from twenty-two yards' distance, but he was no bowler and the ball wandered about erratically. Our theory was something to work on but we never approached a firm conclusion about the way Gleeson bowled. Fortunately for us, Australia did not use Gleeson as aggressively as they ought to have done. He should have bowled to attacking fields with two men close on the leg and off sides, rather like Derek Underwood. He would have been bound to get a lot of bat–pad catches because of our inability to pick him.

The third Test in Melbourne was abandoned to the weather and the series then hinged on the fourth Test in Sydney, which England won by 299 runs on a pitch which finally suited our skills and style of play rather more than the Australians'. Lawry was asked afterwards if he fancied more pitches like it in a Test series and he predictably said no. Equally predictably, Illingworth thought it was just right.

I played well, for 77 in the first innings and 142 not out in the second – I felt relaxed, increasingly confident and in absolute control. In the first innings Luckhurst and I posted our eleventh first-wicket partnership of over a century before I was caught at fine leg hooking Alan Connolly – just after lunch! It was the best innings I had played so far on tour and the second was even better. The pitch was grassy when we won the toss and batted: by the time we had made 332 and bowled out Australia for 236 it had become a fairly typical English result pitch, very dry, encouraging the ball to turn or cut off the seam. In no time at all we were 48–3 with Basil D'Oliveira on his way in – another wicket then and we could have collapsed disastrously. But Dolly is a marvellously calm character, inwardly strong and with a super temperament. We knew a lot depended on us and Dolly made 56 before they got him out, not at all bad considering he came in on a pair. Illingworth made a fine 53, Knott weighed in with 21 not out and we were able to declare, leaving Australia a target of 415 in 548 minutes. There was the inevitable carping from the press about the slowness of my innings but we knew much better than they did how poor the pitch was and how valuable a big innings would ultimately be. In what seemed like no time, Australia were 21–4 and on their way to defeat. Snow undermined them with a splendid spell of 3–13, bowling at a distinctly rapid pace and getting plenty of bite and fizz from a wearing pitch. Ian Chappell got one that kicked and lobbed to second slip via the shoulder of his bat, Redpath could only fend a steeply rising delivery to gully, and Greg Chappell, trying to get behind the rising ball, went too far across and was bowled round his legs. Lever whipped out Doug Walters and it was only thanks to the obstinacy of Lawry and Stackpole that Australia saw out the day. In the morning Snow polished them off, accurate and hitting the seam regularly. He finished with 7–40 off 17.5 overs, and Australia were all out for 116 with Lawry battling on to a courageous unbeaten 60.

Critics are not famous for eating their words and a lot of emphasis was lain, quite rightly so, on Snow's bowling performance. But my innings, the one that was supposed to be too slow, put England in a position where they could not lose and had every chance to push for victory. Bowlers do win matches but batsmen put teams in a position to win, and my innings allowed the middle-order batsmen to play with some freedom when we were almost out of danger. I still rate it as one of the best I ever played for England.

One of the less palatable Boycott myths emerged from that Test match and this may be a good time to put the record straight. I had batted more confidently against Gleeson, though he still gave me some trouble, and the story has gone the rounds that I had worked him out but refused to tell the rest of the team. The usual version is that during our partnership in the Sydney Test, Basil D'Oliveira told me he had worked Gleeson out. I'm supposed to have said: 'I worked him out a fortnight ago, but don't tell the others.' Something like that; the version varies depending on how far the teller wants to use it to prove my selfishness. The fact is that I never did work out Gleeson satisfactorily, I would be very much surprised if Dolly had and, as far as I can recall, no such conversation ever took place. When I sat down to write this book I rang Basil and asked him about it. He cannot remember it either. So another myth has been hawked round cricket, gleefully retold without any substantiation to reinforce the unflattering Boycott image.

Because the third Test in Melbourne had been abandoned without a ball being bowled, it was agreed to schedule an extra Test, at Melbourne. I say agreed, but Ray Illingworth and the vast majority of the players did not agree to it: David Clark pushed it through with some support from Cowdrey. We were livid. Our job, after all, was to win the Ashes and since we were one up in the series an extra Test was obviously in Australia's interests rather than ours. The argument was that receipts had been badly hit by the cancellation in Melbourne, which is okay up to a point but no justification for changing the itinerary of the series in mid-stride. Matches had been abandoned before without anybody slipping in an extra Test – it is part of the risk of any game that is played outdoors. But Clark and Cowdrey got their way and the Australian Cricket Board got another 'gate', which has always seemed to be very high on its list of priorities.

The fifth Test in Melbourne finished as a high-scoring draw, but not before Brian Luckhurst broke the little finger of his left hand while making 109 in the first innings. He did not bat in the second innings, so the old firm of Boycott and Edrich was reunited and we played out time for a draw on the last day. It was dreadfully hot and humid. The Australians slowed the over-rate right down and it was horsework just staying at the wicket. I finished with 76 and Edrich with 74 but I doubt that either of us would have had the strength to bat for a century. It was a mercy when the match finished – we were both saturated with sweat and it was unquestionably one of the most tiring day's cricket I have ever played.

We had a couple of days before the Adelaide Test began in which to rest and recuperate from the steam bath at Melbourne – except that my rest was rudely disturbed by Basil D'Oliveira under the affluence of inkerhol, or something like that. I was awakened by a steady thud, thud, thud on my bedroom wall and wandered blearily next door to find Dolly conducting a drinking party with a few mates from both teams. The repetitive thud was caused by the Aussie Rules football Dolly was throwing against the wall and the room was full of beery bonhomie – it looked as though a bomb had exploded in the very recent past.

Dolly had been regaling the Australians with news of England's impending win in the series, based largely on the fact that they would never get me out. Nice of him to have so much faith in me – but it might have been slightly more justified if he hadn't woken me up in the telling. I wasn't game to mix it with Dolly when he had a few beers inside him. Next morning Bernard Thomas found him looking distinctly the worse for wear and suggested he apologise – as well as forking out some dollars for breakages. Poor Dolly came to see me looking wounded and very sheepish. He apologised profusely and that was that, except that it later transpired he had telephoned his wife at the height of the party and couldn't remember a blind word he had said. Dolly rang again and spent three times longer apologising than he had on making the original call. By the time his wife had finished tearing a strip off him and I'd finished telling him what a dope he was for waking me, his head was probably thumping. Come to think of it, it would have been thumping in any case.

Of all Australian grounds, Adelaide and Sydney are my favourites and I went into the sixth Test really fancying my chances of making a big score. I was batting well, my confidence was high and Adelaide is traditionally the best batting pitch in the country. Runs were hard to come by at first because the Aussies were keen to make a breakthrough and knew they had to win a Test to get back in the series. Edrich and I put on 107, of which I made 58, when I was run out by a throw from Ian Chappell.

Adelaide

I did not believe I was out then and I do not believe it to this day. It was suggested that my bat may not have been grounded but I can't even accept that. Halfway through the run I felt comfortable that I would make it and I relaxed after making my ground in the conviction – the knowledge – that I had beaten the throw. When umpire Max O'Connell gave me out I simply could not believe it and I still maintain that his lack of experience – he was standing in only his second Test at the time – cost me dear. I let the bat slip from my hands and stood, hands on hips, angry and disbelieving, before an interlude of silence was broken by booing and jeering. It has been claimed since that I threw my bat down, but in fact I dropped it in disgust and it lay at my feet until Greg Chappell picked it up and suggested I return to the pavilion, or words to that effect. The distinction between throwing the bat and dropping it may be small but I feel it is important. There was plenty of comment flying about but I did not say a word to anyone – and when the manager suggested I should apologise to O'Connell I refused. I agreed that he should issue a statement from me apologising for my behaviour in showing disgust at the umpire's decision – that was fair enough. When I had cooled down, I could readily accept that my behaviour in the heat of the moment was unacceptable.

But I had not abused the umpire or anything like that, so I did not consider a further or personal apology was necessary. English umpires Charlie Elliott and Arthur Fagg were on the ground, both in good viewing positions and both considerably more experienced than O'Connell. They both thought I was in. And to this day I have never seen a picture which proves I was out: an odd omission by press photographers who were usually pretty quick on the trigger. Max O'Connell made a mistake: it could happen to anybody and I certainly do not hold it against him. But I was the victim and I saw no reason to go around apologising, beyond the expression of regret I had already made – that would have been tantamount to saying I was correctly given out.

On the rest day we were invited to lunch at a winery in the Barossa Valley outside Adelaide. There was still an atmosphere and, apart from Dolly and Richie Benaud, nobody seemed too inclined to talk to me. There was a lot of local sympathy for Max O'Connell, which might have had something to do with the fact that he was a South Australian. It was predictable enough, and so was the reaction of the crowd when I fielded. I was booed every time I touched the ball, though the balance was redressed a bit by support from expatriate English people in the crowd.

Australia were bowled out for 235 in reply to our 470 and Illingworth did not enforce the follow-on, quite rightly in my view, though he took a fair bit of stick for his decision. The sixth Test, remember, came only a couple of days after the steam-bath atmosphere of Melbourne where Snow had bowled 41 eight-ball overs, Lever 37 and Willis 30. In Australia's first innings in Adelaide, Snow bowled 21 overs, Lever 17.1 and Willis 12. Of course, these were eight-ball overs too: the equivalent in six-ball overs would be 28, 22.5 and 16. So the bowlers were very tired, and since Lever had a slightly strained shoulder, it was obvious a lot of work would fall again on the other two bowlers. And being one up, we had only to draw the match.

There was a considerable amount of booing and catcalling as Edrich and I walked out to bat. The crowd was clearly very angry with me and I was determined to do well – there was no way I wanted it to look as though they could get me down. At close of play on the third day we were 47 without loss and next day I feel I played exceptionally well – my timing was right and I hooked, cut and drove to an unbeaten 119, playing very positively. It was my sixth century on the tour, while Edrich and I became only the third pair to create century stands in both innings of a Test against Australia; the others were Hobbs and Sutcliffe and Hutton and Washbrook, so we were in very good company. The South Australian crowd were marvellous at the end. They gave me a tremendous ovation and I appreciated it, knowing how they had felt when I went in.

Barry Richards was positively fulsome. 'While he is stacking up the runs for himself he is at the same time helping the team,' he said. 'He showed us that he can score just as quickly as any other player in the world. He is the most dedicated player in the world and one of the greatest.' I got used to criticism in my career; a bit of praise, especially from a player as exciting as Richards, did not go amiss. The sixth Test ended in a draw, but a freak accident caused me to miss the last day of the match – something lodged under a contact lens and I had to have it removed under a local anaesthetic – but that was nothing compared to the injury which finished my tour with a sickening crack.

We played Western Australia, winners of a sponsored knock-out competition, in a one-day match at Sydney. Not the most important game on the cricket calendar and even less meaningful for us after heavy rain saturated the ground and made pitch preparation well-nigh impossible. The tarpaulin covers had rarely been off the ground in the previous fortnight, the pitch had sweated and the cutter had missed some areas where the grass was ridiculously long. Understandably, the groundsman had devoted most of his time to preparing the pitch for the last Test. Graham McKenzie's first delivery, his loosener, took off from just short of a length and whistled past my chin; his second delivery reared and hit me in the chest; his third took off and threatened to hit me in the face. I lifted a protective arm – and the ball hit me on the left forearm just above the wrist. The crack echoed round the ground, or so they told me later. There was very little doubt that it was broken and X-rays quickly confirmed as much. McKenzie cut down his pace and simply went through the motions after that – had he continued to bowl properly he would have put half the England team in hospital alongside me. The match was abandoned because of rain just before tea and I was out of action for ten weeks.

Adelaide

My tour had finished prematurely and somewhat cruelly, considering I had scored 1553 runs and was only 18 short of Wally Hammond's record, set all of forty years earlier, for the number of first-class runs on an Australia tour. I watched the seventh Test in Sydney from the dressing room and shared the team's elation at a superb victory in very trying circumstances. Ian Chappell, who had taken over as Australia's captain for the first time, won the toss. England were put in and trailed by 80 runs on the first innings but still pulled off a great win thanks to Illingworth and Underwood. Snow hit Terry Jenner on the head and got into trouble with the umpire Lou Rowan and the crowd. Illy finally took the players off the field and there was quite a row in the dressing room because David Clark wanted him to take them straight back out. I had not noticed Mr Clark dodging cans and bottles. The controversies made the win all the sweeter and the lads chaired Illy off at the end, which summed up our feelings about the Ashes series and the captain. 'In my twenty years in the game, nothing has given me so much pleasure,' said Illingworth, and he was entitled to savour every moment of his triumph.

12

Captain

It seems extraordinary to me, looking back, but my honeymoon period as Yorkshire's captain lasted approximately half a season – rather less than that if you take into account an undercurrent of determined opposition which was already established, even if I was unaware of it at the time. By the end of the 1971 season I had become the first English player to finish an English season with an average of over 100, and Yorkshire had suffered one of their worst seasons on record. Contrast the two and you come up with the very obvious conclusion that the success of Boycott and Yorkshire were somehow incompatible and even irreconcilable. The notion was touted freely enough then, especially by those who needed an excuse for their own shortcomings. Blaming somebody else rather than accepting realities is a natural enough trait in anyone, but I don't really accept that it should become part of Yorkshire folklore. The truth is that too many players in the Yorkshire team of the time were not experienced enough, not good enough, not as good as they imagined or not as good as they once were. Getting them to admit it is a different matter.

On 11 May 1971, in his first match as captain of Yorkshire, Boycott scored 110 in one hour forty minutes to help Yorkshire beat Warwickshire by 3 wickets at Middlesbrough.

None of this seemed remotely likely to me at the start of the season. It is hard even now to convey just how much pride, enthusiasm and optimism I had for my new job and the challenge that went with it. Nobody had heard of 'over the moon' then but that's where I was. The world was my oyster, I was at the peak of my career and captain of Yorkshire. There was nothing that we could not achieve, given a willingness to work together. The job wasn't going to be easy and I knew in my heart of hearts that we did not have a particularly powerful squad of players, but hope springs eternal at the start of every season. I would be a pretty unusual Yorkshireman if it did not. My message to the media and the players before the season began was that there was a future at Yorkshire for the younger players, who had to be encouraged to play to their potential – tub-thumping stuff of course but an honest recognition of the fact that we had lost so many experienced players in the recent past. I wonder now if it was misconstrued by some established players as an indication that I intended to get rid of them – a ridiculous notion when Yorkshire needed all the experience it could get.

One of my priorities was to improve Yorkshire's performances in the John Player League. Close's refusal to take one-day cricket seriously had, ostensibly, cost him the captaincy and I knew the Yorkshire public was irked at the runaway success of Lancashire in the limited-overs game. So it clearly made sense to review Yorkshire's whole attitude to one-day cricket. Close had carried the can but the fact is that Yorkshire's attitude as players to one-day matches left a lot to be desired. We had been brought up to win championships – and made a pretty fair fist of it – but we gave precious little detailed thought to the tactics of limited-overs cricket. Our bowlers were resentful of cow-shots and dismissive of the one-day game in general. Fred used to bowl medium-pacers off a short run to two slips; Close himself bowled piddly seamers to a slip in most one-day matches. That sort of attitude at a time when Yorkshire had just made a record loss could cost individuals dear, as we had seen.

That had to change. I spoke to as many players as possible from Kent and Lancashire, easily the best exponents of one-day cricket at the time, and tried to work out a new game-plan as well as a new philosophy. Of course we didn't come to terms with the game in five minutes, but at least we tried to improve our attitude – and the fact that we won five out of the last six JPL matches of the season suggested the light had dawned.

Yorkshire's team at the start of the 1971 season consisted of several promising young players and six, myself apart, with experience and proven ability – John Hampshire, Tony Nicholson, Richard Hutton, Don Wilson, Doug Padgett and Phil Sharpe. Of those, Hampshire, Nicholson and Hutton were very capable players with a lot still to offer; Padgett was almost thirty-seven; Wilson and Sharpe were past their best and unlikely to figure prominently in the long-term future. It wasn't a lot to play with. In fact Ray Illingworth's objective view, two years after leaving the club, was: 'I probably made things more right for Yorkshire than they have ever been. Now they haven't got a side to go with it.' Arthur Mitchell wrote in his pre-season report as coach that some of the known youngsters appeared to be showing improvement but there was no obvious new talent available. And the first-team scorer Ted Lester, a Yorkshire player for over a decade just after the war, wrote offering his advice on the grounds that there was no experienced player I could turn to. Wanting success for Yorkshire was one thing – and I was totally committed to it – but the plain truth was that the squad did not have anything like the right blend of talent and experience. That was realism, not defeatism, and it wasn't long before I put the point to Brian Sellers: Yorkshire needed some new blood, and pretty quickly, if they were to hold their own in the championship and start building for the future. I think Sellers agreed but he was not prepared, as chairman of the cricket sub-committee, to invite new controversy by rocking the boat too much. There had been a furore over Close's departure, and Sellers had come in for a lot of personal criticism; I reckon he just wanted a quiet life for what was left of his association with Yorkshire. I can understand that now, but his attitude did not help me much at the time and it did Yorkshire's long-term future no good at all.

I attacked the Yorkshire captaincy in the way I approached most aspects of my cricket: trying to be meticulous, leaving nothing to chance where it was possible to plan ahead, trying to take an impartial and wholly professional view of the team and the job it had to do. I still have the notes I took into our first team meeting – eight pages of minute scribble covering everything from how they should address me ('Call me Geoff or Fiery or whatever, I'm not bothered about terms like captain or skipper') to travel and hotel arrangements, selling Phil Sharpe's benefit brochures and advice – would you believe it – on relationships with the press.

I also have notes from one of my very early meetings with the Yorkshire committee, including reminders to ask questions like 'Whom do I report to when anything crops up, secretary or chairman?' And 'Do I have a free hand on the cricket field?' There is even a note, suitably underlined under the heading 'Journalistic Licence', which says, 'Both of us should try not to believe anything in the press until we have met and asked the view of the other party.' It all seems so stylised and nit-picking now, though not totally irrelevant. I was clearly very naive if I thought the answers could be written down and observed like the laws of the game.

The press had taken a pretty lively interest in my affairs for some years and that wasn't likely to diminish now I was captain of Yorkshire. Being the spokesman for the team rather than just for my own performance was new ground for me and there were plenty of pitfalls. Peter Johnson of the *Daily Mail* and Howard Booth of the *Mirror* had followed Yorkshire for years, some would say like Burke and Hare, and we usually managed to furnish them with a story a day. They buttonholed me after a Roses match at Old Trafford and we talked about the day's play, constructively I thought, except that I included a throwaway line about Lancashire's wide bowling making it difficult to score quickly. Their newspapers ran headlines screaming that Boycott had lashed out against Lancashire and so on. Since I had not specified that the remark was off the record I suppose I can't complain. But it taught me a lesson – Cedric Rhoades almost went up in a puff of self-righteous smoke and I had to write to him to put the record straight – that relationships with the press weren't going to get any easier with the captaincy. A little later Yorkshire played the touring Pakistanis at Bradford, soon after their manager announced they intended to use county matches as practice for the real thing. We gave them practice – fielding practice – and declared at 422–9 after batting for one and a half days. The Pakistanis were 140–5, still needing 133 to avoid the follow-on, when rain washed out the last day, and their management were very critical of Yorkshire's tactics. Well they might be – instead of meekly allowing them to practise we had reached a position where we could have bowled them out and won the match. But the headlines still placed Boycott in the inevitable 'row', which proved again that when it came to creating a headline around a supposedly controversial character, nobody was going to do me any favours. There was no reason why they should but the realisation was a little hard to take.

My own form that season was superlative. It seemed that every time I picked up a bat I was going to score runs, and amazingly I felt a flow of confidence like never before or since. By the time I had scored 10 or 15 runs, I really felt that I would go on to make a century – and that was probably the worst thing I could have done in terms of feeding the critics with ammunition.

I am convinced, even at this distance, that the sheer elation of being Yorkshire's captain was the root cause of my good form that season. I was on a high, I knew I had to lead by example and every sinew in my body was taut and tuned. A great deal has been said and written since about man-management but that, in an era dominated by the likes of Sellers, Mitchell and Close, was hardly a silken art form at Yorkshire. I gave the team the very best performances I could muster and I expected the same from them in return. Quite simply I expected professionalism, and not least from the senior players. Instead, it became insidiously fashionable to blame me – even in my absences playing for England – for the malaise which overtook Yorkshire's season.

The more runs I scored, the more a contrast was drawn between my personal success and the team's failure, to the point where it was claimed by some warped logical process that Yorkshire's problems were the direct consequence of my performances. And the claim, alas, was originated and advanced by some of the senior members of the team. I know statistics can be made to prove practically anything but they do not support the case against my captaincy that season. I led the side in seventeen championship matches: we won four, drew nine and lost four. Wilson captained the side in six matches without scoring a win, lost four and drew two. Padgett had one drawn match as captain. Since there was no evidence of a wonderful transformation when I did not lead the side, it was claimed as a second line of attack that my batting cost Yorkshire bonus points because I was more interested in my performance than in the prosperity of the team. Let's look at the figures again. Under me, Yorkshire gained 99 bonus points (44 batting, 55 bowling) during the season; under Wilson they achieved 21 (3 and 18) and Padgett's one match yielded 2 bowling bonus points. Again, not a shred of evidence that Yorkshire earned more bonus points in my absence. And the fact is that we did not win a match in which I did not make a big score. In the win over Northants I made 124 not out, over Notts 169, over Middlesex 88 and 112 not out and over Warwickshire 61 and 110. When I was dismissed for 40 against Hampshire at Bournemouth, we were bowled out for 96 in the first innings and lost by eight wickets. I made 111 out of 233 in the second innings. On a flat pitch at Edgbaston, Warwickshire declared at 354–8 and we were 45–6 before I batted through for 138 out of a total of 232. We lost the match by 22 runs after I top-scored in the second innings with 84.

It was suggested, as an implicit criticism of me, that Yorkshire had become a one-man band. It was claimed that I batted as though I was the only batsman in the team, obsessed with the need to make bigger and bigger scores. All I can say is that the facts prove how desperate Yorkshire's need was. I would have been perfectly happy for some other batsman to weigh in with consistently big scores and make my contributions less vital. In the event only Hampshire made more than 1000 runs in the championship. My critics resented my pre-eminence in the team but they didn't do much on the field to challenge it.

Off the field was a different matter altogether. I was not immediately aware of it, perhaps because I wasn't looking for trouble, but some of the senior players were already making a concerted effort to turn the dressing room, and anyone else who would listen, against the captain. Their own performances were inadequate, their results under a new sort of pressure were demonstrably inferior to their reputations, they had to find an excuse and I was the ready-made target. They were, after all, unlikely to blame themselves and they could hardly blame the junior and inexperienced members of the team. It had to be Boycott.

The fact is that for many years, Yorkshire had been carried to a string of successes by men like Close, Illingworth and Trueman – exceptional players with exceptional presence on a cricket field and a match-winning quality that lifted their team-mates and intimidated the opposition. They had good, solid players behind them but on so many occasions they were the chief influence in forcing a draw against the odds or wringing victory out of what might have been a respectable draw. It was marvellous while it lasted, cementing Yorkshire's reputation as a tough unit on the field and a formidably social outfit off it. Nobody in Yorkshire would have complained if it had gone on for ever, least of all those lesser lights who enjoyed the success and the lifestyle without being forced too often into the spotlight and the irksome responsibility of giving a lead. But those days were gone. They disappeared when Close's era ended in acrimony, and those who had been cast in support roles were suddenly exposed as senior players in a Yorkshire squad which was ordinary at best. They did not like the intrusion into their lifestyle and they could not handle the pressures of seeing their performances come under a new, critical scrutiny. Life was so much easier when better players ensured success and evenings were spent basking in reflected glory at the bar or round the piano. Now Yorkshire were struggling and all the publicity was centred on this new captain who did not socialise much and who had a maddening habit of expecting professional performance rather than skill on the banjo. It really was too bad.

The opposition spokesman was Richard Hutton, a genuinely capable all-rounder who played for England in 1971 (on my recommendation to Illy) but whose lasting claim to fame was the fact that he was the son of the great Sir Leonard. Nothing Richard achieved in his career went close to emulating his father and it would have been a miracle if it had, but I suppose the comparison rankled. Had Richard achieved the captaincy of Yorkshire, which his father never did, he could have stepped out of Sir Len's shadow.

Richard went to Repton, a good public school, where he learned the value of contacts and the rudiments of snobbery that come to some people with an expensive if not expansive education. He clearly resented me as some sort of country bumpkin, totally without social graces, whose only claim to distinction was that he showed a mastery of his profession. The notion that I could achieve the captaincy of Yorkshire while he, for all his connections and ambition, could not, was a bitter blow. Hutton's superiority complex became a byword in the dressing room, where he delighted in the smart phrase and the cruel put-down, usually directed at younger players who did not have the nerve or the maturity to come back at him. But they recognised his superficiality; his nickname was Arch, which was short for Archie, a reference to the dummy used by ventriloquist Peter

Brough. Educated Archie might have a public-school background and an air of assumed self-confidence, he might even be able to understand the *Financial Times* and do the crossword, but there was a cruel edge to his so-called humour and evidence aplenty that he regarded most of the dressing room as his inferiors.

I spent several matches away from Yorkshire that season, playing for England or recovering from injury. When I was with the team I spent a lot of time at the crease. There was plenty of opportunity for Hutton to do his worst in my absence from the dressing room or at the bar, where he was always sure of an audience. We were as different as chalk and cheese, but that did not matter to me as long as he did his job. There were obvious signs that he resented any professional criticism and preferred to bowl when and where it suited him, which did not quite square with the self-made propaganda that he was a team man while I was a loner. Some members of the committee, naturally respectful of the Hutton name or simply obsequious, were always ready to listen to his complaints, and the younger players in the dressing room lacked the experience to assess his criticisms of me. And since looking for excuses to explain Yorkshire's lack of success was the order of the day, the older professionals didn't exactly go out of their way to contradict his anti-Boycott theme. John Hampshire and Tony Nicholson were, I believe, rather less interested in what Hutton had to say than they were in doing a job and then joining in at the bar. I certainly did not feel in that first year of captaincy that they were actively against me. But Don Wilson and Phil Sharpe were more receptive – Wilson because he was encouraged by a wife fiercely ambitious for him, and Sharpe because he leaned towards the Hutton image of the public schoolboy motivated by lofty ideals. He had served as vice-captain under Close and must have fancied he was being groomed for the captaincy at some future date. That seemed to have changed, and Boycott, naturally, was to blame.

So long as their lifestyle remained relatively unchanged, so long as they could cruise along and, particularly, so long as they were selected in the team, the senior players might have accepted their lot albeit disgruntledly. But they had a new responsibility to form the vanguard of the team, not simply to slot in as a competent part of it, and it became clear as the season progressed that they were not up to it. Their performances simply did not guarantee them a place in the side. Sharpe was left out of the Sunday league side and eventually Wilson was dropped from the championship. As far as they were concerned, that was interference with the established order of things, and, worse, it came at a time when unflattering comparisons were being drawn between my productivity and their performances. 'Without

Boycott, Yorkshire are like a ship without a rudder,' said Peter Smith in the *News of the World* – the sort of statement which was probably all the more wounding because the facts seemed to bear it out. I have no doubt that the seniors' pride was hurt and I can understand why it should be. But the solution lay in an improvement in their performance and attitude, not in a denigration of mine. I expected more professionalism than I got from them, greater pride in their performance. It was a chilling sign of the times that while I was in my room studying individuals and desperately trying to work out how we could improve our results, Hutton, Wilson and Sharpe were in the bar spreading the gospel that I was the root of all evil.

If they needed ammunition, I unintentionally provided it by being involved in several run-outs during the season. I use the word unintentionally with a purpose, since I can put hand on heart and say I have never run out a partner with malice aforethought or without giving a damn. It may well be that I was too intense about my own performance, too wrapped up with the need to score runs for Yorkshire that season – I don't know for certain and I make no attempt to absolve myself from blame. John Woodford, Doug Padgett and Sharpe suffered unnecessarily and I felt bad about it. The critical interpretation, of course, was that I had done it deliberately and with blatant, conscious disregard for anyone but myself. That is perverse nonsense.

I also learned, long after the anti-Boycott brigade got into their stride, that they resented my association with Ted Lester, to whom I often went for advice and guidance. Ted, I found, had one quality which none of the more experienced players could claim – he was totally dispassionate and objective in his views on the game and on the team. From his vantage point as scorer he could spot aspects of the game that we might overlook and as a Yorkshire player for over ten years, many of them as second-team captain, he certainly had the cricket knowledge to back his views. It seemed only logical for me to make use of his expertise and I was grateful for the help which Ted offered over the years. I still am.

Being captain and most successful player at one and the same time put me under an enormous amount of pressure. It brought a lot out of me but it also took me to the brink of exhaustion by the end of the season.

I visited Australia recently and was struck by the similarity between my situation then and that of Allan Border now. He is Australia's best player, a great batsman by any standards, and the captain of an unsuccessful team. He is trying to build an effective side but has not yet found the depth of quality. Players who looked as though they might make the grade have not progressed, and they need time. And the creeping insinuation is that Border is a fine batsman, a dedicated bloke but not a Test captain. Border was in good spirits when I met him, full of support for his players and optimism for the future. Good luck to him. But I fear the realities of the situation will wear him down eventually and I only hope he does not come to consider himself a failure, whatever other people may say.

Three weeks before the end of the 1971 season I scored 151 in a drawn match against Leicestershire at Bradford Park Avenue. As I came off the field I was approached by the legendary Herbert Sutcliffe, still alert and dapper in his seventy-seventh year, who remarked that he had once finished a season with an average of over 90 and that Bradman had topped an average of 100 in an English season. 'You could do that. You should do it,' said Herbert. It was the first time I had given it any thought but the idea, unlikely as it appeared, was very attractive. After that I scored 453 runs in six innings as Yorkshire lost consecutive matches to Hampshire, Surrey and Warwickshire – perhaps we would have won had I scored fewer! – and reached the last match against Northants at Harrogate with a century average within mathematical reach. Northants were bowled out for 61, we made 266–2 before I declared with 124 not out, and Northants were bowled out again, beaten by an innings and 99 runs in two days. An overdue victory for Yorkshire and an extraordinary end to the season for me with a first-class average of 105.67. Despite all the disappointment and tribulations of the season, I make no apology for being proud of that achievement.

In 1971 Boycott became the only English player to average over 100 in an English season. He repeated this feat in 1979.

Richard Hutton spent much of Yorkshire's innings at the dressing-room window, calling alternately for me to hit out and get out, without a trace of support for his captain nor of recognition of the fact that Yorkshire were on the road to victory. His hostility was fierce and open. It did not, however, prevent him from sitting stony-faced drinking my champagne after the match.

Looking back, I wish I had given up the Yorkshire captaincy at the end of that year. There was no way of knowing it then, even if the attitudes of the troublemakers were obvious enough, but there was to be very little peace for me in charge at Yorkshire – too many poses and too much opposition from men motivated by nothing loftier than sheer envy. Perhaps I could have changed my attitudes to fit in with the anti-Boycott brigade, but all I knew was the professional approach. I could not frequent the bar as they did, or make light of being beaten, or neglect myself to the point where practice and preparation became a chore – after all, we were paid to play cricket and to win as many matches as possible. But I took great pride in being captain of Yorkshire. I felt I had something to contribute and I did not feel that an alternative captain would have done any better than I had, modest as the season was for us. As a player rather than a captain, the years to come would probably have brought me less hassle, less public and private torment, more peace of mind. But I had been asked to do a job and I meant to see it through as best I could. Giving up the captaincy after one deeply disillusioning year would have looked like quitting and that never came easily to me.

13

Conflict

There was no disguising the undercurrent of conflict and dissatisfaction around the Yorkshire dressing room at the end of the 1971 season and I was as anxious as anyone that it should be resolved – the quicker the better. I didn't want it swept under the carpet or concealed in a few well-chosen phrases. I much preferred to drag it out into the open – at least as far as the players were concerned – and get down to brass tacks. Criticism to my face might not be pleasant but it was infinitely preferable to propaganda behind my back. Tony Nicholson thought the same and we arranged a get-together at the house of Sam Wildblood, a loyal Yorkshire member, at a village a few miles from Leeds. It wasn't a team meeting as such and not all the players were able to attend but those that did had every chance to air their grievances. The Yorkshire committee had called a meeting with the players – a rather better publicised one – in an attempt to clear the air and again the players were given every chance to get things off their chest. It might be no coincidence that most of the talking was done by Hutton. My attitude was the same at both meetings. I had set myself high standards which appeared to have paid off professionally and I expected high standards from others. I was not prepared to drop my standards for the sake of a quieter life; any changes in lifestyle and attitude must logically come from those who were not producing the goods. I didn't expect it would win me any new pals, but I repeated my belief that some established players resented any sort of discipline or direction and confused the opportunity to discuss decisions with the right to be consulted. Once Brian Close had made a decision as captain we followed his lead, irrespective of our personal preferences, and I expected the same loyalty. We had to be more professional with a greater emphasis on the playing side than the social side of the game. They had heard it before, some of them without liking it, and both they and the committee now knew precisely where I stood.

The upshot of the meeting was that we should make every effort to wipe the slate clean and pull in the same direction. It's a familiar heart-cry in Yorkshire these days and it is easy to be cynical about it, but I was happy to think that some progress was made towards a new start. Later that evening Don Mosey went on radio with a report of the meeting, including remarks that made it clear that details had already been leaked to him by one or more players. 'As one player said to me, "I don't expect Geoff Boycott will average 100 next year!"' crowed Mosey. So much for team unity. Joe Lister had only recently joined the club as secretary. He had a distanced view of the controversies and no axe to grind, and he was 'nauseated' by Mosey's report. It was a telling reaction to the already established attitude of a journalist later to write what purports to be an unbiased biography of me.

Lister, a Yorkshire player in two matches in 1954 and former secretary of Worcestershire, joined the club as secretary on the retirement of John Nash, one of several significant changes that winter. Brian Sellers resigned as chairman of the cricket committee – worn down, I suspect, by the repercussions of Close's sacking and cynically sacrificed to public opinion by his committee colleagues – and was replaced by John Temple. We did not know much about Temple, who did not have a background as a Yorkshire player, except that it was rumoured and later demonstrated that he carried in his top pocket a little black book which contained all the season's averages. It was pretty obvious that Temple was a reaction to the autocratic Sellers, a much blander character less likely to arouse controversy than the figure whose treatment of Close had already split the club. That was not necessarily a criticism of either man. Positional switches happen all the time in sport. But it suggested ominously, even then, that the cricket chairman might not be the most forceful of characters at a time when Yorkshire clearly needed positive leadership from the top. One journalist had already written that in the present circumstances, Sellers would have 'sacked Boycott or sacked half the team'. I knew just what he meant.

The loss of Doug Padgett was a heavy blow for me and the team. Arthur Mitchell retired as coach and the committee was adamant that Doug should replace him, despite the fact that this would obviously rob us of a very experienced and capable batsman just when we needed all the quality we could muster. Padgett was a very skilful player on poor pitches, a committed team man and a player I could talk to. I pleaded that he should be retained as a player, but to no avail. Doug himself was perfectly willing to carry on and even offered to combine the jobs of first-team player and coach but the club insisted he should captain the second team. The timing was very unfortunate.

Doug's departure and the knowledge that my critics would still leak anti-Boycott titbits to the press made me even more convinced that I needed help and I urged Temple to give Ted Lester a position of more influence and authority. I felt that Ted could be of enormous assistance in handling the press, overseeing the domestic details of moving a county side round the country, anticipating problems and offering advice. In fact I saw his role as akin to that of an England manager on tour, with a responsibility to the side that stopped short of actually handling cricket matters on the field. To that extent, and in 1971 before the idea had become fashionable, I anticipated a move towards team managers in county cricket. I advocated it strongly with Yorkshire, with the firm proviso that the captain should still be responsible for playing matters. Yorkshire turned me down, and when I broached the subject of Ted's status throughout the years of my captaincy their reaction became increasingly touchy. A bit ironic considering developments a few years down the track.

But I already believed that a team manager, with duties clearly defined, could be a huge asset to a cricket team and its captain. 'I myself would like to see the advent of cricket managers who would smooth many a rugged path and leave the players to get on with the game. My experience of overseas tours, very often managed by ex-players, has shown me what it is like to be able to concentrate solely on the game and leave the travelling arrangements, press and TV interviews, payments of hotel expenses and anything which affects the general well-being of the players to the manager. . . . As a captain I would not like to lose any authority on the field of play but I believe the game of cricket could benefit by adopting some ideas from the management of football.' I wrote that in December 1971 and I still believe it.

Yorkshire, as I have explained, was unlike the other first-class counties in that it never offered its players contracts. Availability and retention were based on a yearly agreement whereby an offer (or otherwise) would be made by the club by the end of July. It says a great deal for the inbred loyalty of Yorkshiremen that the system had worked tolerably well over the years, but of course it was hopelessly out of date and the club finally decided to venture a little further into the twentieth century. That was great, long overdue, but it landed me with the added responsibility of negotiating on the players' behalf, and I spent ages trying to thrash out a good deal. I put my own case for a rise very forcibly – I certainly felt I deserved something in all the circumstances – but I battled on behalf of the others too and came up with what seemed to be a reasonable formula. In future, capped players would receive a salary plus match fees and, in the case of capped first-teamers, a bonus based on years of service. All the capped players would be eligible for an ability bonus of £100, £300 or over £300 to be negotiated individually, and bonuses were there to be added if the team did well. I was keen on an ability bonus, not simply because I had a vested interest but because it had always struck me as ridiculous that a young capped player should start out with the same money as an Illingworth or a Trueman. Being involved as captain on the ground floor of Yorkshire contracts was hard work but I did what I could as conscientiously as I could and the agreement forged in 1971 still forms the basis of Yorkshire's contract system.

By the time I returned from a spell in South Africa, the season was drawing very close. Hutton had accepted only a one-year contract, the Yorkshire selection committee had been reduced from an unwieldy twelve to four, which was a distinct step in the right direction, and Joe Lister – with time to appraise the situation – had come up with his own assessment. He advised me to press for more discipline in the team, to chivvy the cricket committee on the assumption that they would do nothing unless pushed, and to remind the players precisely where I stood. He also said he could not foresee an immediate improvement with the staff we had, which was a gloomy projection, if an honest one.

I spent a lot of time before the start of the 1972 season dissecting my own attitudes and trying to work out just how to develop a harmonious relationship with everybody in the dressing room. I could have rolled up my sleeves, marched in and said that anyone who didn't like the way I did things could pack up and leave. It might just have worked. But there had to be a better way than that and I made notes – covering the back of a foolscap envelope – on how best to lift morale. 'Give the players more freedom to bat and bowl as they wish. . . . Do not tell them how to bat, bowl or field. . . . Advise them only if they want advice. . . . Encourage and give them confidence all the time. . . . Tell them they are great. . . .' The list goes on and on and makes wry reading. How defensive I had become under the accusation that our problems were all my fault. I might deny the accusation and even disprove it but it had obviously got through to me. Trying to lift morale had an unfortunate effect right at the start.

I felt confident, not just as a slogan but as a fact which I told the players, that we could win the newly created Benson and Hedges Cup. We had shown every sign of coming to grips with limited-overs cricket, we had exceptionally well-suited bowlers in Chris Old and Tony Nicholson, and it was well within our capabilities to win the five matches that would take us through to the final, especially if we were blessed with home draws. Sure enough, we beat Lancashire by nine wickets in the first match at Bradford.

Don Wilson took 5–26 but for some reason best known to himself the adjudicator Bill Voce made Barry Wood man of the match. Wood, with a score of 31 and one wicket for 11, couldn't believe it himself. When the press asked my opinion I said Wilson should obviously have had the award, thinking that my words would boost his morale at the start of the season, but they weren't quite reported like that. 'Boycott Lashes Voce' thundered the headlines, and Voce vowed he would never adjudicate in another match. It certainly was not what I had intended.

Only Herbert Sutcliffe, with sixteen, and Percy Holmes, with nine, have scored more double centuries for Yorkshire than Boycott with seven.

The simple fact was that just about everything I did now constituted 'news' – what I said, how I acted, whether I succeeded or even when I failed. It had clearly become a source of annoyance to the other players (I can't say I cared for it too much myself) and their feelings became obvious after a match at Middlesbrough. There we beat Gloucestershire, but not before taking some stick in the newspapers for our approach early in the game. The press misread the situation and the lads in the dressing room were livid, so we called the journalists in for a word. They arrived, notebooks at the ready, thinking there was another Yorkshire story in the offing, and instead Wilson, Nicholson and Hampshire launched into them, making the strong point among others that they resented the near-total preoccupation with Boycott to the detriment of the rest of the team. I could not have agreed more. The nature of press coverage set me apart from the rest of the team when that was the last thing I wanted.

In fact, I was so anxious to be seen to be very much a part of the team that I tried to wriggle out of an invitation to play for MCC against the Australians. I was frankly concerned that it would be used as ammunition by my critics in the dressing room, so-called evidence that I would rather play in a 'big' match for MCC than for Yorkshire. I missed enough matches through Test calls without adding that one. When I brought it up at a selection committee meeting there was a long and sometimes fractious discussion and Yorkshire insisted I should play in the MCC game. It was part of club policy, they said, and refused to request my release. I was very annoyed and tried to let the team know what had gone on, but I would much rather have proved my point by staying with the side.

The playing season was highlighted by our successes in the Benson and Hedges Cup, where we won our early matches convincingly and reached the final with a seven-wicket win over Gloucestershire at Headingley. Gloucestershire were bowled out for 131, the pitch was never easy and we had to pace ourselves meticulously after losing three for 50. It was very tense and the big crowd was as keyed up as we were, especially when we were going slowly against Gloucestershire's front-line bowlers.

The lull and the near silence was broken by a raucous voice I've never forgotten: 'Come on, Geoff. They'll sack thee whatever tha does.' A man in front of his time.

We had qualified for the final and everything in the garden looked unusually rosy when Bob Willis took a hand. We met Warwickshire in the Gillette Cup at Headingley and Willis compounded the pain of a four-wicket defeat by pulping the middle finger of my right hand. The pain was excruciating – I have learned since that fingertips are packed with delicate nerve-endings and I can well believe it – and I was rushed off to hospital after emergency work from the club physiotherapist. 'Rushed' may be something of an overstatement. The job of driving me there fell to the young Colt Phil Carrick, who had just taken delivery of a new car and was not about to abuse it on a mercy errand. It was the slowest life-and-death drive imaginable, Phil accelerating at around walking pace and slowing down miles before every traffic light. I pleaded through my pain, I begged and threatened, but he wouldn't go any faster. Whoever bought that car from him got a real, looked-after bargain. I was fortunate at the hospital to catch a surgeon on duty. The finger was a mess of bone and flesh and it took a lot of skill to avoid the necessity of removing the tip altogether. I was in a real state, rude to everybody and mad as hell with the pain and the knowledge that I was going to miss the B&H final after we had worked so hard to get there. The bookmakers had Yorkshire 3–1 to beat Leicestershire; when I was injured the odds swung the other way. It was a cruel mischance and Yorkshire eventually lost in the final by five wickets to a side led, of course, by Ray Illingworth. Leicestershire were 97–5 chasing 137 but they pulled through thanks largely to Yorkshireman Chris Balderstone; another 30 or 40 runs might have won it for Yorkshire and they could have come from me. It was a totally exasperating thought.

Familiar but no less ominous for that were the storm clouds that began to gather again on Yorkshire's horizon. Wilson was left out of the B&H final and was predictably annoyed; the fact that the secretary announced that it was for fitness reasons when Wilson was obviously available did not help. Wilson sounded off to the press, the final was previewed by stories of yet another Yorkshire row and I'm sure that Wilson believed then and now that I was responsible for having him dropped from the side. In fact, other members of the selection committee had come to the conclusion that Wilson simply was not bowling well enough: Billy Sutcliffe was appalled at his showing in the Gillette Cup and the umpire George Pope had told John Temple that Wilson's bowling in a recent match was some of the worst he had seen. The committee was just as concerned at the form, or lack of it, being shown by Phil Sharpe and both were summoned for a discussion and hopefully an explanation. It was suggested, with the B&H final barely a week away, that Sharpe might drop into the second team in search of runs and form, but he did not react kindly to the idea. Wilson was taken ill for a few days, which prompted Lister to try and sweeten the pill of his being dropped, and was finally left out of the squad for the final. He was not bowling well and the consensus in and outside the committee was that in-form seam bowler Howard Cooper was a better bet at Lord's. Sharpe virtually had to be picked because there was no other candidate for captain, though it was proposed that Doug Padgett could come into the side and do the job better. Wilson was left out of the squad because it was also felt, in a particularly convoluted Yorkshire way, that his presence as deposed captain would be a source of embarrassment to the stand-in Sharpe.

When Yorkshire lost the final, Wilson was promptly restored as captain, with Sharpe being dropped to make way for the up-and-coming Richard Lumb. It was clear that Wilson was in the side by virtue of his position as club vice-captain rather than on merit, and after dreadfully heavy defeats at the Oval and in the Roses match he was left out again. I had almost despaired of getting any sense out of the selection committee, who asked my opinions but very rarely took any notice of them when they picked the team, and wondered if there was any point in going to the meetings. But Sir Leonard Hutton had described Wilson's bowling as the worst he had seen by a left-arm spinner on a spinner's pitch at the Oval, so there was precious little chance of him keeping his place. Tony Nicholson took over the captaincy for one rain-ruined match and the pressures on me to return to play mounted to hysteria proportions. My finger was still dreadfully sore. A huge, ugly scab had developed over the tip and the medical advice was that if it was disturbed, there would be no recognisable sinew to sew together and the only way of tidying the finger up would be to lop the end off. I didn't exactly fancy that and there seemed no way I could get back into the middle, despite Yorkshire's repeated requests coupled with a promise that I could bat anywhere in the order I liked just as long as I took the field.

Their view was that my presence was essential to lift the performance and morale of the side. That might have been true, but it could have been pure desperation on their part and certainly it seems ironic in view of later developments and attitudes. John Temple came up with a metal finger-stall which would fit reasonably snugly and protect the fingertip. While Nicholson led the team against Sussex at Bradford, I turned out in the league for Leeds and made an unbeaten 108. Club bowlers and county bowlers are a very different kettle of fish but it was obvious I should play for Yorkshire as quickly as possible. Their next match was at Scarborough against Surrey – fortunately without Geoff Arnold – and I took the plunge with profound misgivings. Not to put too fine a point on it, I was scared to death. One direct hit could cost me my finger-end and I did not have the form or confidence to get forward to the ball. I spent ages at the nets with seam bowlers like Howard Cooper and Mike Bore patiently coaxing me to play forward. My contribution was modest enough, 4 and 19 not out, but we won the match thanks to some determined bowling led by the big-hearted Nicholson and went on to draw with Leicestershire at Leicester. I did myself a big disfavour in that match by scoring 204 not out in the first innings.

I am still not quite sure how I did it. There was probably more will-power than flashing strokeplay involved and I remember being scared silly when Graham McKenzie hit me a glancing blow on the injured finger very early in the innings. It hurt a lot despite the metal protection and I pottered about for at least half an hour trying to get it out of my mind. Fortunately McKenzie could not bowl all day and most of Leicestershire's attack was given over to the spinners, Jack Birkenshaw and John Steele. I didn't exactly crash it about, even if my second hundred came in two hours, but I did make 204 out of our total of 310–7 declared – and that immediately provided ammunition for my critics who claimed firstly that I should have played earlier and secondly that we should have scored more bonus points! Medical history and the statistics of our innings bear out neither claim, but who cares – it was all grist to the malcontents' mill.

They had not been idle, despite the fact that I had missed a huge chunk of the season with my finger injury. While the senior players were selected in the first team and while we had the prospect of winning a trophy, there was peace. Their interests were being looked after. But the cup final was lost, Wilson and Sharpe were dropped from the side because of their inadequate performances and the whisper campaign was stirred up again: Boycott had to go and Hutton was the man to replace him. Fred Trueman documents an incident at the Headingley Test match during the 1972 season which clearly illustrates what was going on behind my back. Says Trueman: 'I was at Headingley for a Test match having tea with some of the Yorkshire committee when Hutton was asked if he would captain the county. He replied, "Yes, on one condition. Boycott is as far away from Yorkshire as possible." The reply was in words I will never forget: "The removal of Boycott will have to be handled as delicately as a military operation."' I was not aware of that conversation at the time, naturally enough, but I think it speaks volumes for the political pressures being built up in the club. Later that season Hutton tried to organise a letter to be sent to the committee expressing lack of faith in the captain. John Hampshire, for one, refused to sign it and the project apparently fell through. No doubt Hutton would protest that he had no captaincy ambitions and was acting in the best interests of the club; no doubt those committee men involved would insist that the interests of Yorkshire cricket were best served by off-the-field machinations. They were, after all, honourable men . . .

My innings at Leicester triggered another series of events which may have assumed a greater importance later in my career than they appeared to have at the time. It brought me into direct conflict with Ray Illingworth.

When he heard that I was to play in league cricket after my long lay-off with injury, Alec Bedser, as chairman of the selectors, phoned me and asked if I felt I was fit enough to play for England! It was an extraordinary question – I hadn't had a bat in my hand for over four weeks and I wasn't exactly bursting with confidence – and I could not in all conscience tell Alec I was ready. He phoned me again after my unbeaten 108: did I feel any better? I had to point out that the finger was still painful, that I couldn't grip the bat properly and that the bowling in the league wasn't exactly Test standard. Had Geoff Arnold not been picked to play for England, I doubted I would have been up to facing him in the forthcoming match against Surrey. Alec accepted my situation. It was flattering to have him contact me and I reiterated my position in a letter which one might have expected to be the end of the matter. As it turned out, England fared badly at the Oval and Illingworth, as captain, was increasingly critical of my absence. When I scored a double century, against Leicestershire of all teams, he went positively bananas and created huge headlines in the press with a very public condemnation of me for not playing for England. Suddenly, England were losing a Test match because of me.

I was furious and made my feelings clear to Bedser when the Test match ended. Illy was quickly on the phone, presumably at Bedser's suggestion, but there was no hint that he regretted what he had said. He was dismissive and quite unrepentant. I was picked in the one-day squad, Illingworth had to drop out because of a leg strain – and then he let it be known that he would probably be fit enough to play in Leicestershire's Sunday league match in the middle of the international one-day series. In other words, having slagged me off to the press for not playing for England, he proposed to play a match for Leicestershire in very similar circumstances. I made my annoyance plain in a meeting with the selectors at Old Trafford. What was sauce for the goose was sauce for the gander.

Just to make the situation even more prickly, Leicestershire needed to win their last Sunday match of the season to take the title – and their opponents were Yorkshire! Illingworth did not play in the game, and Leicestershire lost by three runs. They were subsequently pipped for the title when Kent won their last two games. In an illogical but very obvious way, Boycott had caused the defeat of Illingworth's England and cost Illingworth's Leicestershire the Sunday league title – nonsense, of course, but I reckon Illingworth always saw it like that and never forgave me. I tried to square the situation with him when he went to Old Trafford for treatment during the first one-day international but he was intractable and we ended up having a row. Illingworth and I were friends at the time, improbable as that may sound, but I already knew that he was not a man who liked to be contradicted. He had strong opinions and he expected them to be heeded. Furthermore, he was a Yorkshireman with a long memory . . .

Only Herbert Sutcliffe (twice) and Boycott have scored centuries in four consecutive championship innings for Yorkshire.

By the end of the season, relationships between me and Don Wilson in particular had degenerated to the point where I had no time for him and he barely tried to hide his contempt for me. Even on a professional level, where personal feelings should not have mattered overmuch, Wilson seemed obstructive and uncooperative. If I tried to set a field for his bowling I was interfering; if I let him set his own fields I was taking no interest; if I tried to help the younger players with their technique I was only doing it to prove how superior I was. There was nothing I tried to do that Wilson could not misrepresent and, more often than not, Hutton would be around to back him up. The situation came to a head during Yorkshire's last match of the season at Southampton, where we went with some of the Hampshire players to a do at the White Rose Hotel – of all places – and Wilson launched into a boozy condemnation of all things Boycott. Wilson had an audience, a drink in his hand and a bit of Dutch courage, and I listened, embarrassed if not entirely surprised, while he publicly poured out his grievances. They ranged over everything from my attitude to players, specifically not telling them how great they were, through my effect on Hutton to the fact that he was considering an offer from Derbyshire and would probably become the first in a massive exodus from the dressing room. I was even at fault for not selecting Sharpe in the one-day Fenner Trophy competition 'because he needed the money'. It was fierce and revealing, even allowing for the fact that he had perhaps drunk a bit too much – he was talking at the top of his voice with his arms waving about, extremely agitated. In the end I remember him saying: 'I won't leave, I won't give you that satisfaction. But we'll have you.' My last word was 'You are all wind and piss,' which wasn't very edifying. In the event, Hutton made himself available the following season on a restricted basis and Wilson never departed for the happier pastures at Derbyshire.

The situation was clearly intolerable and not just because of Wilson's outburst. I suppose I could have marched off to the committee and demanded some sort of disciplinary action but I did not see the sense of telling tales out of school and, frankly, I did not expect they would take decisive action against him. When I was elected captain the vote was far from the unanimity that Yorkshire had suggested; it was 7–6 between me and Wilson. So he still had a very strong body of support in the committee, a fact which explained his presence in the team even when he was bowling so badly. In practical terms, that annoyed me more than his attitude. I felt it was professional nonsense to include anyone in the side who was not in form, and that included the vice-captain. The situation certainly affronted Phil Carrick, the other left-arm spinner in contention, and that was just one of the complaints fermenting in the dressing room. Padgett was fed up at not being included in selection meetings, players were annoyed at the attitude of the secretary who seemed to think he had some function to coach and criticise in the dressing room, there was a general dissatisfaction with practice facilities and communications within the club were a bad joke. It probably sounds trivial now but it all had a dreadfully corrosive effect on a team rarely out of the public eye. Nicholson, Padgett and I resolved to put the whole irritating business before the committee. But before we had a chance, I was asked to go along with two or three other players to answer questions at a public forum, a public-relations exercise for the club. Sure enough, the first question on the agenda was 'What's wrong with Yorkshire cricket?' and there were some pretty forthright answers, most of them since forgotten. I suggested that Yorkshire needed to rationalise its tradition of using several grounds and should also involve the captain more in the running of the club. I used the expression 'managing director', which was probably unwise. It was plastered all over the press, half of Yorkshire was up in arms at the thought that it might lose a local county match and the committee were clearly displeased at any suggestion that involved changing the status quo. It might have been a storm in a teacup elsewhere but in Yorkshire it was back-page news. More Boycott controversy.

A meeting with the committee was even more important now but it was not easy to get Yorkshire to agree to that. Nicholson and I went to see Sellers, we lobbied the committee members for Bradford, who imagined we wanted to take matches from them, and finally we managed to see several senior committee members on 20 November. The atmosphere was distinctly cool. The Yorkshire committee was not accustomed to being questioned – certainly not by the players – and this feller Boycott was clearly in favour of changing the Natural Order of Things. Where would it end? The club chairman Arthur Connell made the point icily that in future I might consider club policy before I made public pronouncements. I answered readily enough that I would if I knew what club policy was! Almost by chance it was decided that in future the first- and second-team captains of Yorkshire would be co-opted on to the cricket committee. It was a significant step forward even if it took the club a full year to put it into practice. It was also decided then that Yorkshire would have no nominated vice-captain the following season, which might save a bit of embarrassment, and that immediate steps would be taken to sort out our other grievances. By Yorkshire standards, it was quite revolutionary, even if it was largely a matter of believing it when we saw it.

After the meeting John Temple asked to have a quiet word and informed me out of the blue that he reckoned I would one day become captain of England. It was an extraordinary comment considering that I was very nearly at the end of my tether as captain of Yorkshire. The last two years seemed like a lifetime and we did not appear to be making any progress. I told Temple that I'd had a bellyful of banging my head against a brick wall. I was practically working seven days a week for the club, which would not have bothered me had it shown some positive results. Instead, we were being slammed in the press, a clique of senior players was being downright obstructive and the committee did not seem prepared to back its captain fully. I was close to tears, totally dispirited by the whole situation. 'If you want my resignation you can have it now,' I told Temple, who instead repeated his conviction that I would one day be captain of England. He probably said it in the belief that it would cheer me up but it seemed totally irrelevant. My preoccupation was to make a good job of captaining Yorkshire – and deep down I still felt I could do it. But the politics, the back-stabbing and the manoeuvring were about as much as I could take. I had to leave the room before I broke down completely and I was still in a depressed state when I got home. My mum didn't interfere in matters of Yorkshire cricket, though she took a healthy interest in how I was getting on. She listened to the discussion that followed between a friend and me and agreed that I was too intense, I was spending far too much time brooding about the job as captain and everything that happened was affecting me emotionally. I was so preoccupied by the captaincy that I was neglecting my real job, which was to play cricket. Leave more of the heartburn to the committee and concentrate more of my best years playing well for Yorkshire and England; sound enough advice, but easier said than done.

Tony Nicholson, big and strong, daft as a brush when it suited him and the very best of Yorkshiremen, had suffered a heart attack and very nearly died. That realisation alone would have been enough to speed most men into retirement, but not Nick. He had been awarded a benefit at Yorkshire and he was determined to play through the coming season rather than accept what he called 'charity money'. Tony was a very good bowler who should have played for England but through force of circumstance never did. A wonderful teller of stories and one of life's compulsive moaners, Nick would launch into the most fearful diatribe against everyone and nobody in particular from time to time; anyone who didn't know him would imagine he was a dreadful malcontent. But it was just Nick's way. He did not have a malicious bone in his body and a dressing room full of men like him would have been totally committed to Yorkshire – though decidedly noisy and rumbustious in the process. Tony was out of hospital and doing everything he could to support me when many men in his position would have been looking for support themselves. I told him I was brassed off and thinking of giving up the captaincy but he urged me not to do it. 'There's only one captain in the country better than you. Close's better,' said Nick with disarming finality. 'Have a good Christmas and forget about Yorkshire. It'll do you good.' He might have been my grandad. We went together to see the Yorkshire committee and ended up trying to tie the loose ends on contracts which should have been signed in April! By the time we finished it was three days before Christmas.

Early in 1973 I spent some time on holiday in South Africa, doing a little coaching of schoolkids, playing when I could, generally making an effort to recharge my batteries. It should have been innocent enough – but not for me. A new controversy had already developed and, as usual, it got completely out of hand. Boycott, it seemed, had perversely refused to tour with England and was now sunning himself while the team suffered in the Test series. By the time the facts were explained, the myths and an unflattering image of selfishness had taken hold.

I had received the usual enquiry about my availability to tour India, Pakistan and Ceylon in mid-July and had subsequently informed the TCCB secretary, then Billy Griffith, that I was unable to go. Quite simply, I was afraid for my health: having lost my spleen as a ten-year-old, I had been vulnerable ever since to infections. Whatever the attractions of a tour of the subcontinent, there wasn't a lot to be said for their standards of hygiene. I discussed the situation with my doctor, who strongly advised me against making the four-month tour. Billy Griffith was aware of my health problems, having been manager when I was taken seriously ill in Ceylon on the way out to Australia in 1965, and I had already outlined my misgivings to TCCB assistant secretary Donald Carr. Griffith asked me to reconsider when I first told him I was unavailable and revealed that it was the selectors' intention to make me vice-captain under Tony Lewis, which augured well for captaincy aspirations in the future. But there was still no way I could risk the trip: I had vividly painful memories of earlier health problems. In any case, it was not exactly unusual for players to pull out of India tours: Hutton, May, Washbrook and Alec Bedser had turned them down in the past and Illingworth, John Snow and John Edrich had already declared themselves unavailable for the tour coming up. That, it seemed, was okay.

Griffith accepted my decision and the reasons behind it. Remarks about health fears might not go down too well in India and we were anxious not to offend anybody. So it was agreed that I should decline the tour offer for 'personal and domestic reasons', which was, incidentally, the justification offered by the others who had made themselves unavailable to tour. I really thought that the whole business would end there.

No such luck. In no time at all, and especially when England did badly on their tour, the press was full of stories about how I should have been out there – as if I had simply thumbed my nose at the chance. Tony Greig made a remark about players 'picking and choosing' their tours, and it became fashionable to suggest that I had refused to tour because I was piqued at not being chosen as captain. There was even a belief that I had turned down the tour because I preferred to make more money from business interests in England and then South Africa. It was so much tripe, of course, but it became obvious that I had made a mistake in not revealing the full story right at the outset. The fact is that if I had been involved in some sort of elaborate, self-centred strategy it would have made no sense for me to stay at home. I could have accepted the vice-captaincy and waited for Tony Lewis to fall from favour, as he surely would. I make no secret of the fact that I did not agree with the choice of Lewis as captain but I would not have made that tour under anybody. Ironically, my unavailability opened the door for Mike Denness, who was drafted into the tour party and made vice-captain in deference to his success with Kent that season. Had I gone to India, history might have been written rather differently; there again, so might my epitaph. The press was having a field day, stirring up stories about my supposed dislike of Lewis (I still have a copy of the good-luck letter I wrote to him before the tour) and the fact that I had blotted my copybook with the men at Lord's. It was even suggested that my decision would lead to a major

Len Hutton (twice) and Boycott are the only Yorkshiremen to have scored seven consecutive fifties in first-class cricket.

international row because so many players had 'snubbed' India. When I turned up in South Africa, it looked for all the world as though I was simply doing my own thing and to hell with England. I finally wrote to Griffith, reminded him of my previous problems on tour and the loss of my spleen and asked him to make all the details known to the press. The adverse publicity, built on ignorance of the facts, was more than I was prepared to take.

The obvious question is, why did I not make all the facts known in the first place? Had I known in August what I knew a few months later I would certainly have done so. First of all, I was asked to play down the health-risk angle for fear of offending the cricket authorities in India. And secondly, I considered that my personal medical history was not necessarily public property. Nobody had made a great fuss when Illingworth, Snow and Edrich dropped out and I naively imagined I would be treated much as they were.

I still have a letter which I received from Griffith. He said he would inform the press and added: 'I feel the difficulty about explaining your inability to tour India and Pakistan is that it was not made at the time when the invitation was made to you. I can appreciate, of course, that they are of a very personal nature and might have offended the countries concerned although I feel such reasons were perfectly understandable.' So much for the sound and fury that seemed to have filled most back pages for the past few months. Yet the explanation never really erased the harm done to my reputation by weeks of guesswork and controversy. Whatever else the episode did, it must have confirmed to the authorities at Lord's that they were dealing with a 'newsworthy' and usually 'controversial' character. I don't suppose they were too delighted at that.

When I got back from South Africa it became pretty obvious that my attempts to represent the Yorkshire players' points of view had not gone down too well with the committee. We were still involved in negotiations regarding my contract – chiefly because of problems created by a national wage-freeze – and the attitude of the committee verged on simple bloody-mindedness. I met John Temple, in the car park of a pub called the Brotherton Fox improbably enough, and he coolly informed me that the committee felt I was acting 'like George Best'! As dopey comments go it took some beating but it did indicate how difficult relationships with the committee might be. Some years previously in Australia I had met a Barnsley solicitor, Duncan Mutch, who volunteered his help if ever I needed it. I contacted Duncan, he sorted out the contract difficulties quickly and thereafter became my invaluable helper and adviser. Duncan loved cricket – he was a member of Lancashire as well as Yorkshire and has since become a Lancashire vice-president, not that I hold that against him . . . When I desperately needed the clarity of a legal mind, and the need became more frequent as the years went by, Duncan was an inestimable help.

I signed my contract in April – on Friday the 13th to be precise – amid a blaze of quite unnecessary publicity at Headingley. I accepted a contract for one year because I did not want to commit myself to long-term financial details at a time of wage restraint – and that prompted a biting little letter from the committee. It was written on 15 May, but Joe Lister needed a fortnight before he could pluck up the courage to hand it to me. The committee had already agreed to award me a benefit in the 1974 season and the letter made it curtly plain that since I had not actually signed for 1974 there was no certainty of a benefit. In other words, it threatened the loss of my benefit if I did not toe the line and sign a longer contract pretty smartly. Lister was embarrassed at having to write it and just as reluctant to pass it over, and I can't say I blame him. It certainly was not designed to improve relations between committee and captain even if, when pressed, the official line was that it had never been intended to withhold a benefit and that the club hoped I would play for Yorkshire 'perpetually'! Steady on . . .

14

The Worst of Times

On the face of it, the 1973 playing season was one of the more miserable in Yorkshire's history. We notched up a macabre sort of first when we were beaten by a minor county, Durham, in the Gillette Cup; we were bowled out for only 69 in the Roses match; and we even managed to top that by being dismissed for 43 on a sticky wicket at the Oval. It was the sort of stuff that deepens wounds and brings antagonism to the surface – yet the atmosphere in the Yorkshire team was healthier and more united than at any time since I became captain. The reason for that was quite clear in my book: Hutton and Wilson did not spend much time with the first team.

Hutton had made himself unavailable for most matches in order to concentrate on his business affairs, and Wilson was dropped after a horrendous loss of form which culminated in a nightmare performance at Edgbaston. Wilson struggled for form early in the season but the committee felt sure he would come good if he were given enough bowling. I was under orders to bowl him at Edgbaston, and Temple was there to see the public humiliation of a man who had lost form completely. The ball was reaching the wicketkeeper second or even third bounce; the Warwickshire batsmen plundered Wilson and then treated him with a sympathetic sort of indifference which may have hurt him just as much. It was sad and I sympathised with Wilson as a professional, but the signs of his decline had been obvious for some time, even if not to him.

Billy Sutcliffe had remarked that Wilson seemed to have lost it when he returned from the England tour of Australia two years earlier. His rhythm had gone and his arm was getting lower and lower. Once his performance waned, Wilson lost confidence and that, for him, was the kiss of death. He lived on confidence; he was a madly, maddeningly enthusiastic cricketer at his best, leaping and prancing, waving his arms about – affectionately dubbed in the county's press boxes 'the demented frog'. Wilson earned his reputation in a team which was unquestionably the best in the land. Fred or Illy bowling at the other end, Close perched so close to the bat that he robbed the batsman of oxygen – a ruthlessly created pressure which few batsmen could withstand. And the sight of Wilson gyrating and twisting as though every delivery was certain to take a wicket was unnerving in itself. So Wilson took his share of wickets and helped Yorkshire to win matches, which was precisely as it should be. His strong hitting down the order and his excellent fielding were factors not to be underestimated either. But he was a reasonable rather than an outstanding bowler and when the team changed, when there was nobody to squeeze down the pressure at the other end and no Close waiting to catch pigeons, Wilson's powers waned. He was always a great storyteller, bubbling with enthusiasm and embellishing every tale until it became larger and more impressive than life. Unfortunately, the high quality of his own bowling, firmly fixed in his mind, became the tallest story of all. He could not accept the realities of his decline so he took the easier and obvious way out: he blamed his new captain.

I always believed and still do that Don Wilson at heart was a straightforward, inveterately enthusiastic character, a simple sort of guy in the nicest possible way who would share his last pound. He was not consumingly ambitious – but his wife was, and therein lay the root cause of his attitude towards me. Jill had a very well-developed sense of her own importance and a clear picture of what she thought he should be. The situation was quite obvious to anyone close to the team at the time, but there wasn't a great deal we could do about it. Mrs Wilson was an important factor in the anti-Boycott movement – her influence was insidious, but considerable.

Boycott has scored at least one Test century against all six countries he has played against in Tests.

In the absence for most of the time of Hutton and Wilson, Sharpe enjoyed a good season with the bat, and although I missed several Yorkshire matches through England calls the improvement in the dressing-room atmosphere was tangible and most encouraging. Though I had cause more than once to criticise players for lack of concentration and application, there was certainly no lack of ability. There were so many inexperienced players in the side: Graham Stevenson was eighteen, Arnie Sidebottom nineteen, David Bairstow only twenty-two. They would go on to play for England but in 1973 they had a lot of work in front of them. Phil Carrick, now Yorkshire's captain, was twenty-one and a learner at this time. But they took my criticism on the chin and I think it says a lot for team spirit that we were able to ride the inevitable wave of acrimony that followed our defeat in the Gillette Cup. Everyone wanted to know what was wrong with Yorkshire and it would have suited many people if the answer was Boycott. Before the end of the season Fred Trueman had voiced the opinion, reluctantly of course, that I should be sacked. It wasn't long before Ronnie Burnet joined in the chorus. Burnet's choice as captain was Hutton, but if there was a serious move in that direction inside the club I did not know of it. Hutton's name was linked with the captaincy only once while I was on the selection committee, when it was suggested he might lead a Sunday side in my absence with England. The discussion was brief and Hampshire was given the job.

It must have been galling for the anti-Boycott lobby to read the reaction of the players to their calls for my dismissal. I refused to comment publicly but the players had their say – and it hardly reflected a fractured dressing room riddled with doubts about the captaincy. Tony Nicholson: 'Despite the fact that we are not doing well the atmosphere in the dressing room is magnificent, better than when we were winning championships all the time.' John Hampshire: 'The captain has my full support and the support of us all. We are disappointed at not doing well but the team spirit is still good, the camaraderie is really something.' Younger players took up the theme. David Bairstow: 'Nobody could have any complaints about the team spirit in our dressing room. Geoff is fine, he has been a great help to me.' And Phil Carrick: 'I just don't understand all these claims about dressing-room disagreements and about Geoff as captain. It's as though people were talking about a different dressing room.' The committee weighed in with statements of support via John Temple and although it was unfortunate that the whole unedifying process should be considered necessary, it was a clear rebuff to those critics who rarely saw a match but still felt free to criticise me.

They weren't likely to be put off by anything as inconvenient as the facts, and in early August Trueman was at it again, peddling his anti-Boycott theme at a dinner in Sheffield to mark the end of Yorkshire's long association with Bramall Lane. The ground was to be redeveloped by Sheffield United soccer club and Yorkshire had received notice to quit, which was a considerable wrench after so many years. Bramall Lane's cricket fraternity had become part of Yorkshire folklore and the farewell dinner was planned as a nostalgic get-together to mark the passing of an era. Men in dinner jackets, wives and girlfriends in their finery, a mingling of distinguished Yorkshire players and club members in Sheffield's impressive city hall. I left the dinner around 11 p.m., quite late enough for me, and discovered later that after I'd left Trueman's speech consisted of little more than an attack on me and everything I stood for as captain. It was greeted by an embarrassed silence and when Yorkshire's former left-arm spinner and coach Arthur Booth stood up to reply to the toast he was beside himself with anger. Trueman's misuse of his platform spoiled the whole evening. I wasn't even there but the incident became another example of how the Boycott Controversy was souring the Yorkshire scene. There was plenty of evidence that embittered outside influences were more of a disruptive element than I was, but the headlines always accentuated the Boycott angle. The players' support meant an enormous amount to me but it was not necessarily prominent in the public mind, constantly assailed by stories of rifts and rows.

England's season began with a Test trial at Hove, Lewis's XI versus Illingworth's team, billed as England versus The Rest, which was a fair old waste of time. Illingworth was rightly restored as captain but it was noticeable that an undercurrent of resentment existed from those who had gone to India, directed at those who had not. I felt I had to establish myself in the England side all over again – nothing I could not manage but an extra pressure in the series against New Zealand and the West Indies. One way and another, it was quite an eventful Test summer, encompassing bombs and bruises, runs and recriminations. I felt I played wonderfully well and the press were fulsome in their praise, part of my very best years as a batsman, though I did not have time to take stock and realise it at the time. I wish I had. I don't think it would have made me big-headed but I might have enjoyed the achievement a bit more. Who can say?

During the summer it was very gratifying to read comments from men whose opinions I respect, Ken Barrington and Richie Benaud among others, to the effect that I was the best batsman in the world at the time. During the Test match against New Zealand at Lord's, Neville Cardus came to see me – a compliment in itself – and said he regarded my batting as on a par with the greats he had seen, including Leonard Hutton and Herbert Sutcliffe. 'The world is your oyster. With your skill you can do whatever you like,' he said. It was heady stuff and I was very proud, though probably not taking it all in at the time. Another memorable source of support came from an unlikely if distinctive quarter in the shape of Ron Griffiths, a Barbados-born cricket fanatic who christened me Sir Geoffrey and attracted quite a lot of pleasant publicity. It may seem a little childish, but after all the politicising at Yorkshire it was a welcome relief to receive some praise rather than condemnation. I played most of the shots in those days, including the hook, which I all but removed from my repertoire later. It is a risk shot – and one with potentially costly connotations as we shall see – but I played it quite regularly and I played it well. I hooked down, seemed to have plenty of time to play the stroke and very rarely got into any sort of trouble.

Boycott has scored at least one Test century against all six countries he has played against in Tests.

Run-outs were a different matter and the fact that I was the innocent party didn't make the situation during the first Test against New Zealand at Trent Bridge any easier to take. Dennis Amiss ran me out, calling for two and then turning his back on the second run to leave me stranded, done like a dinner. I was furious. It was the kind of situation which had so often lead to my being accused of selfishness and I felt especially hard done by since I was still anxious to re-establish myself in the side. I waited in vain for some sort of an apology, even an expression of regret. But the atmosphere between us was decidedly icy, and not a word was spoken. Illingworth sensed the mood and brought us together on the pavilion steps before the next Test at Lord's. It developed into a real old ding-dong argument with heated words and accusations on both sides – and although we determined to be professional about it a little of the tension spilled over into our batting. There was still more than a hint of mistrust on both sides when Dennis sent me back in the second Test against West Indies at Edgbaston and I collided heavily with

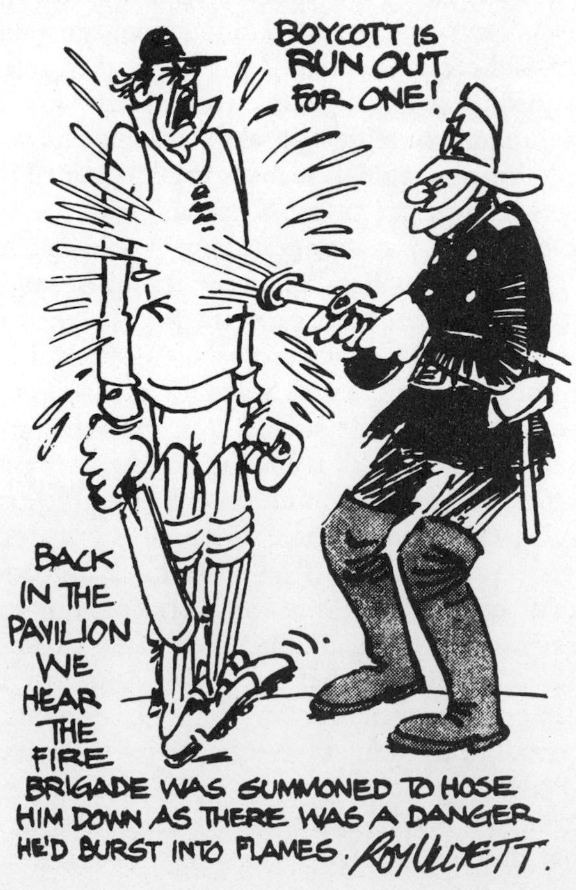

wicketkeeper Deryck Murray. It didn't seem too disastrous at the time but my ribs were badly bruised and I had to have pain-killing injections before I could bat next day, a nuisance I could have done without.

Early in my innings the West Indies appealed for a catch behind off Keith Boyce, Arthur Fagg turned it down and there followed the worst conduct I can remember from a Test team on English soil. Rohan Kanhai was the captain and the ringleader, pouring out a steady stream of invective against me, Fagg and anything faintly non-Caribbean. Fagg had to put up with it all day and next morning he refused to stand until he received some sort of apology.

I admired Fagg's strength of character. The situation was unbelievably tense and strained on the field – you could have cut the atmosphere with a knife. Taking their lead from Kanhai, the West Indians made little attempt to conceal their contempt for the umpire. If an English team had behaved like that there would have been a huge disciplinary reaction; had the West Indies behaved as badly in the Caribbean there is no doubt in my mind they would have sparked a riot. The West Indies' demeanour and many of their remarks were a disgrace. It is probably ironic and certainly sad, but if I had to recall my first encounter with pure racism on a cricket field, it would be from the West Indian team at Edgbaston in 1973.

The third Test at Lord's didn't exactly pass without incident. For a start there was a bomb scare and the match was held up while police searched the stands. I still remember the classic picture of Dickie Bird sitting on the covers, guarding his pitch. The bomb did not go off, but as far as the England captaincy was concerned the balloon was going up behind the Lord's pavilion . . .

Meantime, I plunged straight into another of the widely publicised controversies of my career. I was out in the last over of the day, hooking when the field had clearly been positioned for that shot, and with England needing 453 just to avoid the follow-on. It was a stupid stroke but it didn't come about just because I was feeling careless. Amiss was already out and Brian Luckhurst joined me to bat through to the close. He asked me to take as much of the bowling as I could and I agreed, provided we played reasonably normal cricket. This was, after all, a Test match. Luckhurst was selected as a batsman and the going was no easier for me – I was 15 not out – than for anyone else. I used to hook in those days, not as a violent gesture or as an ego trip but as a stroke selected and played as carefully as any other. I was by no means an instinctive hooker and that was just as well. I played the shot carefully and usually downward, so it was pretty safe. In the last over I hooked Boyce and the ball bounced well in front of Kallicharran, very deep on the boundary at backward square, an obvious and easy single. I set off to amble it, got halfway down the pitch and realised that Luckhurst would not go. He flatly refused and I had time to ask him what the hell he was doing before I remade my ground. I was still angry when Boyce delivered the next ball and I hooked at it – not coolly or thoughtfully but angrily. It was the only time I have ever surrendered my wicket through pure hotheadedness and when the ball landed in Kallicharran's hands I was sure that Luckhurst had done as much to get me out as the West Indies had. Being manhandled by West Indian supporters on the way back to the pavilion didn't help. By the time we got back to the dressing room I was absolutely livid and I launched into Luckhurst in no uncertain terms. As far as I was concerned he was chicken, and I told him so, just looking after number one, refusing a simple run and putting me in a frame of mind where I forgot the basic principles of professionalism. Luckhurst got both barrels.

Illingworth stepped in and told us to cool it. I found it very difficult to calm down and Illy brought in a selector, Brian Taylor of Essex, to act as a witness to the fact that he was handling a very fraught situation. It was a curious thing to do, but Illingworth had already got wind that the captaincy was in the melting-pot and he clearly reckoned he could do without a verbal punch-up. He was looking down the barrel of a second defeat in three Tests and there was considerable speculation about whether he would keep the captaincy on the forthcoming tour to the West Indies. We did not know it then, but his fate had already been as good as sealed by a gathering of the selectors – and some unofficial but influential voices – behind the pavilion during the bomb scare. He certainly did not need any sort of controversy in the circumstances and neither, for that matter, did I. My suicide stroke was unforgivable but I feel that criticism could have been tempered by an appreciation of what provoked it. I like Brian Luckhurst but I could not forgive what I saw as his lack of professionalism.

Later that night I developed a heavy nosebleed in my hotel room and had to go to hospital to have the bleeding stopped. The legend grew that Illy had punched me on the nose but there was no truth in it. We had lunch together the next day, Sunday, at Mike Parkinson's house and if our relationship was a bit strained at first there was certainly no animosity in it. England lost the Test match and the series next day, and later that night Ray called me down to his room. Alec Bedser had already told him that he would not be reappointed for the West Indies tour. The selectors favoured a younger man and had recommended Mike Denness of Kent, captain of a successful side but not a good enough player to get in the present Test team. Denness had gone to India and Pakistan as vice-captain under Tony

Lewis – after I had turned the chance down – and had a good record in limited-overs competitions with Kent. But he also had a very good Kent team laden with experienced players like Knott, Underwood, Luckhurst, Asif, Julien, Shepherd and Cowdrey. I reckoned anybody could win trophies with a team like that. Denness was nowhere near as good a captain as Illingworth and I would back my knowledge against his any day. Illingworth was naturally disappointed and he knew I would be. He wondered if I would actually accept a tour to the West Indies under Denness's leadership, knowing I had little respect for the man as a captain. Denness had not played in a Test match that summer; he was not good enough as a player to command a place; and his success at Kent reflected the quality of the team as much as any qualities of leadership. The professionals in the game knew all this well enough. It was not the first time the selectors had put a whole dressing room in an invidious and potentially fractious position.

I had the gravest misgivings about touring under Denness. I was close to refusing to tour, but friends urged me to go and I agreed against my better judgement. It was a mistake. Looking back, it was one of the worst England tours I have made and Mike Denness was the worst England captain I have played under. My opinion, I know, would be shared by most of the players. Denness was not a Test player and he had little experience of England tours. The more he tried to rule the roost, the less advice he sought or took from more experienced players; and the more he attempted to impose his strictly limited tactical knowledge on the party, the worse matters became. It was a mess from start to finish, an absolute joke – especially with a man of Illingworth's calibre sitting on the sidelines writing for the press.

Denness offered me the responsibility of running the net practices on tour and I refused. My personal standards are high as far as practice is concerned, far too demanding for most cricketers and I knew I would end up involved in rows and frustration. I was co-opted on to the tour selection committee and I resolved to give as much sound advice as I could, but running the nets was to be the responsibility of Denness or his vice-captain Tony Greig. Before the tour party left, Denness made several speeches highlighting the importance of not hooking once we arrived in the Caribbean. I'm not sure how he knew that, since he had never played Test cricket out there, but it was quite obvious that the admonishment was aimed at me. Shades of Lord's and Luckhurst. I knew I would be a prime target for a fair bit of short stuff on the tour, and putting me in a position where I could not play shots without inviting criticism was a pressure I could well do

The highest score of Boycott's career was his 261 not out for the MCC against the President's XI at Bridgetown, Barbados, on 24 January 1974.

without. It was a distinctly shallow thing for a captain to say.

During the first match in Barbados against the Board President's XI I made a conscious effort not to hook and finished with 261 not out. That sounds fine, but avoiding the hook required a lot of effort. It became an intrusion and severely cramped my options. If a bowler knows a batsman will not hook he can bowl short with impunity, and scoring becomes very difficult. Ducking and weaving is one thing but it does not produce runs, a fact easily forgotten when people assess scoring rates against the Holding–Marshall–Daniel–Garner generation of West Indian teams. Observers may not appreciate that point immediately and fully, but a more professional captain would have done. Ironically, I got out in the first Test in Trinidad hooking Boyce. It was not a committed hook or pull shot really, rather an involuntary act of self-preservation when yet another delivery reared off a length. West Indies won the toss and put us in on a damp pitch, a real flyer where the ball sat up and threatened to knock somebody's head off from a good length.

One delivery from Boyce whistled past my chin. I just managed to jerk my head out of the way and I reckon that was as close as I ever came to being decapitated on the cricket field. Too close for comfort. We were bowled out for 131, which was bad enough. Far worse was the revelation that if he had won the toss Denness would have batted! We simply could not believe it – not that he asked anybody's advice. He seemed to think this would be seen as a sign of weakness and in all conscience he might have been right, but at least we might have avoided ludicrous decisions and the tangibly growing antipathy between Denness and his bowlers. He set fields and resented any attempt to change them. Bowlers like Geoff Arnold and Bob Willis were rapidly heading for the end of their tether and I really felt that if matters did not improve soon, somebody would sort him out physically and violently. That prospect was lessened somewhat by the arrival in Barbados of wives and girlfriends. Whatever the demerits of having them on cricket tours might be, I reckon they lifted morale and saved Denness from a thick ear on that tour.

But we could not simply go on disintegrating as a tour party and the obvious man to advise and even lecture Denness on the facts of life was the vice-captain Tony Greig. It looked as though his policy was to sit on the fence, keep his nose clean and wait for Denness to hang himself, whereupon the captaincy would be his. I exploded at a selection committee and told Greig to his face – and in front of Denness and the tour manager Donald Carr – that his attitude was hopelessly inadequate as far as the needs of the team were concerned. He had to take more interest and Denness had to do more listening. It didn't do much for me in the popularity stakes but Greig's performances improved after that. Dennis Amiss baled us out with a superb double hundred in the second Test but nobody was really scoring consistently and it was decided by Denness and Carr that I should bat at four in the third Test at Barbados, theoretically to protect the vulnerable middle order. I did not fancy the idea at all but I wasn't anxious to rock a leaking boat and I went along with it, creating one of the worst hours of my cricketing life. Denness and Amiss put on 28 for the first wicket, then John Jameson sallied in and went at the bowling as though he was playing in a benefit match. Jameson played every extravagant shot in the book, without connecting too often, the ball whizzing off top edges and deflecting off his forearm. It was only a matter of time before he was out and naturally I was padded up ready to go in. Every time it looked as though his end was nigh I was on my feet, pulling on my gloves, picking up my bat ready for the long walk. Then he would escape, the ball would drop short of a fielder or find a gap, and I would sit down again – until the next false alarm. It was totally exhausting. I was up and down ten times in twenty-five minutes and was practically drained by the time I got in. We were 8 for 2 in no time in the second innings, so I expended a fair amount of nervous energy and still ended up facing the new ball both times around.

Batting down the order in a Test match clearly was not for me. I would have been a nervous wreck inside a couple of Tests and there was no evidence that the side benefited from the experiment. Seymour Nurse and Wes Hall approached me while I was waiting to bat and expressed their surprise that I wasn't opening. There was even a hint that I might be afraid of the new-ball fast attack. I wasn't having that. At the next selection committee meeting I announced: 'I'm opening. Let's sort out the rest of the batting order,' and nobody disagreed.

By the time we got to the last Test in Trinidad, relationships between Denness and practically everybody had worn wafer-thin. The press had no time for him, many players found it increasingly difficult to tolerate him and the manager Donald Carr left no doubt that he considered Denness a failure and a mistake. He let it be known, though not to me directly, that his tour report would not be complimentary as far as Denness was concerned and that he would recommend Boycott as a replacement. That may have had something to do with the fact that Denness became more and more aloof from me. He could barely bring himself to pass the time of day with me, and in the field I was invariably positioned as far as possible from the action. At Barbados I fielded at fine leg while Underwood and Jameson patrolled cover and midwicket. I realise I am no greyhound but that was ridiculous! The fact that I was favourite to take over the captaincy was brought home by an odd

little incident on the Saturday night of the Trinidad Test, when I was 92 not out in England's first innings. I received an invitation to join E. W. Swanton for dinner.

Jim Swanton was cricket correspondent of the *Daily Telegraph*, one of the most influential of the press corps and a man with a well-developed sense of his own importance. It would probably be stretching things to say that Swanton's word was law but it certainly carried considerable weight. Being invited to dinner with Jim did not quite bear the significance of an audience with the Pope but it was a strong indication that Boycott was in the establishment's good books. We dined in his room, number 427 I recall, and Swanton asked my opinion about the game, the players and so on. I felt as though I was being vetted and the incongruity of the situation struck me even then. When Swanton broached the subject of the captaincy and asked me who I could best work with as vice-captain if I were given the job, I promptly told him Tony Lewis. It was tongue in cheek, to say the least, but it was obviously just what Jim wanted to hear. Tony Lewis, nice chap,

Cambridge and all that, fine fellow – talk about getting the angels on your side, I had all on to keep a straight face. Part of me was flattered by the situation and part of me was offended. The sober realisation was that all the signs pointed to me being very close to the captaincy of England – and I have never made any bones about my ambition to achieve that. Denness's days were numbered – until fate, Tony Greig and I took a hand in the last Test.

We arrived in Trinidad only 1–0 down in the series, though as professionals we knew it could have been 3–0 on merit. It looked as though we would need a miracle to square the series – and we won the last Test by 25 runs. I made 99 and 112, Greig took 8–86 and 5–70; between us we re-established a man whom neither of us rated or liked in his job as England captain. Had England lost that match, there is no conceivable way in which Denness could have kept the captaincy. I knew the mood and the talk at the time: he was a goner. I was proud of my contribution to England's win, proud of the way I battled it out, even though the press had a go at my 'slow' scoring in the first innings. When we won, they forgot their misjudgement a lot more quickly than I did. But the achievement was bitter–sweet and I would be a hypocrite not to admit that I was torn by it at the end. In the afterglow of victory, Denness accepted the congratulations and as much glory as he could. He praised the contribution made by Greig but he never made one reference to me – it was so obvious that many of the players were embarrassed by it. Shocked, too, by the sudden change in Donald Carr. The man who was going to recommend an end to Denness's captaincy was suddenly beside himself with praise. Denness – a winning captain – had become the best thing since sliced bread. Nobody said much but there were a lot of arched eyebrows around. I felt sick when the significance of the situation sunk in. In simple terms, I had just cost myself the captaincy of England. It would have been the easiest thing in the world to have given my wicket away in the second innings, especially after a big score in the first, and history would probably have turned out very differently. I will not pretend that the thought did not cross my mind at the time, when I was out in the middle taking the flak, but I could not bring myself to give it away. This was England, this was a Test match and I had my standards. But I still believe that keeping Denness in his job was the worst day's work I ever did for England. It comes back to me, not without bitterness, when I read another accusation that I spent all my life playing for myself.

Boycott has scored at least one Test century on all six Test grounds in England.

There was a grim sequel to the series which totally destroyed any possibility of Denness and me seeing eye to eye. We had a one-day match and a three-day match in Bermuda on the way home and I expressed a preference for playing in the one-day game. I'd played in all the Tests, on the field for most of the last one, and I had a slight muscle strain that could do with a bit of rest before we launched into the English season. Denness came to my room and more or less accused me of swinging the lead, of pretending I had an injury just to avoid playing. It was the last straw: 'Get out of here before I do something I'll regret . . .' Man-management was never supposed to be my strong point but that sort of insensitive arrogance took some beating. We barely exchanged a word after that and I don't reckon I missed much.

15

England Lost

To say that I was dispirited by England's predicament would be a considerable understatement. I was dreadfully low when we returned from the West Indies and there was barely time to turn round before the 1974 English season began. Back into harness when I felt I needed a rest to recharge myself physically and mentally, back to the potential hassles at Yorkshire. It did not cheer me up to reflect that Richard Hutton had made himself available for all matches. He would strengthen the team as a player but I had no doubt the disruption would start all over again. Frankly, I was in no mood or emotional shape to take another season of strife. And that was precisely what I got. The season seemed to stagger from one controversy to the next and I'm still not sure whether they were exaggerated or whether it just appeared that way because of my mental fatigue. The effect was the same. I became increasingly despondent, less and less able to take problems in my stride. My form suffered and my spirits flagged until I had to do something drastic.

Every cricketer loses form at some time in his career. Usually he works hard at whatever faults have developed, carefully puts his game back together and picks up where he left off with no lasting harm done. When I lost form, I did so in knee-high type across the sports pages of every newspaper in the country, which did not exactly speed my rehabilitation. I could not string together a run of decent scores on the field and the familiar problems were redeveloping off it: Yorkshire did badly in terms of results and the critics sharpened their knives. One of the fiercest was Don Brennan, a former England wicketkeeper who represented Bradford on the committee and who now replaced Brian Sellers on the selection committee at Yorkshire. Brennan was an argumentative, self-opinionated sort of character who had strong views about virtually everything and did not fancy the idea that others had views of their own. He was obsessed, for instance, with the theory that we should play spinners in our one-day games, though the facts said quite clearly that such success as we had had was achieved with a seam attack. Brennan was no supporter of mine, which did not matter as long as we framed our views around what was best for the team. In fact he went out of his way to disagree with virtually everything I proposed and I walked into selection meetings knowing that Brennan would give me a rough ride just for the hell of it. We fought a running battle all season and it wore me down like water – or perhaps that should be acid – dripping on a stone.

I was selected to play in the MCC match against the touring Indians, and Yorkshire tried to secure my release so I could play in a Benson and Hedges Cup tie. MCC prevailed and I set off to the match in poor form and worse spirits, thinking over some well-meaning advice from Ted Lester that I should 'go for my shots' as one method of rediscovering my touch. It didn't work – a left-arm medium-pacer by the name of Solkar got me out twice and yet another Boycott controversy was up and running.

Solkar had already dismissed me once in Yorkshire's match against India, so his latest success, coupled with the fact that I was in very unproductive form, raised the lurid suggestion that my technique was deficient against left-arm pace bowling. Experts sprang out of the woodwork to reveal they had suspected as much all along. Newspapers printed diagrams showing precisely why Solkar had the Indian sign (*sic*) on Boycott. Most of the diagrams were just infantile enough to be ludicrous, usually depicting a matchstick batsman missing a ball that was either perfectly straight or swung in something approaching a 90 degree arc! In different circumstances it might have been funny but at the time it put me under more stress and increased a sense of creeping suffocation. Just for the record, Solkar's success against me was a reflection of my poor form rather than of his near-hypnotic abilities. I faced left-arm seam bowlers throughout my career and found them no harder or easier to counter than anybody else. Solkar was pretty ordinary when you put him in the company of men like Garry Sobers, Dick Collinge, Bernard Julien, Trevor Goddard, Geoff Dymock, Liaqat Ali and Karsten Ghavri. I faced them all at some stage but Solkar is the only one still dining out on our encounters.

About the same time, and with Yorkshire still struggling to win a county championship match, I ran into difficulties with my benefit – a difference of opinion with the organiser which suddenly landed me and a few close friends with the burden of making arrangements and attending to details. Trying to do that and play at the same time was hopeless, another unforeseen friction in a season that already had far too many. There wasn't much money about in cricket in those days – the Packer revolution and South African opportunities were unheard of – so a benefit represented the only chance a professional had to establish for himself reasonable security. If you made a mess of your benefit year it was the waste of an opportunity that was very unlikely to occur again, and here was I faced with a near-total collapse of plans. The situation was eventually resolved thanks to a lot of hard work from many helpers but it was another pressure, another intrusion to prey on my mind.

Boycott has won four one-day medals in international games for England – once against the West Indies and three times against Australia.

So was the outcome of the match against Lancashire at Headingley, a Roses match that ended in a draw with me 79 not out in the second innings. I put Lancashire in because we were unsure of a relaid pitch and not terribly confident about our batting. The consensus of opinion in the team was that a last-innings target of 244 was beyond us unless we had an exceptional start, which we did not have. The cricket chairman, John Temple, could have discovered our reasoning simply by taking the trouble to walk a few yards and ask. He might have been critical that we hadn't made more attempt to play for a win and it was pretty obvious that Brennan certainly would be, but at least he would have an explanation. Instead, he sounded off to the press and a Yorkshire rift was blazed across the newspapers. Temple was going to summon me to explain, he said. A bit of shoeleather and common sense could have achieved that straight after the match.

As it was, the whole silly business lingered on for several days while I went off to a Test trial at Worcester and made scores of 160 not out and 116. I don't really know how I did it. Perhaps it was just the sight of John Snow racing in or perhaps I was so downright angry at the latest Yorkshire affair. I certainly did not feel that it represented a lasting return to form because my mind was still in a tangle. Batting to me is more than a mechanical use of techniques. I have to feel in a good frame of mind if I am to do well, and I was a long way from that. Garry Sobers did not subscribe to the idea that I was vulnerable to the Solkars of the cricket world, and he ought to know. 'All shots in cricket must first be played in the head and this is where Boycott is having his problems. The moment he believes in himself again the runs will come,' said Sobers, and there was a lot of truth in that.

A letter to Temple and another to the club chairman Arthur Connell sorted out the so-called Roses row. It was mentioned briefly at a selection committee meeting which I did not attend and that was the end of it, though considerable damage had already been done. I was pleading for support and unity while some members of the committee were publicly agreeable and privately poisonous. That was a scenario I had to endure for years and it never got any easier to take.

The atmosphere in the first Test against India at Old Trafford did absolutely nothing to lift my spirits. In fact it made me feel worse. I did not score many runs, I hadn't expected to, and it was glaringly obvious that Denness wanted about as much to do with me as the Black Death. On a personal level I did not give a damn but professionally I felt it was a perverse waste of my experience. When I took stock of my situation I realised, to my horror, that the drive and desire to play for England had gone. There was no satisfaction in it, very little involvement, even less pleasure – and despite what anybody may say they have always been very important sources of my motivation. Yorkshire's lack of success on the field and the infighting off it, benefit problems, lack of form, lack of motivation to play for England – they all mounted up until I couldn't take it any longer. It made sense from everybody's point of view to tell Alec Bedser that I was in no mental or emotional condition to play well for England. I put it all to Alec at Old Trafford and he rang me again before the selectors met to pick the second Test team. There was no point in back-tracking or kidding myself – it was better to leave me out. Ironically enough, when the decision had been made and the team was announced minus me, I did not feel any great sense of relief. Playing for England fulfilled a life's ambition, I took enormous pride in my contribution and it was no easy thing for me to give it away, whatever the reason. When I put the phone down after talking to Bedser my head was spinning: had I done the right thing, had I done a terribly wrong thing? Why didn't I feel better about it? I was low, confused and physically ill by the time I reached Bath for Yorkshire's match against Somerset: it might have been stress-related, I really don't know, but it was real and painful enough.

So was the injury that put me out of the game for ten days and gave the anti-Boycott factions another opportunity to peddle their propaganda. Graham McKenzie broke my finger in a championship match at Leicester, a match which coincidentally marked the return of John Hampshire after injury and Don Wilson from the second team. While I was out injured, the team drew one rain-affected match and lost another by an innings and 83 runs against Worcestershire at Hull. Suddenly the move to remove me from the captaincy reached a new pitch. The clarion call from some senior professionals was 'We need leadership,' when it might logically have been 'We need to improve our performances.' Players and disaffected committee-men buttonholed the press and screaming stories appeared forecasting that I was about to be sacked as captain. It emerged later that Hutton, Wilson and Nicholson had prepared a petition to the committee calling for my removal; Sharpe refused to sign it and it was eventually torn up. But the situation was

g else t cri

Too much bottom hand, captain . . . David Bairstow takes a dim view of a four-iron off the toe.

Time to relax – with a friendly koala on a tour downunder, and in the garden of my home at Woolley in Yorkshire. Makes a change from ducking bouncers . . .

Hello Dennis Lillee. Close encounters of a distinctly unpleasant kind at Perth in 1970, when I first met Lillee and lost my cap, if not my composure. I had the last laugh that time with a century.

That hurt . . . Bob Willis breaks the middle finger of my right hand during Yorkshire's Gillette Cup tie against Warwickshire at Headingley, 1972.

A bouncer from Keith Boyce and a hurried hat-trick from me. One of the unfriendlier deliveries of the 1974 series, bowled in the first minutes of the first Test at Port of Spain.

Duck for safety. Facing Wes Hall at Sabina Park, Kingston, Jamaica, 1968.

Run-out victim with a difference . . . I nip in to run out Garry Sobers in the Lord's Test, 1969. Charlie Davis looks like I sometimes feel.

Sheer horror: Derek Randall is run out in the Trent Bridge Test match, 1977. I could not imagine anything worse.

Adelaide incident, 29 January 1971. Ian Chappell hits the stumps and umpire Max O'Connell gives me out. Hands on hips mean I don't quite agree, and my bat lies on the ground until Greg Chappell retrieves it and suggests that I should make my way elsewhere – or words to that effect.

Geoff Boycott, OBE, 11 November 1980.

revealing: John Hampshire was urging me to return immediately and play in Yorkshire's Gillette Cup tie against Hampshire at Bradford while his senior colleagues were organising a petition to get rid of me as captain. I do not know for certain if Hampshire was aware of the petition but it would be difficult for him to travel and socialise with the rest of them and not be. The senior players, it seemed, were constitutionally incapable of finding any fault with their own performances and practically neurotic about me. Except, of course, when they wanted an innings from me to add a bit of lustre to their own records. I had a net at Hull; the finger was still very sore, but I played at Bradford – knowing that if I did not my detractors would have made great play of it – and we won the tie by 41 runs.

Yorkshire officially denied the reports of my impending sacking as captain, and before the Gillette tie John Temple and Billy Sutcliffe came to me for a long and very constructive chat. It was arguably overdue, since this was mid-July, but I appreciated their friendliness and their concern. I was totally fed up with the machinations going on inside the club and I had even considered giving up the game altogether – the stresses were that intense. Tony Nicholson complained that I did not bowl him enough. He had not long recovered from his heart attack and the fact is that I was terrified that he would collapse and die. Geoff Cope constantly complained that he was not used in the Sunday side and therefore lost money – and again I was cast as the villain with some sort of a down on him. In fact I made him 12th man when I could on Sundays, so he would not lose out financially, but I feared that if he bowled in the limited-overs game he would have to fire the ball in and long-standing suspicions over his bowling action would recur. I did not want to end his career and I told him so, but he was feeling low and receptive to suggestions that I had other motives.

All that may sound rather domestic, even petty, and I suppose that in most circumstances I would have sorted it out logically. But on top of the other traumas of the season it developed an importance and significance out of all proportion. So did an article by Fred Trueman in the *Sunday People* claiming that I was ready to take my benefit money and emigrate to South Africa – total misinformation really too daft to laugh at, but aggravating and upsetting at the time.

Yorkshire's results picked up towards the end of the season when I was at last able to concentrate. I played better and became more positive in my captaincy. We won four and lost two of our last ten championship matches and won three out of four John Player League games. As usual, the politicians went a bit quiet when we were winning.

Wilson, Sharpe and Hutton left the county at the end of the 1974 season and I am sure that to this day many believe I was instrumental in getting them the sack. I can't pretend I was distraught at their leaving – they disliked me personally, created a disruptive atmosphere and didn't exactly shine on the field – but I cannot claim the blame or credit for their departure. The mood in committee was that Wilson was past his best and had to go; he anticipated that with his resignation at the end of August. Sharpe had a year of his contract to run but the committee felt he would not get into the first team next year and his presence in the second team would only deprive a youngster of a place. They gave him the option of leaving on that basis, and he got himself fixed up with Derbyshire. Hutton was sacked and given an *ex gratia* payment in recognition of his services to the club. The decisions were taken at Headingley on 12 September – it's all in the minutes of the cricket committee meeting. I was surprised at that meeting by the weight and vehemence of opinion against me. I didn't imagine for a moment that everything in the garden was rosy but I was frankly surprised to be asked questions like 'Would you play for Yorkshire under another captain?' and 'Do you think the captaincy has affected your batting?' I was even asked 'What do you think of John Hampshire as captain?' – a loaded question if ever there was one. I stuck up for myself as best I could but, as I say, I was surprised at the opposition of some individuals. Eventually I was asked to leave the meeting, which voted to recommend my reappointment as captain for 1975. I learned later that the decision was taken with a one-vote majority. The notion that I had enough clout or influence to dismiss players from the club is laughable.

But the narrowness of the vote to retain me as captain played on my mind. One vote . . . I confess I was surprised and alarmed. Although I had long been used to the sniping from the senior players, I had not been aware that a strong body of opinion inside the committee was ready to give me the bullet. It came as a nasty shock.

On 29 August I received my official invitation to tour Australia and New Zealand with England; by 19 September Donald Carr was in a flap, sending a telegram to my home in Fitzwilliam asking for confirmation, or otherwise, of my intention to tour. The days in between were filled with hours of soul-searching which finally persuaded me to turn England down. It was a decision I never imagined I would make. Had anyone mentioned the mere possibility of it to the kid who played in the South Yorkshire back-streets or the young man who battled his way into the Yorkshire and England sides, he would have been invited to go forth and multiply. I would have considered him certifiable. But the culmination of events, circumstances and attitudes was too much to resist. I knew I could not go to Australia and do a good job for England.

Part of the reasoning, I think, was fairly obvious. I had no confidence in Denness's professional ability and no respect for him as a man and another tour like the previous one to the West Indies was the last thing I wanted. Then there was the Yorkshire situation and not least the realisation that I was close to losing the captaincy. I really needed time to sort out my mind on that one. Other less obvious factors were in play and on my mind, even if most people were unaware of them at the time.

My benefit year had staggered through more than its share of problems and hanging over me, believe it or not, was the threat of a prosecution and the possibility of going to jail! It stemmed from a raffle which we had organised for a car donated by Vauxhall Motors. I am still not aware of all the legal ramifications but suddenly two detectives turned up at my house and informed me that the matter of prosecution was being considered. I nearly had a fit, I could see the newspaper headlines: 'Win a Vauxhall car and visit Geoff Boycott in clink.' I was desperate that the whole business should not get into the papers but I was also aware that I must play fair with those people who had taken part in the raffle. We ended up replacing the raffle with a 'Spot the Ball' sort of competition and the whole thing cost us money. Far worse than that, it played on my mind through the latter half of the season: in fact, it was not until after Christmas that I received a letter telling me that no further action would be taken. The whole affair may seem incongruous now but it was a source of real anxiety at the time. Yorkshire's attitude did not help overmuch. They were drawn into the whole silly mess and Joe Lister gave me a hard time, as he had throughout my benefit year. It even reached a point where Lister would not release my benefit money and I had to ring the club treasurer to get hold of it. Another unnecessary aggravation, another brick in the wall of frustration and worry.

Added immeasurably to that was the constant concern for my mother's health. She developed rheumatoid arthritis soon after my father died and it grew progressively worse to the point where the pain became intolerable. I never saw her cry, she was too strong and proud for that, but I would go home at night and find her sitting in the dark, hunched over like a woman twice her age, moaning to herself with pain. She could not carry a kettle or bring in the coal; there were times when she couldn't even turn a key in the lock. One day she took thirty-two aspirins to try and deaden the pain. She admitted herself that it almost drove her out of her mind. I fixed up for her to see a consultant specialist and she underwent several weeks of treatment at the spas in Harrogate. Wax baths, injections, electrolysis – the specialist tried everything and did succeed in giving her some relief. But she still had her bad days filled with pain, although typically she would insist, 'It's all right. It's not as bad as it used to be.' I was the only member of the family still at home and I clearly did not relish the prospect of leaving her to fend for herself for four months. I doubt if she could have managed. In different circumstances I suppose we could have made arrangements, reached some sort of a working compromise involving friends and relations, but it certainly would not have been easy. I already lacked the motivation to play for England on tour and Mum's condition added to my determination not to go.

I travelled to Lord's on 23 September and explained my situation to Alec Bedser and Donald Carr, trying as far as I could to give all the reasons for opting out of the tour without involving them in every tiny detail. I don't know if they would have appreciated a blow-by-blow account of the machinations at Yorkshire, and I did not, for instance, go into details about my mum's illness. It didn't seem fair to her at the time. They listened, accepted my reasons and subsequently wrote me nice letters expressing their regret and understanding. I put my thoughts in a letter to Alec at the same time and it still says something about my state of mind.

> When we had our talk at Old Trafford early in the summer I tried to explain to you how I felt. It was difficult to explain in its entirety but I had been reluctant to join the West Indies touring party and was only persuaded to go by friends against my better judgement; looking back I was unwise to go to the West Indies and if I had taken a rest over the winter I think I should have been much better equipped at the beginning of the English cricket season. Instead of which I found myself at the beginning of the 1974 season contemplating retiring altogether and it is perhaps not a coincidence that at that time I was just about the same age as Peter May and Ted Dexter were when they retired.
>
> I am thankful that in the last six weeks of the season, having had some rest from international cricket and its resulting tensions, I began to play much better but I still don't feel that I am playing as well as I can play when I am at my normal peak.
>
> I am sure that if I am to regain my form I must have another winter free from cricket at the highest level and that this should enable me to look forward to the 1975 season with more confidence. After ten years in the international arena John Edrich was dropped from the England team and has now returned after two years' respite. His results this season prove how beneficial the break was for him.

You will know some of the pressures to which I have been subjected during the last twelve months and I think you will understand how, for example, the press expect me to turn in a high standard of performance in every match I play, and how they are hypercritical if I fail to do so. By the standards of the press I was a failure in the West Indies although my record there was fairly good. Similarly I have been a failure in their eyes this summer although I did in fact end up as the leading Englishman in the batting averages and began to have some measure of success in leading Yorkshire, none of which has been mentioned in the leading daily newspapers. Consequently the public at large feel I have played badly.

If I were to operate at something lower than my best in Australia this winter the criticism would continue and this would undermine my confidence further. I feel very strongly that this would be detrimental to the team's performance particularly on a long Australian tour and especially if we run into a bad spell.

Please do not think I am taking a selfish view. This summer, because I felt it right to stand down, I lost substantial Test match fees and probably failed to collect a number of additional, sponsored for my benefit, Test runs. This winter I shall lose the tour fees and earnings and the opportunity to add to my total of Test and first-class runs. This is something which goes against the grain but I believe it to be right from England's point of view.

There are, of course, other personal pressures which have played some part in this decision, none of which I have mentioned to you but perhaps it would be right to tell you of my position at home. Since my father died in 1967 my mother has suffered almost continuously and very seriously from rheumatoid arthritis. You will know that I am the only one of three sons still at home and therefore have a responsibility towards her. It is very questionable that she could cope on her own for five months in her present condition, even so, she would not have stood in my way.

I am desperately sorry to have given you this decision and can only hope for some measure of understanding – cricket administrators, press and public alike . . .

Hardly Shakespeare but there again, hardly the sort of letter I ever expected to write. Alec wrote a kind letter in reply, which was typical of the man and very much appreciated in the circumstances. He knew that the decision had not been reached without a great deal of soul-searching and added: 'I fully understand your reasons and I trust your rest from the international scene this winter will bring you back refreshed.'

There was no suggestion at that time that my decision not to tour would have any long-term repercussions. Donald Carr, apparently as understanding as Bedser, asked me if I had any plans to play cricket anywhere in the winter and I told him I had none, though I usually went to South Africa for a few weeks to prepare for the season. Carr mentioned that if I did decide to play cricket anywhere, I should get in touch with Lord's. I barely gave it a thought. By the time I did ask for permission to play, on a tour of South Africa organised by Derrick Robins, England's fate in Australia had been sealed very painfully by Dennis Lillee and Jeff Thomson. All through the winter, the English cricket public was bombarded with stories about the Australian pace attack, just as our batsmen were battered and bruised to the point where the tour party had to send for replacements. Resentment of my decision not to tour grew, fanned by the press and now based on a thinly disguised accusation that I opted out of the tour to avoid having to face the fast-bowling pair. The facts destroy that theory, but so what? Lillee had injured his back in February of 1973 and there was a real possibility that he would never play cricket again, let alone get back into the Test arena. That was the situation when I made my decision. And Thomson was barely heard of. He had made his début against Pakistan at the end of December 1972 and finished up with 0–110 off 19 overs, which did not exactly represent instant stardom. Thommo disappeared from Test cricket until England arrived in 1974. It is surely significant that Alec Bedser wrote to me about him from Melbourne on Christmas Day: 'We've struck a lot of bad luck with injuries as well as coming up against a bowler who is pretty quick,' he wrote. 'Thompson (*sic*) has a curious slinging action and I think because he brings his hand from behind his back it's not easy to pick up as quick as a normal delivery. He is a strong fellow with a very strong back and seems to be able to get lift from a better length than most. He is quicker than the pace Lillee is bowling and he is not slow – so he is quite a handful. . . .' Thomson came as a nasty surprise to England on that tour, but not one that I could have anticipated when I declined the invitation.

That, as I say, was not the view taken by some distinctly scurrilous articles in the press – and when it was learned that I might have gone on the Robins tour, the reaction bordered on hysteria. The invitation to tour was first extended by Robins' captain, Brian Close, in a phone call on 9 February. I wasn't particularly keen and in fact I was having treatment for a touch of tendonitis, but the time was about right for me to start getting ready for the 1975 English season and the tour would provide good, competitive cricket with and against established players. It made sense and I asked Lord's for permission.

Permission was refused. Derrick Robins anticipated controversy by withdrawing his invitation, and the story hit the press in a welter of large, lurid headlines. The fact that England had lost the series despite a win in the last Test did not help: Boycott was cast as the villain who opted out of England on a whim and at his own convenience. I agree that the timing of my Robins request was awful, not that I appreciated it at the time, but I still insist the whole episode was blown out of proportion – and the myth that I was afraid to face fast bowling was just another barb in the armoury of the mischief-makers. Nevertheless, my reputation hit rock-bottom. The critics had a field day and even those who would normally have sprung to my defence felt uneasy and a bit bewildered. I did not exactly feel chirpy myself. The winter's rest that I had tried to give myself seemed to have been eaten up

by controversy. Instead of marshalling my thoughts I found myself even more confused. It seemed that whenever I played for England I was responsible for Yorkshire's lack of success; and if I did not play for England I suddenly became the best batsman in the world who had a sacred duty to be there. Only one thing seemed clear, or at least half clear: captaining Yorkshire and playing for England had somehow become incompatible. I wasn't sure how that situation had come about and it certainly did not affect other county captains in the England side but it sure as hell seemed to stir up all kinds of problems for me.

Yorkshire had already been in a flap about my decision not to tour. The president Sir Kenneth Parkinson and John Temple asked me to explain my decision fully because 'certain committee members feel awkward when they go to functions around the county and don't know the inside story'! That must have been really dreadful for them. As far as I was concerned I had made my explanations in the proper quarter. I trusted Sir Kenneth with confidences but I did not feel so comfortable with Temple, which did not augur too well for the coming seasons at Yorkshire. I was desperately anxious that my winter of 'rest' should not be wasted altogether so I asked for a meeting with Sir Kenneth and Arthur Connell in mid-February 1975.

We met at the offices of the *Yorkshire Post* (Sir Kenneth was chairman of the company), and we thrashed out our views on the state and future of the club. But it was more than a talking-shop – plenty of those had achieved very little – and I went armed with a typed list of ideas and complaints. It struck me that there had not been a single season since I took over as captain when I felt I could trust the whole committee or rely on their support. The fact that I had retained the captaincy by one vote, for instance, was now public property. Information could in many cases be traced back to committee members. That was not supposition: I had a whole list of examples of committee members speaking out of turn at functions, in bars, at cricket dinners. They were undermining the club in general and me as captain in particular and we simply could not go on without a hard look at the situation.

The atmosphere in selection committee was invariably strained. When I walked into the committee room I felt like a boxer entering the ring. Inside the club communications were bad and outside they were complicated by endless statements which some people in positions of responsibility seemed to find it necessary to make to the media. The fact that committee members freely criticised me – except when the press asked them to go on record – inevitably led disgruntled players to believe they could be disloyal too. The list was long and so was our discussion, but I was adamant that the coming season should not be as fractured or fractious as the last four. During a break for lunch I mentioned that I was contemplating quitting international cricket to concentrate on Yorkshire. It was, so far as I can remember, the first time I referred to it, though it was clearly taking shape in my mind. A lot of importance seemed to be attached to the fact that I was away from the county side a good deal playing for England and that it cost the club continuity. It was, at least, a convenient rationale for my critics. Arthur Connell advised me to dismiss the criticisms and the thought from my mind, but it was not that easy.

The Robins controversy broke and, sure enough, Joe Lister and John Temple went into print with personal opinions about my position. Only this time I am pretty sure that Connell gave them a rocket and said things were going to be different in future. The first selection committee meeting of the season dawned with Temple suggesting that we should 'clear the air', and I was more than happy to attempt to do that. What did they want from me and what did I expect from them? In a nutshell, they resented my reliance on Duncan Mutch; they wanted me to instil more confidence into the younger players; and they wanted us to take more risks to win matches, emphasising that they would back me if the policy led to criticism. From them, I expected more confidentiality, closer support and rapport with the players, and a determined effort to confine criticism of the players to the dressing and committee rooms. Only then would we build any sort of trust between players, committee and club members. It all sounds like tub-thumping, rather obvious stuff now. The fact that it actually had to be said is the most significant thing about it.

16

The Best of Times

There is not a shadow of doubt in my mind that 1975 represented my happiest hours in cricket. No amount of success in Test cricket, no time spent in supposedly exotic places on tour, no feeling of pride at an innings particularly well played will ever overshadow the sheer, unadulterated pleasure I got from leading Yorkshire that season. To say that I enjoyed playing cricket would be understating the obvious, but being a Yorkshire player that season was one long, unblemished holiday from politics, backbiting and the wrong sort of pressure. There was no way I could completely distance myself from my situation with England because the press would not let me. They still produced provocative and barbed articles from time to time, and one scribe short of a sensible story even had the cheek to 'dare' me for £100 to return and play international cricket. It filled his back page which was the only recognisable justification for it.

By mid-May – and realising that the England problem would come to a head again when the Test series neared – I was able to ring Kenny Barrington and Alec Bedser and tell them that I did not want to be considered. For the first time in eighteen months I had peace of mind and I was totally enjoying my cricket at Yorkshire, I wanted to make a go of the captaincy, our attitude and results were excellent and the club was finally showing every sign of getting back on its feet. I did not want anything to compromise that. And I wanted them to know before the decision was taken on the captaincy that season. There was no way I was going to be accused of biding my time and then acting out of pique. It may not need reiterating, but I considered by then that I had about as much chance of captaining England as I had of flying to the moon. Okay, I felt I had a lot to offer as a captain and I wanted to prove as much with Yorkshire.

We finished second in the county championship, improved to equal fifth in the Sunday league and had a useful run in the Benson and Hedges

Cup – but the really important thing was the teamwork and camaraderie which flowed through the team and even through the club. Quite simply, it was a pleasure to play. There are many theories on the chicken-and-egg lines about success, whether it is achieved by team spirit or the other way round. All I know is that a basically young and inexperienced Yorkshire team buckled down magnificently to the job. I had cause to reprimand them only twice all season – after we lost to Lancashire following a dreadful performance in the first Benson and Hedges tie and much later in the season when we seemed to be sinking to a defeat against Middlesex at Lord's. My litany was the same: 'You are professional players, you have to be able to look in the mirror every night and ask yourself, "Did I do my best today?" I don't think you would like the honest answer.' It said a great deal for the character and the attitude of these young men that they rarely let me or themselves down. When times were bad it was fashionable to bemoan a 'lack of character' in the Yorkshire team. I reckon that the squad of the mid-seventies had bags of it. It cannot have been easy for them to live under the shadow of interminable Boycott controversies and yet they kept plugging away when weaker individuals would have accepted second best and blamed their inadequacies on me. Some had.

They were a rum lot – young and daft in many ways but suddenly mature enough to take themselves seriously and accept the responsibilities that went with the job and the pay packet. The old Yorkshire teams used to work hard and play hard. The accent seemed to have shifted off the work ethic somewhat in recent years, but we got the balance right again that season. If they relaxed noisily, they had usually earned the right. In fact we lost only one championship match all summer, which would have been unthinkable only a year before. After the years of intrigue and tension, the season was a breath of balmy, fresh air. Not that it was uneventful. With a squad like ours, it was never going to be.

John Hampshire was vice-captain at my request, experienced and a forceful attacking batsman; Chris Old was good enough to be a near-automatic choice for England when fit; Barrie Leadbeater and Richard Lumb were sound, capable players and Tony Nicholson, though close to the end of his career, could still turn in a remarkable performance or two. David Bairstow was and remains my kind of player, full of energy and drive, aggressive and determined to win every match, never short of advice for the bowlers – and for anyone within distant earshot, come to think of it. Bluey's influence as wicketkeeper was massive; measured in decibels it was incalculable.

Bairstow's wicketkeeping improved that season, largely because he often kept to two spinners. It was a long, hot summer, the ball turned on dry pitches and I liked using spinners whenever I could. Our off-spinner Geoff Cope had battled through problems with his bowling action and had revamped it after tuition at my suggestion from Johnny Wardle. Cope was a big spinner of the ball and I probably had more confidence in him than he had in himself: 'Spin it, spin it for chrissake, don't just roll it out.' Geoff was a determined individual in his quiet way. It was a great pity that doubts about the legality of his action finally defeated him. The left-arm spinner was Phil Carrick, as keen as mustard even then, with a great appetite for learning and a willingness to practise. Like most left-arm spinners, he didn't turn the ball as much as the off-spinner but he had a lot of ability and the confidence to use it. Not being played much in one-day cricket probably helped him to learn his trade without the trauma of being slogged unmercifully once a week. He could bat, too, well enough to rate as a genuine all-rounder in terms of the county game.

There are few more committed competitors in professional cricket than Arnie Sidebottom, tall and lean but with a lot of guts and dedication. Arnie had played soccer with Manchester United among others – and he had plenty of ability as a bowler and batsman. No flannel from Arnie; treat him properly and fairly and he would do anything for you. He won an England cap in 1975 and nobody is entitled to be more proud of it.

Graham Stevenson was only a kid, just nineteen and with a round, ingenuous face that lit up like a beacon when he was pleased with himself. That and the fact that he was prone to behavioural irregularities which might have been associated with the South Yorkshire moon soon earned him the nickname of Moonbeam. He had prodigious talent even then, but not much idea how to make the most of it. The trick was to prevent him giving way completely to nerves and I used to stand at mid-off advising him where to bowl. 'If they hit you, it's my fault not yours.' When Stevo went on a Whitbread scholarship to Australia, the feeling was that he was a better cricketer than the guy who accompanied him – Ian Botham! He really did have tremendous natural ability but not much 'cricket brain' to go with it. I tried to help. 'With my brains and your ability, you could be anything,' I used to tell him. It became a stock phrase in the dressing room and Stevo was never afraid of using it in triumph himself.

Yorkshire humour is distinctive, South Yorkshire humour is probably unique – dry as old sticks, very cutting when it wants to be. I remember Stevenson and his South Yorkshire mate Steve (Esso) Oldham tackling the crossword in the dressing room. 'Ey up, Esso, what's a five-letter word meaning "To egg on"?' Oldham thinks deeply, staring out of the window. 'Toast,' comes the reply in good time. 'Toast? How d'ye work that out?' A deep sigh: 'Obvious innit. Two egg on toast, answer "toast".' Stevenson makes to fill in the clue and then: 'Can't be, mate. Got a V in it.' And neither of them batted an eyelid; for any evidence to the contrary it was the most serious exchange in the world. Oldham was a strong, usually quiet character who rarely made a fuss but was nobody's fool. During a Roses match at Headingley, Fred Trueman made one of his extremely rare visits to the dressing room and started to give Oldham the benefit of his advice, something about keeping his bowling arm higher. 'Just as a matter of interest, Fred, when have you seen me bowl?' enquired Oldham. 'I've been here a few times, I've seen you,' protested Fred. 'Then tha must have been up one of them trees over there because we've never seen thee,' said Oldham. The conversation stopped there.

Peter Squires played rugby union on the wing for England and was a marvellous fielder, a promising batsman and quite the untidiest sportsman I have ever met. His cricket bag looked as though it had not been emptied for a fortnight, which was probably the case, and there was no daily certainty that he would have enough kit which was presentable enough to take the field. Nothing seemed to agitate him and he was unfailingly polite, even under pressure. I once described him as an incorrigible partaker of strong liquor with an unreasonable interest in things physical pertaining to the opposite sex – or words to that effect. 'Oh, thank you very much,' says Squires, clearly quite flattered. What can you do?

Arthur Robinson and Howard Cooper may not rank among the greatest bowlers ever to play for Yorkshire but they stand firmly in my estimation as two of the finest characters. They were a little older than the other junior players and a bit more mature, always ready with an observation and clearly in no awe of the captain. If I wanted a forthright answer, which I might not like, I invariably sounded out Arthur and Howard. They would give it to me straight. They were good professionals, too, ready to join in a lark but unlikely to lose sight of their priority to play the game as well as they could. Good, solid cricketers and first-class human beings. I thought the world of them.

My critics have tried to suggest that I was some sort of Svengali figure who surrounded himself with youngsters because he knew they were no threat. It is so much rubbish and an insult to the players who climbed one mountain after another in 1975, played some very good cricket and enjoyed themselves hugely in the process. They were young but they were never weak; they were impressionable but they were not gullible. It was a season to cherish.

The match at Worcester was one of the more expensive draws in my career: I made 152 not out in the first innings and paid dearly for every run. It was my first century against Worcestershire in the championship and completed the set against all counties, so the champagne was a nice thought. The only trouble is – it was on my bill. Rain cut into the first day and there was a dark suggestion that I might get out to avoid paying for the champagne, which had already gone on ice. Next day I pressed on and players periodically nipped out for more supplies. It was becoming ruinous. Thank God for the 100 overs limit on first innings . . . But the party was entertaining. The following day I felt terrible. I had certainly paid more and probably drunk far less than anyone, but I just couldn't take it. 'If you lads can bowl on mornings when you feel like this, you don't deserve a bollocking, you deserve a medal.' Oh, the pain.

Boycott's 152 not out for Yorkshire against Worcestershire at Worcester on 15 May 1975 meant he had scored centuries against all other sixteen first-class counties. The only other Yorkshiremen to complete this set are Herbert Sutcliffe and Len Hutton.

At the end of May we played a friendly match against Scotland in Glasgow and the demon drink reared its head again. I was ill and couldn't take any part in the game, confined to my hotel bed while the locals poured hot toddy into me to effect a rapid recovery. I might well have died from the cure. Boycott and whisky don't mix very well and it took me three days to recover. Significantly, though, there was no criticism from the team about my absence – nobody in the dressing room now trying to upset our applecart.

The only championship defeat of the season was at Scarborough, where we lost by 20 runs despite a valiant 45 from Stevenson in the second innings on a 'sticky dog'. He kept hammering Fred Titmus over mid-off and cover for fours and sixes, many of them straight on to a red-brick toilet which was in obvious danger of demolition. 'I fancied that little feller,' said Stevenson. It was only after the game that we informed him who the 'little feller' was – remarkably enough, he had not known. He went positively ashen when he found out. Had he known all along he was batting against the great Fred Titmus, he would probably have patted every delivery back in frozen respect. That was Stevenson.

Brian Close, by now Somerset captain, gave us a verbal roasting when we played them at Harrogate, insisting we had killed the match by delaying a declaration. It got a lot of publicity and our retort was to take nine wickets before Somerset scrambled to a draw. We enjoyed that. And even when we lost in the Gillette Cup to Leicestershire on a poor Headingley pitch, we made a great attempt to defend a score of only 109. Leicestershire were 86–9 before Graham McKenzie and Ken Higgs pulled them through. 'Yorkshire made a magnificent effort,' conceded Ray Illingworth. 'If Yorkshire were to recruit one top overseas batsman they would probably be an outstanding side.' We appreciated the praise. It certainly made a change.

One of the more remarkable matches of the season was against Middlesex at Lord's, where we established a first-innings lead of 51, made 106 against Titmus and Emburey in the second innings on a 'sticky dog' and looked as though we were going under very meekly. Middlesex, 157 needed to win, were 63–0 at tea. I turfed the visitors out of the dressing room, told the players to pay attention whether they thought they were busy or not – and firmly put them in their place. The performance simply wasn't good enough; the bowling was dreadful and the general application was worse. Middlesex were batting on a tricky pitch and we were making their task shamefully easy. I pointed out what was wrong and how we could put it right – and the lads responded magnificently. Cope bowled Brearley immediately after tea, we attacked them like tigers and when Squires swooped in driving rain to run out last man Mike Selvey, we had won the match by five runs. I simply could not have been more proud of the team. They had taken my criticism on the chin, taken their chance and taken Yorkshire to the top of the championship table for the first time in ages. It was a marvellous vindication of character and ability, and we were even receiving telegrams telling us how good we were!

Rain robbed us against Glamorgan at Cardiff – I am sure we would have won the match without it – and I reckoned we needed to win our last three matches to beat Leicestershire to the title. But one of them was against Lancashire at Headingley and they certainly would not do us any favours. The realist in me feared we might not quite make it. As it turned out, the match was an all-too familiar Roses bore and an inevitable draw after Lancashire left us 260 minutes to score 331. I included in my captain's report a complaint about Lancashire's slow over-rate, pointing out that at one stage Richie Benaud on TV timed an over from Peter Lever at seven minutes and forty seconds. Once, while he was ambling back some forty paces, a vexed voice from the crowd observed: 'Lever, I don't go as far as that for my holidays.' A Yorkshire voice, of course. Victory in our last two matches was not enough to head off Leicestershire, as I feared, but it had still been a wonderful season. 'We are three years ahead of our time,' I insisted. 'A lot of our young players are still that far from becoming accomplished county players and even further from their best.' But I was immensely, unashamedly proud of them and will always remember a season where I rediscovered the sheer delight of playing cricket for a living. I did not look forward or back. I lived every day as it came and treasured it.

At the close of the season, during the Scarborough Festival, we had a team meeting in a private room of a hotel, John Hampshire and myself acting as barmen with contrasting amounts of expertise. After the usual round of drinks I called the meeting to order and made a little speech thanking the boys for all they had done in the summer – Hampshire and I were so impressed we had a little present for everyone. It wasn't Yorkshire style and the embarrassment showed in grins and furtive glances – until we whipped out a cache of soda syphons and sprayed them all for a full five minutes. It was absolute chaos until somebody found a key to the locked door and they had an avenue of escape, bowling Hampshire and me aside and bursting out on to the streets of Scarborough, raucous and ringing wet. Still boys in many ways, but boys who had done a hell of a lot for me in the last six months.

17

England Regained

I was re-elected captain of Yorkshire quickly and unanimously that winter, though it may be significant that two of my most implacable critics, Don Brennan and Robin Feather, did not attend the relevant cricket committee meeting. I doubt it would have been unanimous if they had, though there again they might not have wanted to be seen opposing me as captain when we had just done so well. Yorkshire's success probably put them in a pickle, which is odd on the face of it. Rather more pressingly, five players were considering leaving the club unless their financial arrangements improved – Leadbeater, Cooper, Robinson, Cope and Mike Bore were happy enough with their cricket but not impressed by the cash. The committee insisted they were hamstrung by the wage-freeze but my enquiries showed they could give more money under the merit award which I had negotiated in 1972 – so all the players received an increase of some 27 per cent. It added up to around £800 more than they would otherwise have got – my salary was already fixed – so I feel I did my bit.

It was clearly going to be difficult to maintain our impetus in 1976 but I was optimistic provided we kept our standards and the new-found sense of togetherness. By the end of the 1976 season the club was in a mess again – largely attributable, it appears, to (absent) Boycott. I broke a finger in the Sunday league match against Lancashire on 16 May and just when it had about healed I ricked my back playing an impromptu game of park football with the kids. The combined injuries put me out until 14 July, by which time something unpleasant had hit the fan. Chris Old was injured, John Hampshire's captaincy did not measure up and the results tumbled. So did team spirit. Several players approached me with stories of Hampshire's incompetence or unpopularity; men like Cope, Cooper, Robinson, Carrick and Lumb (who even came to my home) sincerely felt that Hampshire offered too much criticism and too little constructive advice. He had a sharp

In 1976 Boycott scored 161 not out for Yorkshire against Gloucestershire at Leeds – one of six centuries in the match, four for Yorkshire, two for Gloucestershire. This is the only occasion that six centuries have been scored in a match involving Yorkshire.

tongue but no recognisable evidence of a sharp tactical brain. The Yorkshire committee had told me to stay out of the way if I was not playing; that meant I could not offer advice which might have been resented. 'You have to get back quick, because if you don't there will be nothing left to pick up,' said one player with no axe to grind. It was heartbreaking to watch the spirit of the previous season gradually but perceptibly fall apart – and insidiously, inevitably, my critics on the committee began to shift the blame on to me. Ray Illingworth watched Yorkshire's match against the West Indians at Abbeydale Park and warned me later that there was trouble for me 'behind the scenes and beneath the surface'. He did not elaborate but it was ominous if not entirely unexpected news. I was, I suppose, very conspicuous by my absence in view of the team's plight. The whisper was that Boycott's back was taking too long to heal – I agreed – and by the end of June at least one newspaper story appeared to the effect that I was in danger of losing the captaincy. Here we go again.

The depth of the latest malaise was underlined early in July, when Mel Ryan, a former Yorkshire bowler and now committee member for Huddersfield, launched a fierce attack at a meeting of the cricket committee. Ryan expressed a lack of confidence in Temple as cricket chairman, he deplored the lack of rapport between the committee and John Hampshire, and he called for the election of a chairman who had played first-class cricket and would support the captain. Worse, Ryan threatened to resign from the committee and make his attitudes known to the press unless something was done. Nobody had expected Ryan's attack and Temple left the room – somewhat shell-shocked – while a heated debate took place. The upshot was that it would be discussed at a future date. It probably was but nothing definite emerged.

There were more problems at the end of the very disappointing 1976 season: in selection committee Temple, Sutcliffe and Brennan voted to sack five players – Robinson, Cooper, Oldham, Squire and Colin Johnson. Their attitude was that the five were not county players and never would be; somebody would turn up to replace them before the start of next season. I was appalled. It was only a year since we had finished second in the championship and this sort of wholesale slaughter made no sense at all. Anyone with an inkling of the realities at the club could not have put forward an idea like that. To the point – anyone who had seen much Yorkshire cricket would never have suggested it. The debate was heated and sometimes acrimonious, which did not exactly put me in good stead for the future, but I felt I had a responsibility as captain to go in to bat for the players. I admit I was as determined as the men I was arguing against, but since I was close to the team and they seemed remote from the realities, I reckoned I had to be. Padgett, Ryan and I voted against any sackings and the issue went to the cricket committee on a split vote. Four of the players were retained but Squires was not; he left the club against my wishes. I had also recommended Robinson, Carrick and Cooper for first-team caps and Cooper missed out, ostensibly because he was still dogged by a back complaint. The psychology of how far a captain fights for his players, where he insists and where he compromises with a committee, is a very difficult area. Compromise is not my style and I do not claim to be easy to deal with, but I was the only spokesman the rank-and-file players had. Should I agree to their sacking just because they were not as good as players of an earlier generation? Should Yorkshire award caps only to players of the calibre of a Hutton or a Trueman? It seemed to me, all too sadly, that we had slipped back into the bad old days of bloody-mindedness from some members of the committee. They would vote against practically anything that I voted for.

Nine days before my injury against Lancashire made the whole subject temporarily academic, Alec Bedser phoned me to enquire whether I was available for England in the 1976 series against the West Indies. My reply, in a nutshell, was that I wanted to continue the good work with Yorkshire. Next day, selector Ken Barrington and the England captain-elect Tony Greig spoke to me during a Benson and Hedges Cup tie at Hove. Their attitude, again, was that I should make myself available and would be selected. Greig went rather further than that. He confided that Alan Knott was ready to give up any claim to the England vice-captaincy and said that when he was reconfirmed as skipper, he would insist on having me confirmed in the job – for the series against West Indies and, beyond that, on the winter tour of India, Sri Lanka and Australia. Tony had clearly thought out the situation in some detail. He anticipated my reluctance to tour India by promising to have special foods flown in from Australia and said there was no need for me to play in the up-country matches. As captain and vice-captain we could work out that detail between us. It was very tempting and it was meant to be. Greig was down-to-earth enough to realise that he needed the very best team he could muster and he was prepared to be totally pragmatic in search of it. 'If you play well you could confirm me as England captain; if I don't play well and you are standing there as vice-captain, I could cut my own throat,' he said. He had not forgotten the Denness syndrome, any more than I had. But I recognised his honesty and as a professional I respected his point of view. The vice-captaincy was not a bribe. It was a genuine attempt to make use of my experience and expertise and I understood that. I promised to think it over – and then I broke my finger. Nearly nine weeks were to pass before I got back into county cricket and by then England were having a fearful time against the West Indies in the infamous Greig 'Grovel' series. David Steele was called up to face shot and shell – 'the bank clerk who went to war', Clive Taylor called him in the *Sun* – and Brian Close made a dramatic if eventually cruel return to Test cricket. Not unlike the situation in Australia during 1974–5, when England were mauled by fast bowlers – and again Boycott was not there. By the end of the season the knives were out and cutting stories about my courage and right to play for England began to emerge. I had been injured for nearly nine weeks but that was overlooked.

Early in August I received a visit at Bradford from selector Charlie Elliott, a realist not easily swayed by the political fashion of the times, who politely informed me that I was a fool not playing for England. He was adamant that I should play – but he added the interesting rider that he did not feel the winter tour of India was the right time or place to make a return. If you do make yourself available now, said Charlie, the media will crucify you on the grounds that you avoided the West Indies and are now looking for easier pickings. In any case, he thought Alec Bedser and Ken Barrington's attitude towards me was less favourable now: there was a real possibility that if I offered to go, I would be turned down.

Charlie's advice was simply to sit tight on India but to write to Bedser and confirm that I would be available for England next year against Australia. It was an odd situation. I was not falling over myself to tour India, even if I went as a protected species and as vice-captain. The reasons for that are already well documented. But I respected the fact that Greig had bent over backwards for me at our meeting earlier in the season and I knew I could play happily under him. On the other hand, there was the recurrent possibility that the press would pillory me for playing (just as they did for not playing) and the selectors would turn me down in any case. Miles of type, thousands of words, hours of the media spotlight – and no material change in the situation at the end of it. The Yorkshire situation was a bit of a mess again, the England situation was about as straightforward as Spaghetti Junction in a fog. I did what many people do in the circumstances – I opted to do nothing.

By doing that – and not for the first time – I left the field open for the media to speculate and pontificate. Fred Trueman and his sports editor at the *Sunday People* unsuccessfully offered me £500 for an exclusive article while Fred, whose influence as a journalist is apparently beyond compare, promised: 'Once I get you back in the England side, I'll get you the captaincy.' That was very nice of him; neither happened. And I discovered later that my silence gave Tony Greig the false impression that I did not want to play under his captaincy. There had been some talk about the merits of a South African captaining England and he may have been a bit touchy, especially in view of his frank approach to me earlier in the season. I spent some time with Greig at the Waverley cricket club in Sydney before he left for India and he was anxious to know why I had not taken up his offer. When I repeated my conversation with Charlie Elliott, Greig retorted that he was sure he could have got his way and swung the selectors into making me vice-captain on the tour. His strategy, apparently, was to keep them talking for so long that they came round to his way of thinking out of sheer exhaustion. That sounded plausible.

I recall a conversation I had with the Yorkshire players during the many days late that season when my England problem was being plastered over the press. They rarely talked about it – except to take the mickey – but on this occasion the atmosphere became serious and I was glad of that, because I wanted to know how they felt. 'Stay with us,' said one. 'Don't go back unless they make you captain,' said another. 'We need you more than England – but I suppose they need you too,' ventured a third. Howard Cooper's summary still interests me: 'We need you at Yorkshire as our results this season have shown. We won't do as well without you. But I think you've got to play for England – because England needs you and you are the best player.' It looked as though I needed to cut myself in two – if the endless sniping and controversy did not cut me into little pieces.

They probably never imagined it, but the officials and players at the Waverley cricket club, just across from Sydney's Bondi Beach, had an important formative part to play in my decision to return to England's ranks. I wintered there in 1976–7, scored a lot of runs and gradually rediscovered my confidence as a player and a bit more of myself as a person. Waverley was 12,000 miles and thousands of light years philosophically from the politics of Yorkshire and England. The club treated me marvellously and by the time I returned home I felt as though I had taken a rest cure. I was in a great frame of mind, though a little puzzled, perhaps – because I had met Ken Barrington at the Centenary Test and he had repeatedly urged me to make myself available for England, which did not quite square with Elliott's view that he was no fan. I was determined to find out once and for all. The phone to Alec Bedser's home began to run hot and we met, more or less halfway I suppose, at the Blue Boar service station off the M1 at Watford Gap on Tuesday, 17 May. We sat in his car, a white

Princess as I remember, and tried to cut through the fog of half-truth and misunderstanding which invariably seemed to hang over my position. When it came down to it, I was anxious simply to know whether there was any directive from on high that I should not be picked if available for England, and whether, in the unforeseen future, I would be considered as captain on merit if the job became vacant. Alec knew of no directive and said he would seek the views of the Cricket Council if necessary. It was a start. He also told me why I was overlooked as England captain when Illingworth was sacked. 'We thought you were too wrapped up in your own batting,' he said. 'And now?' 'That view has changed, I'm sure of it.' Things might have worked out very differently had I been told that four years earlier. It was the first time I received any sort of official explanation.

Bedser rang me at my home on 26 May 1977 and said he had checked with the TCCB secretary Donald Carr, who knew nothing about any quasi-official attitudes against me. Bedser could not reassure me that no such attitudes existed, he would only find out for sure when he put forward a Test squad for ratification by the Cricket Council. Carr rang me at Bradford the following day and I repeated that the crux of the situation was whether I would be considered for a place and even the captaincy in future on merit. I did not want any guarantees – Carr understandably winced at the word – but I did need reassurance. Carr was anxious that I should not appear to be making conditions before I made myself available and so, for that matter, was I. We seemed to be playing with words but at least we, rather than the media, were discussing the pros and cons. That made a welcome change. Donald reiterated that he was unaware of any high-level 'policy' about my future and added: 'I believe if you made yourself available and if the selectors picked you and if in their view they felt you should be captain at any stage, I would see no reason why you should not be acceptable.'

By now, details of the Packer Circus had broken in the press and the enormity of the situation had rightly consumed most cricket lovers' thinking. I made my position clear when asked: I had been approached by Kerry Packer and I had been inclined to join his players, but I had turned him down when I realised that his contract would cut across my contract with Yorkshire. As the list of players who had joined Packer began to emerge, I felt public opinion becoming better disposed towards me. Even some of my entrenched critics in the press warmed a little. Just a little. Public pressure on me to play for England now became positive and complimentary rather than carping criticism for what I had not done. I listened to ex-Glamorgan captain and ex-Test selector Ossie Wheatley for a long time at Cardiff. He was genuinely interested in my problems and said gently but firmly that I should ring Bedser and say the word. I remember strolling across the ground deep in thought. Would they pick me? What if I failed? What about the pressures from the media all over again? What would happen to Yorkshire? I do not deny that I had a deep-rooted fear of failing in those circumstances, amid a glare of publicity I could not avoid. I rang Alec again from the hotel in Cardiff. We talked without coming to any conclusions. I felt very vulnerable and yet I knew deep down – as I always had – that I wanted to play for England. Those closest to me had sensed the mood for some time – the desire to play for England undermined by a reluctance to jump back into the spotlight and by a fear that I might fail if I did. I don't know if torment is too strong or melodramatic a word but it felt real enough at the time. Friends simplified it: are any of the England batsmen better than you? And I could not honesty believe that they were.

Saturday, 11 June was a rainy, dank day at Headingley and it was not long before play was called off. I went home and rang Bedser with an unconditional offer to play for England if selected. Alec listened politely, without an effusive display of emotion and said he would inform his co-selectors as soon as possible. That was it. I looked at the phone back on its cradle and wondered even then if I had done the right thing. Was it a weight off my mind or a new burden for my back? I honestly did not know. Alec Bedser has said since and quite fondly (I think) that he considers me a fine player if 'a bit potty' as a person. He cannot have found our relationship easy over the years when he was England chairman. I was bedevilled by public personal problems which clearly would not make much sense to him. Yet I respected Alec for his patience and for the consideration he showed me when I was in emotional turmoil. A bit potty? It's a wonder I was not totally round the bend. Jim Swanton wrote at the time: 'He [Boycott] has to defeat his pride, accept the risks of failure and put his complete trust in his talent.' As perceptive a summation of my situation as I have ever read. It struck me as a little ironic and certainly not insignificant that at the start of my career I would have backed my talent to pull me through most situations – and would never have asked to be judged on anything else.

Boycott returned to Test cricket in 1977 after missing thirty Test matches. He scored 107 against Australia at Nottingham and shared a 6th-wicket partnership of 215 with Alan Knott, equalling England's 6th-wicket record against Australia.

Trent Bridge, where I had made my Test début thirteen years earlier, became the scene of my recall, after three years outside Test cricket. This was the venue for the third Test against Australia. The team for the first Test was settled before I phoned Bedser and they left me out of the second to make the point, I suppose, that I couldn't walk back into the side. Fair enough. I changed in a small anteroom off the main dressing room, happy with the relative privacy and pleased to note that there was no forced bonhomie or air of censure from the other players. The atmosphere was good. It felt strange to walk out to the nets, past the groundsman Ron Allsop preparing the Test strip for the following day. I tapped it with my bat: it was as hard as concrete. 'Hell, Ron, it'll be no picnic against their bowlers on this,' I said. Ron grinned and came back at me quick as a flash: 'It's a good pitch for them that can bat. You'll get a hundred on it, you always get runs on my pitches.' Hundreds of spectators behind the nets broke into applause as I approached. It was quite a reception and I was nervous, embarrassed. If I got out, so to speak, during the net practice somebody would shout: 'Don't do that tomorrow, Geoff, we want a hundred from you.' Hundreds, always hundreds – the pressure was on already.

Australia won the toss and batted, which was something of a relief since it let me gently back into the atmosphere. Whenever I touched the ball the Nottingham crowd cheered. They were great, though I felt unusually self-conscious. Australia were all out for 243, and I strode out to open the innings with Mike Brearley, England's captain after the demotion of Packer-man Greig. I have never felt so nervous in my life – very anxious to succeed and very much aware that my failure would be welcomed by some. 'If there are people who do not want an England player to succeed they must have warped minds,' I had already told the press, fully aware that some such people were sitting in the press box. 'Geoff is his own worst enemy,' said one reporter. 'Not while I'm around,' said his mate. Jeff Thomson and Len Pascoe gave me a torrid time, testing my technique and my courage with a flurry of bouncers. They had read that I was supposed to be afraid of pace, and they would have been crazy not to put the theory to the test. Pascoe looked as though he was trying to knock his own toecaps off and umpire Dickie Bird admonished him for bowling too much short stuff. Captain Greg Chappell disagreed, naturally enough. I hung on while we lost two wickets for 53 runs.

Then I ran out Derek Randall on his home ground, in front of his home crowd. I can see it now, me running head-down to safety while Derek gives up the ghost and Rodney Marsh demolishes the stumps. Artless, heartless Boycott sacrificing another victim. If the ground had opened and swallowed me at that moment it would have been a mercy. I have never felt so completely wretched on a cricket field. My own failure would have haunted me but to actually run somebody out . . . And Randall at that. I couldn't have imagined anything worse.

Oddly enough, Derek has consoled me since with the suggestion that if he had run straight and true instead of hesitating he would have got home. He says it was not my fault and I really appreciate that. But I accept every ounce of blame and criticism for what happened. My only explanation is that I seriously underestimated the agility of Thomson, who skipped across to the legside on his follow through and arrowed a throw to Marsh. The only time I had seen Thomson before was a very brief encounter during a charity match in Brisbane.

I was distraught. I had no doubt the crowd would willingly have lynched me but instead of a crescendo of boos, which I expected, there was a hollow, dismayed silence. Greig and Geoff Miller tried to help but were soon gone. I was trapped like a rabbit in the headlights – unable to escape and practically unable to move. For what seemed like an age to me – and it must have seemed a vision of purgatory to the spectators – I could scarcely play a shot other than a regimentally defensive one. And through my pain I caught a glimpse of a young man just to the right of the pavilion, chatting with the crowd and throwing his baby up in the air and catching it like a beach ball. Derek Randall, who else? I have realised since what an enormous help the crowd were to me that day. Their reaction was one of double disappointment – at the departure of Randall and at the predicament of a man they really wanted to support. Their silence was a refusal to condemn. At least it transmitted itself to me that way, and I felt deep inside I could not let them down. Part of me wanted to get the hell out of it, out of the spotlight and the embarrassment. It wouldn't have taken much of an effort to get out and seek the anonymity of the dressing room. But something in my nature would not allow me to let go, not in a Test match, not with England struggling, not against the instincts of the years and my upbringing. Alan Knott came in and talked me back from a state of suspended animation into the land of the living. He got my feet and my brain working again and we took the score from 82–5 to 242–5 at the close. All was forgiven. I went on to make a century and to bat on every day of the Test, which England won by seven wickets. A young man called Ian Botham took five wickets on Test début and the winning run was struck, fittingly enough, by Derek Randall.

On 2 August 1977 Boycott became the only England player to bat on each day of a five-day Test.

I have played in some strange, stressful situations in my time, against intimidatingly fast bowling and with the clock ticking against my team. I don't think there are many permutations I have not encountered in cricket. But that innings at Trent Bridge was the finest I have ever played. Test cricket is hard enough without the extra tensions imposed by circumstances that day – the knowledge that many wanted me to fail, the realisation that more wanted me to succeed, the Randall run-out, all wrapped in a suffocating blanket of publicity. It was my hardest innings, physically, mentally and emotionally, and I did not give it away. I'm proud of that.

The day before the Test match finished at Trent Bridge, Yorkshire's cricket committee met to discuss, among other things, the alarming recent results of the team. In my absence, Yorkshire had lost heavily to Middlesex and Hampshire – both on home soil, where the committee felt the sting of public criticism – and it was decided to seek an in-depth discussion with the captain as soon as possible. So I walked out of the relative euphoria of Trent Bridge into another barmy meeting with the selection committee. 'It's your team and it's your responsibility,' said Mel Ryan. I could hardly believe my ears. There was no logical way that I could explain defeats which took place in my absence. It clearly made more sense to talk to John Hampshire and Geoff Cope, who had led the team. There had apparently been some criticism of the team's off-field behaviour in Kent; I was there but I didn't recall any problems. Explain why Yorkshire lost when you were not there, come on – explain . . . The situation was quite ludicrous and I left the meeting feeling totally flat. Yorkshire had publicly urged me to play for England for the past three years. Every club official asked his opinion had expressed the pious hope that Geoffrey would make himself available. I had feared that if I played for England I would be blamed for results in my absence. I would have liked to be proven wrong but the situation was already clear: two Yorkshire defeats while I was away at Nottingham and the balloon had gone up. Was this going to happen every time I played for England from then on? Is that what I had let myself in for again?

The following morning I set off for Birmingham and Yorkshire's next match against Warwickshire – but not before I received another shock which shook me rigid. My mum confessed that she was having trouble with a lump under her arm and admitted when I questioned her that it had been there for at least a year. 'I didn't want to worry you, you've enough problems of your own,' she said. I'm no doctor but I had heard and read about cancer. I suppose it's the first thing that comes into your mind. It was clearly worrying mum, which was why she hadn't said anything. I bundled her off to a doctor and she came back telling me that he was sending her for tests. Driving down to Birmingham I was totally preoccupied with worries about my mum and the latest madness at Yorkshire. I got a speeding ticket and I don't think I gave a damn. The meeting with the committee was ringing in my ears: 'Talk to them, take them on one side,' said Brennan. 'I don't care if you never score another hundred for England, it's Yorkshire that concerns me,' said Ryan. I scored a century against Warwickshire, which meant that I might achieve my hundredth first-class century in a Test match, which had never been done before. And amazingly, the next Test was at Headingley.

That match at Edgbaston was memorable for an extraordinary innings by Chris Old, who batted at number five in our second innings. Rain had already ruined the game in terms of a result, but Old exploded a century in only thirty-seven minutes, the second fastest in the history of first-class cricket. Wisden has been unfair to Old, suggesting that Warwickshire fed him easy deliveries because they were somehow miffed at the match situation. The fact is that they desperately needed to get their overs-rate up to avoid a fine at the end of the season and they took advantage of a moribund match to do it. No matter, Old's hitting was absolutely extraordinary as the Warwickshire bowlers got through as many overs as possible off two or three paces. It really was something to behold and scorer Ted Lester confessed later that even he had a bit of a job keeping up with it. Ted did a lot better than some.

After the match there was a fair bit of horseplay, led as usual by Bairstow, who managed to make himself pleasantly insufferable. I suggested to the bigger lads – they would have to be – that we should fill a bath with ice and give him a soaking, and they agreed readily enough. Too readily. When the bath was ready I was supposed to push Bairstow in, but they grabbed me instead. The water was freezing cold.

The pressure built from the moment I scored my ninety-ninth century. The very idea that I might pull a century of centuries out of the bag in a Test match was somehow preposterous, unreal, too fanciful to be true. And yet it was also a real possibility, and the media weren't exactly unaware of it. I avoided their attentions as best I could; after all, pressure from the media was one of the reasons I had opted out of England in the first place. Making runs for England was hard enough, thank you. I felt good at net practice on the day before the fourth Test, but the pressure mounted steadily during the day. Letters, cards and telegrams arrived in huge numbers and I was still trying to wade through them much later that evening when we met for our traditional eve-of-Test dinner. We talked through tactics, plans and so on, and when the conversation became more general I asked to be excused. I was very uptight and Mike Brearley recognised as much without question. Off I went. But I couldn't sleep, even after watching the television. At 4 a.m. I sent for the night porter because I could not get the air conditioning to work. The room was as hot as hell – or was it just my nerves? I took sleeping pills, which was most unusual for me, and woke up with a start to discover I was well behind schedule. I rushed to the ground feeling tired and listless, barely had time for a practice knock and prayed gently that we would field so that I would be able to shake myself awake. We won the toss and batted. Sod's law.

Ladbroke's were offering 3–1 against a century from me. What kind of odds is that? Arnie Sidebottom, I later discovered, got odds of 8–1 against and even then only risked £1 – and Arnie has faith! A couple of days afterwards I got the taxi-driver who ferried Pascoe and Thomson to the ground on that first morning. A century for Boycott? No way – we're going to knock his f— head off.

It was a beautiful, warm day for batting; the pitch was good and the crowd was on my side, even if the bowlers most certainly were not. Mike Brearley got out in the first over, an increase of pressure on him which I recognised and understood. After twenty minutes, improbably enough, I felt relaxed and confident, purposeful at least. The ball was hitting the middle of the bat and the tiredness had disappeared, my concentration was good. Len Pascoe bowled me a corker which brushed my left wrist band as I played forward: the Aussies did a war dance and I held my breath. Not out. Ray Bright bowled an arm ball and I went to glance it; it brushed my thigh pad on the way through and the Aussies went up again for a catch behind. Not out again and Bright was having apoplexy. Greg Chappell moved to cool him down and Bill Alley – who knew the language – told him where to get off. Those two incidents have been well documented and I suspect the Australians still think I was out at least once. I'm just as sure I was not. My worst moment came, in fact, when I was in the 70s and I helped a short delivery from Pascoe on its way towards fine leg. I knew as soon as I played it that it was in the air, a bit firmer than I intended, and as I set off for the single I dared not look. Max Walker was patrolling that area; if it carried the crowd would let me know. In the event it dropped short and ricochetted off his knee for four. Breathe again. On 95 I pushed Pascoe into the covers for an easy single. Greg Chappell bowled the next over. Don't hook, even if he slips in the bouncer . . . look for the gap around extra cover or through the on side if he puts it in the slot . . . My mind was working overtime before he bowled the delivery that mattered.

I can see it now in slow motion. I saw it then with an amazing sort of clarity and something approaching elation. As soon as it left his hand I knew I was going to hit it and I knew where I was going to hit it. Long before it pitched I knew exactly what I was going to do, as though I was standing outside myself, watching myself play the shot. It was a fantastic feeling. The stroke was outside to in, the ball hit the middle of the bat and went just past the far stumps on the on side as Graham Roope jumped out of the way. As soon as I struck it I lifted the bat high in the air. In the millisecond that followed I realised what it all meant and my arms folded over my head.

Somehow, I was destined to get a century that day. It was my karma. It must have been written by someone, somewhere before I went in to bat.

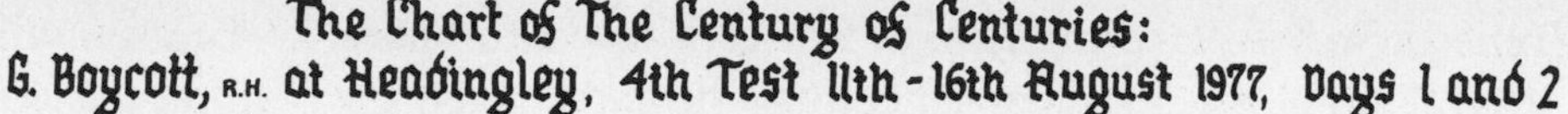

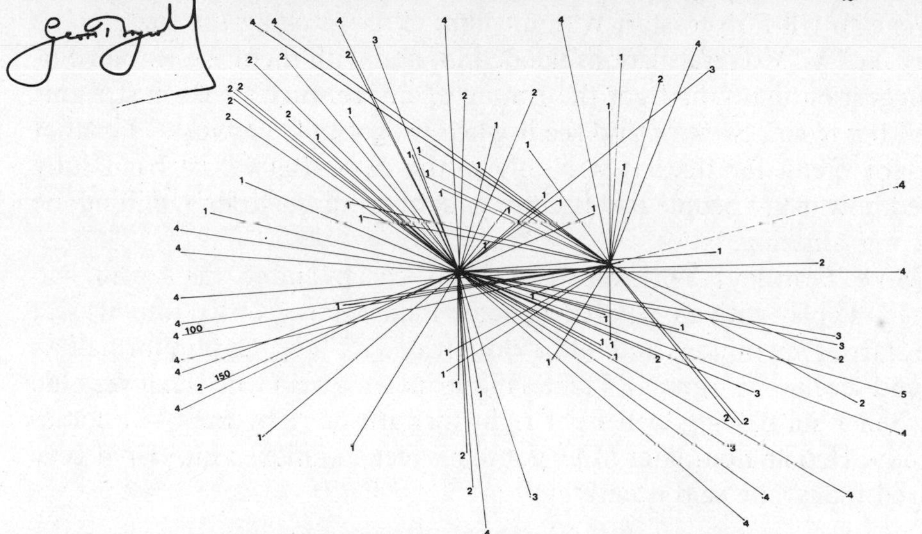

1977 England v. Australia 11th August.

Boycott reached his 100th first-class century on 11 August 1977, against Australia at Leeds. He was the 18th player in the history of the game to complete his 100th hundred and the only player to do so in a Test match.

There is no other explanation for the memory and magic of it. Trent Bridge was my finest century for many reasons; Headingley and my hundredth hundred was the greatest moment in my cricketing career. I may have played better and more importantly but this was the most magical moment of my life. I cannot remember who said what when the crowd flooded on to the pitch; it was like knowing the weather is hot without being aware of the temperature – it was just noise. And I was conscious that I was sharing something important with the people of Yorkshire. My people, right or wrong, good or bad, a source of immense inspiration.

There weren't too many of my rank-and-file supporters in the dressing room that night, not too many personal friends and none of my family. But there were plenty of celebrities from the Yorkshire committee, men who had sharpened the knife for me and would do it again when it suited them. For the time being they were happy to fawn and celebrate as though my success rubbed off a bit on them – Don Brennan, Billy Sutcliffe, Robin Feather, John Temple, Desmond Bailey staggering around with champagne. I would rather have entertained half a dozen real people. 'We must do something, we really must do something,' said Bailey. And they did. A year later those same men voted to sack me from the Yorkshire captaincy. I wonder how they manage to live with themselves.

I telephoned Mike Parkinson and Brian Clough that night. The adrenalin was still running high and I wanted to share it. Brian's wife Barbara said he was in a board meeting – he had arrived late, calling the club chairman to tell him to start without him: 'I'm watching my mate make history on TV.' Congratulations flooded in, and with them the extraordinary suggestion that I had got the timing of my century stroke just right: around ten to six, 'so we could see it when we got in from work'. I cannot claim any credit for that! It was only in the days afterwards that I fully realised how many people had become caught up in the drama, willing me on. It was amazing.

Mike Fearnley, Yorkshire's assistant coach and a man who had watched me play with an expert eye many, many times, settled into his seat at the start of my innings and told a close friend, 'I'll watch him for half an hour and see how he's going.' I take a big stride for a man who is not very tall and when I am playing well I get right forward or right back – it comes naturally. Half an hour later Mike got to his feet and moved on. 'He'll get a hundred today,' he said quietly.

18

'A Bloody Disgrace'

Yorkshire did badly during the Headingley Test. They lost by an innings to Sussex at Hove and inside two days at Worcester. The committee did not see the defeats, of course. They were too involved with the social whirl at Headingley. But it was quite obvious that team morale was at a very low ebb and, inevitably if not logically, I was expected to say why. I could quite understand that the players would not be turning cartwheels in the circumstances but it was clearly impossible for me to go into specific cases. It would have been quite unfair. 'What do you want me to do?' I asked, and there was a deafening silence. What was it Fred was fond of saying? – 'It's no good knocking if there's nobody in.' I gave up in disgust. 'You pressed me to play for England and now you are complaining about Yorkshire's results in my absence. Tell me just what you expect from me.' They had no answer, but I knew deep down what their eventual solution would be.

A five-wicket win over Lancashire at Bradford lifted the mood a bit – Roses wins always do – but it was clear that we could not go on staggering from crisis to crisis. The players were totally fed up and the senior players agreed that we should have a full and frank meeting with the president and the club chairman. They agreed to meet us in private at the Grand Hotel in Scarborough, and the night before I made it clear to the players – Hampshire, Old and Cope – that this was their big chance, perhaps their only one, to get things off their chest. It was vital that the club's hierarchy realised the depth of dissatisfaction running right through the team. I could tell them as often as I liked but there was a possibility they would think the complaints came just from me. Now was the time to put up or shut up – and the players in fact showed a lot of guts when we met Sir Kenneth Parkinson and Arthur Connell, voicing their grievances politely but forcibly enough to leave no doubt whatsoever that player–committee relations had reached rock-bottom. That meeting on 7 September had a profound effect.

In 1977 Boycott topped Yorkshire's batting averages for the fifteenth consecutive season. That year he was also top 'England qualified' batsman in the national batting averages for the seventh consecutive season.

Brennan set rolling a whole series of events which were to have a considerable though not necessarily beneficial influence on Yorkshire history when he said publicly that I should be sacked as captain. In fact, he made his remarks in a radio interview and subsequently tried to prevent them being used on the air, so his was hardly a brave, bold attempt to say out loud what some committee-men were prepared to peddle in private. Predictably, those who agreed with him said nothing once they were confronted with a sense of outrage from the public. Honest and loyal men that they were, they lay low and let Brennan take the flak. He was censured by Connell, but he put a brave face on his isolation and agreed to resign from the selection committee – a distinctly hollow gesture in October when there was nothing to select – provided he was re-elected to the cricket committee the following spring. His mates ran true to form on that one, too; they did not vote for him, and he was absolutely livid. Mel Ryan stepped up his attacks on the running of the club, making little secret of the fact that he fancied becoming cricket chairman himself. And a group of Yorkshire members got together to demand Brennan's dismissal from the committee and to seek a special meeting of the club. The Reform Group was born. Sir Kenneth Parkinson and Arthur Connell watched these developments with dismay, particularly following on their meeting with the senior players in Scarborough. They took the treasurer Michael Crawford into their confidence and determined that positive action must be taken to rescue the club, and quickly. I have no doubt whatsoever that they acted from the very highest of motives. 'In the best interests of Yorkshire cricket' was no pretentious slogan as far as they were concerned. They were genuine men genuinely looking for a solution to strife.

Sir Kenneth was nobody's fool, though he had a deceptively mild-mannered appearance. He worked out the militants on the committee quickly enough: 'I used to think they had a genuine difference of opinion but were thinking of the interests of the club. I now think they are evil-minded people and nothing will satisfy them.' It was painfully clear that there was a huge rift between committee and team. Parkinson, Connell and Crawford determined to bring in a team manager.

The first whiff I got of it was on 24 October at a county captains' meeting at Lord's. Illingworth mentioned, virtually in passing, that he had been approached by Crawford to test his attitude towards the team managership at Yorkshire. Nothing concrete, just a chat. It did not seem very important – Illy had a year of his contract still to run at Leicestershire – and I put it out of my mind. On 31 October, Yorkshire held a secret cricket committee meeting at which the question of appointing a manager was discussed. It was agreed in principle, but the committee later got quite a shock when they realised that events had moved at a gallop. Connell and Crawford contacted Illingworth and offered him the job on a three-year contract from the start of the 1979 season; Norman Shuttleworth was brought in as chairman of the finance committee to discuss details of Illy's salary; and the whole *fait accompli* was presented to the committee on 10 November. Just before I left for that meeting, I received a phone call from Leicestershire's secretary–manager Mike Turner: 'Have you stuffed me, Geoffrey?' I had no idea what he was talking about until he revealed that Yorkshire had signed up Illingworth. Mike seemed to know quite a bit of detail, though there were apparently still a lot of loose ends to tie up. At Headingley I was greeted by Sir Kenneth and Connell who spent fifteen minutes filling me in on the events of the past few weeks. They regarded the recruitment of a team manager as a progressive step, they recognised the need to employ someone who would work closely with me, and they had considered only Illingworth and Brian Close. They saw the importance of moving swiftly, and they also felt there was need for secrecy until the deal was struck. It was so secret that they were still fifteen minutes from telling the Yorkshire committee about it!

My immediate concern was for specifics – not least who would have the final say on team selection and who would take the responsibility that went with it. If the team manager picked the side he should carry the can if it didn't do well, but I could not see Illy falling for that one. 'I picked the right team but it was badly led and we lost.' I could see that scenario clearly. It was evident that details like this had not been finalised, though Illingworth had apparently been told he would be completely in charge. I could not imagine him accepting the job as manager without that stipulation. Sir Kenneth and Connell insisted there was still a great deal of talking to do and emphasised that they felt a team manager would help rather than compromise my position. 'You will have only one man to deal with instead of a selection committee where there are people very obviously against you personally.' I'm quite sure they were sincere.

If I had reservations about the set-up, and there is no denying that right from the start I had, imagine how the committee reacted. News of Illingworth's appointment came as a total surprise and once it sank in there was an enormous amount of hot air flying about. It did not take some long to realise that they were virtually giving away their powers. If Illingworth was to pick and run the team, what was there for the selection committee to do? What, for that matter, would happen to the cricket committee? There were an awful lot of well-developed egos under threat and to say that Illingworth was not received 'with acclamation' would be a considerable understatement. The nub of the problem was power – and it had clearly not been defined, at least not to the satisfaction of the committee, just how much Illingworth would have. Most of the committee, like me, regarded a team manager as somebody who would organise all the fringe areas of the team to allow the captain (responsible to the committee) to get on with playing matters. They did not fancy the idea of a team manager coming in and usurping all their functions, just as I did not fancy any compromise as far as my authority was concerned. Had the roles been reversed, I could not see Illingworth the captain accepting a manager without wanting some straight answers on the interweave of power and responsibility. Those who had made the appointment were anxious that positions should not be struck until people had the chance to talk to Illingworth. Their view was that there was a full year before he took up his appointment and that would be ample time to thrash out the little details. Like who ran Yorkshire cricket . . .

Illingworth did not seem to have any doubts himself. He was interviewed on television next day and stated quite categorically that he would have the final say in matters relating to the team. I rang Connell on that one: Illy was going to have more power at Yorkshire than any individual since Lord Hawke. Connell still felt the matter had to be thrashed out. He was clinging to the belief that everyone would compromise. I know Yorkshiremen and I knew Illingworth, rather better than the men who had taken him on. And Illingworth was never a man to compromise.

We met on 13 November in the players' dining room at Headingley – Illingworth, Sir Kenneth Parkinson, John Temple, Michael Crawford, Norman Yardley and myself. This was supposed to be the meeting at which the incidental problems would be identified and sorted out, where responsibilities would be defined. But it was already obvious that Ray understood he would have full control in team matters, and nothing happened at the meeting to change that view. The president, as usual, was very conciliatory; the pious hope was expressed time and time again that everybody would work together for the good of the club – but there was still the vexed question of Ray's job definition. And if he was overestimating his powers, nobody seemed anxious to tell him.

When I pressed the point about team selection, Illingworth indicated that he would pick a squad of players from whom I could make final choice on the morning of the match. 'If I disagree with your choice too often, I can always give you eleven players,' he said. There did not seem much room there for doubt or misunderstanding: Illingworth's appointment made the selection committee redundant and went a long way towards making the cricket committee superfluous. I doubt that is what Yorkshire wanted – and some committee members played hell about it for a long time afterwards – but that is what they got. Words like 'boss' and 'supremo' were already appearing in the newspapers, which did not go down at all well in the committee room. Ray did not want to give me any choice at all in the teams for one-day competitions, pointing out that he'd had a fair bit of success in them with Leicestershire. I pointed out in return that I had a fair bit of experience as Yorkshire captain, that I had just been appointed vice-captain of England on the forthcoming tour of Pakistan and New Zealand and that I was thirty-seven, not seventeen. At least it looked as though I would be able to exercise some influence when we actually got on the field. Norman Yardley was most insistent on that and as a former captain of Yorkshire and England he should know what he was talking about. It seemed obvious to me that continuity of ideas would be important when Illy took up his job, especially since I would be away playing for England and would miss several Yorkshire matches. 'I'd prefer not to have a vice-captain,' said Illingworth. 'I've got some specific ideas about that.' So it proved.

I tried to anticipate Illingworth's arrival by asking for a 'team manager' in the 1978 season, which would rid me of the cricket committee to a great extent and also bring any obvious practical difficulties into focus before Illy arrived. I suggested Norman Yardley for the job because I really felt I could have worked alongside him – but I might as well have saved my breath. The idea never got off the ground.

Boycott has scored more first-class centuries than any other Yorkshireman. (The next highest scorer is Herbert Sutcliffe.)

Neither did the season as far as I was concerned. I damaged my left thumb in a one-day international against Pakistan at Old Trafford – a troublesome, nagging injury that seemed to take ages to respond to treatment. Meanwhile the Yorkshire committee were unhappy with John Hampshire's attitude when he had captained the side in my absence in the 1977 season. He had made little attempt to get on with the selection committee, and really he did not seem to care too much for the job. At least, that was the cricket committee's view when they argued against Hampshire as vice-captain in April. I stuck up for him and made it clear that I thought he was the man for the job; the committee relented, with the proviso that Temple would speak to Hampshire and tell him to buck up his ideas. Yorkshire did well in my absence. For the first time under Hampshire they put together a sequence of wins in the county championship and the Sunday league. Now there were no near-desperate calls for Boycott to return and rescue the side. On the contrary, my critics inside the committee were quick to point to the results as clear evidence that Yorkshire could do without Boycott altogether.

Boycott: The Autobiography

The suggestion, naturally, found its way into the press, and the back pages again screamed so-called stories about Boycott's future. Most of them were sheer supposition, but from my vantage point on the sidelines it looked as though they were inspired by somebody or something at the club. It was suggested in one newspaper that I was about to move on to Leicestershire in some sort of swap for Illingworth; another suddenly came up with the discovery that I had refused to sign a contract for longer than one year. True enough, but of no significance in relation to the appointment of a team manager. The same report suggested that Yorkshire were in the dark about the progress my injury was making – a mischievous piece of nonsense considering I phoned the secretary virtually every day. Then Illingworth went into print with a suggestion that he might actually play for Yorkshire if the circumstances warranted it – and in another article he championed Hampshire as captain of England in place of Mike Brearley. Here we had Yorkshire's team manager-elect saying that he might play again for Yorkshire, while purposefully sidestepping the question of who would be captain if he did, and advocating Hampshire as a better captain than Boycott. It was not altogether surprising that the press speculated about my future: I was so fed up that I wrote a letter to *The Times*, with Yorkshire's permission, stating categorically that I intended to continue playing for Yorkshire and England 'just as long as I am able to maintain the proper standard of professional ability'. The whole situation seems fantastic even looking back over the years.

Boycott has come top of the national batting averages six times: in 1968, 1971, 1972, 1973, 1977 and 1979.

Yorkshire played Leicestershire on 10 to 13 June and although I was not there it has been suggested to me since, by Leicestershire players, that this was the period when Hampshire and Illingworth established the attitudes and the understandings that would cost me the captaincy of Yorkshire. Illingworth spent a lot of time with the Yorkshire players and passed most of that time in deep conversation with Hampshire. The Leicestershire players were affronted that Illingworth, who was still their captain, was so blatantly anticipating his move to a new county. They were especially dismayed when Illingworth made a declaration which looked far too generous on a flat pitch. A major row developed in the Leicestershire dressing room on the last day. The Leicestershire players questioned very strongly the tactics of their captain, which resulted in Yorkshire looking good at Leicestershire's expense. And his long conversations with Hampshire were not entirely about the weather, as I discovered a few days later at Bradford when I was confronted by Hampshire in a decidedly bad mood. At Leicester, he said, Illingworth had told him that I did not trust him (Hampshire), and that I thought he was after my job. He was obviously angry and I can understand why. Nobody likes to hear that sort of thing, least of all from a third party. 'If you did say that, I never want to play under your captaincy again,' said Hampshire. 'In fact I am not going to. I'm going to the committee. I want a yes or no.'

I denied having said that to Illingworth but I was ready to go to the committee if that was what Hampshire wanted. 'No, don't be a silly bugger. Come and have a drink,' said Hampshire. I couldn't for the life of me remember making any such reference about Hampshire to Illingworth. The fact of the matter is that I regarded Hampshire as something of a fence-sitter, a man who would rarely stand up and be counted. I regarded him as a basically weak individual but I certainly did not consider him untrustworthy. And I could not remember ever having said so. This, after all, was the man whom I had backed as vice-captain when the cricket committee wanted to get rid of him at the start of the season. A man, supposedly, I mistrusted because he was after my job. It didn't make an atom of sense. But I discovered later that Illingworth had said as much again when Hampshire rang him at Worcester. What was Illingworth trying to do? Was this his idea of bringing harmony to the club? I needed this sort of thing like I needed a hole in the head, especially with the media running near-daily stories that I was about to up and leave Yorkshire. After my letter to *The Times* I wrote to the president and chairman expressing my support for Hampshire as vice-captain and adding: 'Any step which weakens the position of either myself or John Hampshire would be disastrous and divisive.' That word 'divisive' was to become pretty familiar in Yorkshire's vocabulary.

Hampshire was not satisfied, and he repeated his threat not to play under me when he encountered the president and Arthur Connell. What must have struck Hampshire was that either I was a liar or Illingworth was. Either way prospects for our future partnership did not exactly look rosy. Illingworth was summoned to explain and he revealed that I had made my comment about Hampshire three or four years previously, an off-the-cuff remark during a meal at his house! That was a time when I was up to my neck in the machinations of Wilson, Hutton and the like. It's quite possible that I said I could not be sure where Hampshire stood, but to represent that as a suggestion of mistrusting him was blowing a harmless comment out of all proportion. Illingworth was bent on making trouble, that much seemed quite obvious. It was also made clear to him that he had been recruited as team manager, not as a player, and the suggestion that he might usurp my position as captain or Hampshire's as vice-captain was not appreciated. That would really have put Illy's nose out of joint, especially when he knew it was contained in a letter from me to the officials of the club. Boycott was clearly too influential and he would have to do something about it. Next day he wrote that in his opinion Hampshire would make a better England captain than me. 'I was one of Geoff Boycott's strongest supporters but doubts have been raised in my mind as to the suitability of his personality for international captaincy,' Illingworth wrote. Perhaps one of my demerits was that I was ready to stick up for myself. Illingworth always had to be right – I doubt very much that he took kindly to being contradicted.

Hampshire and I were told to report individually to the president and chairman at the offices of the *Yorkshire Post*, where Illingworth's explanations were outlined and where I learned to my surprise that Arthur Connell had almost been sacked as Yorkshire's chairman over the decision to appoint Illingworth without full reference to the rest of the committee. Connell was saved only by Sir Kenneth's insistence that he would have to resign as president if the chairman was dismissed. I saw Illy by chance at Headingley and he pledged his support for me as captain – forget whatever I may have read in the press, they had taken his remarks out of context. The usual smokescreen. I reminded him how inquisitive and demanding the press on Yorkshire matters could be and urged him to think twice before he said anything, otherwise there would be no end to the speculation and supposition. 'Unity is the key.' It sounds terribly corny now but that's what I told him at the time. The president telephoned to say that Hampshire was happy with the outcome of their latest meeting and that relations between us should be back to normal. Less than three weeks later we played a championship match at Northampton.

It is still difficult for me to piece together the motivation which prompted Hampshire to stage his infamous 'go slow' in that game. It's hard for me to get inside his head, though it might be suggested there was plenty of room. The facts of the matter are that I scored 113 in just over four and a half hours – pretty grim stuff I confess, but my thumb injury was still giving me a bit of bother and I wasn't playing well at the time. It didn't seem to matter too much because Bill Athey played aggressively and well and we put on 202 on the strength of a splendid century from him. When I was out we needed 33 runs off 10.3 overs for 300 and maximum batting bonus points. Hampshire and Colin Johnson made no attempt and in fact scored only 11.

The visitors' dressing room at Northampton is split in two and it is impossible from the back room to see the play. I was cooling down and undressing slowly after my innings when David Bairstow stormed angrily through from the front section and began flinging off his pads. 'I'm not bloody well going in next, even if one of them gets out. It's a disgrace. You can sack me if you like.' I had no idea what was going on. I had batted eight overs with Hampshire before getting out and he had made no mention to me of slow scoring or of the need to press on. His gesture instead made Yorkshire a laughing stock round the ground. Hampshire faced fifty-nine deliveries and played four scoring strokes, reaching 7 not out by the time the 100-overs cut-off was reached. The mood in the dressing room was murderous and I knew it would be impossible for Hampshire and myself to discuss it in front of the team without creating a mighty row, so I bit my tongue. Hampshire swaggered in without saying a word to me, though he made an illuminating reply when Bairstow – ever the Yorkshireman – taxed him later in the shower. 'It was a bloody disgrace what you did,' said Bairstow. 'What are you talking about? I just couldn't score,' answered Hampshire. 'Come off it. In the nick you're in of course you could,' said Bairstow.

It was entirely significant that Hampshire's first reaction was to deny what he had done. Later, much later, he was to strike a pose as a man steeped in Yorkshire cricket whose big, brave heart was irreparably wounded that day and was finally broken by events. It was good for the self-made image but it did not impress many who knew him. If Hampshire's gesture was so noble, why did he not have the guts to admit to it at the time? That was the Hampshire I knew. And he was not above boasting about it in the bar that night, significantly again when he thought he was surrounded by cronies rather than critics. It must have come as a real shock to him next day when the press announced that Yorkshire would hold an enquiry into the incident and deplored his part in it. Hampshire was not accustomed to being criticised in the media.

Sir Kenneth Parkinson was at the match and he saw the go-slow with as much horrified bewilderment as everybody else. We sat in his car after the day's play and he was still reluctant to believe what he had seen. But he clearly traced Hampshire's attitude back to Illingworth's 'untrustworthy' remark which had done so much damage. Hampshire had seemed to accept my explanation when he left their meeting in Leeds nearly three weeks earlier, but it did not look that way now. The feeling was that we should not rock the boat any more than we had to, in view of the fact that Yorkshire had an important Gillette Cup tie coming up in forty-eight hours. That seemed sensible at the time but the fact that Hampshire escaped immediate disciplinary action did not go unnoticed.

Looking back, it is impossible not to come to the conclusion that John Hampshire saw Northampton as the stage on which to make his bid for the

Yorkshire captaincy. It will be denied until several people are blue in the face but the facts and circumstances support it. For the first time in his career, Hampshire had enjoyed a winning sequence as Yorkshire's captain. The dressing-room atmosphere was favourable – winning captains engender praise rather than criticism – and he had developed a taste for the job. He even enjoyed newspaper reports that Ray Illingworth felt he should be captain of England.

It does not take much mental gymnastics to conclude that Illingworth regarded Hampshire as his first choice to captain Yorkshire. I cannot imagine why anybody would dig up an off-the-cuff remark made in a different context four years previously unless it was to create a division between Hampshire and me. It certainly worked. Hampshire could not believe both of us and it made sense to fall in with the new team manager who would obviously have influence on the choice of captain; and he did not have to look far for support from my critics in committee. He would never have a better chance of ousting me than in the 1978 season.

His personal form was good, his publicity was good – and it went to his head. When I returned, the press turned their spotlight on me, chiefly to speculate when I would be recalled by England. Hampshire slid down the totem pole, he was being overshadowed by Boycott again and the resentment smouldered until it caught flame at Northampton. The combustion may have been spontaneous in that I doubt he spent days planning it, but there was plenty of fuel already laid for the fire. Even before Northampton, his attitude was characteristic of a man who suddenly felt sure of himself and resented my authority as captain: brusque or clever-dick remarks in front of the other players, a nit-picking sort of truculence. The image, and I saw it clearly only later, of a man who suddenly considers himself superior.

By the time of the meeting of enquiry into the go-slow on the afternoon of 20 July, he was not quite so cocky. Perhaps he realised the enormity of what he had done, perhaps he felt he had bitten off more than he could chew – and his courage would not exactly be fired up by press speculation that he might be dismissed from the club. The word 'sack' was bandied about freely enough to upset his father and his young son. By the time Hampshire was called in to face the selection committee – John Temple, Billy Sutcliffe and Ronnie Burnet now sitting as a committee of enquiry – he gave every indication of believing he was about to be dismissed. Which was ironic considering the news I received myself shortly before I went into the hearing in the players' dining room at Bradford's Park Avenue ground.

I bumped into Fred Trueman, who told me he had just come from a chat with several members of the committee. As a distinguished ex-player, Fred was often a party to the attitudes of the inner sanctum at Yorkshire. The following year he was to become the committee representative for the Craven district in North-west Yorkshire. Fred blithely informed me that at least four of the committee had informed him that they intended to get rid of me as captain. 'You know who they are, they've had a go at you often enough,' he said. And he confirmed in a quasi-official manner what had been rumoured round the county for some time: that Illingworth was the means. 'I think he's coming to sack you,' said Fred. 'You can buy me a drink when it happens and say I told you so.' That was on 20 July 1978. I still owe Fred the drink.

'A Bloody Disgrace'

My part in the hearing began in something very close to farce. I had no sooner sat down than Burnet launched into a discussion about my batting and scoring rates in various matches since I had returned from injury. Although called as a witness in the Hampshire business, I felt uncomfortably as though I was in the dock. And they had not even spoken to Hampshire and Johnson yet. Not officially, at least. Clearly, attitudes had already been struck and I protested that the cart was being put firmly in front of the horse. 'If John Hampshire deliberately went slow as a protest against your batting we can't condone that and we shall have to do something,' said Sutcliffe. 'Why don't you ask him?' I replied. Was it that difficult?

On 27 July 1978 Boycott completed his third century in consecutive innings: 113 for Yorkshire against Northamptonshire at Northampton, 103 not out for Yorkshire against New Zealand at Leeds, and 118 for Yorkshire against Glamorgan at Sheffield.

I left the room and returned later to hear a résumé from Temple of the evidence given by Johnson and Hampshire in turn. I already knew Johnson's version; he had given it to me the previous day and he repeated it to the committee when asked. He had intended going for the bonus point but Hampshire told him he had no intention of doing so. Hampshire was vice-captain of the team, so Johnson considered himself under orders and fell in with Hampshire's wishes. I accepted Johnson's version just as the hearing did, and no blame was attached to him.

Hampshire, according to Temple, told the hearing it was difficult and he just could not score. He denied it was a protest over my batting and said he was sorry for what happened. He must have cut a particularly strong figure. Temple then told me they had reprimanded Hampshire – it is recorded in the cricket committee minutes – and added: 'though we cannot condone Hampshire's action, the overall scoring rate of the captain was not satisfactory and he has been notified to this effect. It was nevertheless felt that the scoring rate of some of the earlier batting should have been accelerated.'

I was amazed and furious in turn. I did not claim to be the fastest batsman in the world and I would happily discuss my batting on the day in question, but that was really not the point. I had tried my best that day and Hampshire – on the evidence of Johnson, who had no axe to grind – did not. Surely that was the point at issue as far as Yorkshire cricket was concerned. If they were planning to issue a statement involving me in some criticism, and they were, I would not take it sitting down. Not when I knew that the committee hawks were already trying to discredit and remove me – and one of them was Burnet. I pointed out that in 1962 Trueman had been sent home by Vic Wilson for turning up late to a match in Taunton. And in 1968 he was suspended for one match because Sellers considered he did not try to save a single in a Roses match at Sheffield. That seemed draconian at the time. Now we had a situation where a player had let down the club and his mates and the committee were falling over themselves to implicate the captain instead of backing him. I did not want Hampshire sacked from the club, as some did, but I felt the least he could expect was a suspension and demotion from the vice-captaincy. If not, where would this sort of 'spontaneous' reaction end? 'Boycott Rapped for Slow Scoring' – I could see the headlines again, the stigma of 1967 revisited, as though I had gone slowly on purpose. I knew I had not and I knew who had: Johnson's evidence confirmed it. 'You seem to think we have been unfair,' said Burnet – and I saw red. Fairness was not a word he should have been using to me at that moment. I asked to discuss the matter with the president or chairman, because at least I felt I could trust them; there was precious little trust left between me and some members of the committee. I was so angry I challenged Burnet to his face with examples of his disloyalty, itemising times, places and what he had said against me. He was obviously taken aback but he did not deny the accusations. How could he? 'They were private conversations,' he muttered. As if that made them any less shameful or corrosive. Other committee-men were peddling the same sort of criticism in private and I was sick of the whole business.

The only way I could get a fair deal was to take it to the top – to the president, since a phone call indicated that the club chairman was not at home. Sir Kenneth – a witness at Northampton, remember – was appalled at the idea of censuring the captain in a statement ostensibly about Hampshire. I remember his words: 'Geoff's scoring rate was debatable if you like. John Hampshire's batting was indefensible.' He urged them strongly not to involve me, which left them in a bit of a fix since they clearly wanted to. The next team was picked with Hampshire in it, a decision with which I did not agree; then I was asked to leave the room again while they discussed their statement to the press. When I returned, they had agreed not to say anything. 'The selection committee has considered all aspects of the incident and has conveyed its findings to the players concerned and now considers the matter closed.' The sort of bland non-statement which was bound to excite the curiosity of the press. The committee-men fled as soon as it had been delivered by a distinctly flustered Temple to a distinctly dissatisfied press contingent. They had been hanging around all afternoon – it was around 8 p.m. now – and Temple's ragged throwaway line about wanting to get home to his family didn't exactly smooth things over. Reporters buttonholed me, wanting further details and frankly I saw no reason to protect Hampshire or the committee. The whole hearing was rigged to put me in the least favourable light and I wasn't having it.

In a sense, I suppose I won my point because the truth that Hampshire had been reprimanded was revealed. But I also knew that the gloves were off now, especially as far as Burnet was concerned. The anger on his face at not being able to issue a full, angled statement was eloquent enough. If they could not have a go at me, they would not admit to censuring Hampshire. It would not look good when the time came to make him captain . . .

One aspect of Temple's brief press conference sticks in my mind. He was asked by one reporter if the president had ventured any opinion about the go-slow incident, since he was at Northampton himself. And Temple said: 'He has not voiced any opinion to me today.' Considering that he had spoken to the president for at least ten minutes on the phone and certainly had received his opinions on the issue, that was simply not true. I wondered then at the glibness of it. Had they really reached a point in matters concerning me where they could not recognise the difference between truths, half-truths and plain untruths? And if they could recognise the truth, why were they indifferent to it? The pretence of supporting me would go on after the Bradford meeting but it was largely cosmetic, as indeed it had been for some time. Hampshire, Illingworth and a good number of two-faced committee-men knew what was on the cards.

19

What You Are

Yorkshire might have officially considered the Hampshire affair closed, but it never was – not while there were committee-men gunning for a captain who had 'gone over their heads', and not while Hampshire himself and Illingworth were scheming a change for next season. 'Boycott is too powerful,' said Burnet. 'Boycott is too popular,' said Brennan. And it suddenly became public knowledge that Derbyshire wanted Hampshire to join them as captain next season. Hampshire's position was simple: he would accept Derbyshire's offer unless Yorkshire made him captain. At around the same time Illingworth was interviewed on Sunday afternoon television by Jim Laker, and he pushed Hampshire for the England captaincy in place of Mike Brearley. No room for misquote or misunderstanding there. And Illingworth contacted Robin Marlar of the *Sunday Times*, indicating that it would be 'worth his while' to push Hampshire as the next England captain. The hawks were already working on the rest of the committee, arguing that Hampshire was a better captain than me and that Yorkshire could not possibly risk losing him to another county. They also maintained that I was unpopular with the rest of the players.

Richard Lumb, already miffed by being dropped down the order and playing in only ten Sunday matches, was thoroughly browned off when he was blamed for Yorkshire's defeat in the Gillette Cup quarter-final against Sussex at Headingley. Billy Sutcliffe suggested that Lumb should open in Hampshire's absence through injury. I didn't fancy yet another row so I acquiesced, Lumb scored 10 off twenty-three deliveries and we lost a ten-overs match by nine runs. Lumb received a lot of public condemnation for his innings, blamed me for putting him in first and smouldered. Immediately afterwards Barrie Leadbeater played his first match for nearly three months and scored an admirable 61 at Southampton. Leadbeater was a fine-looking player technically who never scored the runs his style promised; Lumb was nowhere near as aesthetic but he came up with the goods. By way of geeing up Leadbeater, I told him that he was technically the better of the two players who ought to get in the side more often. That was no criticism of Lumb, who clearly made the best of his abilities. My little lecture was overheard by a member and found its way back to Lumb. While I was away at a Test match against New Zealand, John Hampshire advised Lumb and Leadbeater to report my remarks to the committee and they subsequently had an interview with Sutcliffe. Talk about a storm in a teacup. I am perfectly convinced that in normal circumstances the matter would have been killed there and then. But two players complaining about Boycott was too good for the hawks to ignore. I apologised and insisted that I had been trying to be constructive. I might as well have saved my breath. The committee became involved, the matter was blown out of all proportion and we ended up having yet another meeting with cricket committee representatives at the Crown Hotel in Scarborough on 20 August 1978. It was clear by now that the committee was gathering as much evidence as possible to be used in support of a decision to sack me as captain. There was no hint of support.

Certainly there was none from Hampshire, whose attitude was disruptive to my face and openly contemptuous behind my back. The open, genial Hampshire whom the public thought they knew held many a long drinking session with Yorkshire players who were ready to listen to grievances. I know; one player's wife contacted me because she feared her husband was going off the rails! It may be that Hampshire's confidence was stiffened by the feedback he was getting from the anti-Boycott brigade. He went to the chairman and asked for his release in order to captain Derbyshire. The reaction and the confirmation that he was close to the Yorkshire captaincy must have cheered him up no end. It might also explain his increasingly open hostility to me: he knew he had nothing to lose.

I had to have a break, come what may, and I slipped away to Bermuda for a brief holiday, determined to be back for the cricket committee meeting on 29 September where the captaincy would be debated. In fact, it received an important debate before then – at a meeting of the selection committee on 28 September. As a member of the selection committee, I ought to have been at that meeting; Ray Illingworth was not yet an employee of the club, but he was there. And he told Temple, Burnet and Sutcliffe – reassured them might be a better word – that he favoured a change of captaincy and preferred Hampshire for the job. I flew back to England the same day quite unaware that this unscheduled meeting had happened – and with a telegram in my pocket informing me that my mother had died suddenly at home.

It was a shock, of course, but in many ways it was a mercy. Mum had entered hospital in mid-August of 1977, cancer was confirmed and she began a long, eventually hopeless battle against the disease and the indignities that went with a wasting body. That's what dispirited her most, I think, the loss of her physical strength. She was brave and independent and proud of her ability to fend for herself. She always had been. Radium treatment and then chemotherapy did not prevent the cancer from spreading and she hated the side-effects. Throughout the last year she became progressively weaker and there was really nothing anybody could do. The doctors said it was terminal but there was no way of knowing how long she had. It was just a matter of doing what we could. Mum was aware of my problems throughout that season and that probably made her less inclined to lean on me. Her problems were so much greater than mine, God only knows, but she was tough and determined. If I inherited any of those qualities I undoubtedly got them from her and I really wish I had had more time to be with her in the last year. After she was gone it was too late, but I suppose that's often the way. We had no idea at the end how close she was to dying, but I reckon she knew. When I left for Bermuda she gripped my hand very tightly and said, 'Don't let the buggers get you down,' and she had tears in her eyes. It was the only time I ever heard her swear, the nearest I ever saw her come to crying.

Boycott has won nine one-day medals in the Benson and Hedges Cup.

Naturally, I think, in view of what had just happened and of what I'd known for some time, I was not in the best frame of mind when I went to the cricket committee meeting on Friday the 29th. Despite all the pressures which had built up and despite the mounting evidence against it, I still clung to a belief that I would retain the captaincy. After all, and I think I kept recalling this for reassurance, Yorkshire had said that the 'two best brains in the game' would be allied when Illingworth worked as team manager with Boycott as captain. That was next season. Surely they could not renege on that? I left the meeting, as usual, when the question of captaincy came up – and never went back in. The cricket committee went straight into lunch at the end of their meeting and I hung around all afternoon while the general committee ratified the captaincy decision. Hampshire was to take over.

The hawks had a field day in the cricket committee. Sutcliffe made out some sort of case to show I was indecisive and inconsistent as captain. Burnet said that Yorkshire's good results during the season were really a reflection of Hampshire's captaincy. (In fact, we each led the team to five championship victories.) Hampshire would leave if Boycott were re-elected, and so, it was darkly forecast, might several other players. Illingworth's view, even off the record, clinched it. There was some discussion about whether Illy's opinion should be made public, and Temple had to remind the meeting in some alarm that Illingworth's remarks were made in strict confidence. They almost managed to stuff the team manager before he arrived. The atmosphere, I am told, became distinctly lighthearted and congratulatory. Crawford thought it a difficult decision to make, Ryan insisted that their inside information on Illingworth's attitude left no doubt, Feather predictably agreed. Connell made remarks about searching the depths of one's conscience and Sir Kenneth Parkinson said it was time to stand up and be counted. The voting was 10–1 against me as captain and only Sir Kenneth dissented. He had heard their arguments before and he simply could not accept the assertion that everything amiss with the club stemmed from me. He knew my faults but he also knew better than that. And it may be indicative of his closeness to the rank-and-file membership that Sir Kenneth forecast serious opposition from the members if I was replaced a year before the much-vaunted partnership with Illingworth was struck. He felt I should be given at least a year to work with Illy. That had, after all, been the intention when Illingworth was recruited. Times had changed.

It is odd, looking back, but while I was sitting waiting for the decision and trying not to accept what was pretty obvious, I kept reflecting on a pretty disastrous year in one way or another: 'Thank God 1978 is over. I'm quite looking forward to a fresh start with Illy next year – it certainly couldn't be any worse than the year I've just had . . .'

After being told officially that I was sacked as captain I waited behind again and had a word with the president, Connell and Temple. It achieved nothing and I suppose I was foolish to imagine it would, but I do recall Connell denying that Illingworth's opinion had ever been sought. I know better now, and I'm convinced that Illingworth's attitude, the fact that Hampshire threatened to leave and the trauma of almost losing the chairmanship himself in the wake of the decision to sign Illy up had swung Arthur Connell to the point where he voted against me as captain. It was a wearing time and a wearing process, no doubt about that.

During my wait for news I read the day's copy of the *Daily Mail* and turned to the horoscopes, as I often do. There under Libra, my star sign, was the forecast: 'Mercury in your sign makes a favourable aspect of Jupiter and will be helpful for personal hopes and wishes. Put yourself where you will be noticed. You will easily gain the support you need and it is a good time to ask favours.' The day did not quite live up to Orion's expectations.

Eight general committee members voted against the cricket committee recommendation that Hampshire should be made captain – Eric Baines, Dr John Turner, David Welch, David Drabble, Ron Yeomans, Tony Woodhouse, Jack Sokell and Sir Kenneth Parkinson. I later received a letter from Mollie Staines, the Dewsbury representative, saying she had thought it all over and had voted against me but wished me well for the future. I respected and appreciated that. Not surprisingly, the likes of Brennan were wandering about saying that their views had been 'vindicated'. The anti-Boycott camp was crowing. I went on the Parkinson television chat show and gave some of them a piece of my mind, which led to a huffy reaction from the club and a suggestion that I would be disciplined. Letters darted to and fro and I finally went with Duncan Mutch to address the general committee on 23 October. Duncan prepared a dossier of facts, figures, times and places proving that I had not enjoyed the full backing of the committee and that many had in fact waged a smear campaign against me. Some of the committee listened in embarrassment, others who already knew the details rather too well pretended to be bored or blasé. Brennan and Ryan shared a loud joke. The speech took around one and three-quarter hours as I recall and after it nobody asked a question. A typed sheet suddenly appeared and Connell read out to me the committee's view. The sheet had been typed before the meeting – the charade was complete.

Connell's speech was hurriedly amended with the odd deletion and change of tense and became a statement for the press, who had spent yet another day camped out in the crisis centre at Headingley. One phrase was grabbed above all others: 'It is nothing to do with what Mr Boycott has done, or has not done. It is to do with what he is.' I regarded that comment with utter contempt. The presumption of a public comment on my personality as justification for their actions was bad enough. Coming from a body, some of whose members had been scheming against me for years, who posed as strong characters and yet did not have the guts to come clean with the members and the cricketing public about what they were doing, it was disgusting. John Temple unwittingly put so many things in perspective when he later admitted, 'If we'd sacked him a year ago the members would have taken us to pieces. Now we can get away with it.' Not even the usual pretence about what was best for Yorkshire cricket. Frankly, too many of them didn't give a damn as long as they could keep their seats, polish their egos and enjoy some sort of shabby status on the club's back.

Next day I caught the train to London *en route* to England's winter tour of Australia. I was desperately low, what with the insidiously mounting pressures of the last few months, then the death of my mother, then the culmination of the Yorkshire business. England had stripped me of the vice-captaincy and had appointed Bob Willis instead, which didn't exactly help. All I had to do was clear my head, consider my future with Yorkshire and score centuries for England. That's all. I summed it up in a letter to Ted Lester, written on the plane to Australia:

> These last few months have been the worst in my life – constantly watching my mother get gradually worse and finally seeing her deteriorate so rapidly that she was unrecognisable as the strong, determined lady I knew. . . .
>
> As for the Yorkshire issue I am really sorry I was not given the chance to work with Roy. The remarks last season by John Temple and Arthur Connell that he would take the weight off my shoulders and to specifically get the Committee off my back and allow me to captain on the field and bat seem strange after recent events! . . .
>
> John's part in all this has hurt and saddened me – particularly culminating in Northampton. . . . I have failings but I have always tried to keep him involved with team decisions, selection of players, tactics and selection committee views because I genuinely felt it was best for the team. . . . Perhaps he has looked upon it as a weakness in me rather than a genuine desire on my part to cement a relationship and to work as partners.
>
> I can't help feeling that it would have been a lot easier with a loyal Selection Committee and Cricket Committee helping me rather than being divisive, talking about me behind my back and generally downgrading everything we tried to do – John, you and I. It made it so that I was always looking over my shoulder, wondering what I could do to keep peace with them and gain their support – at the same time members and supporters would tell me of remarks they were making and plots taking place. I seemed to have to spend more time concerned with the Committee rather than the players. . . .
>
> I don't know what I shall do now. Take time to think is the most important thing – get over my mum – settle down a bit out here – try and play cricket and see what evolves.

Back in Yorkshire, the row over my dismissal blazed at a sometimes furious level as preparations were made for a special meeting of the club on 9 December. The Reform Group, whom Ronnie Burnet contemptuously dismissed as 'an unruly mob' and who were in fact dedicated Yorkshire members with a heartfelt stake in their club, demanded a meeting which would vote on members' confidence in the general committee and the cricket committee and on the reappointment of me as captain. They had to go to the High Court before Yorkshire would agree to hold the special meeting, although the required number of signatures were on the table. Talk about the club holding its members in contempt. It was an appalling state of affairs. I was in Perth, still desperately looking for batting form after the tenth match of the tour, when I received news of the voting. The meeting expressed confidence in the general committee, by a majority of 1355; expressed no confidence in the members of the cricket committee by a majority of 870; and rejected the call for my re-election by 2224 votes. Clear enough, you may think, but the vast majority of members at the meeting were anti-committee and the votes were decided by proxy voters who traditionally tend to be conservative. Furthermore, the middle ground – the floating voter if you like – had been influenced for the establishment by a letter from Ray Illingworth. It was published when the arguments were at their height and it was a master stroke of duplicity. Illingworth, due to take over as team manager the following season, suggested publicly that the players wanted rid of me as captain. The uncommitted public could hardly ignore that.

Illingworth's letter, dated 10 November, read:

> I have recently returned from holiday and find the controversy about Geoff Boycott still raging.
>
> As you know when I was first offered the job of Manager I said I would serve with any Captain who might be appointed and in particular was perfectly happy to work with Geoff.
>
> Up to now I have therefore kept out of this row, but as things are developing I think I should now let you know that the players are wholeheartedly behind the Committee in the change.

I knew, of course, that some players would back Hampshire as captain but I was surprised to discover that the players 'wholeheartedly' supported a change. And the fact is that they did not. Illingworth did not speak to all the players himself: he asked Geoff Cope to sound them out. I do not know how they all responded but I know for a fact that Chris Old refused to give an opinion to Cope and that several players were never approached.

David Bairstow was not asked his view, neither were Arnie Sidebottom, Howard Cooper, Bill Athey, Jim Love or Kevin Sharp. It is immaterial to suggest that they were not senior players or even all capped players – they were very much Yorkshire's team of the period. And without their knowledge or approval, Illingworth went on record as saying they supported the committee. There was not a great deal they could do about it, unless they wanted to cut their own throats with the men running the club. But they knew it was a put-up job and they would never forget it. A huge body of Yorkshire members suspected it was false and eventually came to know it was – and they never forgave. Hampshire's reign as captain was founded on a lie.

The fact that Illingworth was prepared to issue a letter like that left me in no doubt where he stood and therefore little doubt where I would stand as a player. Illingworth and Hampshire were bound to come to the conclusion that I would make it my business to find out if the letter was accurate. I could only imagine they would close ranks and try to continue to discredit me when they could. It was a fraught situation. In many ways the obvious solution for me – and the one they clearly hoped I would adopt – was to accept an offer from another county and get out of the whole fractious business. I had approaches from Gloucestershire and Northants as well as from wealthy clubs in the leagues, so I would not be short of options or employment. But I loved Yorkshire cricket, still do. I knew that the way back would be difficult for me and I feared that there was more controversy in store, but my heart was with the Reform Group members who had worked so hard for justice and the thousands of members who voted for me. There was no way I could let them down and slink away. At the last minute – not to be perverse but because I wanted as much time as possible to come to an unavoidable conclusion – I telexed Arthur Connell and Joe Lister from Adelaide, accepting the club's offer of a contract:

> After long thought I have reached the conclusion that I owe a debt of gratitude to the members of the Reform Group and all my loyal Yorkshire supporters through the years. I therefore accept the two-year contract offered to me in the terms of that offer which the club has made. I am nevertheless disappointed that a two-year contract was the maximum which the committee was prepared to offer me after 16 full years of loyal service. I hope that the two assurances which you gave over the telephone one of which related to the possibility of a two-year roll-over contract will eventually be implemented.

I sometimes reflect on the mixed reception the news must have had. A lot of members, I know, would have been delighted; some would have been pleased, with reservations in view of the recent infighting and its effect on the reputation of a club they loved. And some people – in high and influential places – would have been mad as hell. They certainly had not finished with me.

— 20 —

The Arts of Captaincy

For a man who dreamed for most of his remembered life of being England's Test captain, I cannot honestly say I got a tremendous thrill out of doing the job. That might be because I didn't exactly shine on results – though we rewrote the record books by losing a Test match in New Zealand – but the real reason is that I got the job by default. Almost literally by accident. I was vice-captain on the 1977–8 tour of Pakistan and New Zealand, and when Mike Brearley's arm was broken in a meaningless match at Lahore, I inherited the post. It was most certainly not the way I wanted to become England captain, for Mike's sake and my own. If I made it, I wanted it to be in my own right, with an opportunity to mould my team and include my kind of players. The team which I captained for four matches – two draws, one defeat, one victory – was not the one I would have taken on to the field had I been given any choice. Brian Rose, Graham Roope and Geoff Miller would not have been in it, Derek Randall would only have been there if his confidence had been high, Mike Gatting would have been discarded, then, as being too young and callow. Barry Wood would have been in my side, so would David Bairstow, Roger Tolchard, David Steele, Peter Willey – men with the necessary strength and character and fighting qualities. A captain must have players in whom he can have confidence. When the going gets tough you can't have men who are upset by plain speaking.

Boycott's first match in Pakistan was England XI against BCCP Patron's XI at Rawalpindi in 1977.

A New Zealand tour is more difficult than many imagine, and arriving there straight from the privations of Pakistan did not exactly help. Physically and mentally we were on a low, and New Zealand is demanding: the pitches are grassy and require technique as well as application, the weather is sometimes foul, and practice facilities, as we soon found, can be a huge problem. Rules are interpreted differently from ours, and poor umpiring can create an enormous build-up of irritation. Nobody doubts the in-depth talent of the West Indies, yet they have lost a series in New Zealand in 1980, when players like Colin Croft and Michael Holding were driven over the top by frustration at bad decisions. Umpire Fred Goodall was at the centre of much of the trouble. After one disallowed appeal, Holding kicked over the batsmen's stumps: Croft got so frustrated that he charged Goodall when delivering the ball. By the third Test match the West Indies refused to play unless Goodall was removed, and a twelve-minute delay followed while officials sorted it out. As the New Zealand team becomes stronger and stronger, so the very real problems of facing them at home are revealed.

England lost the first Test in Wellington because we batted lamentably against some superb downwind bowling from Richard Hadlee and could not make 136 to win the game. We were bowled out in our second innings for 64, which was quite pathetic. The series was squared at Christchurch, where we won by 174 runs after a declaration and where Ian Botham, in his second Test overseas, claims to have run me out on purpose – a story that gets bigger and more fanciful with every telling.

Less than a year later, I set out for a winter tour of Australia under Brearley, having lost the vice-captaincy to Bob Willis. It puzzled me at the time and in a professional sense still does – but then I am no psychiatrist. Alec Bedser came to see me at Edgbaston early in the English summer of 1978 and had told me that Brearley, now recovered from his broken arm, would be reinstalled as captain for the first three Tests. No problem there. And it was pleasing to hear from him that they had received good reports of my captaincy in New Zealand. Alec considered England were lucky to have two very good captains on call and said he hadn't 'given up hope of my being captain one day.'

Boycott's first Test as captain of England, against Pakistan at Karachi, began on 18 January 1978.

Injury had ruled me out for much of the 1978 season and my form wasn't great when I first returned but it got considerably better and I was hurt and disappointed not to win back an England place. Even more puzzling was the lack of contact from Alec Bedser. The press suggested that the selectors felt I needed more match practice, and wanted to try out other players for the forthcoming winter tour to Australia. Whispers were circulating that I had received a bad report from New Zealand. I began to suspect that my presence in the England team would be an embarrassment if I did well while Brearley was still struggling to make runs and cement his place as a player. Three championship centuries regained me a place in the England side for the last two Tests against New Zealand – and it was announced that Willis would go to Australia as Brearley's vice-captain. In view of what Bedser had said five months earlier, I asked for a meeting with him and Doug Insole, the tour manager, to find out just what was going on.

We met at the Carlton Club on 11 September and the upshot was that the selectors felt I should concentrate on my batting through the Australian tour. They had had verbal reports from New Zealand that the captaincy had affected my batting and particularly my scoring rate. Some players weren't happy with me in charge there, though there was nothing on record to that effect. The clinching factor was that Brearley had expressed no desire to have me as his vice-captain; had he done so, they said, it might have been different. So I arranged a meeting with Mike for the following day. I do like to get to the bottom of things. I feel more comfortable – though not necessarily more convinced – when people say to my face what they believe behind my back.

It was an odd meeting and I cannot to this day work out precisely what it proved. Brearley was very ill at ease, which surprised me. He was, after all, rightly celebrated as a man with a talent for dealing with people. Yet he had the gravest difficulty explaining just why he did not want me as his vice-captain. Either that, or I had the utmost difficulty understanding him. He mentioned, for instance, that on the few occasions he had asked my advice I had been brusque and perhaps slightly patronising, as though the answer was an elementary feature of captaincy. Well, perhaps it was. I don't recall specific instances and I don't think he mentioned any. In the end, I got the impression that I was the one who was doing the psychoanalysing, and I reckoned he felt inferior as a player (though certainly not as a man), because my ability and popularity and status were so far beyond his. I think my presence on tour as vice-captain made him unsure and nervous to the point where he took the easy way out and very rarely discussed things with me as captain to vice-captain. Certainly, we had not related much on the tour of Pakistan – at least we agreed on that. I represented a threat and Willis did not. That might be an awful over-simplification of the situation but that's what communicated itself to me. I had been told that Mike was an ambitious and even ruthless man, and I saw nothing at all wrong with that; such men were not unknown where I came from! But he had one devil of a job getting his message over to me that day, and one way or another I suppose our encounter proved his point that we would find it hard to work together as captain and vice-captain.

Kenny Barrington was an easy man to misunderstand at the best of times, a marvellous mixer-up of words who could unwittingly keep an audience in stitches. 'The press went through that food like a swarm of lotuses,' he observed in Pakistan, and Mike Hendrick was once asked if, when he went on shooting forays, he used 'them high-philosophy bullets'. Ken was a brave, stalwart batsman for England and a warm and friendly person. I had the greatest respect and affection for him as a bloke. But he was badly miscast as tour manager in Pakistan and New Zealand. Ken's forte was dealing with net practices and the dozens of associated problems which niggle players on tour. He was under pressure, as it was his first time as manager and Lord's was probably taking a special interest in the team's affairs. But he was plunged into the middle of a near-strike by players in Karachi over the rumoured return of Pakistan's Packer players, and he spent the New Zealand tour acting as though he was trying to qualify for the Diplomatic Corps. He was under pressure, of course, since one can only assume Lord's was taking a special interest in the team's affairs, but the fact is that everything became an exercise in public relations. Nothing particularly wrong with that, except when it overrode every other consideration – and it usually did. I have no reputation as a diplomat, and Ken's total preoccupation with keeping the peace became a positive hindrance to our chances of playing winning cricket.

I met Ken in a London hotel on 13 September, the day after talking to Mike Brearley, and it became obvious that although he had not damned me in any written report as tour manager, his verbal observations did me no good at all. We talked, perfectly amicably, about where he thought I had gone wrong and I think Ken's points were quite revealing.

He had been dismayed, he said, by an incident in Lahore when I had asked the Pakistan leader General Zia-ul-Haq if he could fix us up with some strong drink. It was said as a joke in a country under prohibition and it was accepted as such. But Ken worried about it. The England team had been introduced to the British Prime Minister Jim Callaghan in Karachi and when he asked me if there was anything we wanted, like some beer, I said a couple of cases of wine for the team would not go amiss. He promised to look into it – in fact he sent us two cases. I discovered from Ken that the British Ambassador was miffed because *he* was supposed to look after us and my request might be construed as an indication that he and his staff were falling down on the job. Talk about pettiness – or is it Empire-building?

On that tour I had repeatedly had problems getting decent nets, which I considered were very important, and Ken's attitude was always that we mustn't complain, must never make waves. So we were turfed out of the nets in Auckland to make way for local club bowlers and then spent ages traipsing round Dunedin looking for nets which, as it turned out, had been taken down by the local cricket association before we arrived. The players were moaning and I was livid – surely it was more important to have proper practice sessions for Test cricket than to stay on good terms with inefficient officials? Ken said that my attitude had embarrassed him.

So did my attitude towards umpires who would not give an lbw decision if the ball hit the front pad, even when it was barely out of the crease. And I had had a run-in with the umpire at Christchurch, Fred Goodall by name, who repeatedly no-balled Bob Willis and became distinctly officious when we asked him why. He wouldn't even answer simple questions, and just stared into space. I later gave Goodall no marks in my captain's report, which Ken thought undiplomatic, since Goodall was a leading New Zealand umpire at the time. Ken felt I should mark him higher so as not to offend New Zealand officials. As England captain, I considered it was my job to look after our players, not their umpires.

Ken developed something of a nervous twitch about my conduct of press conferences. The language might not be flowery and the accent might not be refined but the message was clear. The atmosphere seemed healthy enough to me, though Ken said some of the 'quality' papers' men were critical. I still have a letter from Don Cameron, a leading New Zealand cricket writer, who said among other things: 'I enjoyed covering your tour of New Zealand, not the least because your team were a courteous and friendly bunch of players; and more so because it is a pleasure dealing with a captain who not only knows what he wants to say, but can also say it. Press conferences can be a bore, but I must say I enjoyed yours – they had a pleasantly competitive atmosphere.' It just goes to show that there are other interpretations of my attitude, that the critical one is not the only one.

But Ken was clearly living on his nerves. He had talked himself into a belief that something was going to go wrong, and he reached a point, I feel, where he mistook plain speaking for rudeness. (He was not the first person to have done that.) Because we disagreed at a press conference about revealing the nature of a hand injury – the last thing I wanted was to tip Hadlee off to that – Ken said he felt we were 'at loggerheads'. It seemed a gross overstatement to me. Ken also said that some players had moaned about my attitude, which was no doubt true and may be the result in part of the fact that I had inherited Brearley's team. Ken felt I should have socialised more with the players – maybe that was Brearley's way too. But I was not like him and, as I have said, they were not all of them the players I would have chosen to lead. The hardest criticism to swallow was Ken saying I took too long over my runs. Talk about the pot calling the kettle black. But Ken was a selector as well as manager and his views carried weight.

It was an interesting conversation and I consider I learned a lot about the attitudes of others towards me. Many of Ken's criticisms, I'm bound to say, seemed rather petty then and still do, but I know he held them honestly and we parted as good enough friends. One thing did annoy me: at no time on tour, nor after it up until my meeting with Ken himself, were any of these points raised with me. They had fermented beneath the surface and along the corridors of power, but nobody had had the guts to come and confront me with my reputed failings. It makes it that much harder for me to see them as entirely frank or honest men, which is inevitably how they see themselves. It did not do a lot for trust between us.

I often wonder if Mike Brearley went away from our rather stilted meeting in London and put on his thinking cap about me. I rather fancy he did, because after that our relationship improved by leaps and bounds, and I have no hesitation in saying he was the best captain I played under for England. It might be that he felt less threatened when I was not his vice-captain. He treated me fairly – and after what I had been through in some quarters that was one hell of a nice change. Mike's reputation for man-management is no myth. And like the very best of man-managers, I suppose, the men who were being managed never realised it. There was a naturalness about his approach which made co-operation logical. Mike picked my brains a fair bit, he made use of my experience and he made use of my ability, but I never resented either – *we* had a match to win.

By the time I played for England under Mike, I had a well-developed reputation as a player and as a personality. Nobody complained too much about my ability but there were plenty who hardly knew me and yet took a firm view of my personality. Mike may have been wary – that might explain his reserve at first – but I feel he made up his own mind and did not allow prejudice to colour his attitude towards me. His praise was never fulsome and his criticism was never mean. His attitude was balanced and honest and I don't think you can ask for more; certainly, I never did. I suppose that at the end of the day I felt that Mike understood me. He did not always agree with me but he did not try to change me. If I wanted extra nets, he would be the first to make the arrangements; when I appeared undemonstrative on the field he never mistook it for lack of interest. I was a player of the old school, in many ways. Mike has written that he was brought up not to show too much emotion and in that respect we were probably similar. And we both wanted to win for England. I have lost count of the number of times in my life that I have been accused of playing 'for myself' and I can honestly say that it was never in my thoughts as an alternative to the team doing well. Mike never seemed to want to create a conflict between my batting and the best interests of the team. I remember telling him once when I wasn't batting as quickly as we both might like, 'I want to win, y'know.' He just looked at me and said, 'I know you do,' and I really felt that he meant it. It was a simple statement of faith and it meant a lot to me. And Mike knew his cricket: we could always talk sense to each other. If a captain cannot get on with one of his team, he can tolerate him or try to sack him. Burnet sacked Johnny Wardle at Yorkshire; I *could* have tried to get rid of Richard Hutton. But I reckon that is a sign of failure on the part of a captain. I only saw Mike lose his temper twice: once with Phil Edmonds and once with me.

It happened in Sydney just before the second Test match in 1980. I had been out playing golf some time before and had ricked my neck. I really did not feel that I was able to play and when I told Mike he blew his top. When I say that, I mean he went crazy, raging round the dressing room shouting at the top of his voice. It would have been quite a performance from anybody. From him it was amazing. Bernard Thomas quietened him down and we ended our argument on a slightly more composed plane. In a strange way, I admired his general control all the more after this revelation that he could lose his temper like anybody else. And I played in the match, which might prove something. I would have done better in my career if Mike Brearley had captained me more.

My biggest disappointment as far as Mike is concerned is his failure to seek my advice about his batting. Let's face it, he was short of real Test class and although he worked very hard at his game the realisation that he was below par at international level must have caused him a lot of worry. He tinkered with his style, his stance, his back-lift, but nothing really worked. That did not surprise me, because it was all too manufactured. Batting has to feel right and there is no way you can be thinking about technique when you face the next ball. It must not be intrusive. Botham and Willis gave him advice, but he never asked me. A man who could take so much intelligent interest in other people found it hard to talk about his major professional weakness. That was an oddity and a pity. I might have been able to help him but I certainly did not want to embarrass him.

Brearley was the best captain I played under, but Brian Close had more influence on my attitudes and even aptitudes than anyone else. They were as different as chalk and cheese, which may prove, contrary to some theories, that there is no stereotype for a successful captain. Closey was shrewd, physically strong and straight out of the mould that calls a spade a bloody shovel. His idea of man-management was to lead from the front. He would no more think of psychoanalysing a player than he would attempt to spell it. The Yorkshire dressing room under Close had all the appearances of a free-for-all; somebody described it as a 'managerie'. But his critics misunderstood the Yorkshire character and they underestimated Close's powers of command, which we never did. He had to deal with stroppy characters like Jimmy Binks, Fred and Illingworth – there was no way a retiring type would have won their respect or even kept them under control. Brian encouraged his players to throw their ideas into the ring, even if it sounded a bit like the tower of Babel. But then he would take control and make the decisions that had to be made. 'If I have to play any more under Closey, he'll have me in Menston.' The speaker was unmistakably Fred, who then went out and bowled his heart out. Menston was the only psychiatric hospital we knew.

Boycott has won fifteen one-day medals for Yorkshire and England.

So long as Yorkshire kept on winning – and we usually did – nobody seemed to mind too much what sort of means achieved the end. We accepted the character of Close's leadership as perfectly normal, which is not to say that we agreed with everything he said or did. I have never known so many arguments in one dressing room at one time. But I can't help wondering what the 'man-management' gurus would have made of a captain who would finish a team discussion (thinly disguised as a four-way argument) by standing in the middle of the room and announcing: 'That's what we're going to do, so shut up the lot of you. Anybody who thinks he can do this job better than me can have the first punch – and some of you can have two. But you'd better make it count because I bloody well will.' Somehow, I don't see Mike Brearley adopting quite that stance, if only because Ian Botham might have taken him at his word! If the best captains are supposed not to lose their temper, as Mike so rarely did, what would Lord's have made of the following incident? In a match on a turning pitch at Swansea the Yorkshire fielding was dreadful and a lot of catches went down. Close was already fuming by the time he brought himself on to bowl and, sure enough, I dropped a catch in the outfield when I lunged forward and grabbed the ball but knocked it out with my knee. That was just before lunch and most of the players had the sense and experience to disappear fast to the dining room. Not the young Boycott. He was still in the dressing room when Close appeared with steam coming out of his ears, making dark remarks about silly so-and-sos who couldn't even catch a cricket ball. Close had dropped three catches himself. 'If I'd dropped as many as you this morning . . .' I began and I never finished the sentence. Close bounded across the dressing room and pinned me against the door with one hand, my feet several inches from the ground. I closed my eyes and waited for the other fist to arrive but Fred and Illy pulled him off in the nick of time. Now that's what I call man-management. Lord's, of course, had the last word when they stripped Closey of the England captaincy. He had won six out of seven Test matches as captain but he was obviously not a 'good chap'. They cost England a very strong and fine captain. I respected him totally and I think anybody who called himself a professional would have done the same.

The captaincy of Yorkshire and, briefly, of England was very important to me. I have often been asked just why I stuck it out all those years with Yorkshire when the captaincy seemed to be more trouble than it was worth. What on earth is so important about the Yorkshire captaincy anyway? Well, it was my dream to captain the side, always had been. And dreams of Yorkshire cricket were very precious to kids of my generation who didn't have too much else. And in a practical sense I looked on the captaincy as a way of extending myself as a cricketer, reaching out from succeeding as a player, first with Yorkshire and then for England.

Inevitably, I was more of a Close than a Brearley as a captain. I used to study Close's tactics avidly right through the 1960s, trying to work out when and why he would make bowling changes or alter his field, which bowler would bowl at which end and why. When I thought I had the answers I used to try and go one step ahead of him, anticipating his next move just to see if I had got my thinking right. Fielding was rarely an irksome exercise and never a wasted one for me because I was locked in a private, mental contest with a very shrewd captain. Significantly, I think, few people challenged Close's command of the tactics of the game and few have challenged mine over the years.

Boycott appeared in his 100th Test match on 2 July 1981, against Australia at Lord's.

Wanting to become Yorkshire captain was a perfectly natural though by no means inevitable progression as far as I was concerned. As it turned out, it became a source of almost constant pain and in fact cost me three years of playing for England. The emotional pull of leading Yorkshire, plus the fact that I really felt I could do the job, blinded me to practically any other consideration. I did not realise until much later in my life that it might not have been the most important thing in the world; perhaps I would have been happier simply trying to be the best player and fulfilling myself rather than the hopes of others. But I still look back on the Yorkshire captaincy, heartache and all, with a lot of pride. I did it and they can't take that away from me. There are no medals for losing captains but I recall a comment by Sir Leonard Hutton some years ago: 'I think it's not a question of one's ability as a captain. It's a matter of being in the right place at the right time.'

Ian Botham's involvement with the captaincy of England was eventful, sometimes controversial, and eventually painful for him. I don't see how it could have turned out any other way, because he was totally unsuited to the job at the time he was given it. Brearley had retired, Boycott was beyond the pale and there was no candidate more obvious – or more premature – than the phenomenal Both. I did not expect him to turn it down and I knew he would do his best to make a go of it, but it was a crazy selection which reflects no credit whatsoever on the people who made it. For a start, Botham had practically no experience of captaincy. That is not a complete bar, of course. I'm aware that Leonard captained England without captaining Yorkshire, but he had been playing Test cricket for a decade before he became England's first professional captain and he was a decidedly more mature individual than Botham. That was another fundamental drawback to Botham as captain – his lack of personal maturity. Terrorising the dressing room, half-dislocating the odd shoulder and sitting on somebody's chest may be okay for a player of elephantine stature, especially with a captain at hand to call a halt when it threatens to get out of hand. It is no behaviour for a captain who will later have to call for greater discipline and sense of responsibility from his players.

That incompatibility was not Botham's fault. It should have been quite obvious to the men who put him there. His lack of experience coupled with a rumbustious personality really never gave him a chance. So we inevitably hit the sort of situation that cropped up in Trinidad, where Botham threatened that 'heads will roll' if we did not save the Test match, and then proceeded to play one of the most atrocious shots I have seen in Test cricket. He holed out to a delivery from his old mate and adversary Viv Richards. For an unthinking moment it was Botham versus Viv, ego versus ego, and Botham lost expensively. Total immaturity – and what had been the beauty of his game as a player became a millstone as captain. Botham is an undisciplined individual who translates that into unorthodoxy and sheer unpredictability as a player. Good luck to him; it is a great strength. But indiscipline is no qualification for Test captaincy. I told him during a quiet talk in Jamaica that he should not have been given the captaincy until he was thirty-one or thirty-two – because I could not see him growing up before then! He must have thought there was something in it: I'm still here to tell the tale.

Botham's private life is his own business, or should be, and there is no way I will be involved in the many controversies surrounding his off-the-field reputation. I have lived with the media too long not to recognise the superstar syndrome for what it is. But I do feel he mistakenly believes that his fame gives him a right to ignore accepted norms of conduct, and I fail to see how he can protest his right to a private life when he invites the media into it. It does not make sense for Ian or his wife Kath to go endlessly into print asking to be left alone. He will have to accept that if he wants a private life, and I think that is very important, the first steps are up to him. So far, because he is basically a person who enjoys the limelight and the notoriety, he has tended to flaunt himself in the belief that he can switch off the spotlight when it suits him. It is a dangerous illusion. As a celebrity, Botham is vulnerable to the 'birds, booze and drugs' syndrome much loved of some of the popular press. Frankly, I think the birds and booze business is a matter for him and his family. I don't think it has a damned thing to do with anybody else, even if the problem exists – and there aren't too many people who could look in a mirror and be entirely happy with what they see. But drugs? Botham can't expect any sympathy or special treatment there. It's a bad example and quite simply it is against the law.

Botham plans to spend a lot of his time in the near future playing in Australia, and I'm sure that will be good for him. It can be a sort of fresh start for him – new situation, new friends, new media. If he wants it to be. I hope he does not allow himself to be dragged into the media syndrome and recreate in Australia what he would rather leave behind in Britain.

As far as his future playing for England is concerned, I reckon he has as much chance of being captain again as I have. I suspected he might make it once and there is always the possibility that a crisis could arise which might give him another match or two in charge. But it is an extremely long shot. The establishment will have its own view of him now.

Whatever happens, he is already sure of a place in the history of the game – and for all the right reasons. He is one of the greatest players I ever played alongside and I'm glad I was around to see the explosions and to enjoy the sheer entertainment value of the guy. It was a pleasure and a privilege. Botham is my sort of cricketer and, whatever happens to him from now on, I wish him well.

21

Roads to Rebellion

India is not my favourite country. Don't misunderstand me. I have nothing but the fondest memories of the people – their cheerfulness, their sometimes overpowering friendliness and willingness to help, their marvellous enthusiasm for the game. The people of India are great, but conditions in India are not, and I was always decidedly nervous about the prospect of undertaking a long tour and coming away with a serious illness. My medical history after the loss of my spleen was not exactly comforting and neither were reports I'd had of India from older players. It may sound melodramatic but India spelled the end of some careers, and as recently as 1977 Clive Taylor, the cricket correspondent of the *Sun* newspaper, contracted an illness on tour in India which was diagnosed as hepatitis, and died. A tragedy like that sticks in the mind and brings back memories of men like Roy Kilner, who went on a coaching tour to India in 1928, contracted enteric fever and died at his home in South Yorkshire. (Amazingly, 100,000 mourners attended his funeral at Wombwell.) Australia's Gavin Stevens and Gordon Rorke went down with hepatitis in India, had to be sent home and never played again. Fear of serious illness in the subcontinent led me to turn down tours to Pakistan in 1968, India in 1972–3 and again in 1976–7. I crossed my fingers and went to Pakistan in 1977–8 – and ended up being dreadfully ill in Hyderabad, where I was so weak I could scarcely look after myself and I spent four days living on Mars bars. That didn't exactly dispel my misgivings about cricket tours in Pakistan and India – a pity in many ways since as a cricketer I wanted to play in as many countries of the world as I could. Given the chance, I would play cricket on the dark side of the moon.

My view of India changed somewhat in 1980, when we played the Jubilee Test in Bombay on our way back from a tour of Australia. The stay was short, about ten days, and the Taj Mahal Hotel was superb. No problems at all, and everyone was anxious to impress on us just how much conditions in India had improved. Experience showed that in the major cities they *are* very good – certainly far better than whole generations of cricket tourists once had to put up with – but the situation up-country is very different indeed. I didn't fully understand that when I accepted the invitation to join the 1981–2 tour under Keith Fletcher.

There were problems before a wheel left the ground, chiefly because the Indian government began to make noises about refusing entry to myself and Geoff Cook because we had played and coached in South Africa. The Indian cricket board was happy enough to have us but the government obviously felt it had to be seen to take some sort of a stand on the anti-Apartheid front. My views on South Africa and Apartheid were clear enough, insofar as I had thought them through and described them in a book published earlier that year.

I was having a pre-tour break in Hong Kong when the telephone wires began to hum. George Mann, chairman of the TCCB, secretary Donald Carr, Robin Marlar of the *Sunday Times*, who seemed closely associated with the politics of the situation, all called me. Would I give a public assurance that I would not go to South Africa again? Would I condemn Apartheid? The official line was that the TCCB would not bow to political pressure in determining just who was picked in tour parties, but it seemed it would help the Indian government if I publicly disowned South Africa. I refused. I was not prepared to allow any politician to chip away at my rights just for the sake of a bit of window-dressing. It was not up to me to get the politicians off the hook. In the event, the tour went ahead and I took the opportunity in Delhi of giving a copy of my book – Apartheid references and all – to the Indian Prime Minister Mrs Gandhi. 'You caused us some trouble,' she said before moving on. I did not have time to tell her I reckoned she had caused it herself. Within four days of our arrival in India the tour manager Raman Subba Row called me in to counsel extreme caution in discussing South Africa. It appeared I had been overheard talking casually about South Africa to a group of people on my return from practice. 'If anyone says anything about South Africa, pull the blind down and say "I'm not here to discuss it."' he said. That sounded okay but it could make me look a fearful idiot. It was obvious that whatever I felt – and frankly I did not want to be involved in the political business any more than I had to – Subba Row and the TCCB were like cats on a hot tin roof. Playing politics can take up as much of their time as playing cricket.

On 23 December 1981 Boycott passed Garry Sobers's world record of 8032 runs in Test Cricket.

I was still worried about matters at Yorkshire, not least because I had had it confirmed that the committee wanted to pay me up and get rid of me

A feeling in a million – or hundred hundreds at least. The boundary off Greg Chappell which brought up my hundredth first-class century in the Test match at Headingley, 11 August 1977.

Somewhere in the middle of that lot there is a very tired and very proud England batsman.

Congratulated by Graham Roope after the police restored order.

Keep going, Geoff. Alan Knott comes to my rescue.

Look, no helmet. One of the luxuries of Test cricket on the subcontinent, where spinners are still highly prized. Syed Kirmani and Gundappa Vishwanath look on as I make my way to 60 in the first Test at Bombay, 1981.

All the comforts of – Nagpur. Touring on the subcontinent is no bed of roses, even if the mosquito net is efficient, which it rarely is. Life outside the main cities is a constant battle against discomfort and the probability of health problems.

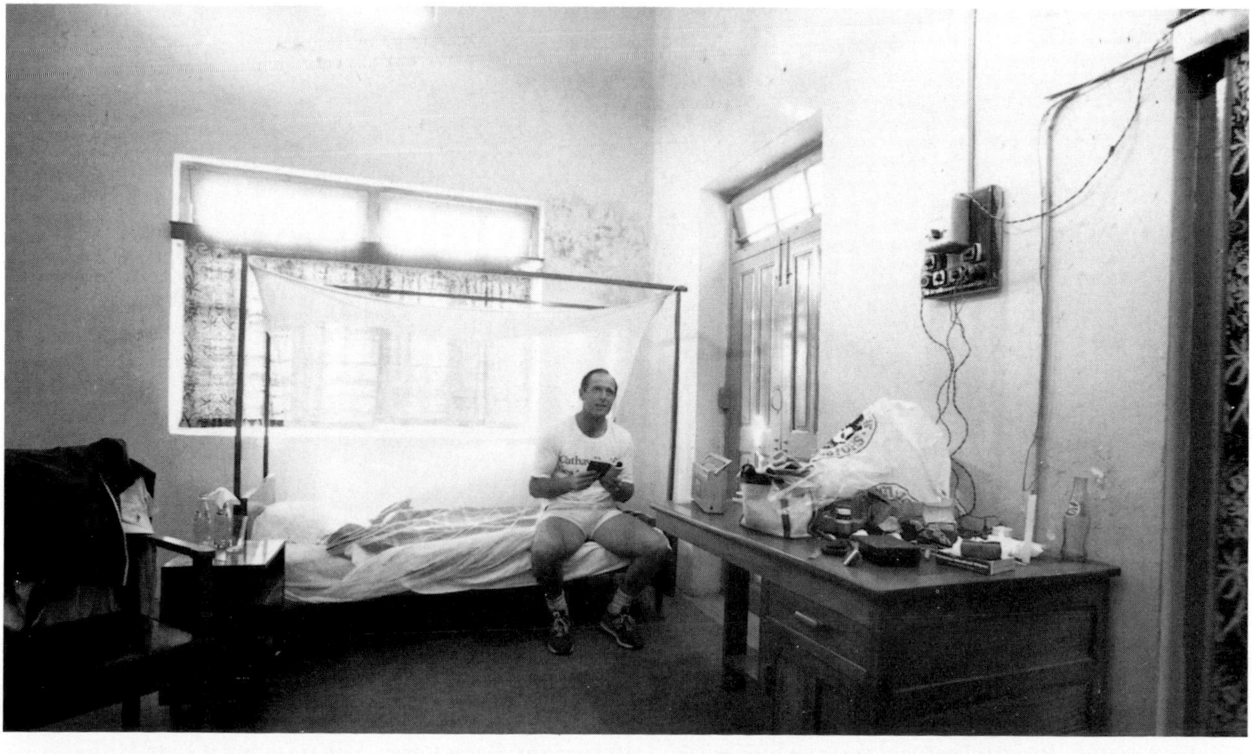

The lonely way: practising before a couple of laid-back spectators in Pakistan.

England captain Boycott leads out the team at Karachi. Left to right: *John Lever, Mike Gatting, Geoff Miller, Phil Edmonds, Derek Randall's head, Boycott, Graham Roope, Bob Willis.*

A rare group picture of the South African 'Rebels' taken in March 1982. All the players have appeared for England, before or since their decision to make the tour. Back row, left to right: *Wayne Larkins, John Lever, Peter Willey, Mike Hendrick, Les Taylor, Chris Old, John Emburey, Arnie Sidebottom, Bob Woolmer, Geoff Humpage.* Seated: *Alan Knott, Dennis Amiss, Graham Gooch, Peter Cooke* (manager), *Geoff Boycott, Derek Underwood, Martin Locke* (assistant manager).

Not quite sure what that will do for east–west relations . . . A message from a fan on the Berlin Wall.

Celebrating with Yorkshire President Sir Kenneth Parkinson.

A.H. Connell, Chairman YCC 1971–9 (left), *and J.T. Temple.*

Yorkshire Reform Group meeting, Ossett, 1983.

J.R. Burnet, M.G. Crawford and J. Lister.

J.D.W. Bailey and W.H.H. Sutcliffe.

Togetherness, Yorkshire style. A friendly word of advice, or perhaps just the latest joke, from ever-involved David Bairstow. Ray Illingworth thoughtful in the background.

irrespective of what the in-depth investigation might say. And conditions as the tour wore on gradually got me down and began to affect my health. One thing for sure – not all the hotels were Taj Mahals!

In Nagpur, for instance, we spent a week at the Circuit House, a sort of government hostel in dilapidated concrete which was eloquently described by Fletcher as 'a spacious cowshed'. The fact that it was the best accommodation in town said a lot for the attitude of our hosts and absolutely nothing for the place itself. It was filthy, black with encrusted dirt and festooned with cobwebs. The beds were all of 5 foot 3 inches long, which left Bob Willis to sleep – when he could – with his great feet sticking miles over the end. The only light in the place was provided by a grimy bulb on a cord, which made it impossible to read or write a letter; and the toilet facilities were dreadful. Primitive would not begin to describe it and the players compensated, typically, by making a joke of the whole situation. Hunting parties went in search of Rodney the Rat and Sammy the Snake, and Botham and Lever became quite expert at catching cockroaches. The knack, apparently, is to leave the light off until you are ready, then flick it on and whack them before they have time to run for cover – a skill no England cricketer should be without.

The highlight of the evening was dinner, not because it resembled the sort of evening meal you or I would expect but because it whiled away some of the tedium enforced by a near-total lack of alternatives. Boredom up-country in India is almost absolute. The food, when identifiable, was monotonous and tasteless. And the sheer repetitiveness of our diet made me realise how right those seasoned tourists were who insisted it was important to be a drinking man in India, not just for the semi-escapism but because the beer itself became an important dietary supplement. A fair amount of nourishment and liquid in a safe, recognisable form. I did not drink myself and I did not feel any the better for it.

Boycott's last Test innings, in 1982, took his Test aggregate to 8114 runs. This world record has since been overtaken by Sunil Gavaskar.

Nagpur was bad, Jammu in its own way was worse. Our beds were damp, an open invitation to pneumonia. And the only solution Subba Row could devise, since it appeared impolite to complain, was to position fan heaters to blow all day on the mattresses in the hope of drying them out. You tried to laugh it off, but the humour wore thin after several trying weeks. Try eating your favourite food every day for a week and the pleasure palls; try eating toasted ham and spam sandwiches every lunchtime for two months and you are quite ready to go round the bend, never mind play cricket. And when you feel off-colour, there is understandably little sympathy from team-mates who don't exactly feel on top of the world themselves. It is difficult to define illness when nobody is well. I felt increasingly sick but that was accepted as normal and nobody was disposed to take too much notice. Perhaps it looked like swinging the lead. I know for a fact that it felt awful.

Just when I was at a low ebb, an incident occurred that was to have the greatest possible bearing on my relations with Fletcher and Subba Row. And, again, it was totally unnecessary. I received copies of the English newspapers in which Fletcher was reported as saying that he had told Chris Tavaré and myself to get a move on during the Test match in Delhi. It was plastered over the back pages – another Boycott row – and I certainly could do without that at a time when my critics in Yorkshire were looking for ammunition against me. Worse still, it was untrue. Fletcher had never spoken to me about scoring rates or anything vaguely similar. Obviously, I wanted to get to the bottom of it and, just as predictably, Fletcher insisted to my face that he had been misquoted. Trouble was, I borrowed a tape recording of his interview to the press and there was absolutely no way he had been misrepresented or misunderstood. I replayed it to him and Subba Row a dozen times and he still made foolish denials. It was ludicrous. I wanted the record put straight; Subba Row seemed to think it was quite out of the question for an England captain to admit to a mistake, much less a lie. My reputation was to be swilled down the drain again just to protect a captain who had sounded off for God only knows what reason, and I was not having that. I stood my ground and insisted on an apology.

Raman Subba Row suffered on that tour from the same obsessive diplomacy that had afflicted Ken Barrington in New Zealand four years earlier. There were no lengths to which he would not go in order to placate the locals and win points as a fine English gentleman, even when that went against the best interests of his own players. Keith Fletcher had been out of Test cricket for almost five years and had lost touch with changing realities – the tour had a tendency to run him rather than the other way round. Between them they spent an awful lot of time tinkering with all the trappings and incidentals of touring rather than getting down to the business of playing good cricket and winning matches. It was obvious after we had lost the first Test in Bombay that it was going to be an uphill struggle: the pitches were bland and it would be the devil's own job to pull a Test back. Yet team selection was awry and too much official time was spent genuflecting in front of local officials instead of tackling problems head-on. I don't know if it impressed the locals but it offended me – there has to be a point at which good manners ends and fawning begins. As a professional trying to win a Test series I expected nothing more from the Indian officials than efficiency and straight dealing. I have no reason to think they expected anything more from us, but I rather fancy they got it. I obtained my apology from Fletcher, too, and it was inevitably blared across the sports pages back in England, which would not suit him or the establishment. It came at a high price – my relationship with the captain and the manager became distinctly distant, not to say icy, after that.

My health degenerated too. I make no secret of my fears about touring India so it is not impossible that the problems were partly psychological, but I was in no mood to analyse myself at the time when my body was telling me something was very wrong. At the end of the Test match in Delhi I awoke in the small hours running a temperature, shaking feverishly and suffering from diarrhoea. The team physiotherapist Bernard Thomas was getting up that morning at 4.30 to visit the Taj Mahal so I did not disturb him. Instead I contacted the hotel doctor, who prescribed tablets and advised me to seek further help next day. A doctor at the British High Commission diagnosed a viral infection and wanted me to stay in his care for a few days while he treated me and ran some tests, but on his return from the Taj Subba Row insisted I fly on with the rest of the party to Calcutta that night. He was impatient and dismissive. My insistence on a retraction from Fletcher had clearly left a bitter taste.

In Calcutta I hardly had the strength to practise in the nets, a few minutes at a time was as much as I could take. I felt terrible when we went into the Test match and got worse as the match progressed. I could not face food for three days and spent most of the game ill in bed at the hotel. Fever, constant diarrhoea, not eating and taking hardly any liquid left me listless and very down. I had to insist on the management getting me a doctor, and desperately wanted to go back to Delhi to see if the British doctor could put me right. I even offered to pay my own fare. But Subba Row would not hear of it; he mentioned my having the next match off and insisted that I would have to go to Madras with Botham, Willis and their wives while the rest of the team moved on to Jamshedpur. As far as I knew, no arrangements had been made for me to see a doctor in Madras.

Subba Row's attitude was pure bloody-mindedness. I did not expect him to sit at my bedside but I did expect him to co-operate, at least, in anything which would get me back on my feet. He obviously did not give a damn. Bernard Thomas advised me to get out of my room if I could – I had only been out for about twenty minutes in three days – and suggested I should go for a walk in the fresh air, though the term 'fresh' is strictly relative when applied to Calcutta. Try to get to the ground, if only to pack your case, said Bernard. I made my way to the ground, set aside some gear so that I could practise in Madras if I felt better and packed the rest. The only place reasonably near by where it was possible to walk without ploughing through thousands of bodies was the Tolly Gunge golf course, and since they were not playing in the match I asked Geoff Cook and Paul Allott if they fancied joining me. Cook wanted to come but he couldn't get out of twelfth-man duties. They thought they should hang around.

I walked a few holes of the course, knocking a golf ball for the exercise, sitting down when I felt wearied. The suggestion that I went off and played a round of golf creates visions of Boycott striding out, marking a card, oblivious to his team-mates or his responsibilities, which is utter rubbish. As far as I was concerned, I was trying to take Thomas's advice and get a bit of fresh air to buck myself up. I saw absolutely nothing sinister in that.

Subba Row was on the phone as soon as I got back to the hotel. Had I been playing golf? After a fashion. 'You went without my permission and the team is very annoyed about it. You'd better come to my room.' When I got there Subba Row had been joined by Fletcher, Willis and Thomas, and the mood was very accusing. I pointed out that Bernard had suggested I get out for a walk and I could only apologise if my actions had been misunderstood. I had not done anything surreptitious. I'd even mentioned it to players in the dressing room and nobody threw their hands up in horror. The fact that they were annoyed and frustrated at not being able to force a win in the Test match was understandable enough but I did not fancy the idea of them taking it out on me. The more we talked the less we agreed. It was a hopeless situation and I'd had a bellyful of it. Subba Row demanded a written apology and said I should apologise to the players. There followed a pathetic discussion about exactly how I should deliver it. In the end I promised a written apology for him, a written apology for the players and a written resignation from the tour.

I went into the adjoining players' room, borrowed a pen from Botham and wrote out my letters of apology and resignation. I stuck the players' letter on the door of the fridge where everybody would be bound to see it (because the fridge contained the beer). Next morning Subba Row and Fletcher came to my room and reiterated their belief that it would be best for everyone if I went home. This was the only time Fletcher came to see me during my illness. Subba Row saw me off at the airport. I reckon he was glad to see the back of me – and the feeling was mutual.

Looking back, I can easily appreciate what a bad impression I must have given that day in Calcutta. Boycott, too ill to field, goes off playing golf while his England team-mates are fighting hard in a Test match. Put as baldly as that, it looks terrible. But the facts of the so-called 'golf' expedition are slightly different and I'm sure the significance of the whole incident was magnified by attitudes which had already been struck. I still do not know what possessed Keith Fletcher to tell the press he had given Tavaré and myself instructions to get a move on when in fact he had never said a word. I do know that he deeply resented having to retract that statement and I know that Subba Row felt just as strongly that I was wrong to insist on an apology. We rarely saw eye to eye on anything after that. My dread of being ill in India probably made things seem worse than they were. I *was* ill and dispirited and disorientated. By the time we got to Calcutta I would have given anything for the luxury of just feeling well again. Heading off to a golf course was a misguided, foolish thing to do in the circumstances but there was nothing underhand or uncaring about it. My health and the troubles at Yorkshire preyed on my mind, there was a lack of consideration from management, and I made a mistake for which I have apologised. I was perhaps unfortunate to be judged by people who had never made a mistake in their lives . . .

The possibility of an English team of near-Test strength making a tour to South Africa was first mentioned to me in December 1980 by Peter Cooke, a cricket fanatic and then manager of a large South African recording company. I was in the republic on holiday before embarking on the England tour of the West Indies early in 1981. We did not discuss any details, just the broad concept, and it stayed that way until Cooke caught up with us at the Trinidad Hilton in February. Then the so-called rebel tour of South Africa began to take shape.

Boycott has scored more runs in Test cricket than any other England player.

The philosophy was simple enough: the tour would involve as many current England players as possible and would be so arranged as not to clash with the county championship season or with Test match tours. It was never intended to be an alternative to established cricket and we genuinely believed that we could fit in a South African tour without breaking our county contracts and without disrupting the international Test schedule. We were not simple enough to believe the tour would be uncontroversial, but we did not look at it from a political point of view. Quite simply, it was a business proposition of the type that might be considered by any professional in any walk of life. Its moral character was a matter for individuals, as it always should be. There was no talk of bridging ideologies or nurturing international understanding. It was a job and it would make money for us – that was the unglamorised and unpretentious truth of the matter.

Robin Jackman was kicked out of Guyana during our Caribbean tour and our sympathies were entirely with him. His crime, it seemed, was that he had had the temerity to marry a South African and attempt to earn part of his living in that country. We sat around not knowing if the Caribbean tour would go on or not, and frankly we were pretty fed up with this latest demonstration of black (political) power on the international cricket scene. There had been no official tour to South Africa since 1964, a lot of people were curious to play there, and in any case five of the tour party besides myself had already signed in principle to undertake a 'rebel' tour. Ian Botham, David Gower, Graham Gooch, John Emburey and Graham Dilley signed statements – which were needed as proof of good faith to prospective sponsors – in Trinidad on 19 February. Peter Cooke came up with a sponsor, Holiday Inns, whose chief stipulation was that the tour party must include myself and Botham as well as other high-quality players. That seemed no problem; I was committed and Botham was especially keen. Plans inched forward steadily during the next English summer, formulated in secrecy because we knew full well it would be impossible to organise a tour in a glare of publicity. Keeping our plans under wraps also allowed players time to consider all the angles and to make up their own minds without interference from the media and the inevitable pressure groups.

The original plan was for a month-long tour beginning in October 1981 and finishing in time for the selected players to join the England tour to India. The Jackman affair made us rather more aware of the political heat likely to be generated and we agreed to postpone the 'rebel' tour until after the official tour of India. Going to South Africa immediately before an India tour would probably be provocative and we certainly did not want to disrupt establishment cricket in any way. On the contrary, we were very anxious to continue playing for England ourselves. Quite out of the blue, the Test and County Cricket Board issued a letter to all contracted county cricketers in August 1981 warning against signing for any representative tour to South Africa. They had got wind of a proposed tour, but not the one we had on the cards. Some seventeen players were already involved in a privately organised tour as the English Counties XI and the TCCB warned that anybody taking part in such tours 'could thereby make himself ineligible for future selection for England.'

That was plain enough but we still felt that if a majority of the current Test team embarked on a South African tour – as free agents breaking no law – it would be morally and practically difficult for the TCCB to take punitive action. We were, I suppose, working on the principle of safety in numbers.

In September, Holiday Inns' representative Stuart Banner arrived in Britain to finalise contracts for a tour which was now due to take place in March after the India tour. Holiday Inns would pay £500,000 for a party of fourteen players plus Bernard Thomas as physiotherapist–manager. I had already confirmed with Bernard that he was interested. The money would be paid into a company in Greenock, Scotland, called Rasip, and that company would move it into the newly formed players' company, Oxychem in London. The contracts envisaged a tour of one month with one major match against a South African XI and included free flights and accommodation for the players, their wives and families or their girlfriends. Those players who had been on the India tour could fly direct to South Africa or return home and then fly out via a European city. It was a good deal.

By this time, the original party of six had been increased by the addition of Alan Knott, Bob Willis and Mike Gatting. I spoke to the players by telephone and they were all anxious to go ahead, but there was no way I wanted to be looking over their shoulders when they finally signed up. The opportunity was there. It was up to each individual to make his own decision whether to sign a contract, and I certainly did not want to appear to be putting anybody under pressure. Everyone had to decide the strength of his own commitment, and naturally Stuart Banner was anxious to judge for himself just how committed individuals were. I left it in his hands and went off for my break in Hong Kong.

Banner told me later that he saw Gooch, Dilley, Knott and Gatting at a London hotel and spoke to Gower, Botham and Willis on the phone. He was very conscious of the sponsors' insistence that Boycott and Botham must be in the tour party. Botham was holidaying with Viv Richards in Antigua and reiterated his keenness to take part. Gooch spoke to John Emburey, who was holidaying in Australia, and Emburey was anxious to be counted in. The only exception was Gatting, whose solicitor advised him he could be in breach of his contract with Middlesex if he went on the tour. Gatting pulled out with a promise that he would not leak details of the tour plans.

On 19 December 1979 Boycott became only the third England player (after R. Abel and Len Hutton) to carry his bat through a completed innings against Australia, scoring 99 not out, out of 215, at Perth.

It was obvious from the TCCB's letter that we might get a rough ride when details of the tour were revealed. It was not impossible that we would be banned from playing for England, and both Gooch and Gower said, reasonably enough, that the cash and conditions should reflect that risk. On 21 November we had a meeting in Willis's room at the Express Hotel in Baroda – Botham, Dilley, Gooch, Emburey, Gower, Willis and myself – to mull over some of the details and the implications. There was no doubting our level of commitment by now. Banner was so confident of us that he assured the South African Cricket Union that the tour would go ahead and the president Joe Pamensky called off the proposed Counties XI tour. But there was a strong feeling that there should be some sort of insurance against the loss of earnings if we were banned by England.

Gower felt that £150,000 spread over three years was a realistic figure if we were banned from Test cricket. Gooch thought £40,000 a year with the prospect of two or three extra years. Dilley mentioned £60,000 up front plus two extra years. The permutations were varied but the point was that players wanted something to fall back on if an England ban was applied. 'It's your future, it's not just a matter of cash on the table,' said Botham. 'You have to think of your families.' Botham was concerned about how far the South African contract would affect existing endorsement agreements and wanted a legal brain to study that for him. He admitted he did not give a hoot about what the TCCB might do but, oddly enough, he was worried about political repercussions. He wondered if the government might refuse to let us back into the country!

The political temperature had certainly risen since the Jackman affair in the West Indies and we had the recent wrangling over Geoff Cook and myself to illustrate how complicated it could all become. That is why the money seemed so important to cover the higher risk of being banned and that is why I was determined to see if there was any shift in commitment. When I asked him directly, Botham insisted he had not changed his mind about making the tour, though he recognised the need for safeguards to protect his interests. Gower said he would accept £50,000 and not press for further options so long as his international career was not affected. 'We don't want anybody jacking out a month before,' said Gooch. 'You're either in or out.'

Every time we had a meeting, it was stressed that players must decide for themselves what they considered to be in their best interests. But it was also important that anyone who felt like pulling out should do so quickly, rather than jeopardise the whole tour by leaving it to the last minute. We felt that Holiday Inns would come up with the extra cash and we finally agreed to put to them a figure of £150,000 over three years. Inside a week their representative Peter Venison was in Bombay with the authority to make decisions.

His offer, outlined on 30 November, envisaged a tour party of thirteen players, eight of whom were already known. The rest had to be signed up by 18 January 1982. Cash up front for the first year would be £45,000 with provision for a second and third year if the players were banned from international cricket. The fee would increase by 5 per cent each year. Wives and girlfriends would accompany the tour, all expenses paid, money would be available in the players' account before the tour started and no tax would be payable in South Africa. All we had to do was to sign – preferably there and then.

David Gower ventured the general feeling that he would rather have time to let his solicitor look at the contract details and implications before finally committing himself to a signature. 'All we are asking for is a bit of grace,' he said. And it was agreed that Venison would take our verbal acceptances back to Holiday Inns and SACU before returning on 18 January to sew up the tour formally. We were that close to sealing it when the venture fell apart.

A week after Venison's departure, Ian Botham announced during the second Test at Bangalore that he was pulling out. He had learned through his agent, Reg Hayter, that new and lucrative contracts had been negotiated in the light of his performances the previous summer against Australia, including a huge seven-year deal with the sportswear manufacturers Nike and a lucrative TV commercial for Shredded Wheat. Financially, it would make no sense for him to go to South Africa now. Botham's solicitor Alan Herd arrived, spoke on the telephone to Venison and later confirmed that Botham was determined not to risk his new-found wealth by joining the tour. We understood that well enough but in view of the long-standing stipulation that Botham and I had to be included, it looked like the end of the tour. The players met in Delhi on 27 December – ironically while I was confronting Fletcher and Subba Row about the so-called instructions to get a move on – and at that meeting Gower said he was going to opt out. Former Derbyshire and England bowler Fred Rumsey had offered him a stake in a travel firm involved chiefly in Caribbean tours and Gower reckoned he would not be welcome in the West Indies if he had taken part in a South African tour.

Venison rang me on 29 December to say that the sponsors knew of Botham's decision and would not accept anyone else dropping out. I had to tell him that Gower had already done so. The tour was off . . . and I left India a week later.

A little over a month later, back in England, weak, listless and still recovering from the viral infection contracted during my India tour, I received a call from Peter Cooke and Joe Pamensky. They were determined that a tour to South Africa should go ahead, whatever the difficulties. New sponsors would have to be found, new agreements would have to be reached and new contracts signed, but they were desperate to see a tour go ahead. I did not think it was possible. There were too many problems to overcome, and in any case there wasn't a lot I could do in England – feeling like death warmed up – while many of the principal players were thousands of miles away in India. If they wanted to set up a tour, they would have to contact the players themselves.

A few days later a newspaper carried a report that I was intending to fly to South Africa to organise and play in a 'rebel' tour, and Donald Carr was on the phone like a shot to check it out. As far as I was concerned the Holiday Inns tour was dead and buried, and I really could not see an alternative being organised, so I was not lying when I told him I had no intention of going to South Africa in a proposed tour. But I rang Bob Willis in India to warn the players concerned and put them on their guard – Carr was on his way with a lot of questions to ask. Willis told me that somebody had already been on to Gooch with suggestions for a new tour and the players were talking about it. Perhaps it was not quite as dead as I thought.

Cooke arrived in England and I reiterated that there was precious little I could do to help him except to furnish him with telephone numbers. I was preoccupied with my health and with the continuing in-depth dramas at Yorkshire, and frankly I still did not believe a tour was possible. My involvement from then on was minimal, though I kept receiving phone calls from players whom Cooke had contacted. He had come up with another sponsor, South African Breweries, and he was pulling out all the stops to recruit players. It seemed to me that the best he could hope for was a sort of Counties XI on the lines of the one which had been mooted some months earlier. I really thought the problems of contacting players up and down the country and half the world away were insurmountable, but I underestimated Cooke's drive and determination.

Slowly the tour party began to take shape, though certainly not without stops and starts. Bob Willis, John Emburey, Geoff Cook, John Lever and Derek Underwood were said to be in; Paul Allott and Chris Tavaré were probables. Graham Gooch and Graham Dilley were out, though Gooch changed his mind and joined up at the last minute. There was talk while he was in India of his getting the England captaincy and that naturally delayed his decision. Tavaré and Allott declined to go, Allott because he reckoned quite reasonably that in the absence of Willis and Lever he would have a good chance of playing for England.

By the middle of February Cooke had signed up Peter Willey, Wayne Larkins and Alan Knott; Mike Hendrick and Dennis Amiss followed soon afterwards. Chris Old and Les Taylor were already in South Africa and were being approached. By 19 February Cooke had all the confirmations he needed to get a written guarantee of financial backing from the South African Breweries and to produce his own contracts for signature. They were agreed between Oxchem (the 'y' had disappeared) and individual players, who would receive 10 per cent of their fee on arrival in South Africa, one-third after the first match, one-half when the tour was halfway through and the rest after the last game.

The England touring party arrived back from India and Sri Lanka on

24 February and Cooke spent the next two days feverishly tearing about getting signatures and making last-minute arrangements. How he managed it without every newspaper in the country breaking the whole, detailed story remains a mystery, but the press were certainly beginning to sniff a 'rebel tour' story afresh. The squad was due to leave for South Africa on Sunday, 28 February, but players were beginning to get educated and inquisitive phone calls from the TCCB, and the departure date was brought forward a day. Barely twenty-four hours before that, Bob Willis pulled out. He felt he had a future in the administration of English cricket, and although he leaned towards making the tour, his wife was firmly against it. Geoff Cook phoned at the last minute and pulled out too. Peter Cooke was close to panic when he called me at my home and urged me to join the tour.

Boycott has reached 50 sixty-four times in Test cricket – more than any other player except S. M. Gavaskar of India.

The last-minute withdrawals had unnerved one or two players, he said. The sponsors were anxious to have as many international players as possible in the squad and from a purely cricketing point of view he needed another batsman now that Geoff Cook had declined. 'I just want to get a team out of the country and I need you to be in it. I want you on that plane,' he said. There wasn't much time to take stock of my position.

As I saw it, there was a very real possibility that I would be out of a job in a couple of weeks' time. On Wednesday, 24 February, it had been leaked in Yorkshire that the in-depth investigation would recommend that I be sacked, which did not surprise me one bit. The newspapers were full of 'Yorkshire to sack Boycott' and my phone was red hot. In no time at all my home was besieged by reporters, photographers and TV cameras, all wanting me to add comment to this impending event. Assuming I had been prepared to play for another county, which was no formality at the age of forty-one, I would still be faced with a block on any more Tests for England. It would not be admitted officially, of course, and I had already received non-committal answers when I spoke to Alec Bedser and the selectors' chairman-elect Peter May. The press had been writing informed articles from the India tour that I had played my last Test match and Keith Fletcher was making provocative noises about wanting Amiss back as opener. Subba Row would do me no favours in his India tour report. It would be back to the Barrington syndrome – nothing too damaging on paper but plenty of verbal advice on how this man should never play for England again. Given a choice I would rather have played for England than gone to South Africa. As it was, I came to the conclusion that I had no choice and very little to lose.

I threw my cricket gear in a couple of cases, packed my bags and caught the 1.06 p.m. train from Wakefield to London *en route* for the 5.15 p.m. Saturday flight from Heathrow to Johannesburg. It was such a rush and I was in such a state that I left my suit covers on the train when I caught a cab to the airport. We travelled first class – Boycott, Gooch, Emburey, Lever, Underwood, Larkins, Amiss, Willey, Knott and Hendrick – and were met in South Africa by Old and Taylor. The Dirty Dozen had arrived.

Virtually as soon as we settled in, Emburey phoned Geoff Cook to find out why he had pulled out at the last minute. Cook, after all, had signed a contract and given a commitment to colleagues. It seemed out of character that he should renege, and he could certainly do with the £45,000 which his contract involved. Cook's experience was to become familiar: he had been put under enormous pressure by Northants and by TCCB members who had contacted him. It was suggested by his club that if he went to South Africa his position as captain and his prospects of a benefit would be in jeopardy. Donald Carr and then George Mann talked about the tour splitting cricket down the middle and Mann even mentioned that Geoff might be needed as England captain. So much for *that* – Geoff never played another Test match. The propaganda and the thinly veiled threats were powerful, and Geoff finally gave way, though he was far from convinced that he had made the right decision and was close to tears when we spoke to him from South Africa. He was upset because he felt he had let us down, and in a sense he had, but it was difficult at the time to withstand the pressures and the personal aggravation involved. Larkins and Willey were incensed when they heard that Cook had denied all knowledge of their involvement in the tour. It seemed like a total betrayal at the time, but looking back it is hard to see what else a captain under pressure from Northants and with his future to consider could have said. The establishment don't exactly play fair – as they would like people to think – in situations like these.

We needed batsmen to balance the team and the word went out to Derek Randall in Australia, where his club side would not release him from his contract; to Paul Parker, who preferred to take his chance of winning an England place; and to Bob Woolmer, who checked with Kent and was warned that his future employment and benefit would be endangered. South African Breweries agreed to sign Woolmer up and compensate him up to £40,000 if Kent eventually refused him a benefit. Arnie Sidebottom was recruited later on the tour when bowlers went down injured and Geoff Humpage joined us, primarily as a batsman, after a fine season in the county championship. Tony Greig, who was playing in Sydney Grade cricket, had sent word that he was available, and the players fancied recruiting Alvin Kallicharran – which led to a strongly worded if brief disagreement with the SACU officials.

It dawned on us that SACU wanted to pass us off as an England team, playing Test matches against a Springbok side, and they could hardly do that if our side included a player like Kallicharran. That was not our purpose and in fact it went against the way most of us saw the tour. We did not react kindly to being used and I told Joe Pamensky so in no uncertain terms, but he made some unconvincing remarks about being overruled by the cricket union.

The story soon became current that I had been overlooked as captain of the team by popular demand. I was supposed to be annoyed that Gooch had been given the job. The fact is that I was pressed to take the captaincy and refused; Gooch then took on the job, but very reluctantly. Once he had it, he did it very well, a firm and resolute character who does not take half-measures once he is committed to a cause. We all respected him for that. The captaincy was first offered to Keith Fletcher, who said he wanted time to think it over and eventually rang back Gooch to turn it down. Fletcher said he would have accepted but for the fact that he was on the verge of a benefit year, which was fair enough. But it did not quite square with his version splashed expansively across the back page of an English tabloid a couple of days later: no mention of benefit cash there, just the rather more pious belief in the sanctity of the England captaincy.

Less than a week after we arrived in South Africa, we each received a communication signed by A. R. Thomas, Deputy Consul-General, passing on a message from the TCCB. It read:

> We must make you aware of the very strong reaction in England and other countries to the proposed participation by you and other English cricketers in international calibre matches in South Africa. In particular, the India and Pakistan tours to the UK this summer could clearly be in danger if the proposed matches take place, thus seriously affecting county finances and the possible future livelihood of fellow cricketers.
>
> If it is still practicable for you to do so, we urge you to reconsider your position and refrain from playing in any such matches.

The letter was signed jointly by Donald Carr and George Mann. And that became rather singular only two days later when Joe Pamensky told us he had received a phone call from Mann urging him to cancel the tour. Mann said that if Pamensky did so, England would propose South Africa for renewed membership of the International Cricket Conference, the gateway to a return to Test cricket.

The probability that such a move would have split cricket far more quickly and acrimoniously than any 'rebel' tour did not seem to concern

Mann overmuch. In any case, Pamensky did not believe him. The best South Africa could hope for in those circumstances was a 4–3 vote against re-entry to the ICC on black–white lines. Pamensky reminded Mann that SACU believed it had a duty to the South African public not to stagnate instead of trusting to proposals, the success of which could not be guaranteed.

We did not expect a round of applause from the media when we became involved, eyes open, in the South African tour. But some of the treatment verged on hysteria, heavily laced with good, old-fashioned hypocrisy. It was particularly unpleasant when it affected wives and families, and I remember Dennis Amiss spending hours on the telephone trying to comfort his wife, who could not take the hostility and 'Blood Money' headlines back in Warwickshire. As a team, we issued a statement and then resolved to say nothing, except insofar as the captain would discuss cricket with the press. Our statement read: 'All players in the South African Breweries English team wish to make it clear that our purpose in being in South Africa is to play cricket and earn our living. Even though we are guests in South Africa we would like it to be known that we do not support Apartheid.' Simple enough, and far too brief for those reporters whose newspapers wanted a daily diet of scandal and controversy. They were hardly there for the cricket and since we would not speak to them they did what a particular type of journalist will always do in the circumstances: they made stories up. It was the worst sort of muckraking, sensational journalism, and several players were extremely bitter by the end of the tour, especially when the same journalists would offer money for exclusive articles. One player was told to name his price for a ghosted book; he refused, and the prospective ghost redoubled his attacks on him.

The saddest comment came from Botham, who was soon quoted in an exclusive article as saying he had turned down the opportunity to join the tour because 'I could never have looked Viv in the eye again.' Botham said it had been his special affection for Viv Richards that had led him to shun the tour and its implied associations with Apartheid in South Africa. This was the same Botham who had been so heavily and enthusiastically involved in arrangements for the Holiday Inns tour; the same man who had looked Viv Richards in the eye after reiterating his support for the tour in the West Indies. It was also the same man who had signed lucrative endorsement and advertising contracts and therefore did not need to go to South Africa for financial security. Nobody begrudged him that. We had accepted his change of mind without acrimony and, despite the reports, without any sort of row. But the suggestion that he had opted out of the tour on moral grounds was unnecessary and puke-making. The players who went to South Africa know Botham's attitude full well and I doubt they will ever forget. 'I won't ever trust Both again,' said Gooch, and I reckon the feeling was unanimous.

On 19 March 1982, the TCCB announced that the 'rebels' had been banned from international cricket for three years. We expected some sort of punishment (though the TCCB legalistically insisted that the ban was for protection rather than as punishment) but three years . . . We were shocked by the severity of the sentence. We enlisted the help of Robert Alexander QC – the man who had appeared for Kerry Packer in his legal battle with the TCCB – and tried to have the ban reduced. Alexander was sure we would win an action for restraint of trade but he also believed that the TCCB, acting as a trades union, would be seen to be protecting the game and that the ban would not be lifted. The TCCB had polished up its legal act considerably since Packer. SACU was prepared to finance legal action and my inclination was to fight the ban, if only to achieve some sort of legal ruling for future generations of professional cricketers; but the majority view was to grin and bear it. We got the distinct impression in our dealings with the TCCB – Gooch, Emburey and I acted on behalf of the players – that they felt themselves that three years was a bit over the top. But the TCCB were under pressure internationally: the World Cup was due in 1983 and the West Indies were due to tour the year after that. If we were not banned there was a good chance that the Windies would come under political pressure from their own governments not to tour. Who says sport and politics don't mix?

It has always seemed deeply ironic to me that when I toured South Africa in 1964, under Donald Carr as manager, and played in front of crowds segregated by virtue of race and colour, and by high wire fences, I was a legitimate England cricketer. An ambassador even. Eighteen years later I played as part of a privately funded team in stadiums where there was no segregation and where cricket people were free to mix as they chose – and I was a 'rebel'. Following the D'Oliveira affair in 1968 the South Africans were told that they could not expect another England team to tour there until cricket was multi-racial at all levels. Cricketers and cricket officials have worked hard to cut through many of the racial laws of the land to make cricket multi-racial. The South African Cricket Union replaced the all-white Cricket Association, and the South African cricket authorities have done everything that was asked of them by the International Cricket Conference and then more. They have shown a lot of courage in the face of a rotten regime and I for one think it should be acknowledged. But one evasion and excuse follows another.

The argument runs that sportsmen can play in South Africa as individuals but not as a team – a handy piece of blatant discrimination since it is impossible for cricketers and others involved in team games to appear as individuals. And the politicking does not stop there. On 1 August 1986 the TCCB met at Lord's and decided to issue a directive to all county players warning them against accepting coaching or playing contracts in South Africa beyond 1987 – even as individuals – because it might jeopardise their future chances of playing international cricket. They believe the ICC is to debate a rule banning all cricketers from going to South Africa on pain of forfeiting their international future. So much for the freedom the anti-Apartheid lobbies claim to hold so dear: the freedom of the individual . . .

22

Collision

The overtures to the 1979 season, Ray Illingworth's first as Yorkshire team manager, were as bland and conciliatory as I always expected them to be. Illingworth had made a few noises in the winter about my attitude needing to be 'right' when I reported back at the club. Fair enough; my attitude was as right as rain. I was anxious to put a poor winter tour of Australia behind me and even more anxious to pick up the pieces after a year of public and private turmoil. I went to the indoor school at Lord's for three days, studying videos which showed clearly that I had got too 'square on' in my stance and was using too much right hand, trying to protect an injured thumb. Once I recognised the problem I could correct it. My form felt good and my head felt remarkably clear, all things considered. At the end of the first-class season I averaged 102, so there was not a lot wrong with my year as a player.

But I knew deep in my bones that I would not be allowed simply to slip back into Yorkshire cricket as a player and do well for myself and the team. Whatever their public protestations, Illingworth and Hampshire knew they began the season sharing the dressing room with Banquo's ghost. As long as I was there, I was a constant reminder to Hampshire of his go-slow at Northampton and to Illingworth of his misleading letter. Sooner or later, I knew, they would have to get rid of me. I was resigned to further trouble. Illingworth took me aside before the season and urged me just to go out and play like a world-class player, to enjoy my cricket and to assume that I would be picked in every Yorkshire match. Just as significantly, in a different way, club officials grilled me about the Reform Group. Could I exercise some sort of influence to make it go away? So long as the club was properly run, I couldn't see any need for a Reform Group but it was certainly not my affair to tell members how to view their own club. It did not take long, in fact, for Illingworth and the Reformers to collide: Illingworth hinted that he might return as a player in June of that year and the Reform Group immediately

The best bowling performance of Boycott's career was 4 Lancashire wickets for 14 runs at Leeds (3 bowled, 1 lbw) on 25 August 1979.

announced its opposition to the idea. It struck me that Illy planned to return as a Yorkshire player as soon as he could possibly wangle it.

Fred Trueman kicked off the season in style when he remarked in April that his one remaining task for Yorkshire, as a newly elected committee-man, was to get rid of Boycott when his contract expired. Here we go again. And antagonism from Illingworth and Hampshire bubbled to the surface well before the season was half over. The team did not win a championship match until 10 July and reached the end of July before winning a second. The brave new world of the Illingworth–Hampshire era was not being vindicated by results. And to make matters infinitely worse, I was doing well – even as a bowler! It was just the state of affairs to set some teeth on edge. Early in July, Illingworth confronted me with the accusation that I was working with the Reform Group against him. Someone had phoned him, or someone had written to complain or yet another someone had claimed I was selling Reform Group ties from the boot of my car! It was baloney and I told him as much. But I also told him I refused to dissociate myself publicly from people who had supported me and fought for me and believed in me; some of them were my friends and I would continue to be sociable to anyone who wanted to be sociable with me.

When Boycott completed the 1979 season with a batting average of 102.53 he became the only player ever to have averaged over 100 in two English seasons.

Hampshire had told me in April that I would be acknowledged as his senior pro and given the respect which that entailed, including taking charge if he was unavailable. When Hampshire was injured for a Sunday match on 22 July, Chris Old was made captain and Illingworth did not even go to the match. Old had to tell me about his promotion himself. Three days later Hampshire challenged Reform Group members at Worksop with: 'I could cheerfully smack him [Boycott] in the gob.' When asked what the problem was, Hampshire repeated this remark and said, 'You people are always giving him big licks.' It was obvious from then on, if it had not been before, that Illingworth and Hampshire did not want me near the team.

The 1980 season began disastrously for the club. We went out of the Benson and Hedges Cup quickly and lost our first six Sunday matches. Public criticism grew and by mid-May Illingworth was issuing curfews and Hampshire was at loggerheads with his bowlers. 'Bowl line, length and straight,' was his only instruction. Not bad advice but there has to be more to captaincy than that. The players urged Hampshire to talk to me on the field, but he rarely did except when the situation had got irretrievably out of control. Illingworth began to moan to the players and hint to the press that Hampshire was not a good captain. So their honeymoon seemed to have ended. Illy used to try and relay tactical instructions to Hampshire from the dressing room via fielders on the boundary. When things began to go wrong on the field the players would say, 'Hey up, the walkie-talkie's broken down.' It was ludicrous.

That did not, of course, prevent some committee-men from continuing their anti-Boycott campaign as though they had nothing better to do. Trueman became so publicly and obsessively critical that my solicitor had to write him a letter about it. And by July the Lancashire committee was remarking on the 'well-known' fact that Boycott and Hampshire would be sacked at the end of the year! I cannot imagine where they got their information from. Speculation was fired when I was left out of the Sunday side as part of an Illingworth 'youth policy', though he took me aside to say there was nothing sinister in it – a reassurance I found hard to believe. While Illy was telling the press that there was a place for Boycott at Yorkshire he was telling Jim Laker – who mentioned it to me after a match at the Oval in July – that I would 'have to go'. Jim, nobody's fool, also made a remark which I found quite extraordinary even by Yorkshire's current political standards: 'Illy's afraid that you might get his job as team manager.' It was the first time I heard the idea mentioned. It had never entered my mind.

But Illy was fast causing strife in the dressing room. He referred to Sidebottom, Bairstow, Stevenson and me as the 'South Yorkshire Mafia' and seemed to spend as much time manoeuvring as he did managing. The media began to speculate strongly about the future of Hampshire and myself, and public reaction forced the club to step in. In mid-July, Hampshire and I were offered new two-year contracts, many months before the matter would normally have been discussed. That upset the rest of the players, who considered we were being given preferential treatment, and Michael Crawford, who had taken over as club chairman from Arthur Connell, had to make gestures of appeasement which were plastered all over the newspapers. What a mess! On 3 September, Illingworth took Old into the empty opposition dressing room at Scarborough and offered him the Yorkshire captaincy; John Hampshire's resignation was announced a week later.

The familiar storm clouds began to gather over the 1981 season in late July, when Illingworth dropped a bombshell by making Neil Hartley captain in the absence of Old on Test duty and with Hampshire injured. Such an elevation of an uncapped player annoyed the more senior players and was almost unprecedented in Yorkshire's history. Hartley was unsure of his place in the side, so it was clear that somebody would have to step down to accommodate him as captain – somebody who had cause to consider himself

On 23 August 1980 Boycott scored his ninth Roses century (135 at Manchester) to equal Herbert Sutcliffe's record against Lancashire. Sutcliffe needed 61 innings to complete his nine centuries, Boycott 45.

a better player. And if the resentment in the dressing room was not already sharp enough, it was reported that Hartley was going out with Illingworth's daughter. This was bound to create friction, anybody with half an eye could see that, and it led pretty quickly to a stand-up row between Illingworth and Bairstow in the bar of the Royal Hotel in Scarborough. Whatever was said was loud and embarrassingly public and the news spread like wildfire. My reaction to it was that if this was man-management at work, we were better off without it. We seemed to have more chiefs than Indians and the latest chief's previous experience of captaincy was with Bingley in the Bradford League. It was unbelievably insensitive to imagine that a Yorkshire dressing room would accept such an appointment unquestioningly.

By early August, Hampshire and I were being left out of the Sunday side – the youth policy again – and Illingworth was under increasing public pressure to justify his record as team manager in terms of a visible improvement in the fortunes of the team. It was generally believed that Illingworth's contract expired at the end of the season. In fact he had negotiated himself a one-year extension, probably at the same time that Hampshire and I had had our contracts lengthened. That was to prove very important.

A week of the Scarborough Festival that year was taken up by the Fenner Trophy knockout competition plus a three-day match against Barbados before Yorkshire played their last home championship match of the season. Going into the last Test against Australia at the Oval, I was informed by Mike Gatting that Illingworth had said I was not required for the Fenner Trophy games. Yorkshire were playing over at Lord's and I was sharing the same hotel – yet the message came via a Middlesex player. Illy was rapidly reaching a point where he barely spoke to me or to any Yorkshire player whom he thought was a friend of mine. This was man-management at its finest. I did not want to miss a whole week's cricket so I asked Illy if I could play in the match against Barbados; the answer was no, because he intended to give all the younger players a go.

When I read the team in the newspaper at home I discovered that Hampshire, Old and Lumb were in it. The only senior player to be left out was me. That did not entirely square with what Illingworth had said and I did not consider I was getting a fair deal. I determined to have it out with Illy at the end of the season. In the meantime, I attended a book-signing session in York and was approached by a television company who wanted an interview. Having okayed it with secretary Joe Lister, I agreed to the interview and was eventually asked why I was not playing for Yorkshire. It must have seemed odd to many people that an England player could not get into the side for the Scarborough Festival unless, of course, he did not want to, which was not my position at all. I told the interviewer I was as perplexed as anybody and did not think it was fair. I would seek a meeting with Illingworth as soon as the season was out of the way. It was not vitriolic stuff – but nevertheless Illingworth immediately phoned Trueman and Brennan for official committee support – which he knew perfectly well he would get from them – and determined to suspend me for the rest of the season. The decision was taken the night before our last home game started at Scarborough. Several players knew about it. In fact when TV cameras appeared with improbable alacrity at the ground next morning, there was a little witch-hunt among the players in the know to see if anyone had leaked the information. Deserving bedfellows.

I was already in the dressing room next morning when Illy came in, took me aside into the shower area and told me I was suspended for the rest of the season and that I should pack my bags and leave. After making a couple of phone calls I asked him precisely why I was being suspended and he referred to my TV interview of the night before. He was obviously trying to suppress his anger but he was red in the face. I hung around outside the dressing room, simply because I had promised Bairstow I would sign a load of bats for his benefit year and since this was the last home match it looked like being my last chance. That done, I disappeared home.

1980 was the eleventh consecutive English season in which Boycott achieved a batting average of over 50, thus exceeding Jack Hobbs's record of ten.

By the time I left the ground, the Reform Group had already begun to collect signatures for a petition against Illingworth, and the TV cameras were rolling. I don't know how they made it to the ground so smartly, but they certainly had plenty to film, what with puzzled and angry members gathering outside the pavilion and spilling further on to the ground. Illingworth said his piece to the press – that I was in breach of my contract by giving an interview without permission – and the whole lurid business was blazed over the newspapers next day – around the time that Illingworth was probably finding out how hasty he had been. For a start, I had had permission from the secretary to give the TV interview (and Lister himself thought it fairly innocuous); and secondly – this is what he did not know – I did not really need it! My contract did not require me to clear interviews with the club, so Illingworth was obviously wrong in suspending me for a breach of regulations.

Illingworth had overstepped his own powers and had put the club in a near-impossible position. Michael Crawford said later that Illingworth required authority from the chairman before he could suspend me and he added that in any case, as chairman, he would 'have advised caution'. The newspapers were again full of showdown stories: should Yorkshire sack

Boycott or Illingworth or both? The local media organised public opinion polls which came down strongly in my favour. Illingworth had a one-year contract to run and so did I. It occurred to one committee-man that sacking either of us would 'cost a lot – and particularly Geoff Boycott – at least £150,000'.

That was a point which communicated itself pretty quickly to the committee when they met, ostensibly to sort the matter out, on 17 September. Instead of coming up with the sack, they announced the institution of an in-depth enquiry into the team's playing record and into ways of improving it. The enquiry committee, which eventually interviewed thirty-three people, was chaired by Peter Dobson, a retired accountant who was independent of the committee, yet a good friend of Michael Crawford. Other members were Phil Sharpe, Don Brennan, John Temple, David Welch, Reg Kirk, Tim Reed and Julian Vallance. I could have taken a shrewd guess at their established attitudes towards me, but what was just as important was that they were all on the committee, and I really could not see the point of the committee investigating the committee. Not if we were to come up with anything genuinely impartial. The enquiry team decided who they were going to see and what they were going to ask. When I finally appeared I was struck by the superficiality of the questions and by the familiar overtones of long-held views. It did not surprise me overmuch when, after issuing a skeleton report with recommendations about committees and so forth, it was leaked to the media that the enquiry committee recommended my sacking. I would have been amazed, in the circumstances, if it had been any other way, and this renewed publicity and speculation hurt me personally and consequently affected my last-minute decision to go to South Africa.

Before the enquiry panel first met, and following a local newspaper suggestion that the players would prefer me as captain, Chris Old was urged by two committee men, David Welch – Rotherham – and John Turner – Wakefield – that self-professed supporter of mine, to take a player's poll. A stronger captain might have refused but Old was under pressure himself, what with Yorkshire's results and the emergence of Hartley as a powerfully backed rival. Stronger players might have declined to vote – and some did – but they were all placed in an intolerable position. They were being pressed to choose between the sacking of a colleague or the manager who had absolute power over them. Who would you have chosen? In this club with a record for not giving a damn what players felt, this new democracy was a bit of a surprise; I do not recall the players being asked their opinion on much else.

Old reported a majority in favour of Illingworth remaining as team manager and a majority in favour of me being sacked from the club. Yorkshire seized another chance to discredit me – would the poll have been revealed had it gone the other way? – and made it public with suitable pronouncements of reluctance. Doncaster's Eric Baines was at the meeting where Burnet spoke so passionately in favour of the poll being released. Baines said they agreed to publish it 'with relish', and he resigned from the committee in disgust. He, at least, retained his honour. I was appalled. Here I was watching a television screen that suddenly informed me – and the world, it seemed – that my team-mates didn't want me. I could not think of anything more hurtful. I contacted a few players and found they were as shocked as me. Whatever their views, they had given them in confidence.

The press amazed me by being as disgusted as I was. Articles and editorials hammered Yorkshire's decision to release the poll and although I will probably never understand how newspapermen think and work, I was genuinely grateful to them for their understanding. In twenty-five years of dealing, sometimes acrimoniously, with the press, it is this support which sticks in my mind. In trying to discredit me, the committee had discredited themselves, and not for the first time. What I also realised as I looked at the howling headlines was that they had finally managed to discredit the name of the club and a membership who deserved far better. Yorkshire's name was being dragged into the gutter by those whose determination to get rid of Boycott had become an obsession. John Hampshire finally left for Derbyshire before the start of the 1982 season; all the other players remained, and so did I.

Chris Old talked himself out of the captaincy before the 1982 season started. He was honest enough to admit publicly that he was ashamed of taking the players' poll, that he had been pressured into it by sources outside the team, and that it had done only harm to the club. He was right, but the admission was not going to go down well with Illingworth or the committee. Chris was on borrowed time and when team performance hit rock-bottom against Northants, ironically on his home ground at Middlesbrough, he was sacked and replaced as captain by Illy. There was no doubt that the team's performances had gone to pot under Old that season, but I'm not sure he received the support he needed. Old certainly did not think so. He was fed up and considering resignation before Yorkshire sacked him.

One of the spin-offs from the in-depth enquiry was the formation of a three-man sub-committee – the press quickly called it a peace-keeping committee – with power to make decisions on a day-to-day basis without

On 20 May 1982 Boycott partnered G. B. Stevenson in Yorkshire's record 10th-wicket partnership, 149 against Warwickshire at Birmingham, Boycott scoring 79, Stevenson 115 not out. The previous record between Lord Hawke and D. Hunter had stood since 1898.

interference (as Burnet put it) from the rest of the committee. Burnet was chairman, the other two were Fred Trueman and Billy Sutcliffe. I met Ronnie at Headingley before the season started and we had a frank talk as we slowly walked round the cycle track.

It was clear from the start that Burnet was the strong man of the three and although we didn't exactly get on like a house on fire I was quite happy with the new arrangement – provided I got a fair deal, was not judged in my absence and could rely on positive action instead of the familiar hollow words. Burnet knew that Trueman was an immovable critic of Boycott – 'looking at you through red-coloured glasses', as he put it – but he was confident he could handle him. The system did work that season. Burnet stopped me once or twice with a word of praise, a note of criticism, and Illingworth was more approachable while he was captaining the side. We probably had more common ground in those circumstances, and since Illy was being judged on his results as skipper, he may have felt more vulnerable. He would be very much aware that his contract, like mine, was due to expire at the end of the season.

We had dinner together in Scarborough towards the end of the season, talking sensibly over Yorkshire matters, and I offered him two pieces of advice. First, it was imperative that whatever the inducement, there should be no more Boycott versus Illingworth stories in the press. If there were, we should both very probably get the sack. And I urged him not to make Neil Hartley vice-captain because giving the job to him would have a dreadful effect on the dressing room and was unfair to the lad himself. Illingworth revealed that Brennan, Feather and Bailey had plans to bring back Hutton as captain; they had even mentioned a young man called Haggas, who was not even in the second team but had been to public school! How Yorkshire history might have been rewritten. I told Illy there were only two candidates for the captaincy next year and there was no way the committee would have me, so he should make a decision to lead the side and get himself into shape during the winter.

Chris Old did not get a new contract – Illingworth did not recommend one – I was given a one-year contract and Illingworth was given a two-year one. Soon after he was reinstalled he made Hartley his vice-captain. 'He won't last two months, he's not good enough,' said a junior player, and sure enough Hartley had to be left out of the side by the middle of July. An unnecessary hassle and embarrassment.

The 1983 season may well be remembered for two features as far as Yorkshire are concerned: we finished bottom of the championship for the first (and hopefully only) time in our history; and Geoff Boycott was reported for scoring too slowly in a match against Gloucestershire at Cheltenham. We also won the Sunday league – but I wonder which event is best remembered before history has time to reduce everything to raw dates and facts. The answer may say a great deal about the club and the men who mismanaged it at the time. The way the Cheltenham affair was handled told me an enormous amount about the ability of a manager to manage. And none of what I learned was to his credit.

A good deal has been written about the match at Cheltenham, where Yorkshire failed by one run to secure a fourth batting bonus point and where, so it came out later, I was supposed to have ignored or rejected Illingworth's instructions to bat more quickly in the best interests of the side. It seems to me slightly crazy that after a match which we lost by five wickets, the only source of heartburn for Yorkshire's captain–manager should be the absence of a bonus point. Be that as it may and accepting that misunderstandings may have occurred, I totally reject the suggestion that I wilfully refused any instructions from Illingworth to bat more quickly. I went, as far as I recall, as quickly as I could, and if that was not fast enough to suit everybody there was nothing perverse about it. Illingworth made no complaint whatsoever to me at the time.

Boycott has scored six centuries for Yorkshire against Gloucestershire – a Yorkshire record.

When I reached the dressing room at the end of the first day – at which point I was supposed to have thumbed my nose at him – Illingworth was nowhere to be seen. Next day he asked me briefly about my innings before we started a Sunday league match which we won by four wickets. I bowled eight overs and scored 39 in the match, a reasonable contribution to the win. On Monday, the afternoon papers in Yorkshire carried reports that Illingworth planned to report me to the committee for 'going slow'. Their inspiration came from him but, again, he never mentioned a thing to me. The first I heard of it in any official sense was in the car going home on Tuesday evening when it was confirmed on the radio that Illingworth had reported me. The story was inevitably plastered over the newspapers until I met with the three-man committee at Headingley on 19 August, six days after my so-called offence.

As I went into the meeting in an upper office of the Headingley pavilion, Illingworth came out. We did not speak and I then listened in growing amazement to Illy's evidence, as reported by Burnet. Illingworth had made a report by telephone on Monday evening – after the inspired newspaper reports – and had been told to put it in writing. His letter, read to me by Burnet, claimed that he had told me during the tea interval at Cheltenham that I was going too slowly (untrue), that I had made no attempt to score a fourth bonus point (untrue) and even (untrue) that I ran out Kevin Sharp on purpose! The letter also claimed that over the previous few innings I had played for myself against the team's interests. I was dumbfounded. Not once – not even when I was supposed to have defied his instructions at Cheltenham – did Illingworth say a word of censure to me. It was the first I had heard of any suggestion that I had batted selfishly that season, and here was the captain–manager claiming I had done so on several occasions. When I told the 'peace-keepers' that Illingworth had never complained about my batting they seemed surprised, so goodness knows what lurid details he had already furnished them with. It was quite preposterous. I noticed through the window that Illingworth was on the ground, talking near the square to the Headingley groundsman. 'There's Illy now. Let's get him in here and sort this out face to face,' I said. But they made no move to do the obvious. Illingworth's letter as read to me rubbished the major scores I had made that season and portrayed my play that season in the worst possible light. He could have walked a few yards into the meeting that day and accused me to my face but he did not do it, and the so-called peace-keeping committee did not require him to. I later asked for a copy of Illingworth's letter but Burnett was unable to let me have one. It had, he said, been torn up and put in a wastepaper bin . . .

Looking back, I am pretty sure that Cheltenham was just another example of the obsession to be rid of me on the part of some members of the committee. On the face of it, the season had gone quite smoothly as far as I was concerned – no Boycott controversies to point to, a good season with the bat. And yet the team under Illy was at the bottom of the championship table. That was not going to go unremarked, not in Yorkshire where the championship is far more important than any one-day competition, so it was imperative to create a smokescreen by levelling the finger at Boycott. Two attempts to do that had already fizzled out embarrassingly: I was scolded for taking the meat out of my sandwiches at Edgbaston and later for swearing at a persistent journalist, though I barely remembered the incident. There was, of course, no known instance of a sportsman – least of all a Yorkshire cricketer – ever swearing at a journalist. The whole thing was a revealing nonsense.

Burnett issued a statement after the hearing saying that it had been decided that my batting at Cheltenham was not 'in the best interests of the side'. He was asked if I had been reprimanded – the word seemed strangely significant to some – and he replied that I had. Odd, that – since I still have a letter from Burnet placing on record the fact that I was *not* reprimanded. We must assume he forgot.

Illingworth seemed to have a bad memory too. The day after the hearing at Headingley I scored 163 against Notts at Bradford – and Illy was incensed at my reception. 'He always gets the applause and I get attacked,' he stormed. The very public criticism of his conduct was clearly getting through to him and after the game he kept repeating to me over and over again that he had not led any journalists to believe he would report me at Cheltenham. He also said that in his letter he had referred only to the fact that we should have had another bonus point and he concluded grandly that he did not bear me a grudge. I knew what was in the letter – and after plunging Yorkshire into turmoil for another unnecessary week *he* did not bear *me* a grudge! It was sick-making.

Yorkshire won the Sunday league that season, a great boost for the young players who hadn't previously won anything with the club. The pity was that Illy, on the balcony at Chelmsford, refused to let some of us savour our moment of triumph. When the crowd in front of the pavilion was chanting for individuals to take a bow, he was telling us to get back into the dressing room. His own media profile was pretty high.

On 3 October 1983, with Illingworth increasingly militant as a result of his position as a winning captain – 'Back me or pay me up' was one of his better-publicised pronouncements – Yorkshire grasped the nettle and sacked me. They attempted a trade-off in the process – henceforth Illingworth would not necessarily travel with the team (some team manager) and the new captain would be the ever-popular David Bairstow. Illy had made it clear he didn't want him as captain but Bairstow was the 'sweetened pill' to get the members to accept my sacking. Not for the first time, they totally misjudged the mood of the Yorkshire membership, either because they did not know what it was or more probably because they were still contemptuous of it.

The club lurched towards a special meeting which had to be put back to 21 January, at more expense, because of a legal wrangle over voting rights. One of the more illuminating facts to emerge was that Joe Lister had already informed the chairman, Michael Crawford, how the voting was going! Another charming insight into the attitudes of management towards membership. The sometimes stormy meeting at Harrogate finally voted to give me a one-year contract (by a majority of 1006) and expressed no confidence in the general committee (majority 31) and no confidence in the cricket committee (majority 788). Even Yorkshire's committee could not ignore the wishes of the members on that scale. The whole lot resigned.

I wonder how many people know to this day that the cost in terms of Yorkshire's reputation as well as finances could have been avoided, at the eleventh hour, by the old committee. I had been awarded a testimonial for the following year and it was perfectly clear that the situation would be impossible – a sacked Boycott attending matches would inevitably have become a focal point for those who disagreed with the committee decision. So on 14 October I met Crawford and Burnet and offered them a compromise. I even drafted a statement – they wanted it in writing – which summed up my position:

> I am glad the club has offered me a contract for next season and I accept the offer with the realisation that at the end of the next cricket season which coincides with my Testimonial year I shall retire as a Yorkshire player.
>
> On occasions in the recent past I have been the focus of factional controversy within the club. I do not wish to comment or be involved except to say that I did not seek or wish to have that brought about.
>
> I am a professional cricketer and I have always served the club loyally.
>
> I am grateful for the support and friendship of so many people which has sustained me as a Yorkshire player over the years and for the goodwill of the committee which has extended my career with Yorkshire for one more year.
>
> I hope that in the months to come everyone will unite in the interests of Yorkshire cricket so that under the captaincy of David Bairstow we may do well.

In other words, let me play through my benefit year and then I will retire – Yorkshire could not have had a clearer offer. My letter was sent to Burnet's home, and he promised to place it before the general committee. At the committee's next meeting, Burnet said that Bairstow believed other players would leave if I was given a contract. Bairstow denies this. Bill Athey left the club for Gloucestershire at this time and Burnet wanted him to say he was leaving because of Boycott. To his credit, because it wasn't true, Athey refused.

And the letter with my offer of an alternative to strife? The general committee did not discuss it and never voted on it. How could they? Burnet never told them about it . . .

Fred Trueman put himself up for re-election to the Yorkshire committee early in 1984 and was rejected by the members in his Craven district, who voted 128–65 in favour of the infinitely less famous Peter Fretwell. It was an extraordinary development for Trueman, one that he clearly did not expect

– and I am quite sure that he blamed me for his embarrassment. Well, Fred had blamed me for virtually everything that had gone wrong with Yorkshire cricket in the previous ten years or more.

Trueman was against my appointment as Yorkshire captain and it was not long after it that a meeting took place at the Scalby Manor Hotel, near Scarborough, to discuss how to put Boycott in a bad light and ultimately to get rid of him. Trueman's solicitor Jack Mewies was there with his client and friend, so were Don Wilson and his wife. From then on, Trueman waged a systematic and virtually unbroken campaign of character assassination against me which reached a very public height during the committee's justification of the decision to sack me and their attempts to hold on to power. It backfired hurtfully on Fred when the Craven district members had their say. But I cannot pretend I feel sorry for him.

Fred was a truly great player. There is absolutely no question of that and as a newcomer to the Yorkshire side I thought the world of him; it was a privilege to play in the same team. But when Fred retired, I began to replace him in the affection of the current Yorkshire membership – and I don't think Fred could stand that. Put simply, I reckon he became jealous of my popularity because he somehow wrongly imagined it diminished his own. He rarely missed an opportunity to put me down. His newspaper articles were usually critical, his after-dinner speeches were rather more forthrightly anti-Boycott and his attitude in committee bordered on the vitriolic. The Yorkshire committee used him whenever they could because he was a big name among the Yorkshire members; Fred let them, and gradually he eroded his own popularity and status in the club. I think members were first disappointed and then frankly offended by the bitterness of his attitude towards me. It was all so unnecessary – even now I doubt that he can bring himself to admit that it was his own fault.

In 1985 Boycott scored over 1000 runs in a season for the twenty-sixth time. Only W. G. Grace and F. E. Woolley (twenty-eight times each) and Colin Cowdrey and C. P. Mead (twenty-seven times each) have exceeded him.

Fred's rejection by the members at the polls hit him hard, a lot harder than he cares to admit. He affects not to care overmuch and says Yorkshire cricket no longer interests him – Fred taking his bat and ball home is a sad sight. Yorkshire hit on a scheme to raise money for the club in 1987 by issuing 200 original certificates at £100 each signed by Fred, Sir Leonard and myself as the pre-eminent players since the war, and an unlimited number of printed ones at £10 each. Fred refused to sign.

Now that I have gone, the Yorkshire public will find another hero, somebody else to identify with. They are generous people with their affection, and that's the way it should be. 'The King is dead, long live the King' – it's a natural progression.

★

The Yorkshire establishment of the late seventies and early eighties spent a considerable amount of time pouring scorn on the Reform Group as a non-representative gang of glory-seekers. Burnet's 'unruly mob' were a noisy nuisance who had no right to challenge the wisdom of the elected committee and even less chance of changing the Natural Order of Things. They were upstarts, discordant and disruptive, beneath the committee's contempt and insignificant except inasmuch as they would not go away. By the early months of 1984, that established Yorkshire committee had been swept away by men who represented the Reform Group view and philosophy. Defeat was stinging and near-total. And all because the old Yorkshire committee had lost sight of the fact that it was dealing with a strong body of its members.

Ronnie Burnet lost in Harrogate to Roy Ickringill; Fred Trueman lost in Craven to Peter Fretwell; Bob Platt lost in Huddersfield to Tony Ramsden; Billy Sutcliffe was defeated in Leeds by Tony Vann; Tim Reed lost in Sheffield to Tony Boot; and Eric Burgin lost to Terry Jarvis; Desmond Bailey was beaten by Peter Quinn in the North Riding; Mollie Staines went down to Philip Ackroyd in Dewsbury; Michael Crawford and Norman Yardley resigned from the club completely. In Wakefield I won the seat ahead of John Turner. I had never made a secret of the fact that I intended to stand for the committee one day; my sacking from the club brought that plan forward, and Wakefield was my home district. It was as uncomplicated as that.

The snide and sneering view of the Reform Group and its members was that it was a breakaway group committed entirely to – and very probably led by – Geoffrey Boycott. I never orchestrated the group's activities so I cannot take credit for the landslide success it eventually achieved. But I am grateful to this day for the support and reassurance which I received from so many people. Some of them – like Peter Briggs, Sid Fielden, Bob Slicer, Reg Kirk and Peter Charles – became known through the media or as members of the committee and I will never underestimate all they did for me personally. For every one of them, there were dozens, hundreds and ultimately thousands of people who had a like view of Yorkshire cricket and were not prepared to pay up and then shut up while the Yorkshire committee lectured them on the best thing for their club. Yorkshire never came to terms with the fact that they were dealing with members; they stupidly and rigidly insisted that if they could get rid of the Reform Group they would get rid of the problems, whereas it was perfectly obvious that the opposite was the case. Had the old committee taken genuine steps to remove the causes of genuine grievance, they would have got rid of the Reform Group because it would have been redundant. The Reform Group was not the cause of Yorkshire's problems; it was a consequence of mismanagement over many years.

The sacking of Johnny Wardle did not drive Yorkshire members to the barricades but it made them think. The cruel treatment afforded Brian Close led to the formation of an Action Group and to a demand for change, though I do not recall any cheap remarks about Closeshire. My removal from the captaincy, though backed by the members, led to a vote of no confidence in the cricket committee. The warning signs were plentiful, but a committee with an exaggerated idea of their own importance refused to believe themselves anything but infallible. They attacked me and they attacked those who had the temerity to support me as foolish; in fact they were attacking their own members, and Yorkshire members are not fools. I may have been the catalyst but the Yorkshire committee brought the house down around their own heads by treating members with contempt.

In 1985 Boycott scored his 100th century for Yorkshire, 103 not out against Warwickshire at Birmingham. Only Herbert Sutcliffe (112) had previously reached 100 centuries for the county.

In fact, the Reform Group and their supporters were a very significant reminder of the fact that Yorkshire's members are not to be trifled with. They were ready to get off their backsides and fight, ready to spend their time and their money to oppose what they saw as injustice in the club they love. The Reform Group was fortunate at the time to have the help of legal brains like Duncan Mutch and Matthew Caswell, both Yorkshire members who, incidentally, gave their services entirely without payment. And when the crunch came, a group which could probably number its paid-up membership only in hundreds was backed and supported by Yorkshire members in their thousands. Like it or not, the old committee had to concede that the group reflected the view of the membership far more accurately than they did themselves. Had they considered that earlier, a good deal of strife could have been avoided.

For my part, I can only marvel at the enormous energy of the Reform Group and their supporters. As a member of the committee, I hope I shall never forget that example of the commitment of the Yorkshire public. And I will always be grateful to thousands of people, whom I shall never know, for their support and faith in me.

Ray Illingworth never made the transition between superb captain and successful team manager. I doubt that he ever will, because his years at Yorkshire proved conclusively to me that he is temperamentally unsuited to being a team manager.

That has nothing whatsoever to do with Illy's knowledge of the game. His record as a captain speaks for itself; it is excellent and he has every right to be proud of it. But a team manager's job is very different from that of a captain and I don't think Illy can come to terms with that.

When Illy arrived at Yorkshire in what was for him the new field of management, it was soon obvious that he did not want to help his captains so much as to control them. He was insistent, then and now, on absolute power over the teams, and when results were bad he changed the captains. It was no coincidence that while he was manager Yorkshire went through five. Illingworth fretted at what he saw as inferior cricket brains. He always felt he could do better on the field than they could – and he was undoubtedly right. But that is something which team managers have to come to terms with – the captain is not really supposed to be an extension of the manager's personality. Illingworth wanted a robot as captain or a junior Illingworth. He wanted to lead the side by remote control, and that is simply never going to work.

The captaincy was just too much for John Hampshire, who had little feel for it and less tactical awareness. Hampshire's captaincy was wooden, with few original ideas. Chris Old was an easy-going character who did not fit in with Illingworth's precise views on the game. The harder Illy tried to impose his views on Old, the worse things became. David Bairstow and Richard Lumb flitted across the captaincy scene while Illingworth tried to find a suitably malleable character; Neil Hartley's elevation caused problems which should have been foreseen and avoided by a mature, thinking man. But Illingworth is a cricket man to the point of insensitivity and tunnel vision.

'Never argue with Illy. Illy's always right.' They told me that when I first went into the Yorkshire dressing room and I came to know exactly what they meant. Once he had a bee in his bonnet, it was impossible to shift him. He was intractable and he did not take kindly to being contradicted. The process of self-justification went on long before and long after the event but it always worked to Illy's satisfaction.

The Yorkshire dressing room under his management became split, and if Illingworth did not create all the divisions he certainly cultivated them when it suited him. It was noticed and it cost him trust – and he was never going to achieve much without that. As I watched him work with captains and players and as I learned more about his dealings with me, I realised that Illy's feel for cricket was infinitely better developed than his feel for people. That might not be decisive in a captain but it is an enormous drawback in a team manager. I might have been able to work with him as captain because we share a lot of common ground as far as cricket tactics and attitudes are concerned. But looking back, I don't think I would have put up with his overwhelming desire to be boss for very long. Illy was as bad a team manager as he was good a captain.

The revolution of 1984 completely changed the face of the Yorkshire committee, to the extent that a body which had once been dominated by ex-players was now packed with representatives of the rank-and-file membership. They might not have the same cricket expertise as many of their predecessors – much good that had done Yorkshire – but they certainly had the club at heart and a willingness to listen to the members. And that made a refreshing change.

Boycott scored his fifteenth century against Nottinghamshire, 125 not out at Scarborough in 1985. This is more centuries against one county than any other Yorkshire player. Herbert Sutcliffe is next with ten against Leicestershire.

Apart from myself, there were only four ex-players on the new committee. Phil Sharpe and Bryan Stott publicly opposed a contract for me as a player and won their district elections by small majorities. Brian Close replaced Don Brennan, who retired through ill health, and Bob Appleyard came on in place of Robin Feather. Both Close and Appleyard told their members they would support a contract for me; at the first general committee meeting after the elections they reneged on their election promise and voted against. It was hardly the best way to prove their good faith with the people who had elected them. In fact it smacked ominously of the high-handed attitudes which had caused an upheaval in the club.

Close was elected cricket chairman and soon threatened to resign unless he got the sub-committee he wanted. His first season in the job was barely ended when he approached David Bairstow and urged him to say publicly that he wanted rid of me from the team. Bairstow refused – and in no time Close was manoeuvring to reinstall me as captain and get rid of Bairstow because he was 'not good enough'. When I refused the job, Close said Bairstow should continue as captain but cease to be wicketkeeper, which Bairstow predictably and angrily rejected. Close's logic took a bit of following but his attitude was clear enough: he liked his own way. He resigned from the cricket committee and the ex-players – Sharpe, Stott and Appleyard – went with him. From then on, if there was an objection to be made, they voiced it; if there was an opposite view to be taken, they adopted it. Close could command a fair amount of newspaper space on the strength of his reputation and he rarely missed an opportunity to have a go at the chairman Reg Kirk. But the heavy artillery was reserved for attacks on my position as both committee member and player. They wanted me off the committee and preferably out of the club, and the campaign to discredit my dual role gathered pace.

In the history of Yorkshire cricket there have been five men before me who have served on the committee at the same time as being players: Lord Hawke (1892–1911), the Hon. T. S. Jackson (1899–1907),

T. L. Taylor (1902 and 1906), W. E. Harbord (1935) and A. B. Sellers (1947 and 1948).

One of the most vociferous critics of the dual role was Sid Fielden, the Doncaster policeman who had fought long and very loudly for me in the past. I appreciated Fielden's help, even when others warned me that it was close to being an obsession with him, but his attitude changed completely when I got on the committee. Fielden seemed to expect a promotion for his eloquent part in overturning the old committee, and he was clearly annoyed when he was not made chairman.

He saw himself as the champion of Boycott the underdog, and he enjoyed the public notoriety that went with it. When I was no longer cast as the underdog, when I could make out my own case on the committee, Fielden may have felt he had lost some sort of starring role. Whatever the reasons, he quickly and publicly ceased to be a celebrated supporter of mine and became a critic. His change of heart was quite startling in its suddenness; his change of face was rather more subtle. Fielden said in public that he disagreed with the dual role but would always support my having a contract as a player. His attitude in private was somewhat different . . .

23

Last Days

The writing was on the wall – and in the crystal ball – long before the Yorkshire committee met in September of last year and officially announced that I had been sacked as a player. There were the usual expressions of regret, of course, familiar and mealy-mouthed references to my services with the club and the pious statement, the same old worn-out refrain, that the decision had been taken 'in the best interests of Yorkshire cricket'. It was pure window-dressing. The decision to sack me was taken with relish, the culmination of a campaign that had been waged for too many of my twenty-four years with the club and which had barely slackened in the past year. Nothing I might have done in 1986 could save me. My opponents on the committee were resolved.

I knew all this perfectly well and it was interesting in a painful and gruesome sort of way to see the year unfold towards its inevitable climax. In November 1985 I had visited a medium, who had told me that big changes were on the way in my life and to beware of a titled man who would do me harm. By early 1986 the message was even more clear: 'Watch out for another man who will attack you. Keep a still tongue and do not be provoked into a confrontation; he will be amazed because he wants to upset you. I see him with papers all the time. During the events of the next few months keep your own counsel. You may want to speak your mind but a still tongue is best for you. In six months' time something important will occur. . . .' In fact, the wheels were already in motion. It was becoming clear to anybody, even then, that I was on the way out.

Gradually and by an improbable mix of circumstances, the number of people on the committee who might support me had been whittled down. Terry Jarvis in Sheffield had been replaced by Tim Reed, a member of the committee that sacked me in 1983. Jarvis lost by two votes and six votes were spoiled, four of them having been cast in Jarvis's favour. Peter Fretwell resigned his seat in the Craven district, worn down and tired of all the hassles, and was replaced by a Brian Close supporter, Anthony Roberts. Reg Kirk surrendered the chairmanship of the general committee, harassed and pilloried by his critics and increasingly disillusioned; he finally resigned from the committee just before the annual meeting in 1986. Then Huddersfield member Tony Ramsden died suddenly and Bob Platt (who had voted to sack me in 1983) got back on the committee despite a brave attempt by Tony's widow to defeat him. Mrs Carol Ramsden lost by six votes, hardly a landslide victory. But it was enough, of course, to pack the opposition benches. Four probable supporters lost in twelve months was the equivalent of eight votes changing hands. The residue of the old Reform Group and the Members Group had lost its numbers on the committee and the composition of the sub-committees immediately reflected that. Brian Walsh took over as chairman, Close replaced Tony Vann as cricket chairman, Tony Cawdry replaced Peter Charles in finance and Sid Fielden became Public Relations and Fund Raising chairman instead of Peter Quinn.

Boycott is the leading run scorer in post-war English cricket.

One look at the composition of the influential cricket committee left no doubt that my days were numbered, whatever happened that season on the field. Tony Vann probably would support another contract for me when the time came and Tony Woodhouse might. But Close, Bryan Stott, Bob Appleyard and Phil Sharpe would not. They held the majority. It was really only a matter of waiting for the season to end.

I was working in the West Indies when the annual meeting was held in Sheffield on 22 February 1986. The club had pushed the dual-role legislation relentlessly all winter. It had suddenly become the most important issue facing the club, or so they would have everybody believe, and I was not surprised that it went through by 3370 votes to 310. The size of the majority was a revelation but so was the fact that only 35 per cent of the membership had taken the trouble to vote. It looked disturbingly like a drift back towards the days when apathy left the door open for all kinds of extraordinary and ultimately wounding decisions. So many men who had fought hard for a new vision for Yorkshire cricket had disappeared, surprised and dispirited in many cases to discover that their opponents were skilled political animals with an insatiable determination to be proved right and to wield power. The Reformers and their supporters were basically decent men and women reacting to the mismanagement of the club. They did not consider they had a God-given right to run the club and, frankly, I do not think most of them minded whose name went on the committee roll as long as the job was done properly. Their opponents minded a lot.

Close, Appleyard, Sharpe, Stott and Platt gathered in a bar at the

Queen's Hotel in Leeds soon after the annual meeting. 'We've got them by the balls and we should squeeze 'em,' said Appleyard. 'They're finished.' 'They', of course, were those Yorkshire members who had supported me. Appleyard's attitude was typical of the private policy of the newly constituted committee, whatever its public pronouncements. And his gleeful conviction that policy would become fact was based, unanswerably, on numbers.

At the end of March I read in the newspapers that Phil Carrick was to be appointed vice-captain for the season. As senior professional, I had more or less fulfilled that role for the past few years so the press naturally represented this as a snub to me. Whether or not it was matters rather less than the way it was done; the information was leaked at a sponsor's function and I was never told officially that the change was to be made. A small point, perhaps, but I had hoped Yorkshire had learned something about treating its players decently.

It had not, apparently, grasped the real significance of the anger and disruption of the previous stormy years. At the pre-season luncheon, a traditional get-together of players, committee and press in an atmosphere of goodwill which would (hopefully) last for the rest of the season, the new committee wheeled in some invited guests. Ronnie Burnet, Arthur Connell, Norman Yardley, Michael Crawford – it was like some grotesque scene out of *Animal Farm*. I was amazed. Whatever one's opinion of these men as men, the fact is that what they stood for had been rejected by the Yorkshire membership. They had lost office most reluctantly in a bloody and very public revolution and here they were being welcomed as distinguished servants of the club! I wonder what the rank-and-file membership made of that. Perhaps someone, somewhere who had given years of service to Yorkshire without involving the club in controversy might have been glad of the recognition and a free lunch. The audacity and arrogance of those invitations was breathtaking and left no doubt in which direction the new hierarchy was moving. The personnel might be different but in attitude and assumption the wheel was very close to coming full circle. The club did not appear to have learned a thing. 'This is a cricket club, not a debating society,' said David Bairstow with more than a hint of exasperation. I understood his message but I wonder how many others did.

Boycott has scored more runs in first-class cricket than any other living cricketer.

As far as I was concerned, the cards had been dealt by the time of the annual meeting and it was just a matter of waiting to see how my opponents played them. The familiar pattern of whispers, innuendo and contrived circumstances would follow until the decision to sack me seemed unavoidable and even justified. Then there would be crocodile tears.

Close played his part, particularly through the newspapers. It was inevitable they would want to talk to him and equally inevitable they would ask him about me. Faced with a question, it is only natural that he would offer some sort of reply. But the references to me were invariably critical, though put in a tone of regret and an apparent desire to be constructive. Close told one newspaper that I would be welcomed as a player provided I made a contribution. I cannot offhand remember the last time when I failed to do that. I had to make a contribution to the social side of the team, said Close, and pass on my experience to the lesser lights. Putting those in the same breath suggested I did neither. 'If he does and does it well, there's no reason why he shouldn't have another year with Yorkshire,' said Close. Just for the record, I finished the season with more runs than most despite a depressing run of injuries and the reluctance, on more than one occasion, of Close to pick me in the side. Perhaps I should have concentrated on my 'social contribution' instead.

Close also made enormous capital out of the decision which would eventually prevent anyone – which specifically meant me – from serving on the committee while still a player. Close's version was that this would come as a profound relief to David Bairstow, who had for years been hamstrung by my presence as player and committee man in the dressing room and would henceforth blossom into a freed man and a happier personality. If Close actually thought that, he knew very little of the nature of our Yorkshire dressing room or of the character of Bairstow. 'He will know that he can operate without interference and without worrying that a member of his team has more power and authority than he has,' said Close. And again: 'He has been a captain with handcuffs on but now he will be in command. . . .' The fact that Close was jumping the gun somewhat since the dual-role legislation did not come into force until the end of the season was neither here nor there. The words sounded good, a familiar mixture of drum-beating and Boycott-bashing, even if they didn't make an atom of sense: David Bairstow does not sit and cower under the supposed influence of anybody. The idea that he was intimidated or particularly influenced by the fact that I was on the committee is laughable. Bairstow is a strong character, a man who could not be persuaded to take the easy way out, as Close himself had discovered in 1984 when he wanted Bairstow's help against me. As a matter of record, I turned down a place on the cricket committee specifically because I did not want to spread the idea that David was under pressure from me. The invitation was extended at the start of the 1985 season but I knew it would very quickly be used as propaganda by those who were anxious to convince the public that I was determined to be more powerful than the captain. It was a notion that should have been dispelled years ago and David Bairstow himself did not believe it – but it was another piece of scaremongering.

Close's public stance in these matters was all the more revealing because although he kept saying that his door was always open, actually he made no effort whatsoever to inform me of the so-called hopes and requirements that appeared under banner headlines in the newspapers. The impression created was that I knew what was expected of me – a more social disposition and so on – and the inference was that I didn't give a damn. Close never once mentioned his expectations to me. He simply conducted a campaign of self-publicity and subtle denigration through the columns of whichever newspaper happened to knock on his door. That was provocative, pretentious and quite unnecessary. It made sense only if it was part of a policy to put me in a bad light and perhaps goad me into a reaction which would then be reported as another Boycott (not Close) controversy. Putting me in a bad light was, of course, the point of the exercise.

Boycott has scored nine centuries for Yorkshire against Derbyshire – a Yorkshire record.

The press sometimes helped. I recall, for instance, the match against Derbyshire at Sheffield in June when we struggled desperately against Michael Holding. Nobody exactly blasted him round the field but the press singled me out for criticism of 'slow scoring'. It was even suggested that Bairstow had reacted angrily and shown his displeasure by weighing into the bowling when he came in. It had overtones of Cheltenham 1983 and Harrogate 1985, another stylised Boycott story which would make a good headline. In fact there was absolutely no criticism of my batting approach from the dressing room. The lads appreciated the difficulty of the situation and the aggression shown by Bairstow was simply a matter of taking what advantage he could against the spin bowler. Revealingly, Bairstow telephoned Close to impress on him that the criticism of me was unfounded and that there was no bad blood between us. He made his point again when he saw Bryan Stott next day. Bairstow is no mug: he sensed the mood of the anti-Boycott brigade on the committee and felt it important for my sake to put the record straight.

But the mud from that kind of incident often sticks and there are those who are mighty glad of it. Against Middlesex at Lord's in mid-June I made 69 on a dreadful pitch and was pilloried in the Sunday newspapers for scoring too slowly, killing the game, playing for myself, etc., etc. As it turned out, 69 was top score in the first innings, so was the 31 I made in the second, and Yorkshire won the match by 69 runs. My Sunday newspaper critics had, of course, long since lost all interest in the match. But that did not prevent Close arriving hot-foot to find out what was going on, and it took a full report from Bairstow to convince him that he shouldn't believe everything he reads in the Sunday papers. Bob Appleyard rang Close (though I was not supposed to know that) and told him he should take strong action and discipline me for slow scoring. The niggling and nit-picking went on.

Another development in mid-July strengthened the conviction that this was to be my last season with Yorkshire. The president, Viscount Mountgarret, and Walsh came to see me at Headingley and announced that the management committee had proposed that Close should take my place on the overseas tours sub-committee at the Test and County Cricket Board. In fact, notification of the proposal had already been sent out to the committee, most of whom probably knew about it before I did. According to the president and Walsh, they had intended telling me first but the secretary had been very quick off the mark sending out the information . . .

They were obviously ill at ease and a little shamefaced, suggesting that the decision was taken largely because they did not know what my plans were for the following year. I could hardly make those until I knew what Yorkshire's plans were for me but the logic of that was not really material. In any case, they were unlikely to discover my plans unless they asked, and Close's nomination was already a *fait accompli*. There was some convoluted argument about my not being able to serve on the TCCB sub-committee if I was not on the Yorkshire committee, but that didn't hold water; there were several instances of counties being represented by men who were not serving committee members. It was all something of a charade and they could not even play their parts convincingly. Boycott's influence or participation had to be minimised and this was another step. I did not bother to press the point that Close had made one overseas tour over thirty years ago whereas I had done ten far more recently and might conceivably be more use to the sub-committee – what was the use?

So far there was no criticism in public of my attendance record at Yorkshire's public relations committee, though that was likely to be just a matter of time. Predictably, Fielden brought it up just before the 1987 district elections in which I was standing as a candidate for Wakefield. It did not do the damage he hoped. I missed all four sub-committee meetings in 1986, one because I was not informed that it was taking place (I have the secretary's written apology) and the others because it was impossible to attend. They were held on days when I was training or playing – the fixture list was readily available – and I could hardly split myself in two. In fact, the sub-committee meetings could not have been scheduled less conveniently for me if somebody had tried. If I wanted to make it difficult for anyone to attend meetings I would also arrange them during his unavoidable working hours. I do not suggest Yorkshire should have planned their sub-committee meetings round my availability, but I don't think they should have planned them to try and prove the impracticability of my dual role either.

It was indicative of the intensity of the moves against me that any praise, however oblique, brought an angry reaction. Tony Vann wrote to the *Yorkshire Post* congratulating me and Paul Jarvis for our performances in the matches against Middlesex and Surrey, both Yorkshire victories. He suggested I should be judged on performance, as Close had promised at the start of the season. That was hardly fifth-column propaganda, but Appleyard and Fielden immediately attacked Vann in committee, told him he should not speak out of turn and demanded a public apology! I wonder if they would have done that had he suggested I should be sacked forthwith . . .

Boycott has scored eight centuries for Yorkshire against Warwickshire, sharing the Yorkshire record with Herbert Sutcliffe.

Close announced in due course that the question of the captaincy would be discussed not at the contracts meeting in September but in November when, according to him, the club would have a clearer picture of who was available for the next season. That may not have seemed significant in some circumstances. I knew then that it meant no contract for me and goodbye to Bairstow as captain. The only reason for splitting the contract and captaincy decisions was to avoid hitting the public with two potentially unpopular developments at the same time.

Less than two years earlier, Close had said publicly that he thought I should take over the captaincy. That being so, how could he support a situation where Yorkshire dispensed with Bairstow as captain and sacked me at the same time? It was politically important to separate the two decisions, even if they had been taken in principle months before they were admitted to or announced. Bairstow could not help but come to the same conclusion.

Injuries are the bane of a professional sportsman's life. I have had my share over the years but on balance I have not been particularly injury-prone. In 1986 I did struggle a bit against injury, which was bad and frustrating enough; what made it worse was the knowledge that my critics would seize on any opportunity to make injury a sign of advancing years and therefore another argument for the proposition that I should be sacked as a player. The club's attitude towards my fitness and availability became illuminating, bearing in mind the muttered suggestion, prevalent in the past, that I had chosen my games and used injuries as an excuse for opting out.

I suffered a hamstring injury early in the season which kept me out for some time, and in early July I scored a century against Leicestershire at Middlesbrough – the 150th first-class hundred of my career – after being hit on the left hand by Philip DeFreitas. The hand was broken, though X-rays taken at the time did not show it, and of course nobody knew, least of all myself or anybody picking the side. Yorkshire played a NatWest Trophy tie against Middlesex at Headingley and won after the match spilled over into the second day. I went to London to do a TV interview and headed back early to have treatment at Headingley from the Yorkshire physiotherapist so that I would be fit to play against India. He told me nobody else had checked on the state of my injury. I joined the Yorkshire players in the pub where they were celebrating their win over Middlesex and told Bairstow I was available for the game against India, then forty-eight hours away. Bairstow was surprised; he said they had not expected me to be available but that he would get in touch with Close, for whom I had already left a message through Joe Lister saying I was fit and available for selection.

There was still no word from Lister or Close the following day when I went to Headingley for nets. The official word, which Lister left with his staff when he went into meetings, was that I had been left out to recover from my hand injury. If I was not to play against India I needed permission to play in league cricket, and in any case I wanted some sort of explanation for being left out despite the fact that I was fit and ready to go. A management committee meeting was in progress and I hung around into the evening. Walsh came out and told me that Close had given a full explanation to the cricket committee and I had better speak to him. Chance would be a fine thing . . . I eventually knocked on the committee room door and asked to speak to Lister.

I felt I had been avoided and treated shabbily and I told Lister as much. I asked to see Close, Lister still being pretty uncommunicative, and told him how I felt. Close said it was good that I should feel disappointed – rather trite and patronising – and said they had not known I was fit when they chose the team. It was too late to change and in any case they wanted to give one or two younger players a run out against India. I couldn't help thinking that the attitude would have been rather different if Yorkshire had been facing a black fast bowler; they might well have waited on my fitness then. While Yorkshire played India I made 95 not out for Castleford against Doncaster; the official version, remember, was that I had been left out of the team in order to recover from injury.

Later in the season, after my hand injury had been diagnosed as a break and the injury had healed, I told Close I had tested it in the league with Castleford and was fit to play. Yorkshire were at Bournemouth at the time and Close said he would contact Bairstow regarding the team for the next match at Edgbaston. He never did. Bairstow heard of my situation from Doug Padgett, who was aware I was fit and wanted to know whether I was in the first or second team. Close later told me that his car had broken down, which delayed his telephone call to Bournemouth and caused him to miss Bairstow by minutes. Whichever way it was dressed up, the fact is that I was fit and available and had been left out of the side.

That may not seem over-significant – it has happened to other players after all. But in the context of what I knew and suspected about the cricket committee's attitude towards me it added up to another useful piece of anti-Boycott propaganda. The decision to offer me a one-year contract was explained in part because of my age and the fact that I was 'more susceptible to injury'. Giving the impression that I missed matches because of injury would not harm their cause at the end of the season. Moreover, the less I played the less opportunity I had to make out a case for a renewed contract by batting well, which had been a fairly reliable response to pressure from the critics in the past. When they came to make an official case for not re-engaging me, as they surely would, they would point to fewer runs and evidence of injury to help justify their decision. The fact that I had spent hours chasing around, phoning around and hanging around to establish my fitness would be conveniently overlooked and the public would not know the facts in any case.

Boycott has scored six centuries for Yorkshire against Somerset – a Yorkshire record.

The whisper campaign went on all summer, a constant wearying catalogue of innuendo and misrepresentation with very few opportunities missed to create a mood in which I could be sacked with a minimum of reaction. In mid-July, Fielden swore to my face he would support a renewal of my contract. By 10 August at Scarborough he was buttonholing members behind my back and regaling them with his opinion that 'Boycott plays for himself all the time – the sooner he goes the better we'll be.' He picked out my innings against Leicestershire as the most selfish he had ever seen. I played it with a broken hand, as he then knew, but cricket knowledge, after all, was never Fielden's strong suit. All over the county, people began telling me about the propaganda dished out by Fielden, the president and the ex-players on the Yorkshire committee when I was not there to defend myself. The knife was in from the start. The fork soon followed.

A reference suddenly appeared in one newspaper, for no apparent reason, to the fact that I was Yorkshire's highest-paid player. The report went on to say that there was a move to have me paid on a match-by-match basis next year. Another report forecast confidently that I would not get a contract at all. The source was Close, the press informant who usually asked to be anonymous was Fielden.

Long before the end of the season, the president of the club buttonholed a radio journalist and told him that Yorkshire simply had to get rid of 'this fellow Boycott'. The same president took delight in taking anyone who would listen across to the club shop and urging them to buy a book recently published and strongly critical of my so-called attitudes. Not bad for a man who is supposed to be above the politics of the club – and hardly a step towards the peace and conciliation to which he so often paid lip-service.

Bairstow did not escape. By the time the NatWest quarter-finals came round at the end of July, Appleyard was already touting his belief that if Yorkshire lost, Bairstow should be replaced as captain for the rest of the season by Neil Hartley. The press who follow Yorkshire aren't stupid – they keep their ears to the ground and are receptive to the undercurrents at the club. Goodness knows they've had enough practice. So it was significant that stories began to appear forecasting that this was to be my last season, followed not long afterwards by strong suggestions that Bairstow was on thin ice. Illingworth was a frequent visitor to matches and always seemed to be in deep conversation with Close. It did not take a huge intellect to conclude that if Bairstow were to be replaced as captain, the chief candidate to replace him would be Hartley, whom Illingworth had already championed for the job. Illingworth's presence in the dressing room, incidentally, did not always go down well with players who found his visits embarrassing at best.

Early in September, Close finally said he wanted a word with me prior to entering discussions in the cricket committee. What did I think of the suggestion, bearing in mind that I had suffered from injuries during the year, of being contracted on a match-by-match basis in future? I had heard whispers and frankly I did not like the idea one bit. The money did not matter, except insofar as everybody should be properly paid for doing a job, but the principle was all wrong. The sudden interest in my injury record was exaggerated, if not entirely unexpected. Sidebottom and Sharp had been injured for long periods during the season – it's an occupational hazard and I doubt that any sensible person would attach blame. My professional instincts told me that anyone paid on a match-by-match basis would put staying fit before any other consideration, so the difficult catch might not be attempted for fear of picking up an injury. Not my way of playing the game.

Boycott has scored 151 first-class centuries. Only Jack Hobbs (197), Patsy Hendren (170), Walter Hammond (167) and C. P. Mead (153) have scored more.

Neither is lack of continuity, the possibility of playing one match then missing a couple, then trying to pick up the pieces again. There was no way I could see myself keeping any sort of form in those circumstances, assuming for instance that Yorkshire wanted Martyn Moxon and Ashley Metcalfe to open the innings and me to substitute for them when they were injured or unavailable through possible Test calls. If the match-by-match suggestion was an oblique way of replacing me as an opener it was scheming and unnecessary, and I told Close as much quite forcibly. Given that the club wanted to look to the long-term future and putting aside the fact that I considered myself the best opener on the books, I could see a situation where I would bat at three, with Kevin Sharp at four and Richard Blakey or Phil Robinson at five. That seemed to me to be the best alternative, and it was based on performance and on logic, not on politics.

Close remarked that if I was not going to play one-day cricket regularly I should not expect to be paid the same money. He also pointed out that I was being paid more than the captain, which was a potential source of embarrassment. It was necessary to point out to him that my salary level had been accrued over some twenty-four years with Yorkshire and was likely to be relatively high. In any case money was not the prime concern, provided that any offer was not downright derisory. If anyone was harping on about money, it wasn't me. Close made noises about having only one vote and I put it to him straight that what he wanted would most likely go through the cricket committee. People like Stott, Sharpe and Appleyard would probably vote against me, but he had the status and influence to carry the committee with him. Through the years I had known Close, I had disagreed and sometimes argued with him, others had given him a fair bit of stick, but I had never known him to be vindictive or petty. He hadn't even bothered to reply to some of the wounding criticisms levelled at him in public by one or two so-called mates from the past. All I wanted now was to be judged on cricket sense, not politics and the memory of old controversies. I believed that Close was a big enough man to do that and far too knowledgeable to lend his support to any plan to make Hartley captain. I told him so – it was a discussion long overdue.

Boycott has scored five centuries for Yorkshire against Glamorgan, sharing the Yorkshire record with Percy Holmes and Herbert Sutcliffe.

Later that day, Appleyard asked me to sign some autographs, and since I was in the mood for plain speaking I determined to have one or two things out with him – having first made it clear that I knew he was no supporter of mine and that we did not see eye to eye on most things from cricket to fund-raising. Appleyard protested that it wasn't so, but that is by the by. I told him straight that I knew he wanted rid of Bairstow as captain, a move that might get a measure of support, but that it would be crazy to put Hartley in his place. Hartley simply was not good enough to be sure of his place in the team and there was no evidence that he had exceptional leadership qualities to compensate. The team was not good enough to carry a batsman and there were better players available than Hartley, already thirty years of age and unlikely to improve.

Since he had often criticised my performances, I pointed out to Appleyard that we had won only two championship games that season without the help of a declaration, both on difficult pitches, and that I had top-scored in both. I felt I was still the best bad-pitch player at the club – with my experience I ought to be – and perfectly capable of holding my place on merit as one of five batsmen. Yorkshire might talk about dropping me down the order but there was no cricket logic in suggesting that I should be sacked or play on a match-by-match basis. Prejudice was something else, of course, and my views probably wouldn't matter because critics like him would have the numbers to get rid of me. Appleyard insisted that my views were important because I was the one closest to the players, but it was only words. As far as changing his opinion was concerned I might as well have saved my breath, and I knew that well enough.

By now, the fact that Bairstow was likely to lose the captaincy at the end of the season was Yorkshire's worst-kept secret. Nobody would admit to being the source, but stories appeared regularly in the press and the conviction that he was to go became bolder and firmer by the day. It certainly can't have done anything for Bairstow's morale or judgement and, knowing only too well how he felt, I had a lot of sympathy for him. The die was probably cast at the end of August, when Bairstow blew his top about a team selection: Close sent Chris Shaw off to play in the Under-25 final when Bairstow needed bowlers for a Sunday League game – and the story got in the newspapers. There was no way Bairstow would survive after such a clash.

The matter of his successor was not proving as clear-cut as some had imagined and there was even talk of the job being offered to me. I saw reports that I was practically prepared to stand on my head to get the captaincy back, which was total rubbish. My name probably got a mention in high places simply because it was becoming increasingly obvious that there was considerable opposition to Hartley. Players expressed their distaste for the idea of him as captain and at least one journalist who was asked his opinion by Close and the president told them flatly that Hartley was not the man. Phil Carrick's name began to creep into consideration and by chance, or mischance in Bairstow's case, Carrick suddenly looked the part in the last match of the season against Northamptonshire at Scarborough.

Bairstow broke a finger in the game and Carrick took over as captain. On a good pitch and for no reason directly attributable to Carrick,

Northants were bowled out and had to follow on. That doesn't happen too often in Yorkshire cricket these days and because the club's major sponsors were throwing a reception in the evening, there were plenty of committee members at the ground to associate captain Carrick with an extraordinarily successful day.

It was a very simplistic view, of course, but the skates were already under Bairstow and the situation was ripe for a contender to step into the spotlight. Next day, incidentally, Yorkshire failed to bowl out Northants a second time and the match was drawn – but by then most of the committee had gone home so Carrick was not associated with 'failure'. Hartley slipped dramatically in the captaincy stakes and Carrick was installed as favourite to take over when Bairstow was replaced. It fell neatly into place for him when he could least have expected it after a season in which he took only 31 championship wickets at 45.54 each and was considered by some to be an expensive luxury in the side. Carrick himself appears to have had misgivings about his future with the club, because he had talks with Derbyshire about the chances of joining them if his contract at Yorkshire was not renewed. Instead of sacking him, as he feared, Yorkshire made him captain.

Yorkshire's last match of the season was at Scarborough against Northants, and although nobody said so officially it was plain to me that it would be my last if the anti-Boycott campaigners got their way. Miracles do occur but not often enough to be relied on. There was very little in the game as far as the championship was concerned, since both counties were in mid-table, but it turned out to be one of the more bizarre matches I have played in. In a twisted sort of way it just about summed up many of the ups and downs of my career. Nothing, it seems, was ever going to be simple for Boycott.

In Boycott's last innings for Yorkshire, on 10 September 1986 against Northamptonshire at Scarborough, he made 61 before being run out.

I began the match with 931 first-class runs for the season and the prospect of completing 1000 for the twenty-fourth time in twenty-four years. That was important to me and I make no apology for saying so. Having set a standard over the years I had no intention of letting it slip if I could avoid it and the fact that this was likely to be my last season at Yorkshire added a fair bit of spice. Motivation has never been a great problem for me and I certainly didn't lack any at North Marine Road. We batted first and I made 61 before I lost my wicket – and whoever writes the script on occasions like these clearly has a wicked sense of humour. Someone else in my position might have been dismissed obstructing the field or hitting the ball twice; it was quite melodramatic enough for me to be run out.

Jim Love got a thick edge down to wide third man and turned for a second run which would have been routine except for a brilliant pick-up and throw from Allan Walker. I was heading towards the bowler's end so I wasn't in any obvious danger but Jim would never have made it to safety and he pulled up. There was no way I could back-pedal in time – so I was run out for 61 when I felt capable of scoring a century and when I needed only 8 runs for 1000 in the season.

How did I feel? I suppose I should say I was totally philosophical, chalked it up to experience and reflected on the glorious uncertainty of cricket. The fact is that I was an immediate mixture of anger and disappointment – as everybody is when they are run out – and I would probably have wrung Love's neck if I could have got close enough. But that mood passed, there was no point in dwelling on it and not the slightest suggestion that Love had run me out on purpose or with malice aforethought. At tea, I stayed out of Love's way, not because I was particularly angry with him but because he was in the middle of an innings and I didn't want my presence to embarrass him or confuse his priorities for the side. When he was finally out for 109 I made a point of telling him I thought it was a very good knock, which it was. It struck me then that Love did not mention the run-out. I thought he might have had a word of explanation or even apology but he never did and I was disappointed in him. There again, the psychology of run-outs is complicated: there is no normal and acceptable reaction and I of all people should understand Love's predicament rather than represent his silence as indifference. It's a strange situation and one not easily explained in terms of black and white – not that that has ever stopped the critics.

Yorkshire declared at 352–7 and there seemed no reason on that pitch why Northants should not make a lot of runs in turn. Instead they collapsed, made only 197 in the first innings and were 158–4 at the close on the second day after following on. I was fielding on the fine-leg boundary near the end of Northants' first innings, and Bairstow – off the field nursing his broken finger – came and asked me if I thought we should enforce the follow on. If I had been selfish I would have advised Bairstow to bat again so that I could score 8 runs and, quite incidentally, Kevin Sharp could make the 42 runs he needed for 1000 in the season – the critics would have loved that. There was no question of it, of course; Yorkshire's best chance of winning the match was to bowl Northants out a second time and I had no reservations in advising Bairstow to put them in again. I was aware of the irony of the situation but in terms of professional cricket there was no choice needed. By the end of the day, Northants were 3 runs ahead with four wickets down. If things went well next day, Sharp and I could still reach 1000 runs and Yorkshire could win the game.

That night, we attended the sponsors' reception and then went off in a group for an end-of-season team dinner, joined by Arnie Sidebottom and Paul Jarvis, who were not playing in the match but were determined to recoup some of the cash they had paid out during the season. The dinner was financed from the fines players had coughed up for breaking team rules – bowling wides and no-balls, being late in the dressing room and so on. The biggest culprits during the season always tend to have the most fun at the end.

Boycott finished his first-class cricket career at 5.21 p.m. on 12 September 1986 at Scarborough.

Like a lot of good nights, it was followed by a remorseful day. Geoff Cook had a broken finger, but even so we could not take the six wickets we needed to stand a chance of winning the match. Northants soldiered on and on until the game was well beyond our reach – 422–8 before Cook declared at 5.21 p.m. Not a lot for the committee to rejoice at there, but most of them were long gone by then.

There was an inevitable air of anticlimax in the dressing room, not least on my part. If this was to be my last appearance – and that was the odds-on probability – I would have liked it to end rather more memorably. Most of all, I think I would have liked to finish with a bat in my hand, not wandering off the field at the end of a particularly frustrating day with a lot of people still confused by the finale. Spectators hung about, wondering if Yorkshire would bat again, even the umpires waited in the middle until ten minutes had elapsed and it became obvious that the match had finished. David Bairstow was anxious that Sharp and I should go out and start a second innings. He was convinced that he had a right to ask Northants to field for the last half hour, and as it turned out he was correct. Both captains have to agree to call off play at 5.30 p.m. on the last day. Somebody in the dressing room pointed out that the umpires were still in the middle; somebody else pointed out that several Northants players had already changed out of their cricket clothes. I wasn't sure that the championship rules allowed us to carry on and, in any case, it struck me as being clearly against the conventions of the game. Make no mistake, I would dearly have liked to go out for as long as it took Sharp and me to score the runs we needed for 1000. But in all my career I have tried to play the game properly and professionally – nobody has had to give me anything as a batsman and I would not expect them to. I could not see any credit for cricket in a staged and contrived end to the season, my last or not.

In a romantic and ideal world Geoff Cook would probably have come into our dressing room and offered to field for half an hour. But cricket is our living and I have absolutely no criticism of Cook or Northants that day, even if spectators have told me since that they think their attitude was less than sporting. Cook did not know, any more than anyone else did officially, whether Geoff Boycott was in his last season for Yorkshire. As captain of Northants he probably would have cared rather less about that than the achievement of his own side in battling for a draw, and rightly so. As far as figures go, it was certainly not Cook's job to furnish anybody with the opportunity to complete 1000 first-class runs in a season. Had the situation been different, had Cook known for certain that it was my last game or had Yorkshire been batting, Northants are the kind of team that would have co-operated to the full. I have no axe to grind with them whatsoever.

The fact that I had failed to score 1000 first-class runs for the first time in twenty-four years with Yorkshire was plain enough and disappointing enough. The fact that I would be sacked in a fortnight's time was not yet official policy, so it was hard for the players to treat the last day at Scarborough differently from the last day of any season. They are not the sort of people to indulge in long and embarrassing farewells and they could hardly say 'See you next season' with conviction. The whole subject was awkward, so it was pointedly avoided. Richard Blakey, the baby of the team and a youngster with enormous potential, commiserated with me for not reaching 1000 runs. 'It's a lot of runs, that,' he mused. 'How many times have you done it?' I'm not quite sure he believed I had only failed to do it that once and he looked even more thoughtful when I told him 1000 first-class runs a season was well within his capabilities. 'If you stay clear of injury and play most of the championship games, it's a piece of cake for a player with your ability. It's only about 25 an innings after all. If I played thirty innings and couldn't make 1000 runs I'd chop my bat up.' Young Blakey had probably never thought of it quite like that.

The players drifted away one by one, snatching a last drink at the bar, packing their gear in the boot, leaving the dressing room looking as though a wastepaper basket had exploded. I was about the last to leave and by then the ground was all but deserted. I couldn't help thinking that if the committee had handled my last appearance better, informing everyone that it was to be my last game, they might have filled the ground and made money for the club. Never mind. I think Scarborough has a special appeal for cricket fans in Yorkshire. There always seems to be a special sort of atmosphere about the place, especially at the end of a season. Something nostalgic, pausing to look back and ready to look forward. It's a ground I have always enjoyed playing on. The 100th Scarborough Festival had finished, Sir Leonard Hutton was in his presidential year at the club and I was literally and figuratively on my way out. It was a long drive home. The phone rang later that night and I was offered a place in the Castleford team next day if I fancied a match. A kind offer, but I had to refuse; I just didn't feel like it. If I was to play my last innings in 1986, I wanted it to be with Yorkshire.

The meetings of the cricket and general committees were still a fortnight away and the gap was filled to a considerable extent by newspaper speculation that I was to be offered the captaincy in Bairstow's place. Most of the guesses at my attitude were imaginative, to say the least. I apparently vacillated between dumb insolence and a grovelling desire to grab the captaincy as a means of staying at the club. The newspapers' brainwaves did not come from me.

What intrigued me more was the conviction in most reports that I would carry on at Yorkshire. I knew that several players had buttonholed Close and the president on my behalf; journalists had been asked how they thought the public would react to certain courses of action, and although I do not necessarily believe all I read in the press I know it can be an indication of what's in the wind. As far as I could judge, there was no indication from any of the diehard anti-Boycott committeemen that their attitude towards me had softened. 'Boycott's getting the boot,' said Close at a lunch table when Yorkshire played a benefit match in Hertfordshire on 15 September. That did not sound very conciliatory to me. The impression that I would stay at Yorkshire, even as captain, was created by journalists applying their own logic. But since the hawks were keeping quiet officially, I wasn't fooled for a second. Tuesday, 23 September was still pencilled in for the execution.

I arrived at Headingley for the general committee meeting at around 4.30 p.m. and was awaiting the 5.00 p.m. start when Close came over, sheaf of papers under his arm, and gave me the news. 'Unfortunately, you will not be getting a contract, Geoff. I thought I would tell you before the general committee meeting and thank you for all you have done.' Close told me it was a majority decision of the cricket committee. 'It wasn't just your ability. It was felt your age was a factor – there are a number of youngsters we want to give a chance to. Some of them asked me at the end of the season if they would get a chance and we had to take that into consideration. We might lose some of them.' I asked Close if he agreed with the decision and he smiled without saying anything. 'Have Hartley and Love got contracts?' Yes. 'Why do you keep moderate players like them?' He just shrugged and smiled again.

The last item on the general committee agenda was the cricket committee's report on contracts and Walsh asked me to leave while it was discussed. In the past, I had stayed in the room when players' contracts were being discussed – I was an elected committee member, after all – but never took part in the talks and never voted. I suppose I could have insisted on staying this time. In the event, I heard all I wanted to hear.

It was impossible not to, since I was standing in a quiet corridor just along from the meeting room and the sound of voices carried clearly from behind the closed door. Close's tones wafted along: 'Geoff Boycott is a good player, you can't take his record away from him. But over the past few years he's shown a lack of consideration and thought for others in the team . . . Whenever Geoff Boycott is around it creates an atmosphere which stifles discussion. I noticed that myself when I was in the team with him, and it's not the best atmosphere . . . The last two seasons he hasn't played on Sundays, he's been a part-time player. His age is against him . . . When he is criticised he immediately turns to criticise other players for lack of ability. In the teams I have played in we always defended one another all the time . . . We have to look to the future with our youngsters . . .'

It was not a fire and brimstone speech and it did not need to be. Close knew that the die was already cast and that the numbers would push my sacking through. The usual format for criticism of me: Boycott is a good player (as if that were practically immaterial) but . . . and then a litany of prejudiced opinions masquerading as 'facts'. Predictable enough.

Peter Quinn spoke up for me, asking if Yorkshire could afford to lose a batsman of Boycott's ability. Being a cricket argument, it was not likely to carry much weight. Then Fielden joined in, the very same Fielden who had repeatedly assured me of his support as a player and had stressed publicly during the dual-role controversy that although he was against my having a dual role in principle he would be in favour of my being given a new playing contract. I could not make up my mind if he was two-faced or ten-faced. 'I will not criticise Geoffrey,' he began with all the unctuousness of a born actor. The use of the Christian name was offensive in the circumstances. He read out his ideal batting order – even the formality of sacking me had to become a stage production with Fielden at its centre – and finished by announcing grandly: 'I have every confidence in that team.' Naturally, it did not include my name and, revealingly, it did not include David Bairstow's either. With Close in the room, Fielden sounded very much like Uriah Heep. It was no more than I had expected and yet it was still profoundly disappointing to hear it for myself. People had told me what Fielden said about me behind my back and I had to believe them even if he denied it to my face – there was too much evidence to do otherwise. Now I was hearing it for myself, and although the circumstances were unfortunate, I knew at least that I would not have to rely on reports second-hand for confirmation of what I knew.

Stott was true to type and pattern. Boycott was a very good cricketer, still a good batsman, he said, but . . . he creates an atmosphere and makes other players feel inferior. 'We need dedicated, happy cricketers pulling one way,' he intoned. I could almost hear the background of angels. And when it was pointed out that most of the members seemed to want me to continue as a player, Close reminded the meeting sharply that 'The club is run by you the committee for the members, not by the members themselves.' It sounded horribly like the motto and attitude of a committee discredited a few years previously.

Walsh urged the committee to support Close and the cricket committee's view, suggesting that they were faced with the choice of doing nothing (i.e. giving me a contract) or being positive (that is, investing in the youth of the club and giving Boycott the boot). As chairman, there was not the slightest doubt where he stood. 'I would like us to consider the interests of the club,' he declared. There really must be a handbook of useful clichés for moments like this.

There was even a moment of light relief, at least it would have been amusing had it not been quite so nonsensical. In the circumstances it was black humour at best. The cricket committee had recommended an extension of Neil Hartley's contract to the end of 1988 and this was challenged on the grounds that Hartley was thirty years of age, had never scored 1000 first-class runs in a season for Yorkshire and had just completed a season wherein he scored 676 runs at an average of 26. If Yorkshire had a policy of encouraging youth and ability, Hartley did not noticeably qualify on either count.

Close jumped on to his high horse and announced that he would regard it as a personal insult if Hartley were not given the contract as suggested. He got into the team, said Close, because of his commitment to Yorkshire cricket. 'Neil Hartley is a trier who will do anything you ask of him,' said Close. 'If you gave him a brush he would sweep up.' Now the advantage of that was not immediately obvious to me but the sheer incongruity of the situation was. Outside in the corridor I had to try very hard to suppress my laughter. Fielden added his support for Close, pointing out that Hartley's manner was good and that he was always willing to meet the sponsors, which was a big help to the public relations and fund-raising committee.

Fair enough as far as it goes but hardly the basis on which to get a contract, let alone have one extended for an extra year. I hadn't heard any word about Hartley's ability as a player used to justify his new contract – just some twaddle about him being a good lad and handy with a brush! If that is the basis of Yorkshire's blueprints for the future then God help the county.

It would be farcical and even funny if it were not so damned serious. Close could not have championed Hartley more passionately if he had been Illingworth himself. His old mate and adviser Illingworth, that is.

Peter Charles pointed out that the club did not have adequate cover for the position of opener if it sacked me and then lost Moxon or Metcalfe for any reason. He moved an amendment, seconded by Tony Boot, which would offer me a contract for another year. It was defeated by twelve votes to nine at 8.00 p.m. I know the time because I looked at my watch. After twenty-four years I was out in the cold as well as the corridor. My supporters in that vote were Peter Charles, Tony Vann, Roy Ickringill, Philip Ackroyd, Robert Hilliam, Peter Quinn, Jack Sokell, Tony Boot and David Drabble, and although their stand will not make life any easier for them on the committee in future I shall always be grateful for their backing.

Walsh emerged into the corridor and told me how the voting had gone. He said he was going to say a few words to the media paying tribute to my record with Yorkshire. 'My record doesn't need any words from you,' I said. 'It will stand up on its own.' I was tired of the pretence and I really didn't want him to choke himself saying something uncritical of me.

Walsh wondered if I wanted to go back into the meeting – did he think I wanted to run away? – but I was still the committee representative for Wakefield and I had a couple of points to make. First of all, I thought it was high time the club ended the speculation over the captaincy in fairness to Bairstow, who must be hurt and upset by the constant uncomplimentary speculation in the press. And secondly I urged a suitable gratuity for Graham Stevenson, who had not been given a contract and was leaving after eight capped years with the club. Close said both matters would be discussed by the cricket committee and resolved by the time of the next general meeting. That was six weeks away and six weeks is a long time when your future is hanging by a well-publicised thread. Ask Bairstow.

I learned later that discussion of my future at the cricket committee was cursory at best, which did not really surprise me. The ex-players had made up their minds and had only to put up their hands without the tiresome formality of giving reasons which they had already exchanged often enough among themselves. Vann and Tony Woodhouse tried to put the case for a contract for me but they were wasting their breath – at least one ex-player spent that part of the meeting gazing out of the window. Oddly enough, Close told the press that the voting in the cricket committee was 4–1 against my having a contract, so clear-cut that he did not have to vote himself. I don't know if that was an attempt to put himself in a neutral light but it wasn't true. No vote was actually taken because it was obvious how the committee was aligned. Had a vote been cast, it would have been 3–2 against me without Close's vote and 4–2 with it. His figure of 4–1 appears in the minutes and is a figment of somebody's imagination.

After the general committee meeting broke up, I made a point of thanking and shaking hands with all those who had supported me for another year. They were pretty deflated and a bit defeated. They didn't quite know what to say to me, which was natural enough, but I wanted them to know that I appreciated everything they had done. Close came over and offered his hand but I simply could not take it. 'Don't be a hypocrite, Brian. That's one thing I am not.' He turned on his heel and walked off without another word.

Five of us went off to a fish and chip shop in Headingley, from where I telephoned my friend and adviser Matthew Caswell to let him know what had happened and to thank him for all his efforts. Without him and thousands of like-minded supporters, I would have been finished three years earlier. They had extended my career by that much and I will always be conscious of what I owe them. The press described our fish and chip meal as The Last Supper: the only man who might have made it complete was Sid Fielden. Judas was missing again.

The newspapers went to town next day with news of my sacking, background and in-depth articles tracing the good, bad and ugly years at Yorkshire. I had read most of it before but what was particularly fascinating now was the attitudes attributed to those who had made a campaign out of getting rid of me. The columns were awash with crocodile tears. I have never known so much regret expressed to disguise so much delight. The spokesman of those who had connived at getting rid of me, had worked assiduously at it and had finally succeeded, now found it necessary to cloak the whole thing in a sickly sauce spiced with the odd strident but familiar and frankly discredited phrase. 'For the good of Yorkshire cricket' cropped up endlessly. Other arguments were dredged from the archives to justify a decision which could not be defended on professional grounds.

Close floundered somewhere between remorse and vindication. 'I know a lot of people think I'm a tough guy but underneath I am a soft old bird and it wasn't easy,' he sobbed. It certainly wasn't easy; it took Yorkshire years. 'In some respects I would have loved Geoffrey to have gone on breaking records but in reality I had to say that his retention would not have helped us. . . .' The specious suggestion was that he had to be talked into supporting my sacking when it was perfectly clear he supported it wholeheartedly. 'Boycott has also played only seventeen first-class innings for Yorkshire all season,' said Close. 'He has had "soft flesh" injuries and they don't improve with age.' Predictably, he was making the accusation that age and injuries were upon me. No mention, of course, of the fact that he had left me out of at least two championship matches and that I could have made a greater contribution to Yorkshire had he not left me out of the Sunday League. No mention of the fact that, with limited opportunity, I had just scored more first-class runs than anybody in the club with the exception of Ashley Metcalfe.

Close trotted out the old chestnut that the club was somehow intimidated by the very presence of Boycott, which says dismissively very little for the character of professional cricketers and especially of Yorkshiremen. 'For several years it's been difficult for players in the team overshadowed and kept in a backwater by Geoffrey's presence,' he said. And again: 'We just couldn't carry on with a cult figure grinding out his personal glory while the rest of the players simply made up the numbers.' I wonder how many people realise the contempt for the masses that goes into statements like those, the veiled suggestion that anyone who supported me was an easily impressed idiot and only my critics had the wisdom to spot the truth. Close was telling the majority of the Yorkshire membership that they were fools. Furthermore, he was telling a generation of players that they were weak and spineless, totally blinded and intimidated by this Boycott who was a mixture of Merlin and Svengali. But I know them and do not agree: I have a lot more faith in their character than he has. If Yorkshire players have an inferiority complex, I suggest they see a psychiatrist; I don't think many will.

Boycott has scored 1000 runs in a season for Yorkshire nineteen times – only Herbert Sutcliffe (twenty-one) and David Denton (twenty) have done so more often.

When I first started with Yorkshire the outstanding figures in the club were Trueman, Close, Illingworth and Binks; when I made the England side I was plunged into the company of men like Dexter, Cowdrey and Barrington. They were all imposing men and some could be difficult, some downright bloody awkward. But I never felt inferior to them as men, I never felt superior. I just got on with the job of playing the game and the business of earning a living. If anyone had explained my failures by saying it was his fault or his or his, I might have been tempted to agree but it would not have been so. Any more than he or he or he could take the credit when I did well.

If Yorkshire's players were so intimidated by me, how come several of the senior players urged me to take on the captaincy when the possibility was floated in the press? And how come so many of the younger players sought my advice? I believe that if Bairstow had been given the chance to name his successor he would have opted for me, and I know that many players supported the notion of me taking over as captain. I will not name names because there is the nasty business of victimisation to consider. I know who they are – that's what makes Close's claims such a nonsense.

Over the years since they came in the team I had been approached by most of the youngsters for advice and I can remember the guidance I gave to Blakey, Booth, Jarvis, Pickles, Swallow, Shaw and Dennis. I was invited to the Yorkshire Second XI dinner at Edgbaston and well remember being stripped and thrown in an icy bath after the Colts' match at Hull in May of last year. That was routine horseplay, common to any dressing room on the county cricket circuit and I attached no special importance to it. But it is hardly the conduct of youngsters who were frightened to death of a 'cult figure'. Close either does not know what my relationship is with the players or he did not care, so long as he could propagate the myths that suited his argument. It was the same old suggestion that had been put forward by the 1983 committee, who were discredited and voted out by the members.

When the cricket committee were discussing an *ex gratia* payment to Graham Stevenson after the 1986 season, Close gave his opinion that Stevo would have been a better player handled properly. 'Boycott used to take the mickey out of him,' he recalled, as though that – and therefore I – had stunted Stevenson's development. I have a soft spot for Stevo, I knew how to handle him and he responded to me. Only a very ignorant or very prejudiced man would suggest otherwise, and Close was not at Yorkshire when Stevo played under me. But the comment was indicative of the anti-Boycott attitude to which Close subscribed. His determination to make me the whipping-boy destroyed any pretence of objective judgement.

It was a ridiculous state of affairs, but the level of politicking by former players on the committee had reached such a level that I hardly dared offer advice to some players for fear that it would be purposely misrepresented. It might be treated as a challenge to the authority of the captain or even of Close himself. On a more practical level it might be twisted to look as though I was doing it out of self-interest. If I told Martyn Moxon to tighten up his game, for instance – and that would have been sound advice – my critics would have said I was trying to make him defensive and stodgy. If batsmen took my advice and it didn't work for them, I might be accused of feeding them false advice so that I would do well by comparison. It sounds quite pathetic, I know, but that was the stage the whipping-boy syndrome had reached.

Close even made reference to players leaving the club – 'so many players have left and become stars elsewhere' – with the obvious implication that they had left because of me. The only player who left and became a 'star' with another county during my playing days at Yorkshire was Bill Athey, now with Gloucestershire and back in the England side for the Ashes tour of

Australia. To the best of my knowledge, Athey has never gone on record as saying he left Yorkshire because of me, though I know the committee would have liked him to. Where were the other departed stars? Close was talking rubbish, but never mind – some mud might stick.

And there was, predictably, the tired old stuff about me batting for myself, going too slowly, costing the club bonus points and victories. Clearly, I was responsible for everything that was wrong with the club. Ronnie Burnet could hardly keep the gloating out of his voice, even in print. 'He should have gone three years ago. His batting has been a disaster for the side and a good example of how averages can be misleading. If he scored a hundred . . . it made it difficult for Yorkshire to win the game because at his normal rate it takes him around eighty overs and that is too slow,' said Burnet. The way he talks, you would think there was no batsman at the other end, which was probably indicative of his total preoccupation with me. The facts do not bear out Burnet's theory, but since when did the facts matter once men like him had taken a stance?

It is a wry reflection on the level of cricket logic in Yorkshire's decision to sack me that the cricket committee later came up with a singular recommendation on the Palmer Report into the future of the game. It urged that the championship should be played over three days but on uncovered pitches and with the system of batting bonus points discontinued. So much for the smokescreen about my batting costing bonus points – the same people were about to recommend no batting points in future. And as they plumped for uncovered pitches with one hand, they sacked their best bad-pitch player on the other. For the good of Yorkshire cricket, of course.

The decision to sack me was predictable but the amount of sanctimonious nonsense and propaganda that accompanied it didn't make it easier to stomach. Close was telling the media: 'It will be all right if you fellows don't make too much of it', because he knew I still had a fund of popular support: local radio stations carried out a phone-in poll and they came out in favour of another contract for me, by 4–1 in the Sheffield area and 2–1 around Leeds, which is a pretty accurate barometer of the public mood on Yorkshire cricket. The feeling was that had there been a referendum among Yorkshire members, I would have won.

But there was to be no fight this time. It would not be fair to go back to the public again and recreate the open acrimony of a few years before, whatever the outcome. 'There is no point in going back to the members – they have had enough of politics,' said Peter Briggs and he was right. I'd had a bellyful of politics and I could understand that the public was weary of it. People had their lives to lead, their jobs, their families. Getting involved in another Boycott controversy had as little appeal for them as it had for me.

There was still an ironic little twist to the tale, as there will no doubt be others. Close very publicly offered me a seat on the cricket committee. It looked like a remarkable peace offering and there was no doubt that Close wanted it to appear as such. I turned it down because it would not have achieved anything – a purely cosmetic gesture which had little sincerity behind it and which would not alter the realities of the situation one bit. The ex-players on the cricket committee had made it abundantly plain that their attitude towards me was not going to change. Voting Boycott down in committee would have been an endless source of amusement and satisfaction.

It was even suggested that since I now had time on my hands I would be in a position to watch more Yorkshire cricket than most and would therefore be an invaluable source of first-hand information and advice. A dangerous area, that. I could see a situation where the ever-present Boycott would again be blamed if the team did not do well. My presence would intimidate somebody for sure.

Within a week of my sacking, Derbyshire and Glamorgan were on the phone to ask about my plans for the future. Several newspapers had suggested, in a smart and snide way, that no other county would have me and subsequently found some inventive reasons for my not signing. I considered the approaches, of course, and I'm bound to say it was comforting to have them. I particularly appreciated the written offer from Derbyshire. But at the end of the day there was no way I could play for anyone but Yorkshire. I just couldn't see myself pulling on another county's sweater – it wouldn't have felt comfortable. Tim Hudson wanted me to play six matches at the Birtles Bowl at £200 a time but jazz-jackets and brass bands weren't my style either.

Boycott is the third highest run-scorer for Yorkshire – only Herbert Sutcliffe (38,558) and David Denton (33,282) have scored more.

The season had not quite blown itself out; there was still the ritual business of sacking David Bairstow from the Yorkshire captaincy months after the intention had been made plain. The lad must have been thoroughly sick of the situation, though of course any sign of short temper or disgust on his part would be offered as evidence that he lacked the 'man-management' qualities a captain needs. When he was at his most vulnerable emotionally, Yorkshire asked him to resign.

Close contacted Bairstow on 14 October, four days before the cricket committee was due to meet, and told him that he would not get a single vote in support of another year as captain. Far better, said Close, to do the 'decent thing' and resign the captaincy – an ironic choice of phrase from a man who had been reduced to tears in similar circumstances sixteen years earlier. I doubt if Close would have seen anything 'decent' in the invitation to resign which he himself had received, but that was long before he became a member of Yorkshire's committee. Close told Bairstow that if he resigned, he would do his best to make sure he stayed on the same salary level; if he did not resign, he might not get the same support and there would be no guarantees about his financial future. It was a powerful if totally cynical argument to present to a man who already knew he was to lose the captaincy anyway. Incidentally, when I was sacked as Yorkshire's captain I stayed on the same money. I did not see any reason why a different attitude should be taken to Bairstow.

The cricket committee subsequently met and, no resignation having been received from Bairstow, discussed the relative claims of Hartley and Carrick to the captaincy. Relative is probably the right word: it was perfectly clear that neither was an automatic choice. Close asked if anyone supported another season for Bairstow. Sure enough, nobody did. No vote was taken because Close feared that a decision would be leaked to the press before the ratifying general meeting which was still a month away, but it was obvious that the decision to dismiss Bairstow had been taken. Strangely, the story of Bairstow's sacking appeared in the press two days before the general committee meeting, underwritten by comments from Close himself. The same article confidently announced that Carrick was hot favourite to get the job. So now we know. After a good deal of toing and froing in conversation, the cricket committee voted 5–1 to make Carrick captain. Appleyard stuck by Hartley, and Phil Sharpe was absent. Close went off to phone Carrick with news of his elevation and then went to the general committee with his sub-committee's recommendation! It was just as well that the general committee did not throw the recommendation out, though there was never a chance of that.

The proposal to accept the captaincy recommendation, seconded by Fielden, was carried by twelve votes to seven, which was hardly a landslide and reflected genuine misgivings among members of the general committee. Perhaps because of that, Viscount Mountgarret suggested that the actual voting figures should not be made known. I could not agree with that and I told him forcibly that I would tell my Wakefield members how I voted simply because they had a right to know. I voted for David Bairstow.

There was a decidedly heated exchange in which I described the president's arguments as 'crap' – not the most diplomatic of language I agree but a pretty accurate reflection of the way I felt at the time. The Yorkshire committee could do with more public accountability and more open government, not less. So many of the lessons of the past had not sunk in.

I rang Carrick a few days later, told him how I had voted and offered him any help I was able to give. He said he would take me up on it when he had time to collect his thoughts. Those members who attended a meeting in Wakefield found out how I stood as far as voting for the captaincy was concerned. Since I was due to stand for re-election at the next annual meeting they were naturally inquisitive about my future plans and I told them two counties had made enquiries. I also assured them that I wanted to continue as their committee representative and in fact completed the formalities for my renomination. The papers were handed in by me at Headingley two days later. That opened the possibility that I might play for a rival county while serving on the Yorkshire committee, an angle not overlooked by the press. As chairman of the public relations committee, Fielden was asked what the situation was and was quoted as saying: 'There's nothing in the rules to prevent him doing this but I think it would be wrong.' I rang the club secretary and lodged an official protest at Fielden's apparent confusion of the public office and the private opinion. I rang Fielden and told him it would be a good idea if he confined himself to expressions of official Yorkshire policy and kept his personal opinions out of my business. Fielden simply protested that he had been misquoted – the usual bolt-hole.

Bob Platt rang Guy Willett, the Derbyshire chairman, urging him to take me on – because that would make it easier for Yorkshire to get rid of me altogether! And Viscount Mountgarret sounded out the press: what would the reaction be to turfing Boycott off the committee if he became a player with another club? They were still preoccupied with me, still desperate to stick the knife in as though there was nothing else at the club which demanded their attention. It was quite ridiculous that the president should involve himself in cloak-and-dagger manoeuvrings, and I said as much when I ended newspaper speculation that I was about to play elsewhere.

Boycott is the eighth highest run-scorer in first-class cricket. Only J. B. Hobbs (61,237), F. W. Woolley (58,969), E. H. Hendren (57,611), C. P. Mead (55,061), W. G. Grace (54,896), W. R. Hammond (50,551) and H. Sutcliffe (50,138) have scored more.

There is a deeply ominous side to that sort of attitude which goes far beyond my personal annoyance and could have long-term effects on Yorkshire as a club. An example presented itself after the 1986 season. Peter Hepworth is a batsman with the Ackworth club, son of my long-time friend George Hepworth and a genuine enough prospect to be given several matches in Yorkshire's Second XI in the 1986 season. He was not offered a contract at the end of the season and decided to seek his future elsewhere since other counties were interested in him. When he informed Yorkshire of this, Joe Lister invited him for an interview with Close 'before you finally commit yourself'. Peter went to the interview and subsequently affirmed his decision to sign for another county, in his case Leicestershire. His mind was made up when Close told him: 'Now that we've got rid of Boycott, there'll be more chance for you.' I wanted Peter to try his hand with Yorkshire. I am concerned for the future of the club and I do not like to see young potential leaving. But Peter was saddened and disillusioned by the club's attitude towards me as put over by Close. His father was concerned that Peter might not get a fair deal at Yorkshire because he was seen as a family friend of mine. I never advised Peter to leave – I wanted him to stay. And yet when the argument was put forward – puerile and shameful as it was – I could not dismiss or discount it, because I have a sneaking suspicion it might be true. For the good of Yorkshire cricket, of course.

Career Record 1962–1986

Compiled by Roy D. Wilkinson

Debut for Yorkshire: *v* Pakistan at Bradford, 16 June 1962
Capped: 2 October 1963 **Captain**: 1971–8
Debut for England: *v* Australia at Nottingham, 4 June 1964 **Captain**: 1977–8

First-class Matches

Batting and Fielding

Season									Century	How Out						
(tours in brackets)	M	I	NO	Runs	HS	Average	100s	50s	P'ships	c	b	lbw	st	r.o.	h.w.	Catches
1962	5	9	2	150	47	21.42	–	–	–	3	2	2	–	–	–	4
1963	28	43	7	1628	165*	45.22	3	11	5	19	10	7	–	–	–	12
1964	27	44	4	2110	177	52.75	6	11	11	26	8	5	–	1	–	6
1964–5 (South Africa)	15	25	5	1135	193*	56.75	4	6	6	15	2	3	–	–	–	7
1965	26	44	3	1447	95	35.29	–	10	2	23	8	6	–	4	–	14
1965–6 (Australia and New Zealand)	13	21	2	784	156	41.26	1	7	5	13	3	2	–	1	–	6
1966	28	50	3	1854	164	39.44	6	10	8	31	11	2	1	2	–	11
1967	24	40	4	1910	246*	53.05	4	13	12	16	11	7	2	–	–	8
1967–8 (West Indies)	11	16	2	1154	243	82.42	4	6	9	7	3	2	–	2	–	2
1968	20	30	7	1487	180*	64.65	7	4	9	16	3	4	–	–	–	10
1969	23	39	6	1283	128	38.87	3	6	6	21	6	6	–	–	–	9
1970 (Ceylon)	1	2	–	7	7	3.50	–	–	–	1	1	–	–	–	–	–
1970	25	42	5	2051	260*	55.43	4	12	9	26	3	5	2	1	–	12
1970–1 (Australia)	12	22	6	1535	173	95.93	6	7	11	14	–	–	1	1	–	6
1971	21	30	5	2503	233	100.12	13	6	14	16	5	1	1	2	–	6
1972 (South Africa)	1	2	–	148	107	74.00	1	–	–	–	1	1	–	–	–	2
1972	13	22	5	1230	204*	72.35	6	4	3	8	5	3	–	1	–	5
1973	18	30	6	1527	141*	63.62	5	9	8	18	1	2	1	2	–	6
1974 (West Indies)	10	16	3	960	261*	73.85	3	4	6	10	3	–	–	–	–	3
1974	21	36	6	1783	160*	59.43	6	8	8	19	6	5	–	–	–	7
1975	19	34	8	1915	201*	73.65	6	8	10	18	2	5	–	–	1	14
1976	12	24	5	1288	207*	67.78	5	2	5	12	1	4	–	2	–	7
1977	20	30	5	1701	191	68.04	7	7	10	14	4	5	1	1	–	8
1977–8 (Pakistan and New Zealand)	13	20	3	867	123*	51.00	3	5	4	10	4	1	–	2	–	4

Season (*tours in brackets*)	M	I	NO	Runs	HS	Average	100s	50s	Century P'ships	How Out c	b	lbw	st	r.o.	h.w.	Catches
1978	16	25	1	1233	131	51.37	6	3	7	15	5	1	1	2	–	3
1978–9 (Australia)	12	23	3	533	90*	26.65	–	4	2	11	1	7	–	1	–	5
1979	15	20	5	1538	175*	102.53	6	7	8	8	2	4	1	–	–	4
1979–80 (Australia and India)	8	15	4	599	110	54.45	2	3	4	8	2	1	–	–	–	3
1980	17	28	4	1264	154*	52.66	3	8	5	16	3	3	–	2	–	14
1981 (West Indies)	9	17	2	818	104*	54.53	1	7	5	9	4	1	–	1	–	2
1981	16	28	2	1009	137	38.80	3	3	6	17	4	4	–	1	–	6
1981–2 (India and South Africa)	12	21	5	905	105	56.56	2	7	6	10	1	4	–	1	–	4
1982	21	37	6	1913	159	61.70	6	10	10	13	6	10	2	–	–	10
1983	23	40	5	1941	214*	55.45	7	4	8	18	4	10	1	2	–	17
1984	20	35	10	1567	153*	62.68	4	9	10	18	2	3	–	2	–	13
1985	21	34	12	1657	184	75.31	6	9	3	19	–	2	–	1	–	10
1986	13	20	1	992	135*	52.21	2	8	4	10	5	3	–	1	–	4
Totals	609	1014	162	48426	261*	56.83	151	238	239	528	142	131	14	36	1	264

Bowling

Balls	Maidens	Runs	Wickets	Average	Best in Innings
3693	183	1459	45	32.42	4:14

For Yorkshire – County Championship Matches

Batting and Fielding

For Yorkshire versus	M	I	NO	Runs	HS	Average	100s	50s	Century P'ships	c	b	How Out lbw	st	r.o.	h.w.	Catches
Derbyshire	35	53	13	2693	169*	67.32	9	12	13	23	7	7	1	2	–	16
Essex	18	31	1	1566	260*	52.20	3	6	6	19	4	6	–	–	1	9
Glamorgan	22	35	5	1542	156*	51.40	5	9	9	20	2	7	1	–	–	8
Gloucestershire	28	42	7	2070	177	59.14	6	8	11	21	7	5	1	1	–	6
Hampshire	17	28	1	1103	115	40.85	3	5	5	16	4	5	–	2	–	5
Kent	17	31	5	1253	148	48.19	3	9	4	17	6	2	–	1	–	10
Lancashire	35	53	5	2509	169	52.27	9	12	11	29	9	9	–	1	–	9
Leicestershire	25	42	9	2195	204*	66.51	7	10	9	20	8	4	–	1	–	14
Middlesex	22	41	6	2133	201*	60.94	6	11	7	18	7	7	1	2	–	9
Northamptonshire	22	33	4	1302	220*	44.89	4	6	7	18	3	4	1	3	–	18
Nottinghamshire	30	53	10	3303	214*	76.81	15	9	18	31	2	3	1	6	–	16
Somerset	18	30	7	1608	139*	69.91	6	6	5	13	3	4	1	2	–	11
Surrey	24	42	7	1527	142*	43.05	2	10	4	23	4	4	2	2	–	11
Sussex	14	22	7	1099	164	73.26	4	5	6	9	–	6	–	–	–	4
Warwickshire	27	48	1	2445	180*	66.08	8	16	10	20	11	5	1	–	–	13
Worcestershire	15	23	3	1137	184	56.85	4	5	4	11	4	5	–	–	–	7
Totals	369	607	101	29485	260*	58.27	94	139	129	308	81	83	10	23	1	166

Bowling

Balls	Maidens	Runs	Wickets	Average	Best in Innings
1585	85	560	24	23.33	4:14

For Yorkshire – other First-class Matches

Batting and Fielding

For Yorkshire versus	M	I	NO	Runs	HS	Average	100s	50s	Century P'ships	c	b	How Out lbw	st	r.o.	h.w.	Catches
Australia	4	6	1	417	122	83.40	2	3	1	3	–	2	–	–	–	3
India	1	2	0	29	15	14.50	–	–	–	–	–	2	–	–	–	–
New Zealand	2	2	1	107	103*	107.00	1	–	1	1	–	–	–	–	–	3
Pakistan	3	4	0	160	128	40.00	1	–	1	1	3	–	–	–	–	2
South Africa	1	2	0	26	22	13.00	–	–	–	–	–	–	–	2	–	–
Sri Lanka	1	1	0	43	43	43.00	–	–	1	–	1	–	–	–	–	–
West Indies	5	9	1	320	93	40.00	–	3	1	5	2	1	–	–	–	–
Cambridge University	9	12	3	787	207*	87.44	3	3	3	6	3	–	–	–	–	7
International XI	1	1	1	24	24*	–	–	–	–	–	–	–	–	–	–	2
MCC	12	20	3	840	123	49.41	2	5	2	10	3	4	–	–	–	8
Oxford University	6	8	0	332	89	41.50	–	4	4	7	1	–	–	–	–	9
Totals	45	67	10	3085	207*	54.12	9	18	14	33	13	9	–	2	–	34

Bowling

Balls	Maidens	Runs	Wickets	Average	Best in Innings
343	21	105	4	26.25	2:10

First-class Centuries (151)

For Yorkshire (103) versus

Derbyshire (9)

133 at Scarborough, 1971
149* at Abbeydale Park, Sheffield, 1974
151* at Leeds, 1979
167 at Chesterfield, 1979
154* at Scarborough, 1980
122* at Chesterfield, 1981
112* at Abbeydale Park, Sheffield, 1983
169* at Chesterfield, 1983
153* at Harrogate, 1984

Essex (3)

260* at Colchester, 1970
233 at Colchester, 1971
121 at Chelmsford, 1972

Glamorgan (5)

102 at Harrogate, 1967
156* at Middlesbrough, 1976
118 at Abbeydale Park, Sheffield, 1978
134 at Leeds, 1982
101* at Sophia Gardens, Cardiff, 1984

Gloucestershire (6)

177 at Bristol, 1964
125 at Bristol, 1968
141 at Bristol, 1975
161* at Leeds, 1976
140* at Cheltenham, 1983
126* at Bradford, 1984

Hampshire (3)

111 at Bournemouth, 1971
105 at Southampton, 1972
115 at Middlesbrough, 1985

Kent (3)

148 at Bramall Lane, Sheffield, 1970
101 at Abbeydale Park, Sheffield, 1983
104* at Tunbridge Wells, 1984

Lancashire (9)

145 at Bramall Lane, Sheffield, 1963
113 at Manchester, 1963
131 at Manchester, 1964
169 at Bramall Lane, Sheffield, 1971
105 at Leeds, 1972
101 at Manchester, 1973
105* at Leeds, 1975
103* at Manchester, 1976
135 at Manchester, 1980

Leicestershire (7)

165* at Scarborough, 1963
151* at Leicester, 1964
132 at Leicester, 1968
114* at Bramall Lane, Sheffield, 1968
151 at Bradford, 1971
204* at Leicester, 1972
127 at Middlesbrough, 1986

Middlesex (6)

151 at Leeds, 1964
112* at Leeds, 1971
182* at Lord's, 1971
175* at Scarborough, 1975
201* at Lord's, 1975
117 at Lord's, 1977

Northamptonshire (4)

220* at Bramall Lane, Sheffield, 1967
124* at Harrogate, 1971
113 at Northampton, 1978
138 at Northampton, 1982

Nottinghamshire (15)

103 }
105 } at Bramall Lane, Sheffield, 1966
169 at Leeds, 1971
100 at Worksop, 1971
129 at Bradford, 1973
139 at Abbeydale Park, Sheffield, 1975
141 at Bradford, 1976
154 at Nottingham, 1977
129 at Scarborough, 1978
175* at Worksop, 1979
124 at Bradford, 1981
214* at Worksop, 1983
163 }
141* } at Bradford, 1983
125* at Scarborough, 1985

Somerset (6)

105* at Leeds, 1969
122* at Taunton, 1972
139* at Harrogate, 1977
130* at Harrogate, 1979
129 at Weston-super-Mare, 1982
114* at Leeds, 1985

Surrey (2)

142* at Bradford, 1974
135* at Leeds, 1986

Sussex (4)

164 at Hove, 1966
100 at Bradford, 1968
117 at Leeds, 1974
122* at Scarborough, 1982

Warwickshire (8)

136* at Birmingham, 1966
180* at Middlesbrough, 1968
110 at Middlesbrough, 1971
138* at Birmingham, 1971
104 at Birmingham, 1977
115 at Birmingham, 1978
152* at Leeds, 1982
103* at Birmingham, 1985

Worcestershire (4)

152* at Worcester, 1975
159 at Abbeydale Park, Sheffield, 1982
105* at Harrogate, 1985
184 at Worcester, 1985

Australians (2)

122 at Bradford, 1964
103 at Scarborough, 1977

New Zealanders (1)

103* at Leeds, 1978

Pakistanis (1)

128 at Leeds, 1967

Cambridge University (3)

141* at Cambridge, 1973
140 at Cambridge, 1974
207* at Cambridge, 1976

MCC (2)

123 at Lord's, 1966
102* at Scarborough, 1968

For England (22) versus

Australia (7)

113 at The Oval, 1964
142* at Sydney, 1970–1
119* at Adelaide, 1970–1
107 at Nottingham, 1977
191 at Leeds, 1977
128* at Lord's, 1980
137 at The Oval, 1981

India (4)

246* at Leeds, 1967
155 at Birmingham, 1979
125 at The Oval, 1979
105 at Delhi, 1981–2

New Zealand (2)

115 at Leeds, 1973
131 at Nottingham, 1978

Pakistan (3)

121* at Lord's, 1971
112 at Leeds, 1971
100* at Hyderabad, 1977–8

South Africa (1)

117 at Port Elizabeth, 1964–5

West Indies (5)

116 at Georgetown, 1967–8
128 at Manchester, 1969
106 at Lord's, 1969
112 at Port of Spain, 1974
104* at Antigua, 1981

For England versus

Rest of the World
157 at The Oval, 1970

For MCC (13) versus

Combined XI

156 at Hobart, 1965–6

New South Wales

129* at Sydney, 1970–1

Queensland

124* at Brisbane, 1970–1

South Australia

173 at Adelaide, 1970–1

Western Australia

126 at Perth, 1970–1

Eastern Province

193* at Port Elizabeth, 1964–5

South African Invitation XI

114 at Cape Town, 1964–5

Western Province

106 at Cape Town, 1964–5

Barbados

243 at Bridgetown, 1967–8

Guyana

133* at Georgetown, 1974

Leeward Islands

165 at Antigua, 1967–8

President's XI (2)

135 at Bridgetown, 1967–8
261* at Bridgetown, 1974

For England XI (8) versus

England Under-25 XI
147* at Scarborough, 1970

The Rest

160*
116 at Worcester 1974

South Australia

110 at Adelaide, 1979–80

Tasmania

101* at Hobart, 1979–80

India Under-22 XI

101* at Pune, 1981–2

NWFP Governor's XI

115* at Peshawar, 1977–8

United Bank XI

123* at Faisalabad, 1977–8

For Other Teams (4)

An England XI *v* Rest of the World XI

115* at Scarborough, 1968

Northern Transvaal *v* Rhodesia

107 at Pretoria, 1972

T. N. Pearce's XI *v* West Indies

131 at Scarborough, 1966

D. H. Robins' XI *v* West Indies

114 at Eastbourne, 1973

Grounds in Yorkshire

Batting and Fielding

									Century			How Out				
Ground	**M**	**I**	**NO**	**Runs**	**HS**	**Average**	**100s**	**50s**	**P'ships**	**c**	**b**	**lbw**	**st**	**r.o.**	**h.w.**	**Catches**
Bradford	42	72	11	2861	163	46.90	10	12	15	38	8	9	2	4	–	24
Harrogate	16	23	7	1419	153*	88.68	6	6	8	9	5	1	–	1	–	9
Hull	5	10	0	346	95	34.60	–	3	1	7	2	1	–	–	–	1
Leeds	59	94	20	4824	246*	65.18	19	17	26	44	13	15	–	2	–	20
Middlesbrough	20	35	3	1719	180*	53.71	5	10	9	17	4	7	2	1	1	6
Scarborough	45	77	16	4032	175*	66.09	12	22	12	33	14	8	3	3	–	27
Abbeydale Park, Sheffield	15	24	4	1381	159	69.05	6	4	8	10	4	5	–	1	–	10
Bramall Lane, Sheffield	29	47	5	1998	220*	47.57	7	8	6	27	6	5	–	4	–	12
Totals	231	382	66	18580	246*	58.79	65	82	85	185	56	51	7	16	1	109

Other Grounds in UK

Batting and Fielding

									Century			How Out				
Ground	**M**	**I**	**NO**	**Runs**	**HS**	**Average**	**100s**	**50s**	**P'ships**	**c**	**b**	**lbw**	**st**	**r.o.**	**h.w.**	**Catches**
Basingstoke	1	1	0	53	53	53.00	–	1	1	1	–	–	–	–	–	–
Birmingham	19	34	7	1716	155	63.55	6	9	7	15	5	6	1	–	–	10
Bournemouth	4	8	0	360	111	45.00	1	2	2	5	1	2	–	–	–	1
Bristol	7	10	3	704	177	100.57	3	2	5	3	2	2	–	–	–	3
Cambridge	9	12	3	787	207*	87.44	3	3	3	6	3	–	–	–	–	7
Arms Park, Cardiff	1	1	0	80	80	80.00	–	1	1	1	–	–	–	–	–	1
Sophia Gardens, Cardiff	5	8	3	291	101*	58.20	1	1	1	1	–	4	–	–	–	1
Chelmsford	4	7	0	394	121	56.28	1	2	–	3	2	2	–	–	–	2
Cheltenham	2	3	1	332	140*	166.00	1	2	2	1	–	1	–	–	–	–
Chesterfield	19	27	6	1367	169*	65.09	3	9	7	11	4	4	–	2	–	6
Clacton	1	2	0	5	4	2.50	–	–	–	1	–	1	–	–	–	–
Colchester	2	2	1	493	260*	493.00	2	–	4	–	–	1	–	–	–	1
Dartford	2	4	0	92	50	23.00	–	1	–	3	1	–	–	–	–	–
Derby	1	2	0	27	20	13.50	–	–	–	1	–	–	1	–	–	–
Eastbourne	1	2	1	188	114	188.00	1	1	1	–	–	–	1	–	–	2
Folkestone	1	2	0	70	61	35.00	–	1	–	2	–	–	–	–	–	–
Gillingham	1	2	0	85	55	42.50	–	1	–	1	–	1	–	–	–	–
Gloucester	1	2	0	34	24	17.00	–	–	–	2	–	–	–	–	–	–
Gravesend	1	2	1	48	27	48.00	–	–	–	1	–	–	–	–	–	2
Hinkley	1	2	0	73	56	36.50	–	1	–	–	2	–	–	–	–	–
Hove	6	9	4	422	164	84.40	1	2	2	4	–	1	–	–	–	1
Ilford	2	3	0	20	9	6.66	–	–	–	3	–	–	–	–	–	–
Kidderminster	1	1	0	60	60	60.00	–	1	1	–	–	1	–	–	–	1
Leicester	14	23	4	1080	204*	56.84	3	5	6	12	5	2	–	–	–	8
Leyton	2	4	0	149	68	37.25	–	1	–	4	–	–	–	–	–	1
Lord's	41	72	7	2889	201*	44.44	7	14	16	46	12	7	–	–	–	10
Luton	1	2	0	71	68	35.50	–	1	–	2	–	–	–	–	–	–
Lydney	1	1	0	1	1	1.00	–	–	–	1	–	–	–	–	–	–
Maidstone	1	2	0	34	25	17.00	–	–	–	1	–	–	–	1	–	1
Manchester	24	37	3	1647	135	48.44	6	7	9	19	5	9	–	1	–	6
Northampton	8	12	1	396	138	36.00	2	–	2	8	1	1	–	1	–	8
Nottingham	16	27	3	1101	154	45.87	3	5	6	14	5	3	–	2	–	7
Oxford	6	8	0	332	89	41.50	–	4	4	7	1	–	–	–	–	9
Southampton	4	6	0	226	105	37.66	1	–	1	3	1	1	–	1	–	2
Swansea	4	7	0	268	83	38.28	–	3	1	7	–	–	–	–	–	2
Taunton	8	14	3	591	122*	53.72	1	3	1	5	1	3	–	2	–	6
The Oval	20	38	3	1700	137	48.57	4	8	2	23	6	4	1	1	–	8
Tunbridge Wells	1	2	1	163	104*	163.00	1	1	2	–	1	–	–	–	–	3
Weston-super-Mare	2	3	0	212	129	70.66	1	1	2	1	1	–	1	–	–	–
Worcester	8	14	2	908	184	75.91	4	2	3	8	2	2	–	–	–	1
Worksop	8	14	4	932	214*	93.20	3	5	4	9	–	–	1	–	–	1
Totals	261	432	61	20401	260*	54.98	59	100	96	235	61	58	6	11	–	111

Summary

Batting and Fielding

Grounds in	M	I	NO	Runs	HS	Average	100s	50s	Century P'ships	c	b	How Out lbw	st	r.o.	h.w.	Catches
Yorkshire	231	382	66	18580	246*	58.79	65	82	85	185	56	51	7	16	1	109
Rest of UK	261	432	61	20401	260*	54.98	59	100	96	235	61	58	6	11	–	111
All UK	492	814	127	38981	260*	56.74	124	182	181	420	117	109	13	27	1	220
Australia	41	75	14	3322	173	54.45	9	20	22	43	5	10	1	2	–	17
Ceylon (now Sri Lanka)	1	2	0	7	7	3.50	–	–	–	1	1	–	–	–	–	–
India	9	16	6	766	105	77.60	2	6	6	6	1	3	–	–	–	3
New Zealand	10	15	0	354	77	23.60	–	3	–	10	2	1	–	2	–	6
Pakistan	6	9	3	577	123*	96.16	3	3	4	2	3	–	–	1	–	1
South Africa	20	34	5	1487	193*	51.27	5	7	6	20	3	5	–	1	–	10
West Indies	30	49	7	2932	261*	69.80	8	17	20	26	10	3	–	3	–	7
Totals	609	1014	162	48426	261*	56.83	151	238	239	528	142	131	14	36	1	264

Bowling

Grounds in	Balls	Maidens	Runs	Wickets	Average	Best in Innings
Yorkshire	1094	63	413	14	29.50	4:14
Rest of UK	1146	62	363	15	24.20	2:10
All UK	2240	125	776	29	26.75	4:14
Australia	452	6	275	4	68.75	2:32
Ceylon (now Sri Lanka)	18	1	5	0	–	–
India			*Did not bowl*			–
New Zealand	234	19	71	1	71.00	1:27
Pakistan	32	0	5	0	–	–
South Africa	564	24	262	8	32.75	3:47
West Indies	153	8	65	3	21.66	1:9
Totals	3693	183	1459	45	32.42	4:14

Summary – All First-class Matches

Batting and Fielding

For	M	I	NO	Runs	HS	Average	100s	50s	Century P'ships	c	b	How Out lbw	st	r.o.	h.w.	Catches
Yorkshire	414	674	111	32570	260*	57.85	103	157	143	341	94	92	10	25	1	200
England	108	193	23	8114	246*	47.72	22	42	46	104	30	27	2	7	–	33
Other Teams	87	147	28	7742	261*	65.05	26	39	50	83	18	12	2	4	–	31
Totals	609	1014	162	48426	261*	56.83	151	238	239	528	142	131	14	36	1	264

Bowling

For	Balls	Maidens	Runs	Wickets	Average	Best in Innings
Yorkshire	1928	106	665	28	23.75	4:14
England	944	45	382	7	54.57	3:47
Other Teams	821	32	412	10	41.20	3:69
Totals	3693	183	1459	45	32.42	4:14

Test Matches

Batting and Fielding

For England versus	M	I	NO	Runs	HS	Average	100s	50s	Century P'ships	c	b	How Out lbw	st	r.o.	h.w.	Catches
Australia	38	71	9	2945	191	47.50	7	14	17	38	9	12	1	2	–	12
India	13	22	3	1084	246*	57.05	4	2	7	10	3	5	1	–	–	7
New Zealand	15	25	1	916	131	38.16	2	6	6	12	6	3	–	3	–	5
Pakistan	6	10	3	591	121*	84.42	3	3	3	3	3	–	–	1	–	–
South Africa	7	12	2	373	117	37.30	1	2	2	8	1	1	–	–	–	2
West Indies	29	53	5	2205	128	45.93	5	15	11	33	8	6	–	1	–	7
Totals	108	193	23	8114	246*	47.72	22	42	46	104	30	27	2	7	–	33

Bowling

Balls	Maidens	Runs	Wickets	Average	Best in Innings
944	45	382	7	54.57	3:47

Tours

MCC to:
South Africa, 1964–5
Australia and New Zealand, 1965–5
West Indies, 1967–8
Ceylon and the Far East, 1970
Australia, 1970–1
West Indies, 1974

England to:
Pakistan and New Zealand, 1977–8
Australia, 1978–9
Australia and India, 1979–80
West Indies, 1981
India, 1981–2

South African Breweries to: South Africa, 1982

Limited-overs Matches

Batting and Fielding

	M	I	NO	Runs	HS	Average	100s	50s	Century P'ships	c	b	How Out lbw	st	r.o.	h.w.	Catches
Internationals	35	33	4	1074	105	37.03	1	9	4	17	4	6	–	2	–	5
Gillette Cup and NatWest Trophy	40	39	4	1378	146	39.37	1	9	4	15	7	8	–	5	–	9
Benson and Hedges Cup	57	55	9	2052	142	44.60	3	16	4	26	8	5	2	5	–	14
John Player Special League	163	157	24	5051	108*	37.97	2	37	19	84	28	5	3	13	–	69
Totals	295	284	41	9555	146	39.32	7	71	31	142	47	24	5	25	–	97

Bowling

	Balls	Maidens	Runs	Wickets	Average	Best in Innings
Internationals	168	1	105	5	21.00	2:14
Gillette Cup and NatWest Trophy	468	14	238	8	29.75	2:12
Benson and Hedges Cup	378	4	227	2	113.50	1:16
John Player Special League	911	11	611	14	43.64	3:15
Totals	1925	30	1181	29	40.72	3:15

Results as Captain

	Matches Captained	Won	Lost	Drawn
For England	4	1	1	2
For Yorkshire	121	39	21	61
For Other Items	5	2	0	3
Totals	130	42	22	66
		32.3%	16.9%	50.8%

How Out

A Yorkshire Comparison

(all first-class matches)

	G. Boycott	%	L. Hutton	%	H. Sutcliffe	%
caught	528	61.97	378	52.28	514	53.26
bowled	142	16.67	205	28.35	255	26.42
lbw	131	15.37	94	13.00	140	14.51
stumped	14	1.64	20	2.77	25	2.59
run out	36	4.23	20	2.77	28	2.91
hit wicket	1	0.12	5	0.69	3	0.31
obstructing the field	–	–	1	0.14	–	–
Totals	852	100.00	723	100.00	965	100.00

Man of the Match Awards

For England

105 versus Australia at Sydney, 11 December 1979
86 versus Australia at Sydney, 26 December 1979
70 versus West Indies at Lord's, 30 May 1980
75* versus Australia at Lord's, 4 June 1981

Gillette Cup

146 versus Surrey at Lord's, 4 September 1965
92 versus Durham at Chester-le-Street, 18 July 1979

Benson and Hedges

75* versus Gloucestershire at Leeds, 28 June 1972
56* versus minor counties (North) at Leeds, 27 April 1974
59 versus Nottinghamshire at Barnsley, 21 May 1975
102 versus Northamptonshire at Middlesbrough, 30 April 1977
73 versus minor counties (East) at Newcastle-upon-Tyne, 14 May 1977
74* versus Essex at Barnsley, 23 May 1977
53* versus minor counties (North) at Newcastle-upon-Tyne, 12 May 1979
82 versus Leicestershire at Leicester, 22 May 1982
106 versus Northamptonshire at Bradford, 19 May 1984

Index

Picture Acknowledgements

Section 1 Pages 1–7 inclusive, Author's Collection. Page 8 top, Express Newspapers PLC. Page 8 bottom, Sheffield Newspapers Ltd. *Section 2* Pages 1, 2 top, 3, 4 top left, 8, Author's Collection. Page 2 bottom, Express Newspapers PLC. Page 4 top right and bottom, Sport and General. Page 5 top, Photo Source (Central Press). Page 5 bottom, Daily Mirror/Syndication International. Page 6, Press Association. Page 7, Patrick Eagar. *Section 3* Page 1, Ken Kelly. Pages 2, 3, 4 top, 5 bottom, 7, Author's Collection. Page 4 bottom, Telegraph and Argus, Bradford. Page 5 top, reproduced by courtesy of ITN News. Page 6 top, Sport and General. Page 6 bottom, Patrick Eagar. Page 8, Photo Source (Keystone Press). *Section 4* pages 1, 3 top, 4, 8, Patrick Eager. Pages 2 top, 6 centre, bottom left and right, 7, Jack Hickes Photos Ltd. Pages 2 bottom left, 6 top left and right, Yorkshire Post Newspapers Ltd. Page 2 bottom right, Press Association. Page 3 bottom, Graham Morris. Page 5, Author's Collection.

Cartoons by Roy Ullyett/Express Newspapers, PLC.